GLOBAL MIGRANTS, GLOBAL REFUGEES

GLOBAL MIGRANTS, GLOBAL REFUGEES

Problems and Solutions

Edited by
Aristide R. Zolberg
and
Peter M. Benda

Berghahn Books
NEW YORK • OXFORD

Published in 2001 by

Berghahn Books

www.berghahnbooks.com

© 2001 Aristide R. Zolberg and Peter M. Benda

Library of Congress Cataloging-in-Publication Data

Global migrants, global refugees : problems and solutions / edited by Aristide
R. Zolberg and Peter Benda.
    p.   cm.
Includes bibliographical references and index.
ISBN 1-571-81169-9 (alk. paper) — ISBN 1-571-87170-2 (pbk. : alk. paper)
    1. Emigration and immigration. 2. Immigrants. 3. Refugees.
    I. Zolberg, Aristide R. II. Benda, Peter.
JV6032.G58   2000
325'.09'049—dc21   99-045870

British Library Cataloguing in Publication Data

A catalogue record for this book is available from the British Library.

Printed in the United States on acid-free paper.

CONTENTS

List of Illustrations   vii

Acknowledgments   ix

List of Abbreviations   x

Introduction: Beyond the Crisis *by Aristide R. Zolberg*   1

PART ONE   Diagnosis: Is There a Migration "Crisis"?

1. Population Growth and International Migration: Is There a Link? *Mary M. Kritz*   19

2. Ecomigration: Linkages between Environmental Change and Migration *William B. Wood*   42

3. Conflict and Forced Migration: A Quantitative Review, 1964–1995 *Susanne Schmeidl*   62

4. Managing Migration: The Role of Economic Policies *Philip L. Martin and J. Edward Taylor*   95

5. Current Dilemmas and Future Prospects of the Inter-American Migration System *Robert C. Smith*   121

PART TWO   Implications for U.S. Policy

6. Protection and Humanitarian Action in the Post–Cold War Era *Gil Loescher*   171

7. Reforming the International Humanitarian Delivery System for Wars *Thomas G. Weiss*   206

8. U.S. Foreign Policy, Democracy, and Migration *David P. Forsythe, with Gary Baker and Michele Leonard*   243

9. Migration and International Economic Institutions   271
    Leah Haus

10. Development Assistance and International Migration   297
    Richard E. Bissell and Andrew S. Natsios

11. After the Wars Are Over: U.S. Policy in Reconstruction   322
    Elizabeth G. Ferris

Notes on Contributors   350

Index   357

LIST OF ILLUSTRATIONS

FIGURES

1.1	Trends in Mexico's Total Fertility Rates, U.S. Immigration, and per capita GNP, 1973–1993	35
3.1	Refugee Migration by Region, 1964–1995	66
3.2	Internal Displacement by Region, 1964–1995	67
3.3	Number of Refugee-Sending Countries by Region, 1964–1995	68
3.4	Number of Countries with Internal Displacement by Region, 1964–1995	69
4.1	The Migration Hump	106

TABLES

1.1	Classification of Sending Countries by Mid-1980s Rates of Natural Increase and U.S. Permanent Immigration in 1989–1993 Period	24
1.2	Classification of Sending Countries by Late 1980s Total Fertility Rate (TFR) and U.S. Permanent Immigration in 1989–1993 Period	26
1.3	Classification of Sending Countries by 1985 Population Size and U.S. Permanent Immigration in 1989–1993 Period	27
1.4	Classification of Sending Countries by 1989 Population Density and U.S. Immigration in 1989–1993 Period	28
1.5	Correlation Matrix (pairwise) and Standardized Zero-Order Regression Coefficients of Country Characteristics and U.S. Immigration (1989–1993)	31
1.6	Ordinary Least Squares (OLS) Regression of U.S. Immigration in 1989–1993 Period on Population and Other Covariates	32
3.1	List of Forced Migrations by Country of Origin	86

3.2   Pooled Time-Series Analysis of Effects of Explanatory   89
Variables and Interaction Terms on Change in Refugee
Stock, 1971–1990

9.1   Immigration to the United States for Selected Years,   275
1910–1995

9.2   Nonimmigrants Admitted to the U.S. for Selected Fiscal   276
Years, 1985–1995

ACKNOWLEDGMENTS

The papers collected together in this volume emerged from a three-year project undertaken by the New School University's International Center for Migration, Ethnicity and Citizenship with the generous support of The Pew Charitable Trusts' Global Stewardship Initiative. The project officially concluded in June 1997; the papers that now appear as chapters in this volume were authored during 1995–96, and revised by the authors in 1997–98. With certain exceptions, they have not since been revised again to take into account intervening events, some of them quite significant, bearing on the general problems and developments under examination.

The editors wish to thank a number of scholars and scholar-practitioners who served as discussants at two workshops that took place at the New School, at which early drafts of the papers commissioned for the Pew project were presented and discussed. We are grateful to Tom Callaghy, Robert Latham, Chris Mitchell, and Hania Zlotnik for having served as discussants at the first of these workshops, which took place in September 1995; and to Leon Gordenker, Arthur Helton, Kathleen Newland, Astri Surhke, Georges Tapinos, and Warren Zimmermann for having played a comparable role at a second workshop in October 1996. We also wish to acknowledge and thank those who agreed to serve as discussants and panel moderators at the concluding conference for the Pew project, which took place at the New School in April 1997, among them Howard Adelman, Héctor Cordero-Guzmán, Robert DeVecchi, Enid Schoettle, Michael Teitelbaum, and Roy Williams.

A special debt of gratitude is owed to Warren Zimmermann, who as Distinguished Fellow at the New School from 1994–97 played an instrumental role in helping guide the Pew project. Finally, we are grateful for the support we received throughout the course of this project from a small but dedicated group of ICMEC graduate student program and research assistants, including Luis Franco who helped considerably in preparing this manuscript for publication.

LIST OF ABBREVIATIONS

AICF	American Immigration Control Federation
AID	(U.S.) Agency for International Development
ARENA	National Republican Alliance Party (El Salvador)
CAPEL	Center for Electoral Promotion and Assistance
CARE	Cooperative for Assistance and Relief Everywhere
CBI	Caribbean Basin Initiative
CIA	(U.S.) Central Intelligence Agency
CIS	Commonwealth of Independent States
CNN	Cable News Network
CRS	Catholic Relief Services
CSCE	Conference on Security and Cooperation in Europe
DAC	Development Assistance Committee
DC	developed countries
DHA	(United Nations) Department of Humanitarian Affairs
DPA	(United Nations) Department of Political Affairs
DPKO	(United Nations) Department of Peacekeeping Operations
DRC	(United Nations) Disaster Relief Coordinator
EC	European Community
ECHO	European Community Humanitarian Office
ECOMOG	Economic Community of Western African States Monitoring Group
ECOSOC	(United Nations) Economic and Social Council
ECOWAS	Economic Community of West African States
ECU	European Customs Union
EEC	European Economic Community
ERC	(United Nations) Emergency Relief Coordinator
ERP	People's Revolutionary Army
EU	European Union
EZLN	Ejertico Zapatista de Liberacion Nacional (Zapatista Army of National Liberation, Mexico)
FDI	foreign direct investment
FDR	Frente Democratico Revolcionario (Mexico)

FMLN	Frente Farabundo Marti para la Liberacion Nacional (El Salvador)
FRY	Federal Republic of Yugoslavia (Serbia and Montenegro)
FY	fiscal year
G-7	Group of Seven (industrialized nations)
GAO	(U.S.) General Accounting Office
GATT	General Agreement on Tariffs and Trade
GDP	gross domestic product
GIS	Geographic Information System
GNP	gross national product
HDI	Human Development Index
HUMPROFOR	(United Nations) Humanitarian Protection Force
IASC	(United Nations) Inter-Agency Standing Committee
IBRD	International Bank for Reconstruction and Development
ICEM	Intergovernmental Committee for European Migration
ICITAP	International Criminal Investigative Training Program
ICJ	International Court of Justice
ICMEC	International Center for Migration, Ethnicity, and Citizenship
ICRC	International Committee of the Red Cross
ICVA	International Council for Voluntary Agencies
IDENT	(U.S. Immigration and Naturalization Service) Automated Biometric Identification System
IDP(s)	internally displaced person(s)/people
IFE	Instituto Federal Electoral (Federal Election Institute, Mexico)
IFES	International Foundation for Electoral Systems
IFI	international financial institutions
IFOR	Implementation Force (in the former Yugoslavia)
IFRC	International Federation of Red Cross and Red Crescent Societies
IGO	intergovernmental organization
ILO	International Labor Organization
IMF	International Monetary Fund
INGO	international nongovernmental organization
INS	(U.S.) Immigration and Naturalization Service
IOM	International Organization for Migration
IRC	International Rescue Committee
IRCA	(U.S.) Immigration Reform and Control Act
IRI	International Republican Institute
ISI	import substituting industrialization
JNA	Yugoslav People's Army
LDC	less developed countries
MICIVIH	(United Nations) International Civilian Mission in Haiti
MINUHA	United Nations Mission in Haiti
MNF	multinational force

MSF	Médecins Sans Frontières (Doctors without Borders)
NAFTA	North American Free Trade Agreement
NATO	North Atlantic Treaty Organization
NDI	National Democratic Institute for International Affairs
NED	National Endowment for Democracy
NELM	new economics of labor migration
NGO	nongovernmental organization
NICs	newly independent countries
OAS	Organization of American States
OAU	Organization of African Unity
OCHA	(United Nations) Office for the Coordination of Humanitarian Affairs
ODA	Overseas Development Assistance
OECD	Organization for Economic and Cooperative Development
OEEC	Organization of European Economic Cooperation
OERC	(United Nations) Office of the Emergency Relief Coordinator
OFDA	(U.S., Agency for International Development) Office of Foreign Disaster Assistance
OHCHR	Office of United Nations High Commissioner for Human Rights
OLS	ordinary least squares
ONUMOZ	United Nations Operation in Mozambique
OPDAT	(United Nations) Office of Professional Development and Training
OPEC	Organization of Petroleum Exporting Countries
OSCE	Organization on Security and Cooperation in Europe (formerly CSCE)
OUNHAC	Office of the United Nations Humanitarian Assistance Coordinator
PAN	Partido Accion Nacional (National Action Party, Mexico)
PRD	Partido Revolucionario Democratico (Democratic Revolutionary Party, Mexico)
PRI	Partido Revolucionario Institucional (Institutional Revolutionary Party, Mexico)
PRM	(U.S. Department of State, Office of) Population, Refugees and Migration
PVO	private voluntary organization
RAW	replacement agricultural workers
RNI	rate of natural increase
RPF	Rwandan Patriotic Front
RTA	regional trade agreements
SAP	Structural Adjust Program
SFOR	Stabilization Force (in the former Yugoslavia)

SOPEMI	(OECD) Système d'Observation Permantente des Migrations (Continuous Reporting System on Migration)
SRSG	Special Representative of the (United Nations) Secretary-General
TFR	total fertility rate(s)
TPS	temporary protected status
U.K.	United Kingdom
U.S.	United States
UN	United Nations
UNAMIR	United Nations Assistance Mission in Rwanda
UNDP	United Nations Development Program
UNDRO	United Nations Disaster Relief Office
UNGCI	United Nations Guards Contingent in Iraq
UNHCHR	United Nations High Commissioner for Human Rights
UNHCR	United Nations High Commissioner for Refugees
UNICEF	United Nations Children's Emergency Fund
UNITAF	United Task Force (U.S.)
UNMIH	United Nations Mission in Haiti
UNOSOM	United Nations Operation in Somalia
UNPREDEF	United Nations Preventive Deployment Force (in Macedonia)
UNPROFOR	United Nations Protection Force (in the former Yugolsavia)
UNREO	United Nations Rwanda Emergency Office
UNSCOM	United Nations Special Commission
UNSMIH	United Nations Support Mission in Haiti
URNG	Guatemalan National Revolutionary Unity
USAID	United States Agency for International Development
USCR	U.S. Committee for Refugees
USG	United States government
USTR	(Office of) United States Trade Representative
WFP	World Food Program(me)
WTO	World Trade Organization

INTRODUCTION: BEYOND THE CRISIS

Aristide R. Zolberg

The massive movement of human beings across international borders has come to be regarded as one of the most intractable problems the United States and the other affluent democracies face in the strange new post-Communist world. Long a marginal subject even for demographers and social scientists, international migration quickly ascended to the status of a security issue, imperatively requiring attention in the highest places. This atmosphere of crisis also prompted the inclusion of international migration among the subjects covered by The Pew Charitable Trusts' Global Stewardship Initiative, whose organizers commissioned the project reported on in this book.

However, one of our most significant findings is that recent developments in the sphere of international migration, including both voluntary and forced movements, do not provide evidence of a "crisis," and that this holds as well for realistic projections into the near future. In this light, the widespread talk of a "crisis" appears as an irrational phenomenon, akin to the bizarre "panics" that perennially erupt in the economic sphere (Kindleberger 1978). Yet this cannot be dismissed as merely an unfortunate misperception. As the Nobel medal economist Amartya Sen has pointed out with regard to the "population bomb," "the emergency mentality based on false beliefs in imminent cataclysms leads to breathless responses that are deeply counterproductive" (Sen 1994: 71). Indeed, the prevailing sense of an "international migration crisis" has profoundly inflected the consideration of policy alternatives. In particular, it has been invoked to justify draconian measures to protect national borders, even at the expense of other considerations, notably humanitarian obligations toward refugees and generous policies of family reunion. Accordingly, the "crisis" specter must be exorcised at the outset.

As late as 1991, a review of global population issues from a security perspective published in *Foreign Affairs*—originally presented a couple of years earlier to a U.S. Army Conference on Long Range Planning—attributed a limited role to migration and suggested that, overall, "the demographic significance of international migration has decidedly diminished" because "the territories of the globe are now divided among standing governments, virtually all of which limit the absorption of new citizens from abroad in some fashion." Consequently, "opportunities for voluntary migration for most inhabitants of the Third World remain very limited," and "Increasingly, therefore, twentieth-century emigration has become a response to catastrophe ..." (Eberstadt 1991: 125). The author acknowledged that although in proportional terms, emigration from the Third World today is much lower than from Europe at the turn of the century, the impact of migration can be large on both senders and receivers. For example, "For a country accepting migrants, national security may be affected greatly by the manner in which the state encourages newcomers to involve themselves in local economic and political life" (126). However, the case he cited in support of this point is not a western nation but Saudi Arabia, where the presence of unincorporated foreigners is a source of political trouble. Indeed, Eberstadt drew an explicit contrast between Saudi Arabia and the United States, whose "universalist" tradition insures that newcomers are effectively socialized into the mainstream political culture and are therefore unlikely to become politically problematic.

The following year the same journal published "The Population Threat" by Michael Teitelbaum, a distinguished demographer who subsequently became the Acting Chair of the United States Commission on Immigration (Teitelbaum 1992–93). Pointing out that recent demographic trends were "revolutionary, a virtual discontinuity with all human history" (64), Teitelbaum nevertheless quite explicitly rejected "exaggerated visions of global apocalypse" arising from population growth (77). He contended that the sustained high rates of fertility and urban growth that occur in many developing societies both contribute to environmental degradation and limit the capacities of these societies to adopt sound developmental strategies, and suggested that "Many (though not all) nations with rapidly growing populations and significant rural-to-urban migration are also producing large numbers of international migrants, whether as temporary workers, permanent immigrants or refugees" (66). In conclusion, Teitelbaum urged the incoming Clinton administration to resume U.S. support for population-limiting programs in the developing world, which had been terminated by President Reagan in 1980.

The subsequent abrupt militarization of international migration discourse inside the Beltway is largely attributable to the influential pronouncements of the distinguished naval historian Paul Kennedy who, having disposed of the Great Powers, went on to educate policymakers on how to prepare for the twenty-first century. Sweeping aside the balanced assessments of Eberstadt and Teitelbaum, in 1993 Kennedy singled out the "global population explosion" as one of the most challenging issues, and suggested that in view of the imbalances in demographic trends between "have" and "have-not" societies, one should expect "great waves of migration in the twenty-first century" because "desperate migrants are unlikely to be deterred" by immigration policies (Kennedy 1993: 44). Citing as evidence the difficulties France encountered in ridding itself of unauthorized immigrants and the United States in keeping them out, he further pointed to the 15 million living in refugee camps, "hoping for somewhere to go…. While they, and those already on the move via Mexico and Turkey, may encounter obstacles, many of them are getting through."

A year later, in "Must It Be the Rest Against the West?" a co-authored article published in the *Atlantic Monthly*, Kennedy went even farther and evoked an impending apocalypse: "Many members of the more prosperous economies are beginning to agree with Raspail's vision of a world of two 'camps,' North and South, separate and unequal, in which the rich will have to fight and the poor will have to die if mass migration is not to overwhelm us all" (Connelly and Kennedy 1994). Jean Raspail, a conservative French essayist usually published in *Le Figaro*, set forth his vision in *The Camp of the Saints*, a 1973 novel in the scatological tradition of Louis-Ferdinand Céline. In this dystopic tale, a teeming horde of Third World paupers from the shores of the Ganges somehow manages to commandeer a huge flotilla of derelict ships and sets sail for the promised land of affluent Europe. As the bloodthirsty invaders approach the northern shores of the Mediterranean, preparing to land on the French Riviera, the white world falls prey to a collective paralysis induced by political correctness. According to Raspail's blunt diagnosis, the whites have lost their "racial will" to fight for survival. The French army flees to a northern redoubt, abandoning the south and leaving the population to scramble for refuge. The scene is reenacted elsewhere as the successful invaders inspire imitators in other parts of the Third World. The only successful hold-outs are the Afrikaners and the Australians, still in possession of their "racial will." Alas, as we now know, not for long: about the time the novel was published Australia elected a Labor government that relinquished the traditional "White Australia" policy, and two decades later, even the Afrikaners succumbed to the liberal virus….

When published in the United States by Scribner's in 1975, Raspail's novel evoked dismissive outrage from mainstream reviewers. The *New York Times*, 13 August 1975 (32), intimated that reading the novel "is like being trapped at a cocktail party with a normal-looking fellow who suddenly starts a perfervid racist diatribe." In the same vein, *Time*, 4 August 1975 (63–64) suggested that "This bilious tirade would not be worth a moment's thought if it had come off a mimeograph machine in some dank cellar. Instead, *The Camp of the Saints* arrives trailing clouds of praise from French savants … with the imprint of a respected U.S. publisher and a teasing prepublication ad campaign ("The end of the white world is near"). Before the book is called 'courageous' or 'provocative,' a small distinction should be made. The portrait of racial enmity is one matter. The exacerbation is quite another." The *Wall Street Journal*, 30 July 1975 (7–8) was somewhat more mixed. Highlighting Raspail's "contempt for the weakness of pity and charity, in the vein of Ayn Rand; a belief that the West is paralyzed by neurotic guilt, self-hate, and loss of nerve," its reviewer characterized the novel as a "bitter, ugly, possibly destructive book, with patches of bad writing (or translation)," but granted that it "nevertheless has moments of appalling power and occasionally a terrible beauty."

As against this, the ascending neoconservatives were quick to identify a soul mate, and the *National Review* launched a contrarian campaign on the novel's behalf. Evoking the scandals triggered by the avant-garde works of James Joyce and Igor Stravinsky earlier in the century, senior editor Jeffrey Hart ("Raspail's Superb Scandal," 26 September 1975: 1062–63), reported that "In freer and more intelligent circles in Europe ... the book is a sensation and Raspail a prize-winner.... Raspail is to genocide what Lawrence was to sex." Returning to the fray a few months later (5 December 1975: 1412), Hart included *The Camp of the Saints* in an intellectual "survival kit" for conservatives, along with *1984* and James Burnham's *Suicide of the West*. Hailing its author as "a great poet of civilization," he declared that "By presenting his powerful image of the anti-civilizational, Raspail reminds us who we are and of what Western civilization consists. His *Camp of the Saints* is the most powerful political fable of our time."

After going into paperback in 1977, the novel quickly faded from the mainstream publishing scene, but was reprinted in 1982 by the "Institute for Western Values" and in 1987 by the American Immigration Control Federation, a Virginia-based lobby devoted to its eponymous cause. After Raspail's vision was excavated by Connolly and Kennedy and endowed with unprecedented respectability, the book was again reissued in the mid-1990s, this time by the Social Contract Press of Petroskey, Michigan, operating under the umbrella of a publicly supported foundation "called simply 'U.S.,'" which itself reportedly receives support from the Laurel Foundation, controlled by Cordelia Scaife May of the Mellon family (Cockburn 1994: 225). Proudly excerpting the *Atlantic Monthly* article on the book's cover, the publishers hailed the article in their foreword as one of "two recent seminal events" that "helped focus attention to the wider issues involved," the other being the passage of Proposition 187 in California (Raspail n.d. [1973]: viii). They chose as cover illustration a photograph depicting a formidable group of blanket-clad Orientals huddled on a beach, with a tiny cargo ship in the distant background. This was immediately recognizable as a dramatic scene from the widely reported incident involving the *Golden Venture*, a rusty tramp steamer transporting nearly 300 Chinese seeking to enter the United States surreptitiously, which ran aground off the borough of Queens in New York City in the early hours of 6 June 1993. The implications were clear: Raspail's doomsday prophecy has come to pass, the dreaded invasion has begun, whites must get their guns and prepare to defend their race.

Restating in more sensationalist form some of the arguments previously set forth in *Preparing for the Twenty-First Century*, in "Must It Be the Rest Against the West?" their December 1994 article, Connolly and Kennedy accepted Raspail's premise "that a combination of push and pull factors will entice desperate, ambitious Third World peasants to approach the portals of the First World in ever-increasing numbers." Indeed, they argued that "the pressures are now much greater than they were when Raspail wrote," not only because of the additional people on the planet, but because of the communication revolution as well as the prospect of widespread chaos in the developing world, as depicted by Robert D. Kaplan in the same magazine earlier in the year (Kaplan 1994). In the intervening period, the magazine published yet another article warning against the harmful consequences of immigration, this time the threat posed by the resettlement of Hmong refugees from Southeast Asia in Wausau, Wisconsin (Beck 1994). Around the same time, it was also suggested that the international migration crisis was exacerbated by the onset of environmental degradation and scarcities, either indirectly, by way of the contribution of such conditions to violent conflict or simply by forcing people to move abroad in order to survive (Homer-Dixon 1994), and the Sierra Club in effect joined the anti-immigration camp, a move which subsequently led to internal turmoil (Bouvier and Grant 1994). Having participated in numerous Washington seminars and workshops around this time, I can testify firsthand that these shrill warnings had an electrifying impact on foreign affairs and defense officials saddled with the task of thinking about the "new" international and security issues and formulating appropriate policy.

The academic literature evolved in a parallel manner, albeit in a more moderate vein. In 1992, MIT political scientist Myron Weiner proclaimed in *International Security* that international migration had become "high international politics" and cited in support of this assertion numerous instances in which it created conflicts within and between states, notably the exodus of East Germans that brought down the Berlin Wall; the presence of foreign guest workers in Europe, which fostered the emergence of radical right-wing parties; and the invasion of Rwanda by Tutsi refugees based in neighboring Uganda. He suggested that the international economy approach is inadequate for the analysis of such problems, and that it is necessary to supplement it with a "security/stability framework for the study of international migration that focuses on state policies toward emigration and immigration as shaped by concerns over internal stability and international security" (Weiner 1992–93: 95). This seminal article was subsequently incorporated in the same author's *The Global Migration Crisis* (Weiner 1995), published in a popular college-level political science text series, and whose cover pictures a rusty ship covered with people.

Bringing the apocalypse yet closer to home, in 1995 as well Random House published the decade's anti-immigration blockbuster, *Alien Nation: Common Sense About America's Immigration Disaster* (Brimelow

1995). Peter Brimelow's ultimate nightmare is that, unless drastic countermeasures are adopted, the "colored" groups—African Americans, Asians, and Hispanic—will achieve a majority by the middle of the twenty-first century. His overblown tirade signaled the ascent to respectability of an explicitly white-supremacist position, echoing the rantings of the late British ultra-Tory Enoch Powell—whom the author acknowledges as a mentor—and France's Le Pen, but hitherto restricted in the United States to shadowy groups. Indeed, Brimelow's principal contention, that the 1965 reform of American immigration policy was a misguided effort, whose consequences jeopardize the survival of the Anglo-American race, turning it into the "Alien nation" of the title, is lifted straight out of Lawrence Auster's *The Path to National Suicide*, a pamphlet published in 1990 by the American Immigration Control Foundation of Monterey, Virginia, the very organization that reissued Jean Raspail's novel three years earlier. Yet whereas the obscure original— cited by Brimelow with due acknowledgments and even a free advertisement—could only be obtained from the AICF (for a mere $3.00), its derivative elaboration was issued with considerable fanfare by a leading publisher and widely reviewed in the foremost newspapers and magazines, propelling its author to immediate notoriety as a daring reactionary talking head.

Presenting himself as a sort of refugee who came to America with his twin brother in 1967 "when for various reasons we decided all was lost in England" (221), Brimelow views the United States as a fragile lifeboat "that is towing the economy of the entire world" but whose scuttles were opened to let in a multitude of colored aliens, and as a result "is now developing an ethnic list, and may eventually capsize" (18, 249). On page 38, this miscegenetic vessel, part lifeboat and part tugboat, "is starting to rock"; by chapter 11, disaster is near, pulling up the ladder may be necessary, and even those whose families made it into the lifeboat only a few generations ago must concur in keeping out everyone else. To avoid alienating the landlubber market, Brimelow intersperses his nautical jeremiad with the makings of an alternative nightmare, resulting in an even more egregiously mixed metaphor: "By allowing its borders to vanish under this vast whirling mass of illegal immigrants, the United States is running on the edge of a demographic buzz saw. One day, it could suddenly look down to find California or Texas cut off" (35). Over the past thirty years, legal immigration created numerous ethnic enclaves, "turning America into a sort of Swiss cheese" (37). Albeit meant to terrorize, the resulting picture is comically bizarre: America featured as a life-cum-tugboat made of Swiss cheese, its scuttles wide open, running full speed ahead toward a whirling buzz saw. This ridiculous construction makes the respectful attention the book was accorded the more puzzling.

Why, then, has the talk of a "crisis" benefited from such a receptive hearing? In the article cited earlier, Amartya Sen suggests that western anxiety over population growth in the developing world arises from "the psychologically tense issue of racial balance" at the global level. Viewed in this light, works such as *The Camp of the Saints*, "Must It Be the Rest against the West?" and *Alien Nation* can be seen as the most recent expressions of the "fear of population decline," which has gripped the West since the beginning of the twentieth century (Teitelbaum and Winter 1985).

This concern initially surfaced in France, which precociously completed its "demographic transition" and achieved "zero population growth" as early as 1850. In the wake of its subsequent defeat by Prussia in 1870–71, depopulation came to be viewed as a form of "unilateral disarmament," and therefore as a threat to national security. Concurrently, westerners were becoming more aware of the immense size of Asian populations; ironically, even as Europeans and Americans stimulated Asian emigration by massively recruiting Chinese and Indians for work in their proliferating plantation colonies and to develop their infrastructure, they began voicing concern over being swamped by "Asian hordes." Fear of the "yellow peril," as voiced by the German emperor at the time of the Boxer Rebellion, prompted the rapid construction of a world-wide fence to prevent Asians from immigrating into the white world (Zolberg 1997). The "psychologically tense issue of racial balance" was exacerbated in the initial decades of the twentieth century when it became evident that because of the disparities in growth rates, Europe's proportion of world population would henceforth irreversibly decrease (Barraclough 1967: 65). Japan and the United States, which were still gaining, peaked around 1950.

Although Sen correctly points out that the white "sense of a growing 'imbalance' in the world, based on recent trends, ignores history and implicitly presumes that the expansion of Europeans earlier on was natural, whereas the same process happening now to other populations unnaturally disturbs the 'balance,'" (63)—in fact, the Asian and African shares of world population are presently still below their 1650 or 1750 level—there is no gainsaying that if world population is grouped into conventional "racial" categories, which is the common practice in public discourse among Europeans and their overseas offshoots, "white decline" is a genuine historical trend.

As Teitelbaum and Winter point out, European policy responses to this decline in the early decades of the twentieth century focused mostly on increasing fertility by a combination of carrot and stick: encouraging births by way of tax relief or even positive child allowances; providing childcare facilities for working mothers, notably in France; and simultaneously, enacting draconian prohibitions against abortion and birth control devices, notably diaphragms (in the pre-pill era). For the better part of a century, French demographers and decision makers thought that the country's demographic vitality might be revived in part by encouraging immigration from more fertile neighboring countries—notably Belgium (Flanders), Italy, and Spain; however, it became evident that the immigrants rapidly adopted France's own fertility practices, and in any case, the source countries shortly also completed their "demographic transition." By the final decades of the twentieth century, however, In France and elsewhere, immigration came to be seen as part of the problem rather than of the solution. Anxiety over decline of the "white race" in the world as a whole is replicated at the national level on both sides of the Atlantic. In the United States, for example, some demographers estimated as early as 1982 that under ongoing immigration conditions, and taking into consideration disparities in fertility rates, "non-Hispanic whites" would decline from 80 percent of the total in 1980 to 50 percent a century later (Teitelbaum and Winter 1985: 115). By the time of *Alien Nation* a dozen years later, however, the Sierra Club moved the deadline down to the 2050s (Bouvier and Grant 1994: 76).

* * * *

HAVING OVERCOME the "anxieties" indicated, we can approach more realistically the question, How problematic is contemporary international migration from the perspective of the affluent democracies and more specifically, in keeping with the objectives of the present study, from the perspective of the United States? Rapid population growth in many of the world's poor countries is itself a well-established given; but there is considerable contention over the putative consequences of this phenomenon for international migration. We have seen that Connelly and Kennedy, for example, surmise more or less explicitly the operation of a causal chain: population growth in poor countries induces a massive disposition to emigrate; most of those who aspire to leave have the wherewithal to do so, so that this massive disposition is translated into a massive capacity to go; and hence potential receivers face a steadily mounting immigration challenge, requiring the militarization of controls—"the rich will have to fight, and the poor will have to die ..." (Connelly and Kennedy 1994: 62).

However, Sen questions the solidity of the third link in the chain, contending that vast uncontrolled flows are unlikely to occur because immigration is in fact severely controlled by the countries to which people might want to go. Although this observation is in keeping with Eberstadt's earlier point, it has been sharply challenged by respected authorities. For example, Douglas Massey, a leading specialist on U.S. immigration and the coauthor of a major theoretical statement on international migration elaborated on behalf of the International Union for the Scientific Study of Population, has repeatedly expressed considerable skepticism regarding the effectiveness of U.S. regulations in determining the level and composition of U.S. immigration in the twentieth century, both legal and unauthorized (Donato et al. 1992; Massey 1995; Massey and Singer 1995). In the same vein, the editors of a recent comparative study of immigration policy and policy outcomes in nine industrialized democracies conclude that "the gap between the *goals* of national immigration policy ... and the actual results of policies in this area ... is wide and growing wider in all major industrialized democracies" (Cornelius et al. 1994: 3). Their book's perspective is well illustrated by a cover photo entitled "Too hungry to knock," depicting a group of young men jumping down on the northern side from the border fence separating the United States and Mexico. I shall return to this important issue later on.

Sen suggests further that the second link in the causal chain is quite weak as well: the large movements from south to north that have in fact taken place in recent decades "owe more to the dynamism of international capitalism than to just the growing size of the population of the third world countries. The immigrants have allies in potential employers...." But these employers tend to be quite selective in their sources, usually drawing their workers from a relatively small number of countries selected on the basis of a variety of criteria, notably proximity— when there is a sharp economic differentiation between the receiver and the sender—or other "traditional" sources such as former colonies. The dynamics involved are well documented in the present volume by Robert Smith's study of how U.S. policies and practices contributed to the development of an inter-American migration system, linking the United States with Mexico, the Caribbean, and Central America. Another case in point is the Philippines, which constitutes a major source of American immigration in recent decades. Although the origins of this stream can be traced to the country's past colonial relationship with the United States, within that framework recent movement is accounted for in large part to its emergence as an important source of specialized labor, notably nurses trained in English "on demand," with an eye to filling prospective jobs in American hospitals.

Approaching the subject as an economist, Sen neglects the additional movements from south to north that have been generated by the dynamics of the international *political system* (Zolberg et al. 1989). As with labor migrations, these movements tend to follow previously established connections between the sending and receiving countries, which in some cases played a role in the conditions that generated the refugees in the first place, as for example France and later the United States in Indochina. As with economically driven migrations, refugee movements induced by persecution and violence do not automatically result in "immigration pressure" on the affluent democracies.

Indeed, as indicated by Susanne Schmeidl in her chapter, the vast majority of refugees remain in their region of origin within the developing world—now also in the post-Communist world—and usually close to the borders of their source country. The rare exceptions are attributable to initiatives by western receivers, mostly connected with Cold War policies, to take in for resettlement large waves of refugees from distant countries, or to the fact that some of the western receivers in effect constitute "first asylum" countries by virtue of their geographical proximity to the refugee-generating conflict (as with Cubans and self-propelled Central Americans in relation to the United States, or Bosnians and Albanians in relation to European Union countries). Overall, refugee resettlement added approximately 20 percent to the U.S. immigration intake from 1945 to date (Zolberg 1995). In a similar vein, William Wood's contribution examines the phenomenon of "ecomigration," and concludes that environmental degradation does exacerbate conflicts in the arid regions of the developing world, thereby contributing to massive uprooting and refugee flows. However, this has little or no impact on the north, and he therefore concludes that "The use of environmental concerns to justify immigration restrictions plays more on perceptions than realities, especially in North America."

More generally, Mary Kritz has subjected the relationship between population growth and U.S. immigration to an arduous statistical examination. One of her key findings is that countries with the highest population growth rates account for only 1 in 17 U.S. immigrants; conversely, 2 out of 5 come from countries with lower growth rates. Similarly, most U.S. immigrants do not come from the countries with the highest total fertility rates. However, population *size* is positively correlated with U.S. immigration: nearly 3 out of 5 come from the 25 largest countries in the world. As one would anticipate on the basis of common sense, distance does act as a deterrent. In short, absent established connections of the sort noted earlier, the dynamics of world population of themselves do not generate intense "immigration pressures" on the United States. As against global demographic dynamics, the strongest correlate of current U.S. immigration is immigrant stock in the United States, as measured by the distribution of foreign-born. In short, today as in the past, "immigration begets immigration" (Hansen 1961 [1940]: 7). It is noteworthy that Kritz's conclusions have been verified by Hania Zlotnik for the world as a whole on the basis of her elaboration of the most precise set of international migration statistics available to date (Zlotnik 1997, 1998).

As a number of sociologists have pointed out, the tendency for immigration to generate immigration is well accounted for by the formation of "networks," particularly those elaborated on the basis of kinship (Massey et al. 1993). However, the presence of networks alone does not automatically result in international migration: while they foster a disposition to migrate, and a lowering of the costs involved—by providing financial sponsorship, know-how, the assurance of hospitality, and the likelihood of psychological support—an additional necessary condition is the *possibility* of movement. Looking back on the twentieth century as a whole, it is evident that much of the world's population was immobilized for long periods of time by the country of origin's prohibitions against departure, usually founded on a combination of economic and political motives. At the same time, however, many of the potential immigration countries also adopted highly restrictive policies designed precisely to prevent "networks" from resulting in immigration. This was the case, for example, of the United States in the 1920s. In short, "immigration begets immigration" only if states do not seriously interfere with the process.

In this respect, one of the major changes in the world at large is the liberalization of exit; this is true not only of the former Communist countries, nearly all of which maintained draconian prohibitions on exit—except for groups considered "undesirable," or on whose behalf western countries obtained special treatment—but, more importantly, of the entire postcolonial world. It is often forgotten that prior to independence—generally gained between 1947 (India and Pakistan) and the 1970s (Portuguese colonies in Africa)—the movement of European colonial subjects to their respective metropoles was severely restricted, and this was even more true for movement to foreign states, which required obtainment of a passport. The sense of "crisis" undoubtedly is attributable in large part to the fact that the liberalization of exit world-wide shifted the burden of control on potential receivers. But although this quite abrupt turn of events caught many of them by surprise, it is highly unlikely that developed states lack the resources to deal with this matter. Indeed, one of the most striking developments of the last few years is the generalization of "remote control" by way of visa requirements and the like prior to embarking from the south to the north, an approach which was pioneered by the United States in the 1920s, when it effectively ruptured the networks that fostered ongoing immigration (Zolberg forthcoming 2002).

In conclusion, there is no gainsaying that in recent decades, the "South"—which has now been joined by the "East" as well—has generated masses of persons driven by economic circumstances to migrate, and who have the minimal capacity for overcoming the costs of doing so. Concurrently, these unfortunate world regions have also experienced severe conflict, which has generated a considerable number of refugees. However, these processes foster huge internal migrations as well as south-to-south movements, and eventuate in south-to-north migration only when certain facilitating conditions occur in the north. These include (1) the presence of employers who have an interest in recruiting foreign labor from less developed countries, and the clout to persuade their governments to adopt policies to that effect, or at least not seriously interfere with the market forces that induce workers to relocate in one way or another where jobs are to be found; (2) foreign policy considerations, or occasionally historic ties of obligation to particular groups, that dispose a given northern country to go beyond the very limited obligations of asylum arising from adherence to the contemporary international refugee regime, and agree to admit a group of refugees for permanent resettlement; and finally (3) a positive stance on the part of the receiving state toward family reunion initiatives generated by earlier immigrants, or at least relative permissiveness in relation to them.

Albeit significant, these facilitating conditions hardly amount to an "open sesame." Although this scheme leaves out of account illegal immigration—much of which begins as legal entry, followed by overstaying—its importance has been vastly exaggerated. In the United States, for example, it is currently estimated that the net yearly residue of undocumented comings and goings amounts to some 300,000, which represents an increment of a little over one-third above legal immigration. While this is a significant and worrisome proportion, it does *not* amount to a "loss of control over our borders." Considering that immigration control is undoubtedly more problematic in the United States than in most other affluent democracies, because of the long land border with a much poorer country and the long-established tradition of laissez-faire with regard to entry by way of that border, as well as widely publicized laxity in the enforcement of measures designed to deter access to the U.S. labor market (employer sanctions), we are very far from the Raspail nightmare.

In the final analysis, the "crisis" bubble does not survive statistical tests. Although it has become fashionable to refer to the present as "The age of migration," (Castles and Miller 1993), Hania Zlotnik's carefully constructed overview of international migration for the 1965–96 period reveals that at both times a little over two percent of the population in all the world's countries was foreign-born. In short, this indicates that over these three decades, migration grew at about the same rate as world population. However, the proportion of foreign-born in developed countries grew from 3.1 to 4.5 percent, whereas among developing countries, it decreased from 1.9 to 1.6 percent; although this does indicate that migration has become a more salient phenomenon in the North, this is the result of increased migration *within* the North as well as from south to north.

The most dramatic change took place in western Europe, where the proportion of foreign-born climbed from 3.6 percent to 6.1 percent, representing a relative increase of nearly 70 percent. When this quantitative change is combined with a shift in the immigrants' countries of origin, from largely western Europe itself to a more mixed combination that includes prominently the eastern and southern Mediterranean rim, one can understand that it amounts to a major social transformation. While the transformation is irreversible, it is also evident that European states quickly took steps to narrowly limit future immigration, notably by tightening up procedures for family reunion and for asylum. Although none has achieved the tacit objective of "zero immigration," the tide has clearly been effectively stemmed. North America, over the same period, grew from 6.0 from 8.6 percent, a substantial but much less dramatic increase. In the United States, the 1965 baseline is an oddity, because the proportion of foreign-born in the total population reached its lowest point since the statistic began to be recorded in 1850; although annual arrivals in recent years equal the historic records of the immediate pre–World War I years, the weight of immigration today in relation to U.S. population is only about one-fourth what it was at the record level. We are *not* living in an unprecedented "age of migration."

A more measured view is appropriate with regard to refugees as well. Contrary to the widespread notion that the situation has steadily worsened, and in particular that the end of the Cold War has unleashed a myriad new refugee-generating conflicts, Schmeidl reports that whereas the number of refugee-producing countries and the world's total refugee stock doubled between 1970 and 1990—a development clearly associated with the Cold War—in the 1990s the number of refugees declined, and from the middle of the decade on the number of refugee-sending countries declined as well. Concurrently, the number of internally displaced peaked at 27 million worldwide in 1994, but dropped by 6 million the following year (thanks largely to reduced numbers in Africa and Afghanistan). Moreover, contrary to Kennedy's analysis, population in itself plays a minimal role in generating refugee flows: in Schmeidl's study, none of the population variables could significantly predict refugee migration once political factors were controlled for.

The more measured vision of global migrants and global refugees elaborated in this study also provides the makings of a more effective and humane consideration of appropriate solutions. Our contributions fall broadly in two categories, dealing respectively with the alleviation of conditions that foster unwanted economically driven movement toward the United States, and with the alleviation or prevention of refugee-generating conflicts in the developing world.

With regard to the first, the leading theme, set forth by Philip Martin and Edward Taylor, is that "there are solutions, but no quick fix." Arguing that the policy with the best track record for accelerating stay-at-home growth is free trade, they recognize that helpful trade and investment policies may have counterproductive effects in the short term, especially if the wage gap between sending and receiving countries is very large and there are well-established migratory networks. Warning of a possible "migration hump" in the near future. they insist on the need for persistence in the appropriate policy direction, notably at the level of the "inter-American migration system." These short-term problems might be mitigated by bilateral assistance directed at employment generation and resource conservation among U.S. neighbors, as called for by William Wood and Robert Smith.

Even if free trade were to achieve the hoped-for reduction in inequality between countries, and thereby provide new and more rewarding work opportunities in the source countries, realistically this would occur only over the long term. In the intervening period, is there any alternative to the policing of borders? Taking the bull by the horns, Leah Haus systematically examines to what extent it would be possible to manage economic migrations multilaterally by way of international economic institutions. Her contribution highlights the difficulties involved, notably because of the opposition of the United States to the International Labor Organization's (ILO) initiatives throughout the Cold War. There are some indications, however, that some amelioration might be achieved at the regional level, within the framework of the European Union, and as far as the United States is concerned, the North American Free Trade Agreement. The end of the Cold War might also provide opportunities for a new start at the ILO level.

Although, as noted earlier, refugees do not "threaten" the affluent democracies because the growth of refugees worldwide seems to have reached a plateau, and most refugees remain in their regions of origin, their predicament is acute, and the fact that they are deprived of the protection and assistance residents rightly expect from their respective states—indeed, the refugees' states of origin are often the source of their predicament—creates irrefutable obligations for the international community as a whole. If the refugees are not provided opportunities for resettlement in the north, then the north must help them and their host countries in the south. But as with economic migrations, one should also consider solutions that attack the problem at its source.

Four of the contributions address themselves to various aspects of these issues. Paralleling the notion that development will alleviate economically driven migrations, democratization is likely to reduce forced movements since most of the contemporary refugee-generating conflicts have been caused or exacerbated by authoritarian rule. In this light, independently of ethical reasons for supporting and fostering democratization worldwide, the United States should do so on "realistic" grounds. However, as discussed by David Forsythe, the promotion of liberal democracy is difficult, because we don't know for sure how it comes about; and policies to this effect tend to be diffuse, because they sometimes conflict with other U.S. objectives and interests. He further points out that much of what passes for assistance to democratization in fact consists of assistance to market reform—which some argue will foster democratization—but which is hardly the same thing. In the same vein, he suggests that democratization policies of international organizations are limited and inconsistent.

So in the short term, we are left with the prospect of continuing forced migrations, and must face the problems of dealing with them more effectively. Indeed, it might be suggested on the basis of Schmeidl's analysis of post–Cold War conflicts and other observations that "democratization" produces a "refugee hump" which somewhat parallels the "migration hump" induced by free trade. There is growing evidence that management of ethnic and national differences from above, under western colonial rule as well as under Communist rule, tends to exacerbate tensions between groups, in line with the old Roman principle of "divide in order to rule." Authoritarian rule acts in effect as a "lid," which maintains these tensions under control, and thereby enhances the dependency of members of these groups, and especially threatened minorities, on the rulers' benevolence. However, when the lid is suddenly lifted, these tensions are given free play, with little or no opportunity for the groups involved to learn to manage conflict.

Reviewing recent attempts to prevent conflicts by way of humanitarian intervention, and attempts to substitute humanitarian assistance for political and military intervention, Gil Loescher concludes that most of them have been largely ineffective. Hence there is a need to develop more systematically temporary protection arrangements for the kinds of large-scale refugees flows many regions of the world are now experiencing. Guidelines to this effect can be drawn in part from UNHCR practice in the developing world since the 1960s. Beyond this, however, the tendency for western countries to focus exclusively on refugee situations that are thought to affect their security and to limit their assistance to countries that are perceived to be geopolitically important leads to neglect of other situations, sometimes more acutely threatening for the populations involved. Hence there is no choice but to revise and expand the protection side of the international refugee regime, and link it more effectively to institutions dealing with the assistance side.

The assistance side itself is considered by Thomas Weiss, who focuses on the critical difficulties of delivering assistance under conditions of late-twentieth-century internal wars; and by Richard Bissell and Andrew Natsios, who address themselves to the specifics of how the range of development assistance resources provided by the United States can best be spent in different types of emergencies, and in the face of the steadily increasing role of nongovernmental organizations. Fortunately, wars sometimes do end, and refugees sometimes do go home; and it is therefore fitting that the final chapter, by Elizabeth Ferris, should deal with repatriation and reconstruction.

References

Barraclough, Geoffrey. 1967. *An Introduction to Contemporary History*. Baltimore: Penguin Books.

Beck, Roy. 1994. "The Ordeal of Immigration in Wisconsin." *Atlantic Monthly* (April).

Bouvier, Leon F., and Lindsey Grant. 1994. *How Many Americans? Population, Immigration and the Environment*. San Francisco: Sierra Club Books.

Brimelow, Peter. 1995. *Alien Nation: Common Sense About America's Immigration Disaster*. New York: Random House.

Castles, Stephen, and Mark J. Miller. 1993. *The Age of Migration: International Population Movements in the Modern World*. New York: Guilford Press.

Cockburn, Alexander. 1994. "Follow the Money." *The Nation* (September), 225.

Connelly, Matthew, and Paul Kennedy. 1994. "Must It Be the Rest Against the West?" *Atlantic Monthly* (December): 61–91.

Cornelius, Wayne A., Philip L. Martin, and James F. Hollifield. 1994. *Controlling Immigration: A Global Perspective*. Stanford: Stanford University Press.

Donato, Katharine M., Jorge Durand, and Douglas S. Massey. 1992. "Stemming the Tide? Assessing the Deterrent Effects of the Immigration Reform and Control Act." *Demography* 29: 139–57.

Eberstadt, Nicholas. 1991. "Population Change and National Security." *Foreign Affairs* (Summer): 115–31.

Hansen, Marcus Lee. 1961 [1940]. *The Atlantic Migration, 1607–1850.* New York: Harper Torchbooks.

Homer-Dixon, Thomas. 1994. "Environmental Scarcities and Violent Conflict: Evidence from Cases." *International Security* 19, 1 (1994): 5–40.

Kaplan, Robert. 1994. "The Coming Anarchy." *The Atlantic Monthly* (February).

Kennedy, Paul. 1993. *Preparing for the Twenty-First Century.* New York: Vintage.

Kindleberger, Charles P. 1978. *Manias, Panics, and Crashes: A History of Financial Crises.* New York: Basic Books.

Massey, Douglas S. 1995. "The New Immigration and Ethnicity in the United States." *Population and Development Review* 21, 3 (September): 631–58.

Massey, Douglas S., Joaquín Arango, Graeme Hugo, Ali Kouaouci, Adela Pellegrino, and J. Edward Taylor. 1993. "Theories of International Migration: A Review and Appraisal." *Population and Development Review* 19, 3 (September): 431–66.

Massey, Douglas S., and Audrey Singer. 1995. "New Estimates of Undocumented Mexican Migration and the Probability of Apprehension." *Demography* 32: 203–313

Raspail, Jean. N.d. [1973]. *The Camp of the Saints.* Petoskey, MI: The Social Contract Press.

Sen, Amartya. 1994. "Population: Delusion and Reality." *New York Review of Books,* 22 September, 62–71.

Teitelbaum, Michael S. 1992–93. "The Population Threat." *Foreign Affairs* (Winter): 63–78.

Teitelbaum, Michael S., and Jay M. Winter, eds. 1985. *Fear of Population Decline.* New York: Academic Press.

Weiner, Myron. 1992–93. "Security, Stability, and International Migration." *International Security* 17, 3 (Winter): 91–126.

———. 1995.*The Global Migration Crisis: Challenge to States and to Human Rights.* New York: HarperCollins.

Zlotnik, Hania. 1997. "Population Growth and International Migration." Paper. International Migration at Century's End: Trends and Issues. Barcelona, May.

———. 1998. "International Migration 1965–96: An Overview." *Population and Development Review* 24, 3 (September): 429–68.

Zolberg, Aristide R. 1995. "Response: Working-Class Dissolution." *International Labor and Working-Class History* 47 (Spring): 28–38.

———. 1997. "Global Movements, Global Walls: Responses to Migration, 1885–1925." In *Global History and Migrations,* edited by Wang Gungwu, 279–307. Boulder, Colo.: Westview Press.

———. Forthcoming (2002). *A Nation by Design: Immigration Policy in the Making of America.*

Zolberg, Aristide R., Astri Suhrke, and Sergio Aguayo. 1989. *Escape from Violence: Conflict and the Refugee Crisis in the Developing World.* New York: Oxford University Press.

PART ONE

DIAGNOSIS: IS THERE A MIGRATION "CRISIS"?

– *Chapter 1* –

POPULATION GROWTH AND INTERNATIONAL MIGRATION: IS THERE A LINK?

Mary M. Kritz

Introduction: Population Growth and Immigration

Since the 1950s, the world has experienced historically unprecedented rates of population growth and even optimistic population projections envision an increase of the world's 1998 population of 5.9 billion to between 8 and 9 billion by the year 2025. Since the 1950s, the world has also experienced increased international migration, leading to public debate in the United States and other countries over the causes of immigration and over the policy and administrative actions that should be taken to regulate it. Speculation has subsequently arisen regarding whether and how population trends and U.S. immigration are linked.

Some analysts claim that there is a direct link between rapid population growth and international migration. For instance, Matthew Connelly and Paul Kennedy argued in a 1994 *Atlantic Monthly* article that rapid population growth in developing countries underlies global migration trends. That article raised alarm with its claim that "Many members of the more prosperous economies are beginning to agree … the rich will have to fight and the poor will have to die if mass migration is not to overwhelm us all" (62). Kennedy (1993) elaborated upon the impact that demographic change might have on international migration in his book *Preparing for the Twenty-First Century*, arguing that if growth in material resources fails to keep up with demographic growth, this will create strong pressures for immigration to developed countries. He also noted that "While it is clear that nations nowadays make greater efforts to restrict immigration (and, in some cases, to prevent emigration), desperate migrants are unlikely to be deterred.... Enhanced efforts to control migration, therefore, are unlikely to succeed in the face of the momentous tilt in the global demographic balances" (Kennedy 1993: 44–45).

The notion that population growth in poor countries is a root cause of U.S. immigration trends is often made by other influential voices as well. For example, in his 1993 book *Around the Cragged Hill*, George Kennan argued that

> Billions ... of people live outside our borders.... A great number of them ... look enviously over those borders and would like ... to come here.... Just as water seeks its own level, so relative prosperity, anywhere in the world, tends to suck in poverty from adjacent regions.... Given its head, and subject to no restrictions, this pressure will find its termination only when the levels of over-population and poverty in the United States are equal to those of the countries from which these people are now so anxious to escape.

While there is no gainsaying that U.S. immigration would increase if "subject to no restrictions," such a situation is completely unlikely to arise in the foreseeable future; hence by gratuitously evoking this eventuality and associating it with a water-pressure metaphor, the elder statesman of American foreign policy legitimizes alarmist nightmares of the United States being swamped by foreign hordes.

Given the growing credence within the foreign policy community that rapid population growth in developing countries fuels migration to the United States and other developed countries, it is important to assess whether there is any empirical basis for such a claim. Hania Zlotnik (1994) attempted to do that by looking at the origins of migrants to Northern America, Oceania, France, and western Europe in the 1960–91 period. That study showed that during that entire period, most European migrants were more likely to originate in other developed than in developing regions. Zlotnik (1994) also found that among migrants who did originate in developing regions, out-migration flows were higher in the 1980–90 period from regions where population growth rates were falling, namely Latin America and Eastern and Southeastern Asia, than they were from regions where population growth rates remain high, namely sub-Saharan Africa, northern Africa, and western Asia. Of the receiving regions examined by Zlotnik, only North America, i.e., Canada and the United States, received the majority of its migrants from developing regions.

Since Zlotnik's work (1994, 1996) indicates that developing regions are not a major source of migrants to western Europe, it may be useful to look more carefully at inflows to North America which receives large numbers of migrants from regions of the world that have high population growth rates. Of the two North American receivers, the United States receives far more migrants than Canada, averaging about five migrants for every one received by Canada in the 1980s.[1] Indeed, the United States has received more migrants than any other country for a number of years and draws some migrants from almost every country in the world. Given the size and diversity of the U.S. flow, analysis of its correlates can provide insight into the causes of global migrations. If one finds little evidence that levels and trends in U.S. immigration are linked to levels and trends in population growth in sending countries, then such a finding would cast doubt on the merits of the argument that demographic change and international migration are linked.

There is, of course, a large body of literature that focuses on how demographic and economic inequalities contribute to international migration. For instance, scholars routinely cite improved communication and transportation linkages as determinants of whether migrations take place from less developed countries (LDCs) to developed countries (DCs) (Golini 1993; Hofstetter 1984; Stahl 1988; Teitelbaum 1986). Michael Teitelbaum and Sharon Russell (1994) take identification of the mechanisms a step further by arguing that while economic, demographic, and political differentials between countries may create the potential for international migration, other mediating forces determine whether LDC to DC migrations actually take place. They cite several possible mediating factors, including technological advances in transport and communication, labor recruitment, social networks, trade competition between countries, government migration policies, and violence or tensions within countries.

Yang (1995) examines the role of several of these mediating forces, along with socioeconomic inequalities and world system linkages, in shaping U.S. immigration in the 1982–86 period. Of the structural and mediating factors examined by Yang,[2] the strongest relationship is found for size of immigrants' ethnic community in the U.S., which has a positive and significant effect on immigration volume. The effect of U.S. involvement in the politics and economy of the sending country is also positive and significant while the effects of modernization, political freedom, and population size are significant but negative. However, Yang does not look directly at population growth as a determinant of migration but combines it along with three other population indicators in a population pressure index. The latter, in turn, is combined into a composite index of modernization that also includes indicators of economic development, quality of life, and social opportunity. Unfortunately, one cannot determine the contribution of a single factor from this composite measure.

In the present essay, I extend Yang's work by looking at the determinants of U.S. permanent migration for a more recent period, 1989–93, and by focusing on the role of population growth. Rather than using composite indices, which obfuscate interpretation of findings when the relationships of different indicators to the underlying dimension vary, I use discrete indicators of population and economic conditions in sending countries. The broad question addressed in my analysis is whether there is any evidence that countries that differ in their levels of population growth also differ in the volume of migrants they send to the United States. I also evaluate whether three other dimensions of population— total fertility rate, population size, and population density—are directly linked to U.S. immigration and look at how selected other factors mediate the relationship of population growth and U.S. migration. Finally, I briefly evaluate whether there is any evidence that immigration from Mexico to the United States slowed after its population growth rates started to fall in the mid-1970s.

Is There an Empirical Link between U.S. Immigration and Population Pressure?

I use U.S. permanent immigration data for the 1989–93 period, the latest five-year period for which INS published statistics were available, to evaluate how migration volume is shaped by population growth and selected other characteristics of sending countries. Total migration to the United States is not adequately represented by data on permanent immigration because an unknown number of illegal migrants enter annually, as well as other foreigners on non-immigrant visas which authorize them to reside and work. Since these migrants are not evenly distributed across all senders, statistics on permanent migrants underestimate migration flows from countries that send large numbers of illegal and/or temporary migrants to the United States.[3]

In the 1989–93 period, the United States received 6,332,843 permanent immigrants, 43.9 percent of whom consisted of illegal migrants and their dependents who regularized or converted to permanent immigrant status under the Immigration Reform and Control Act (IRCA) of 1986. Because the IRCA adjusters artificially inflate permanent migration in the year in which migrant status is regularized, I remove this group of immigrants from the database[4] and focus on the remaining 3.6 million immigrants from the 112 countries in the study period.[5] Since the bulk of the migrants regularized came from Mexico, removing them from the database has a minor effect on the migration volume data of most sender nations.

Tables 1.1 through 1.4 provide summary data on U.S. immigrants for two sets of countries: the 112 countries for which the INS published data in the study period and the 165 countries that were potential senders of migrants. During the 1989–93 period, just over 99.5 percent of all U.S. immigrants came from the 112 countries. All countries, however, are potential senders and, therefore, summary measures are calculated for the larger universe of countries in order to see whether their inclusion strengthens or weakens the argument that population growth contributes to migration. The calculations for the 165 senders were based on the assumption of zero migration from the 53 countries not listed by the INS as migrant senders.

Table 1.1 provides statistics that allow us to assess the relationship between population growth and U.S. immigration. I measure population growth by a country's rate of natural increase (RNIs) in the mid-1980s. The RNI measures the difference between birth and death rates and is not affected by net migration. Since several developing countries experience substantial immigration (e.g., OPEC oil producers) or emigration (e.g., countries with small populations), their annual population growth rates are affected by international migration. The statistics in Table 1.1 show that over half (51.3 percent) of migrants originated in countries that had moderate to high RNIs (2.1–3.0 percent, col. b). However, only 5.8 percent of migrants came from the twenty countries with the highest population growth rates (3.0 percent or higher) and a substantial percentage (42.9 percent) came from countries that had lower growth rates (2 percent or lower).

Although Table 1.1 indicates that a relatively large number of U.S. immigrants do come from countries with high rates of natural increase, if we consider all 165 countries that are potential senders, we find less support for the population pressure argument.[6] A comparison of the bracketed and unbracketed statistics in columns c and d shows that of the twenty-eight countries that had the lowest population growth rates in the mid-1980s (i.e., under 1 percent), twenty-six sent migrants to the United States. At the other end of the population growth continuum, there were also twenty-eight potential senders, but only twenty of those countries sent migrants. Moreover, only forty of the seventy-two potential senders with moderate to high population growth (2.1–3.0 percent) sent migrants to the United States. Countries in each growth rate group are identified in column f and those that are not major senders are listed in parentheses. A review of the latter indicates that most of the non-senders are rapidly growing countries in sub-Saharan Africa or the Middle East.

Given that the number of countries in each growth rate group differs as well as the odds that a country sends migrants to the United States, it is instructive to look at the average number of migrants produced by the 112 senders and the 165 potential senders (col. e). The calculations for the 165 senders are shown in brackets. For the 112 senders, countries in the moderate to high population growth category (2.1–3.0 percent) produced the largest average number of migrants (46,463), followed by countries with moderate to low growth (1–2 percent) which had an average of 40,463 migrants. The sending countries with the highest growth rates, in contrast, sent only 10,521 migrants, on average. For the 165 potential senders, the largest average number of migrants came from the moderate to low growth countries (26,505) and the smallest number came from the high growth ones.

TABLE 1.1: Classification of Sending Countries by Mid-1980s Rates of Natural Increase and U.S. Permanent Immigration in 1989–1993 Period

Annual Population Growth Rate Group[2]	Total # of Immigrants by Growth Group (col. a)	% of all Immigrants from Countries in Growth Group (col. b)	# of Countries in Growth Group[3] (col. c)	% of Senders in Growth Group[3] (col. d)	Average # of Immigrants per Country in Growth Group[3] (col. e)	Countries in Growth Rate Group[3] (col. f)
under 1.0%	502,944	13.9	26 (28)	23.2 (17.0)	19,344 (17,962)	Germany, Denmark, Nethl, Czech, Spain, Sweden, NewZealand, Poland, Greece, Canada, Yugoslavia, Bulgaria, Norway, Uruguay, France, Austria, Hungary, Switzerland, Japan, Portugal, UK, Romania, Italy, Belgium, Finland, Ireland, (Malta, Luxemburg)
1–2%	1,049,6725	29.0	26 (37)	23.2 (22.4)	40,372 (26,505)	Thailand, HongKong, StKitt, Bahamas, Cuba, Chile, Israel, Australia, Argentina, China, Grenada, Antigua, Trinidad, Singapore, KoreaRP, StVincent, Haiti, Barbados, Dominica, USSR, Iceland, Macau, Jamaica, SriLanka, ElSalvador, Taiwan (NethAnt, Cyprus, GuineaBiseau, Gabon, Mauritius, Seychelles, NewCaledonia, Suriname, Martinique, Gambia, Guadeloupe)
2.1–3.0%	1,858,520	51.3	40 (72)	35.7 (43.6)	46,463 (25,813) [21,277][4]	Egypt, SaudiaAr, Guyana, Bangl, Somalia, Tonga, Malaysia, Iran, Afghn, Samoa, Myanmar, Bolivia, DomRep, Indonesia, Colombia, Philip, SierraLn, StLucia, Albania, Ethiopia, Fiji, Vietnam, Venezuela, CostaR, Beliz, Panam, Guaetmala, Ecuad, Seneg, Peru, Mex, Morocco, India, Lao, Kampuc, CapeVrd, Lebanon, Brazil, SAfric, Turk (Chad, Vanuat, Moxmb, Mongol, Papua, Maldiv, Cotelv, BurkF, Nepal, Lesot, Guinea, Comor, Djib, Brunei, Mali, UAEmirates, Tunis, Bahrain, FrPoly, Qatar, Congo, EqGuin, CenAfricanRep, Angola, Bhutan, Burundi, Niger, KoreaDP, Togo, Mauritania, Madagascar, Yemen)
over 3.0%	210,420	5.8	20 (28)	17.9 (17.0)	10,521 (7,515)	Kuwait, Syria, Liberia, Nigeria, Sudan, Honduras, Zimbabwe, Iraq, Paraguay, Jordan, Libya, Ghana, Nicaragua, Uganda, Yemen, Algeria, Cameroon, Pakistan, Kenya, Tanzania (Zambia, Swaziland, Malawi, Benin, Rwanda, Botswana, Zaire, Oman)
Total	3,621,556	99.9%	112 (165)	99.9% (99.9%)	32,336 (21,949)	

[1]IRCA adjusters are not included in permanent immigration data for the period in question.
[2]Population growth rates are for the 1984-1985 period as estimated by the United Nations and in the Population Reference Bureau Data Sheet.
[3]Numbers in parentheses in columns "c," "d," and "e" correspond to the total number of countries (165) for which population growth rates are available. Data on both population growth and U.S. immigration are available for only 112 countries. Countries with data on population growth but not on U.S. immigration are listed in parenthesis in Column "f." The latter account for less than 0.5% of all U.S. immigrants.
[4]Average number of immigrants for the total number of countries for which population growth rates are available but with Mexico excluded.

The Link between U.S. Immigration and Other Population Dimensions

Although population growth is the element of population that tends to be identified as an underlying stimulant of migration, it may not be the best indicator of population pressure. In this section, I look at three other population indicators—total fertility rates (TFRs), population density, and population size—to determine how they are related to U.S. migration. Using the same approach as followed for population growth in Table 1.1, countries are cross classified by their population indicators and immigration levels in the 1989–93 period. While TFRs measure population growth potential, population size and density capture indirectly the relationship of population to resources. The world's countries vary widely in population size and density, but these dimensions tend to be ignored in today's international system which has countries as its building blocks.

Table 1.2 shows variations in U.S. immigration by total fertility rates. Countries with TFRs of 3 to 4.5 children per woman produced 44.9 percent of all migrants while countries with lower TFRs sent an additional 40.0 percent.[7] Since 48.5 percent of the 165 potential senders had TFRs higher than 4.5, these statistics tell us that most U.S. migrants do not come from countries that have the highest TFRs. A comparison of the average number of migrants sent per country (col. e) by TFR group indicates that the thirty-five countries with below replacement fertility (under 2.1) sent an average of 19,752 migrants to the United States while those with the highest TFRs (over 6.0) sent an average of 5,908 migrants. Moreover, while almost all countries that have low fertility sent some migrants to the U.S., only about half of those in the high fertility categories (4.5–6.0 and over 6.0) did so. To the extent that there is an observed relationship, it appears to be curvilinear with countries in the moderate fertility category producing more migrants than either the highest or lowest fertility countries.

Table 1.3 suggests that there is a direct relationship between population size and U.S. migration. Fully 58.5 percent of migrants came from the twenty-five largest countries in the world, all of which have populations over 32 million. At the other end of the size scale, the thirty-four smallest countries, which had populations under 4 million, produced only 12.4 percent of U.S. immigrants. The range in the average number of migrants (col. e) from countries in different population size groups is substantial, varying from 2,022 migrants per country for the smallest size group to 89,636 per country in the 32 to 80 million size group. Removing Mexico from the latter group, a reasonable thing to do given its disproportionate contribution to U.S. immigration, reduces the average number of migrants per country to 72,410.

Population density is also linked to U.S. immigration. Table 1.4 shows that 40.6 percent of immigrants in the 1989–93 period came from countries with population densities of 175 or more persons per square kilometer, although only 24.6 percent of all countries fall into that density group.

TABLE 1.2: Classification of Sending Countries by Late 1980s Total Fertility Rate (TFR) and U.S. Permanent Immigration in 1989–1993 Period

TFR Group[2]	Total # of Immigrants by TFR Group (col. a)	% of all Immigrants from countries in TFR Group (col. b)	# of Sending Countries in TFR Group (col. c)[3]	% of Senders in TFR Group (col. d)[3]	Average # of Immigrants per Country in TFR Group (col. e)[3]	Countries in TFR Group (col. f)[3]
under 2.1	691,320	19.1	30 (35)	26.8 (21.2)	23,044 (19,752)	Finland, Czechoslovakia, Greece, Hungary, Japan, Sweden, Switzerlnd, Canada, Austria, Australia, Italy, UK, StKitt, Ireland, NewZeal, Germany, France, Cuba, Norway, Nethln, Belgium, Urug, Spain, Portugal, Barbados, Yugoslavia, Poland, KoreaRP, Singapore, Taiwan, Denmark, Antigua (Malta, Luxemburg, Mauritania, NethAn, Martinique)
2.1–3.0	726,376	20.1	17 (21)	15.2 (12.7)	42,728 (34,589)	Uruguay, StKitt, Ireland, Guyana, Bahamas, HongKong, Jamaica, Argentina, USSR, Romania, Dominique, Thailand, SriLanka, Iceland, Chile, China, StVincent (Suriname, KoreaDP, Seychelles, Guadeloupe)
3.0–4.5	1,626,550	44.9	25 (29)	22.3 (17.6)	65,062 (56,088) [45,666][4]	ElSalvador, Panama, Myanmar, CostaRica, Venezuela, Albania, Brazil, Mexico, StLucia, Indonesia, Ecuador, DominicanRep, Lebanon, Malaysia, Fiji, Macau, Peru, India, Israel, Vietnam, Trinidad, Kuwait, Colombia, Turkey, Philippines (Bahrain, Brunei, Tunisia, Cyprus)
4.5–6.0	317,394	8.8	21 (36)	18.8 (21.8)	15,114 (8,817)	Bolivia, Belize, Grenada, Bangladesh, Lao, Cameroon, Guatemala, Hondur, Jordan, Paraguay, CapeVrd, Morocco, Nicaragua, Zimbabwe, Egypt, Libya, Kampuchea, Tonga, Haiti, SouthAfrica, Samoa (UAEmirates, EqGuinea, GuineaBiseau, Chad, Botswana, Vanuatu, SaoTome, Qatar, PapuaNG, CenAfricaRep, Mongolia, Gabon, Lesotho, Congo, Bhutan)
over 6.0	259,958	7.2	19 (44)	17.0 (26.7)	13,682 (5,908)	Ethiopia, Afghanistan, Uganda, Sudan, Algeria, Liberia, Syria, Iraq, Pakistan, Senegal, Ghana, Kenya, Somalia, Iran, SierraLeone, SaudiArab, Tanzania, Nigeria (Mozambique, Zaire, Rwanda, Mali, Djibouti, SolomonIs, Yemen, Benin, Malawi, Swaziland, Gambia, Mauritania, CoteIvoire, BurkinaFaso, Oman, Zambia, Togo, Comoros, Madagascar, Maldives, Angola, Burundi, Niger, Nepal, Guinea)
Total	3,621,598	100.1 (%)	112 (165) (N)	100.1 (%)	32,336 (21,949)	

[1] IRCA adjusters are not included in permanent immigration data for the period in question.

[2] The total fertility rate measures the number of children that a woman will bear by the end of her reproductive life based on current age-specific fertility rates. Data are for the mid to late 1980s as estimated by the United Nations.

[3] Numbers in parentheses in columns "c", "d" and "e" correspond to the total number of countries (165) for which fertility rates are available. Countries with data on total fertility but not on U.S. immigration are listed in parentheses in Column "f".

[4] Average number of immigrants for the total number of countries for which fertility rates are available but with Mexico excluded.

TABLE 1.3: Classification of Sending Countries by 1985 Population Size and U.S. Permanent Immigration in 1989–1993 Period[1]

Population Size Group[2]	Total # of Immigrants by Size Group (col. a)	% of all Immigrants from Countries in Size Group (col. b)	# of Sending Countries in Size Group (col. c)[3]	% of Senders in Size Group (col. d)[3]	Average # of Immigrants per Country in Size Group (col. e)[3]	Countries in Population Size Group (col. f)[3]
under 1,000,000	99,088	2.7	16 (49)	14.3 (27.7)	6,193 (2,022)	Guyana, StLucia, Macau, Belize, StKitt, Antigua, Tonga, CapeVerde, Bahamas, Barbados, Fiji, Samoa, Grenada, Iceland, Dominica, StVincent (Qatar, Tuvalu, Maldives, Luxemburg, EqGuinea, Djibouti, Nauru, FrPoly, Malta, Swaz, Burund, Surinam, NCaledonia, Bahamas, Vanuatu, Liechenstein, Guadeloupe, SaoTome, Cyprus, HolySee, Seychelles, GuineaB, Martinique, Byelorus, Gabon, Gambia, Monaco, SanMarino, Solomon1s, Ukraine, NethAntilles, Comoros, Kiribati)
1–4,000,000	351,048	9.7	18 (31)	16.1 (18.1)	19,503 (11,324)	Uruguay, Lebanon, Libya, Ireland, Panama, Kuwait, Paraguay, Jordan, Trinidad, Laos, Albania, Jamaica, Nicaragua, NewZealand, SierraLeone, CostaR, Singapore, Liberia (Bhutan, Mauritania, Yemen, PapuaNewGuinea, Oman, UArabEmirates, Congo, Togo, CentAfricaRep, Mauritius, Mongolia, Lesotho, Botswana)
4–8,100,000	505,148	13.9	17 (28)	15.2 (15.8)	29,715 (18,041)	Austria, Honduras, Senegal, Norway, HongK, Haiti, Yemen, DomR, Finland, Switz, Somalia, Bolivia, Kampuchea, Israel, Denmark, Guatemala, ElSal (Burundi, Benin, BurkF, Niger, Guinea, Malawi, Rwanda, Chad, Tunisia, Zambia, Mali)
8.1–15,000,000	181,845	5.0	16 (20)	14.3 (11.3)	11,365 (9,092)	Ecuador, Netherlands, Portugal, Cuba, Syria, Belgium, Ghana, Sweden, Chile, Greece, SaudiArabia, Cambodia, Bulgaria, Afghanistan, Zimbabwe, Hungary (Mozambique, Cotelvoire, Madagascar, Angola)
15–32,000,000	367,420	10.1	20 (23)	17.9 (13.0)	18,371 (12,972)	Sudan, Iraq, SriLanka, Venezuela, Australia, Yugoslavia, Uganda, Romania, Kenya, SouthAfrica, Peru, Algeria, Czechoslovakia, Tanzania, Colombia, Canada, Malaysia, Argentina, Morocco, Taiwan (Nepal, KoreaDP, Taiwan, Zaire)
32–80,000,000	1,434,196	39.6	16 (16)	14.3 (9.0)	89,637 (89,637) [72,420]	Mexico, Iran, UK, Germany, Italy, Ethiopia, Poland, Philippines, France, Vietnam, Spain, Turkey, Myanmar, KoreaRP, Thailand, Egypt
over 80,000,000	682,854	18.9	9 (9)	8.0 (5.1)	75,873 (75,873)	USSR, China, Indonesia, Bangladesh, India, Japan, Brazil, Pakistan, Nigeria
Total	3,621,599	99.9 (%)	112 (176) (N)	100.0 (%)	32,336 (20,577)	

[1] IRCA status adjusters are not included in permanent immigration data for the period in question.
[2] Data on population size in 1985 are from the United Nations. Data for Taiwan and other countries with missing data are from the World Population Data Sheet of the Population Reference Bureau. Data for Taiwan and "e" correspond to the total number of countries (176) for which data on population size are available. Countries with data on population size but not on U.S. immigration are listed in parentheses in Column "f."
[3] Numbers in parentheses in columns "c," "d," and "e" correspond to the total number of countries (176) for which data on population size is available but with Mexico excluded.
[4] Average number of immigrants for the total number of countries for which 1985 population size is available but with Mexico excluded.

TABLE 1.4: Classification of Sending Countries by 1989 Population Density and U.S. Immigration in 1989–1993 Period[1]

Population Density Group[2] (persons per square kilometer)	Total # of Immigrants by Density Group (col. a)	% of all Immigrants from Countries in Density Group (col. b)	# of Countries in Density Group (col. c)[3]	% of Senders in Density Group (col. d)[3]	Average # Immigrants per Country in Density Group (col. e)[3]	Countries in Density Group (col. f)[3]
Under 16	369,614	10.2	17 (36)	15.3 (21.1)	21,742 (10,267)	Sudan, Algeria, Paraguay, Libya, NewZealand, Iceland, Bolivia, Guyana, SaudiArabia, Belize, Australia, Somalia, Finland, Norway, USSR, Canada, Argentina (Gabon, Botswana, Zaire, Suriname, Mali, Oman, Yemen, Vanuatu, Angola, PapuaNewGuinea, CentAfricaR, Mongolia, Mauritania, Niger, Congo, EquatorialGuinea, SolomonIs, Chad, Zambia)
16–49	879,396	24.3	29 (43)	26.1 (25.2)	30,324 [20,451] [12,655]	Ethiopia, Iraq, SouthAfrica, Nicaragua, Chile, Yemen, Tanzania, Kampuchea, Kenya, Zimbabwe, Afghanistan, Panama, Jordan, Mexico, Ecuador, Colombia, Honduras, Liberia, Iran, Senegal, Fiji, Laos, Peru, Uruguay, Bahrain, Venezuela, Brazil, Sweden, Cameroon (Emirates, Burundi, Qatar, CotelVoire, BurkinaFaso, Guinea, Madagascar, GuineaBissau, Swaziland, Djibouti, Benin, Tunisia, Bhutan, Mozambique)
50–100	297,286	8.2	22 (29)	19.8 (17.0)	13,513 (10,251)	Spain, Indonesia, Turkey, Uganda, Guatemala, CapeVerde, Austria, Bulgaria, Morocco, Ireland, Samoa, Egypt, Ghana, Greece, Malaysia, Syria, Yugoslavia, Romania, CostaRica, Myanmar, SierraLeone, Cuba (Gambia, Kiribati, Lesotho, Cyprus, Togo, FrPolynesia, Malawi)
101–174	602,688	16.7	16 (21)	14.4 (12.3)	37,668 (28,699)	Kuwait, Tonga, DominicanRep, Hungary, Dominica, China, Czechslovakia, Pakistan, France, Portugal, Switzerland, Poland, Albania, Thailand, Nigeria, Denmark (Luxemburg, Guadeloupe, Nepal, Liechenstein, SaoTome)
175 or more	1,469,205	40.6	27 (42)	24.3 (24.6)	54,415 (33,337)	StVincent, Lebanon, UK, Belgium, Netherland, Antigua, Israel, Philippines, Haiti, SriLanka, Grenada, Japan, Bangladesh, Vietnam, ElSalvador, HongKong, Germany, Jamaica, StKitt, StLucia, Singapore, KoreaRP, India, Barbados, Italy, Trinidad, Taiwan (Maldives, Mauritius, Bahrain, Malta, KoreaDP, Taiwan, Comoros, Rwanda, Nauru, SanMoreno, Martinique, Seychelles, Burundi, Tuvalu, NetherlandsAntilles, Monaco)
Total	3,618,189	100.0 (%)	111 (171) (N)	99.900.0 (%)	32,596 (21,159)	

[1] IRCA status adjusters are not included in permanent immigration data for the period in question.
[2] Data on population density in 1989 are calculated from data provided by the United Nations and the World Population Data Sheet of the Population Reference Bureau.
[3] Numbers in parentheses in columns "c," "d," and "e" correspond to the total number of countries (171) for which data on population density are available. Countries with data on population density but not on U.S. immigration are listed in parentheses in column "f."
[4] Average number of immigrants for the total number of countries for which 1989 population size is available but with Mexico excluded.

Countries with population densities under 16 persons per square kilometer, in contrast, were less likely to send migrants to the United States. A comparison of the average number of immigrants per country (col. e) by density group shows that the group of countries with densities below 100 produced 10,000 to 13,000 migrants on average, with Mexico excluded, while those with densities above 100 produced just over 28,000 migrants on average. In addition, high density countries (over 100 persons per square kilometer) are more likely to produce migrants than low density countries (less than 50 persons per square kilometer).

Population and Other Mediating Factors in U.S. Immigration

In this section, I look at the relative importance of the four population indicators examined in Tables 1.1 to 1.4 and four additional factors that are often identified as migration determinants: distance between the sending country and the United States; the presence in the United States of other foreigners from the sending country; economic growth in sending countries; and social welfare. Distance is often used in migration models as a proxy for economic and social costs associated with long distance migration. In a world of growing interdependencies, those costs should be decreasing but nonetheless may be significant and deter migration. From a conceptual standpoint, migrant stock serves as a proxy for social networks, which play an important role in migration processes (Gurak and Caces 1992; Massey et al. 1993). Economic growth and social welfare in sending countries are often cited as important determinants of migration by economists (Martin and Taylor, this volume).

Measuring these factors is not straightforward nor are data available for all countries. I use Fitzpatrick and Modlin's (1986) estimates of distance between New York City and the capital cities of sending countries. This is a straight line measure that does not reflect actual air travel distances that might be covered by migrants. Although New York City is used as the U.S. referent point, this does not bias estimates as much as might be suspected for migrants from Asian countries since the measure is Geographic Information System (GIS) based and uses the shortest distance between most Asian countries and the United States, which is across the North Pole.

For the measure of immigrant stock, I use the number of foreign-born counted in the 5% Public Use Microdata files from the 1990 U.S. Census. Although there is some overlap in the period covered by this measure and the five-year measure of U.S. immigration volume, this should not present a problem given that immigration volume is fairly evenly distributed across the five-year period and highly correlated with volume of prior years.

The effects of economic growth and human welfare in sending countries are examined by two measures: growth in gross domestic product per capita in the 1980–88 period and score on the human development index (HDI) in 1991. Developed by the UNDP, the HDI compares countries on three aspects of human welfare: longevity, knowledge, and income. Longevity is measured by life expectancy at birth; knowledge by adult literacy and mean years of schooling; and income by a measure that adjusts per capita income for purchasing power.[8] However, both the economic growth and HDI data are missing for several countries and, therefore, only subsets of countries can be examined. The correlation matrix for the eight measures is shown in columns 1–8 of Table 1.5.

To address the question of the relative importance of population pressure and other forces in U.S. migration processes, the last column of Table 1.5 shows the zero-order standardized regression coefficients between each factor and U.S. immigration volume in the 1989–93 period. Standardized regression coefficients express the unit change in standard deviations, which allows one to evaluate the contribution of each factor relative to others. In particular, the larger the size of the coefficient, the stronger the relationship of a given factor to the dependent variable. A comparison of the standardized coefficients in Table 1.5 indicates that foreign-born stock in the United States is the strongest correlate of immigration—a one standard deviation change in foreign-born stock is associated with almost three-quarters of a standard deviation change in immigration. All of the other factors except population density also have strong and significant relationships to immigration. Factors showing positive relationships, by order of importance, are sending country population size, growth in GDP per capita, and HDI. Negative relationships occur for TFR, RNI, and distance.

The zero-order standardized coefficients suggest that rapid population growth does not underlie U.S. migration. Although population growth is significantly related to migration, the direction is negative rather than positive, which indicates that countries growing more rapidly actually send fewer migrants. Population size is the only population dimension that has a strong positive relationship to migration. It is also interesting to note that economic and social welfare in sending countries is positively associated with U.S. migration, rather than negatively, as often claimed.

Since it is plausible that the relationship of population growth to migration is mediated by distance, migrant stock, and economic and social welfare, I next look at whether the relationship of population growth to migration changes after controlling for these dimensions. Because Mexico, Vietnam, and the Philippines[9] exert strong outlier effects on the relationships, they were removed from the database for the models estimated in Table 1.6. Including them would actually strengthen the argument that population growth is not a critical dimension shaping U.S. immigration.

Model 1, Table 1.6, shows that migration volume in the 1989–93 period is negatively related to a country's population growth, as measured by its

Table 1.5: Correlation Matrix (pairwise) and Standardized Zero-Order Regression Coefficients of Country Characteristics and U.S. Immigration (1989–1993)[a]

Variables	1	2	3	4	5	6	7	8	Standardized Regression Coefficient (R)[b]
1. Rate of natural increase (1990)	—								-.175* (3.1)
2. Total fertility rate (~1990)	.85***	—							-.241** (5.8)
3. Population size (1985)	-.08	-.12	—						.630*** (39.9)
4. Population density (1989)	-.18*	-.20*	-.02	—					-.022 (0.0)
5. Distance	.29***	.32 ***	.11	-.00	—				-.15* (2.2)
6. Foreign-born stock (1990)	-.39***	-.39***	.39***	-.03	-.26***	—			.716*** (51.3)
7. Growth in GDP per capita (1980–88)	.05	-.03	.32	.14	.41***	.09	—		.193* (3.7)
8. HDI (1991)	-.66***	-.86***	.03	.16*	-.33***	.33***	-.04	—	.190** (3.6)

[a]Three countries (Mexico, Vietnam, and the Philippines) are dropped from these calculations because they exert strong outlier effects on the coefficients. Asterisks indicate significance levels: * < .05, ** < .01, *** < .001.
[b]These models include only a single covariate in each model.

Table 1.6: Ordinary Least Squares (OLS) Regression of U.S. Immigration in 1989–1993 Period on Population and Other Covariates[a]

Covariates	Model 1	Model 2	Model 3	Model 4
Total fertility rate (~1990)	-2963.23**	-1902.77	719.35	—
Population size (1985, in 000s)	193.64***	202.86***	137.23***	129.62***
Distance (in 000s)		-2706.23**	-975.07	-2919.88**
Foreign-born stock (1990, in 000s)			2561.00***	2050.90***
Growth in GDP per capita (1980–88)				952.73
HDI 1991				-5022.70
Number of cases	162	161	161	102
R^2	42.7***	45.6***	66.2***	69.1***

[a]Three countries (Mexico, Vietnam, and the Philippines) are dropped from these models because they exert strong outlier effects on the coefficients. Asterisks indicate level of significance: $* < .05$, $** < .01$, $*** < .001$. Regression coefficients are unstandardized.

TFR, but positively related to its population size. Indeed, these two population dimensions account for 42.7 percent of the variance in migration volume, with population size being the most important of the two measures (see bracketed figures in last column of Table 1.5). After controlling for distance in Model 2, the effects of population growth are no longer significant, which is consistent with the fact that countries located at greater distances from the United States tend to have higher TFRs (see zero-order correlation matrix, Table 1.5). Distance itself, however, is significantly related to migration volume and in the expected negative direction. Population size remains significant after controlling for distance.

Foreign-born stock is added in Model 3 and is positively related to migration volume, net of other factors included in the model. While population size remains significant in that model, the relationship is weaker than in the first two models and distance becomes insignificant. Since countries located at greater distance from the United States also have lower foreign-born stock (zero order correlation = -.26, Table 1.5), this finding tells us that level of prior migration rather than geographic distance is a key factor shaping U.S. migration.

Model 4 shows the relationships between economic and social welfare of sending countries and U.S. immigration. The TFR measure is not included in this model because it is highly correlated with HDI. Data on both HDI and growth in GDP per capita are available for only 102 countries and, therefore, the findings presented in Model 4 are not directly comparable to models 2 and 3 which were calculated for 161 countries. Keeping that constraint in mind, Model 4 shows that neither economic or social welfare has a significant relationship to migration. The HDI index, however, is in the expected negative direction, indicating that as social welfare improves, U.S. immigration decreases. Growth in GDP per capita, in contrast, has a positive rather than negative relationship to migration. The effects of distance are negative and significant in Model 4 and the relationships of migrant stock and population size to migration remain strong.

Although the findings in Table 1.6 have limitations, they provide little support for the claim that population growth fuels U.S. migration. Indeed, the only population dimension that shows a consistent and positive relationship with migration is country population size. That relationship, however, is mediated by migrant stock and is reduced by the sending country's level of economic and social welfare. Moreover, the effects of sending country population size are small relative to those of existing migrant stock in the United States. There is a significant zero-order relationship between a country's TFR and migration but the direction is negative rather than positive and appears to be accounted for by the fact that countries located at greater distance from the United States have higher fertility levels.

Mexican Trends in Population Growth and U.S. Immigration

The analysis presented thus far is based on analysis of cross-sectional data. One criticism of cross-sectional analyses is that relationships might differ if examined in a dynamic framework. To determine whether that is the case, in this section I look at whether there is any evidence of a link between demographic change in Mexico and Mexican migration to the United States in recent decades. Mexico is the largest sender of migrants to the United States, producing between 20 and 25 percent of all migrants in recent years. According to the rapid population growth argument, today's babies become tomorrow's immigrants when they reach adulthood and find no jobs waiting for them. In the case of Mexico, fertility rates were high down to the early 1970s but began a sharp descend after that point. If reductions in population growth are related to emigration, one would expect to see a decline in Mexican emigration starting in the mid- to late 1980s, since new entrants into the labor force started to moderate then.

For this part of the analysis, I compiled data on Mexico's TFRs in the 1958–78 period (Nuñez, Mendoza, and Bustillo 1982), U.S. immigration in the 1973–93 period, and Mexico's per capita income in the 1973–93 period. Figure 1.1 shows graphs of trends in these three factors and reveals no correlation between them. The beginnings of a downward trend in Mexico's TFR in the early 1970s can be detected in Graph A, but that decline was not accompanied by decreases in U.S. immigration in the late 1980s (Graph B), as should have happened if population pressures cause emigration. Throughout the period, Mexican migration rises and falls and shows no relationship to trends in either fertility or GNP per capita (Graph C). Thus, not only was declining fertility in Mexico in the early 1970s not accompanied by decreases in U.S. migration fifteen years later, but, to the extent that any change in migration volume occurred, it was toward an increase rather than a decrease in migration in the early 1990s. Had illegal migrant status adjusters been included in the analysis, the trend toward increasing migration from Mexico in the late 1980s would be even stronger.

Figure 1.1: Trends in Mexico's Total Fertility Rates, U.S. Immigration, and per capita GNP, 1973–1993

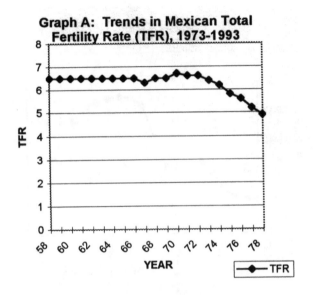

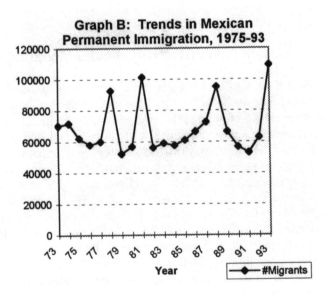

(continued on next page)

Figure 1.1: Trends in Mexico's Total Fertility Rates, U.S. Immigration, and per capita GNP, 1973–1993 *(continued)*

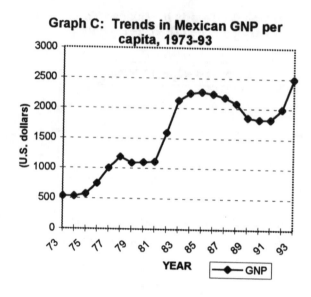

Graph C: Trends in Mexican GNP per capita, 1973-93

Summing Up: Population Trends and Future Migration Patterns

Proponents of the claim that population growth fuels global migrations argue that economic and other inequalities stemming from rapid population growth underlie contemporary migrations from developing countries (LDCs) to developed countries (DCs). Since the United States is the major world recipient of migrants from developing countries, I examined whether there was any evidence that differentials in population growth and other population factors were correlated with U.S. immigration in the 1989–93 period. Since other work (Zlotnik 1994, 1996) shows that most migrants to western Europe originate in developed regions rather than developing regions, a finding of no relationship for the United States would indicate that the population pressure thesis has little merit. In other words, if population pressure is not driving immigration to the two developed regions that receive the bulk of today's immigrants, then the population pressure claim can be called into question.

My analysis provides no support for the claim that population growth drives U.S. immigration. Indeed, migrants are more likely to come from countries with low to moderate population growth rates than they are from ones with the highest growth rates. A similar pattern is found for total fertility rates (TFRs): countries with intermediate TFRs are most likely to send migrants to the United States, and countries with low to moderate TFRs are more likely than ones with high TFRs to send migrants. I also looked at Mexican migration to the U.S. in order to evaluate whether fertility declines in Mexico, which started in the early 1970s, were accompanied by decreasing emigration to the United States in the late 1980s. That analysis showed that not only was there no decline, Mexican emigration actually increased in the late 1980s.

Population size is the only population dimension that consistently showed a positive relationship to U.S. migration. Although findings were not presented in the paper, I also looked at the relationship between population size and a country's emigration rate. That analysis reveals that while large countries do send the largest number of migrants to the United States, they actually have lower emigration rates than smaller countries. In other words, population size is positively linked to the number of migrants that a country sends but negatively associated with its emigration rate. This finding indicates that although a relatively large number of people in large countries are able to obtain permanent resident visas, their overall odds of getting one are actually lower than those of nationals from smaller countries. Thus most of the large country effects observed in this essay probably results from the fact that there are simply more people in a large country who are able to develop the family relations, skills, or other ties that enable them to qualify for a U.S. permanent residency visa.

Since continued population growth will lead to significant increases in the population size of many countries, is it plausible that countries that move into the "large" population size group will send increasing numbers of migrants to the United States in the years ahead? I would argue that this is unlikely to occur because migration flows are relatively stable across time and it is very difficult for a country that is not already a major sender to become one. European countries historically sent large numbers of migrants to the United States and many of them continue to be well represented in today's flow. In addition, large numbers of migrants have historically come from Mexico and other countries in the Caribbean Basin. Those flows are facilitated by short distances to the United States and extensive family ties. Large numbers of migrants also come from Asian countries with which the United States has had close geopolitical ties (e.g., the Philippines, South Korea, Vietnam). Although my analysis shows that about two-thirds of the world's countries send some migrants to the United States, most of these countries send a relatively small number and it is difficult to envision a scenario whereby their numbers would increase. It is also difficult to envision a scenario whereby currently underrepresented countries would become major senders, although "diversity" visas are allowing some new senders to emerge.

Undoubtedly, this analysis has many limitations and thus those who believe that rapid population growth underlies international migration, as well as a host of other problems, will likely not be convinced by findings. To evaluate fully the proposition that rapid population growth fuels international migration, we would need net migration data for all countries in the world, as well as data on other factors examined in this study, including economic and social welfare, distance between sending and receiving countries, and migration policies. It would also be useful to have data on transnational and other flows between countries in order to evaluate how they shape migration flows. Unfortunately such comprehensive data do not exist and, therefore, we need to rely on other techniques and data that allow us to analyze parts of the global migration system (Zlotnik 1987, 1994, 1997).

Whether comparable findings would emerge for the world as a whole if comprehensive data were available remains to be determined. I noted at the outset of this essay that the United States receives more migrants from developing countries than any other developed country. Thus it is likely that there would be even less of a relationship between population growth and international migration if net migration data were available for all countries given that a significant share of movements occur between countries that have similar demographic indicators. Indeed, most of the world's migrants probably move from one LDC to another, and significant numbers also move from one DC to another. In addition, growing numbers of persons are migrating from DCs to LDCs. The presence of migration flows in these different directions would probably dwarf contemporary movements from LDCs to DCs.

The main goal of this chapter has been to evaluate the correlates of U.S. migration. By questioning the claim that rapid population growth is linked to trends in the U.S., I have not meant to question the concern of many that rapid population growth poses many problems for development. Nor should the findings be construed as favoring a particular position with regard to levels of U.S. immigration. To the extent that this analysis has anything to say with regard to immigration policy issues, the message would be that geographic proximity and established migration flows are major elements that shape U.S. immigration flows. In the U.S. policy context, which emphasizes family reunification, the latter will likely continue to be key elements driving immigration in the years ahead even if reductions in rapid population growth and economic development occur.

Notes

1. In the 1990–94 period, the U.S. received nine migrants to every one received by Canada but the ratio was four to one or lower in the 1960–79 period (Zlotnik 1997).
2. Yang looked at nine factors, four of which were indices that included several different indicators, many of which measure different dimensions. The four clusters were identified by factor analysis and measure the concepts of

U.S. economic, military, and cultural involvement in the sending country; modernization; economic growth; and political freedom. The other five factors in his model are discrete variables: migration cost as measured by distance to the United States; population size of the sending country; percentage of migrants from a given country who are professionals; size of the immigrants' ethnic community in the U.S.; and emigration policy of the sending country.

3. Since a growing proportion of permanent immigrants consists of foreigners who adjust status within the United States and most of those who do so enter under an authorized non-immigration visa, it could be argued that countries that send large numbers of temporary migrants are adequately represented in the permanent immigration data, albeit with some distortion due to the lag time between arrival as a temporary immigrant and adjustment to permanent immigration status. If this assumption is correct, only illegal migrants entering without legal authorization are underrepresented in the permanent migration statistics since they are probably less likely to regularize their status than temporary migrants.

4. Removing the IRCAs is the best strategy given that their year of arrival is unknown but, according to IRCA legislation, they had to have arrived in the United States prior to 1 January 1982. This being the case, they would be responding to different origin context conditions than immigrants newly admitted for permanent residence in the 1989–93 period.

5. In the case of a few countries that send a small number of immigrants, the INS does not include their immigration data for all five years. If the time series was incomplete for four of the five years, I substituted the annual four-year average for the missing year.

6. In addition to the 165 countries for which RNI data are available, there are several other small sized units, largely islands or dependencies for which data are not available. Excluded units include: Bermuda, Guam, American Samoa, Cook Island, Isle of Man, Cocos Isles, French Guiana, Christmas Island, Turks and Caicos, Norfolk Island, Channel Islands, Aruba, Greenland, St. Pierre, U.S. Virgin Islands, Montserrat, Holy See, Tokelau, Falkland Islands, Gibraltar, etc. None of these units have large populations although several of them may experience emigration. The former Soviet Union continues to be treated as a single unit in INS annual reports.

7. Ideally, the TFRs for the period fifteen to twenty years prior to the immigration period would be used based on the argument that high fertility today creates tomorrow's immigrants. On the other hand, countries that have high fertility today also had high fertility in the 1960s and almost all developing countries had high fertility in the 1960s. This being the case, there would be insufficient variation to detect a pattern if the 1960 rates were used.

8. The HDI index was introduced by the UNDP in its *Human Development Report 1990* and updated and modified in each of its subsequent annual reports. For a discussion of HDI measurement and subsequent adjustments, see *Human Development Report 1992* (UNDP 1992: 91–96).

9. These three countries sent the most migrants to the United States in the 1989–93 period, which is why they exert strong outlier effects of model estimates.

References

Connelly, Matthew, and Paul Kennedy. 1994. "Must it be the rest against the West?" *Atlantic Monthly*, 274, 1: 61–84.

Fitzpatrick, Gary, and Marilyn Modlin. 1986. *Direct-line Distances*. Metuchen, N.J.: Scarecrow Press.

Golini, Antonio. 1983. "Population Vitality and Decline: The North-South Contrast." In *The Changing Course of International Migration*, edited by OECD. Paris: OECD.

Gurak, Douglas, and Fe Caces. 1992. "Migration Networks and the Shaping of Migration Systems." In *International Migration Systems: A Global Approach*, edited by Mary M. Kritz, Lin Lean Lim, and Hania Zlotnik. London: Oxford University Press.

Hofstetter, Richard R. 1984. "Economic Underdevelopment and the Population Explosion—Implications for U.S. Policy." In *U.S. Immigration Policy*, edited by Richard R. Hofstetter. Durham: North Carolina: Duke University Press.

Kennan, George F. 1993. *Around the Cragged Hill: A Personal and Political Philosophy*. New York: W.W. Norton.

Kennedy, Paul. 1993. *Preparing for the Twenty-First Century*. New York: Random House.

Massey, Douglas, Joaquín Arango, Graeme Hugo, Ali Kouaouci, Adela Pellegrino, and J. Edward Taylor. 1993. "Theories of International Migration: A Review and Appraisal." *Population and Development Review* 19, 3 (September): 431–66.

Nuñez, Leopoldo, Doroteo Mendoza, and Emiliana Bustillo. 1982. "Fertility Trends at National Level 1970–1979." In *The Demographic Revolution in Mexico 1970–1980*, edited by Jorge Martinez Manautou. Mexico: IMSS.

Stahl, Charles W. 1988. "Introduction." *International Migration Today*, Vol. 2, *Emerging Issues*. Edited by UNESCO and the Centre for Migration and Development Studies, University of Western Australia.

Teitelbaum, Michael S. 1986. "Intersections: Immigration and Demographic Change and Their Impact on the United States." In *World Population and U.S. Policy: The Choices Ahead*, edited by Jane Menken. New York: W.W. Norton and Co.

Teitelbaum, Michael S., and Sharon Stanton Russell. 1994. "International Migration, Fertility, and Development." In *Population and Development: Old Debates, New Conclusions*, edited by Robert Cassen. New Brunswick: Transaction Publishers.

UNDP (United Nations Development Program). 1992. *Human Development Report 1992*. New York: Oxford University Press.

Yang, Philip Q. 1995. *Post-1965 Immigration to the United States: Structural Determinants*. Westport, CT: Praeger.

Zlotnik, Hania. 1987. "The Concept of International Migration as Reflected in Data Collection Systems." *International Migration Review* 21, 4 (Winter): 925–46.

———. 1994. "International Migration: Causes and Effects." In *Beyond the Numbers: A Reader on Population, Consumption, and the Environment*, edited by Laurie Ann Mazur. Washington, D.C.: Island Press.

————. 1996. "Migration to and from Developing Regions: A Review of Past Trends." In *Alternative Paths of Future World Population Growth*, edited by Wolfgang Lutz. Laxenburg, Austria: International Institute for Applied Systems Analysis.

————. 1997. "Population Growth and International Migration." Paper presented at the Conference on International Migration at Century's End: Trends and Issues. Barcelona, Spain, May.

– *Chapter 2* –

ECOMIGRATION: LINKAGES BETWEEN ENVIRONMENTAL CHANGE AND MIGRATION

William B. Wood

Introduction

Environmental factors influence migrations and migrants alter environments. This obvious and simple conclusion covers a range of complex and dynamic relationships that span regions and history (as well as prehistory). Projections that sea level rise will send millions in search of higher ground and fears that uncontrolled illegal immigration are ruining pristine first world environments are stimulating interest in the connections between environmental trends and migration patterns. Anti- immigrant rhetoric and apocalyptic forecasts of environmental disaster, though, may also be obfuscating a rational policy discussion of environmental impacts and migration flows at subnational, national, and international levels.

Evidence to support the potentially dramatic influence of environmental change on cross-border migration need not be dependent upon global warming trends. Indeed, focusing attention primarily on such a long-term and worldwide phenomenon could mask the more immediate reality of many, dispersed, and localized ecological crises and the fact that there is usually no simple relationship between environmental causes and societal effects. Numerous historical and current cases of how environment-based woes—in conjunction with other socioeconomic and political variables—affect vulnerable societies and, hence, migration have

---

The views in this essay are those of the author and do not necessarily reflect the views of the U.S. Department of State.

been documented (Homer-Dixon 1994; Myers and Kent 1995). The more difficult debate is over what governments might do about it.

While initial papers on "environmental refugees" captured some media and policy interest, they were not based on any comprehensive review of environment-societal interactions underlying current migration flows (El-Hinnawi 1985; Jacobson 1988, 1989). A recent review of conditions generating more than 25 million "environmental refugees" has helped fill this gap by going beyond environmental disasters and discussing the migratory implications of demographic "pressure points" and natural resource degradation (Myers and Kent 1995). A series of reports by the Universities Field Staff International and the Natural Heritage Institute also have helped document examples of environmental influences on mass migrations in India, Brazil, sub-Saharan Africa, and Haiti (see citations for Maloney and Catanese). This essay on "ecomigrants" does not add to this growing body of empirical research on environmental stress, but instead attempts to frame the environment-migration linkage around a different set of overlapping questions:

- What is an appropriate framework for thinking about environment and migration linkages?
- Why the term "ecomigrants" instead of "environmental refugees" to describe environment-influenced migrations?
- How do migrants modify landscapes and conversely how are they influenced by environmental conditions, and what regional patterns will likely emerge from future ecomigrations?
- What is the relationship between natives and new ecomigrants over use of natural resources?
- How do government economic policies, which can stimulate rapid exploitation of natural resources, encourage ecomigrations to resource frontiers (such as a rainforest) and across international borders?
- How might international ecomigrations, particularly to the United States, directly or indirectly affect national environmental protection efforts (i.e., is it reasonable that the banner of environmental quality be used to justify severe immigration restrictions)?

This essay explores these questions and argues that a coherent debate about them requires a broad sustainable development context in which migrants live and move under an infinite variety of conditions at the family, local, subnational, and international levels. A portable "environment and society umbrella" is described here to help conceptualize environmental and socioeconomic linkages, and their current and future influence on migration subnationally and internationally. The essay then discusses how governments manipulate environment-influenced migrations and migrant-influenced environments. The umbrella analogy will be unsatisfactory to policymakers who want narrow cause-and-effect answers about the environmental merits or sins of particular groups of migrants and prefer to classify migrants into neat categories—political refugee, economic migrant, natural disaster victim—but it does provide a more accurate image of the interconnected causes and consequences under which each migrant moves.

Environment Influenced Mobility

Third world population mobility involves widely varied spatial patterns and durations: "circular migrations" between rural and urban areas, "seasonal migrations" (rural-rural and rural-urban), government-organized relocation schemes, and international labor flows. Despite growing international concern about environmental problems, until recently little attention has been paid to the impact of rapidly changing environmental conditions on migrants and even less on the impacts of modern migration flows on environments.

A 1996 international symposium, "Environmentally Induced Population Displacements and Environmental Impacts Resulting from Mass Migrations," was a notable effort to engage governments on possible prevention and mitigation strategies (UN High Commissioner for Refugees et al. 1996). By categorizing "environmentally induced" migrations by magnitude, acute versus slow onset, and likelihood of return, the symposium report offers an analytical structure for determining which agencies might need to intervene and how they might do so in a constructive manner. The report also notably addresses the complex migration-environment interface in a holistic manner, notes the need to use new remote sensing tools for monitoring the causes and consequences of environmentally influenced mass migrations, and offers some pragmatic measures to tackle the difficult task of restoring an area's ecological stability following a major refugee influx.

This type of interdisciplinary, intergovernmental approach, though, has been the exception. Apart from unilateral governmental responses, migration analysis itself has been generally preoccupied with narrowly defined economic and, to a much lesser extent, political, cultural, and, more recently, global economic inequities; place-specific "environmental" contexts have been largely ignored (Brown 1991). "Ecological push" factors, while associated with "primitive" migrations, have been treated as largely irrelevant to economics-driven "modern" migrations (Peterson 1975). This dearth of *eco*migration analysis is understandable because modeling complex ecosystems and mobile populations is difficult: cause and effect relationships between environmental variables and migration are hard to quantify and are tied to economic, political, and cultural factors. Environmental change, as a proximate "push" factor in migration, must be discussed in relation to income inequity, changing land uses, government development schemes, and ethnic conflicts (Suhrke 1992).

Discussions of migration-environment interaction, also fall under a higher profile debate over influences of population-environment changes on political stability. That debate, with some notable exceptions (particularly recent field studies led by Homer-Dixon), has been driven more by simplistic generalizations than solid empirical research on the nexus between population growth and distribution, environmental degradation, and economic development (Martine 1995). Notwithstanding the stark imagery of a disembarking mass of humanity evoked by Connelly and Kennedy (1994), the notion that "population pressure" in distant lands leads straight to an uncontrolled influx across the borders of industrialized countries is not borne out by a comparison of worldwide demographic trends and United States immigration statistics (Kritz 1995). Just as there is no simple correlation between high population growth rates in poor countries and immigration to European and North American countries, there is unlikely to be one between "environmental pressure" (however it is defined) in many, but not all, poor countries and the entry of their citizens into wealthier countries. Part of this, of course, can be explained by the wide gulf between desire to emigrate and permission to immigrate.

Scientists tend to study particular aspects of natural ecosystems; even when they look at the role of people in these ecosystems, it is usually on their impact on specific fauna and flora. A more systematic approach to studying both ecosystems and migrants would reveal some interesting insights into the viability of vulnerable habitats. If environmental conditions change drastically for whatever reasons—a new predator species, destruction of ground cover, prolonged drought—an organism that has successfully adapted to a particular ecological niche either adapts, relocates to a similar niche elsewhere, or dies out. An accurate assessment of those changes cannot be made by studying a species in isolation, but as part of a dynamic ecosystem with some unpredictable variables. Migration analysis might also benefit by better understanding the complex social and ecological habitats that migrants leave behind, pass through, and settle into.

Migrants must also deal with a bewildering array of socioeconomic, cultural, and political systems as well as environmental ones. Every person, then, moves within broadly defined sets of "environment and society habitats," with some external factors highly localized and others global, and each factor influencing individual decision making in unique ways (people do not necessarily respond to the same stimuli in the same way). Rather than use the term "habitat," which has an environmental deterministic ring, the analogy of an "environment and society umbrella" is used here because it gives the desired image of an encompassing structure and portability, the latter being the key criterion in assessing migration.

Eco Definition

Recent evidence suggest that our homo erectus ancestors may have migrated out of Africa and into Asia as long as two million years ago (Sawyer 1995). The simple tools they brought helped them make these unknown environments more habitable, setting the stage for future cradles of civilization. A recurring irony of diverse civilizations (based largely on the creation and expansion of cities, fueled by rural to urban migration), is how often their transformed environments became uninhabitable because of misguided resource management. How many of our descendants will also attempt migrating to some distant place where natural resources might be more abundant, the climate less harsh, socioeconomic opportunities more promising, and governments less abusive of human rights?

For the past decade "environmental refugee" has been used to define those who have been forced to flee from an environmental disaster (El-Hinnawi 1985; Jacobson 1988; Myers and Kent 1995; *Refuge* 1992). But, as even some of those who use the term acknowledge, it is a poor choice to describe those involved in a much broader and more pervasive phenomena (McGregor 1993; Wood 1995). The widely accepted definition of a "refugee" is someone who is fleeing persecution or war, has crossed an international boundary, and usually has been granted political asylum; the primary push factor is thus political, not environmental. If this definition is accepted, then it follows that an "environmental refugee" is a refugee whose moves are determined by environmental factors.

True "environmental refugees" do exist as a small subset—not an additional set—of the 14 to 19 million "official" refugees (estimates vary); they would be those who are victims of explicit "ecocidal" activities of oppressive regimes, such as the Marsh Arabs in southern Iraq or perhaps refugees who cannot be repatriated because their homelands are littered with landmines. Many refugees suffer from the purposeful destruction of their communities in wars and internecine ethnic conflicts. Combatants have burned crops, bombed dikes, and mined fields to obstruct enemy movements and terrorize civilian populations, but this ecological destruction is less the root cause of refugee flight and more the means of military oppression. Refugees themselves have an environmental impact on the common property resources of locales they flee into, but these have often been exaggerated; efforts to minimize such negative impacts need to involve both the refugees and local communities in food security and public health projects (Jacobsen 1994).

More importantly, "environmental refugee" is far too narrow: ecological factors at least partially and indirectly affect most types of migrants, not just refugees. This essay refers to environmentally influenced migration as "ecomigration" (Wood 1995). Ecomigrants, unlike "environmental refugees," are not necessarily violently displaced. They are closely entwined with the expectation-raising and frequently disruptive process of economic development. The root word "eco" (Greek, "house") for both economics and ecology, indeed, suggests a shelter encompassing the moves of ecomigrants; an image perhaps more like an umbrella than a house. It is less useful to neatly separate the economic and ecological spokes of this umbrella (the tendency of the social and physical sciences) than to appreciate how they reinforce each other, positively and negatively, within the same "eco" umbrella: when it is strong and large (especially relative to others), many people crowd under its canopy; when it is weak and several spokes fail, the umbrella collapses, and people flee in search of a new "eco."

Ecomigrants would include those who move voluntarily to new areas to exploit natural resources. All too often, however, these same ecomigrants are forced to leave when the resources they depend on are destroyed or severely degraded. While international attention on tropical deforestation has highlighted systematic violence against indigenous Indian tribes, as well as the imposed corruption of their traditional ecomigrant cultures, the plight of the incoming modern ecomigrants is given much less sympathy. In-migrants to resource frontiers are often blamed for uncontrolled deforestation and loss of indigenous environmental knowledge (linked to the recent commercial and scientific interest in tropical biodiversity); indeed, they are part of the problem, but more as a desperate consequence than a willful cause (Wood 1990).

Shifting cultivators epitomize the crisis facing traditional ecomigrants. Under normal conditions, they grow a mixture of crops at one site for several years. When thin tropical forest soils are depleted of nutrients, these ecomigrants move on; under unstressed conditions, shifting cultivators will return to the original site after 10 to 20 years. Sustained use of their forest, however, is forever altered when other factors intrude, including: encroachment by sedentary peasant farmers, creation of vast timber cutting concessions, conversion of large areas into plantations and cattle ranches, and war. These ecomigrations become more desperate, with some breaking out of the cycle completely by moving to nearby towns and cities. Once urbanized, they become part of a pervasive pattern of modern ecomigration.

Frayed Umbrella

The central migration issue governments must face, then, is not whether people will continue moving and transforming the areas they live in— they will do both, with gusto—but how seriously the global "environment and society" network is threatened, how that process affects current and future migration options, and, finally, how governmental policies have served to either restrict or encourage migration flows in reaction to environmental and societal pressures.

The analogy of a frayed umbrella can help explain these dynamic interactions. Each of us—like Joe Bfstplk, the L'il Abner cartoon character who was followed everywhere by a dark rain cloud—carries our very own "environment and society umbrella" as we move among different locations (daily, seasonally, or even permanently).⟨Our place and person-specific umbrellas mutate in form and size, depending on the socioeconomic, political, and environmental conditions that affect us personally and collectively. Aggregate sets of umbrellas form local and regional patterns and trends that help determine global population distribution. ⟩

While umbrellas in the same area may share similar characteristics, no two will be alike because the "same" environment might affect neighbors or even members of the same household quite differently, in part depending on their socioeconomic status. A humanitarian crisis is akin to the simultaneous destruction of numerous umbrellas, whose owners must discard them in the midst of a storm. Technical and societal innovations give potential migrants the knowledge and means to repair or even broaden their umbrellas' canopy, but this capability is not shared equally. The wealthy and privileged can create a durable, encompassing cover; the poor have little, if anything, to protect them and thus are much more susceptible to both natural and man-made disasters. While survival skills under one umbrella may be unsuited for those in other locations, rich ecomigrants can quickly retrofit their umbrellas to meet new conditions while the poor usually cannot. Moreover, women and children tend to be disproportionately threatened by environmental changes and have to overcome additional cultural and security obstacles as ecomigrants than do men (Cutter 1995).

Each extended umbrella has a multitude of spokes. Some spokes relate to environmental conditions that influence, to varying degrees, all migrants and potential migrants—air and water quality, land availability or degradation, resource exploitation, locational attributes, etc. Most spokes, however, relate to socioeconomic, cultural, and political aspects of migration—employment opportunities, kinship networks, administrative jurisdictions, migration and squatter laws, housing availability, etc. The umbrellas of white-collar workers in the first world may have a dominance of socioeconomic and technological spokes, while the third world peasant's umbrella may have many environment-shaped spokes. While the composition and strength of the spokes varies, all are linked within the umbrella canopy, in both obvious and subtle ways. Thus, sector-specific governmental actions may not just affect one or two spokes, but alter the structure of the whole umbrella. Indeed, policies that have had the most profound influences on shaping ecomigrations often have nothing explicit in them about either migrants or environments; rather they are focused on land tenure, resource export subsidies, or crop prices.

The infinite variety of umbrellas helps explain why a comprehensive migration theory has proved elusive. Before putting the umbrella analogy away, it should be added that the umbrella represents only the relatively objective, external factors that affect an individual's decision and/or ability to move. Forced migrants have little, if any, choice about exchanging the tattered umbrella of the here and now for the hoped-for sheltering umbrella of the there and future. The voluntary migrant, in contrast, still maintains some ability to explore other umbrella designs (be they few or many) or to leave those options closed, ignore the rains of change, and remain sedentary.

Umbrella Economics

Efforts to explain migration flows with just a few of the umbrella spokes (such as perceived wage increases) may suggest minimal influences of environmental factors on economics-determined migration flows, but these may not give adequate weight to the natural resource basis of economic activities. Environmental factors have had profound, but grossly underestimated, impacts on national and regional economies and thus indirectly have been of great influence on migration flows. For example, the rapid growth of third world primary cities (perhaps the greatest migration of all), is a major consequence of resource exploitation policies—dating back to the beginnings of colonialism—that initially channeled international trade through coastal villages, evolving them into port towns, colonial capitals, and, today, sprawling megalopoli. Migrants, rural to urban and international, have been an integral part of this urbanization/international trade revolution.

Traditional economic analysis tends to assume a uniform environmental space, yet the reality is very different: environmental factors are highly varied within and among states. Migration flows are attempts to capitalize on the inequitable distribution of both economic opportunities and natural resources. When combined with international economic interdependence and improved transportation and communication networks, these inequities have led to the policy dilemma of "unwanted immigration" (Martin and Taylor 1995; Papademetriou and Hamilton 1995). An interesting arena of research would be on the relationship between the "indirect migration management tools" of trade, investment, and aid (Martine 1995) and their impact on an area's environmental conditions and hence ecomigrations.

As with the theoretical argument that "unwanted immigration" should decrease both the labor surplus in the sending country and the labor deficit in the receiving country (and hence eventually shrink the wage gap between them and lower migration pressures), it would seem logical that international ecomigration should ease environmental stress at the place of origin and perhaps increase it at the destination. This hypothesis would be useful to explore, but it would have to be carefully focused on specific local conditions in areas of very high out- or in-migration because the overall environmental impacts (positive and negative) of current international migrants pales in comparison to the likely impacts of internal migrants and residents (Hugo 1995). The lack of such empirical work, though, has not stopped speculation on the "environmental consequences" of immigration.

Any discussion of ecological factors in third world migration must be placed within an economic and political context (Leonard 1989). Poverty and unsustainable living conditions above all else push most ecomigrants, whether to a third world city or out of one. Although poor living conditions can be superficially measured by per capita incomes, public health indicators—particularly infant mortality rates—may better reflect the close ties between poverty and degraded environments. Two-thirds of third world populations reside in rural areas, often engaging in subsistence farming, but ever-increasing numbers are moving to cities. For them, "environmental pressures" are not an abstract concern, but a harsh everyday presence, influenced by misguided government policies on two of the most critical natural resources, arable farmland and water. Rural to urban migrations are often tied to land use pressures, including shortsighted government agrarian policies, declining productivity or prices, and highly restrictive land tenure.

One of the benefits of recent work on environmental or "green" economics and efforts by the World Bank to encourage better accounting of natural and human resources in national economic statistics is a nascent awareness of the true costs of resource degradation (Repetto 1990; World Bank 1992). Much harder to measure is the human cost of ill-planned resource exploitation, for which migrants serve on the front lines. Migration flows to, from, and within resource frontiers reflect the consequences of both explicit environmental regulations as well as others that implicitly affect resource use, such as land clearing stipulations for tenure or mining subsidies (Godfrey 1990). These policies directly or indirectly modify one or several of the umbrella spokes of those living in a given place or region, causing an influx of those hoping to take advantage of the perceived opportunity. When governmental policies result in broken spokes (e.g., the natural resource is exhausted or the price of a key commodity drops sharply), those same in-migrants must reassess their current status, look around at umbrellas in other locales, and, if need be, move once again.

Ecomigration Patterns and Predictability

Regardless of the particular cause of their movement, ecomigrants are buffeted by a variety of environmental stresses and threats to vulnerable biophysical and socioeconomic systems (Kasperson 1994). Ecomigrations are grouped here into three causal categories: "natural" disasters (such as the 1995 Kobe earthquake or the 1995 Yangtze flood); "urban industrial" disasters (such as a Chernobyl or Bhopal); and resource-based exploitation and degradation. Although given much less international attention, ecomigrations falling under this final category have played a far more significant historical role (Myers and Kent 1995; Wood 1995). While specific future ecomigrations may be difficult to pinpoint, generalized environmental trends, such as recurring severe droughts and sea level rise—both of which are likely by-products of global warming—will directly affect food availability in poor, food-deficit countries and the livability of densely populated areas, resulting in predictable out-migration surges (Doos 1997).

Natural disasters represent a clash between social and ecological systems. Regardless of their specific cause or frequency, the growing socioeconomic impact of all disasters will likely spur an increase in population mobility (Burton, Kates, and White 1993). Four types of hazards—floods (40 percent), cyclones (20 percent), earthquakes (15 percent), and drought (15 percent)—account for 90 percent of the world's natural disasters and thus are also the major disaster-based causes of ecomigrations. Disaster-prone areas, such as the Bangladesh delta or China's Yellow River valley, are often densely populated because fertile, silty soils allow for intensive agricultural production. Grim alternatives force disaster victims to risk the high likelihood of future disasters by returning to dangerous areas.

The long-term influences of climate change on population movements will vary greatly by region; some global environmental changes will be systemic (such as greenhouse gases) and others cumulative (such as deforestation) in their consequences on societies (Kasperson 1994). Global warming, with accompanying weather fluctuations and sea level rise, will disproportionately affect low lying coastal regions and may play havoc with agrarian economies. Much of the focus on global climatic changes has focused on aggregate impacts, ignoring the more complex implications on interregional migration flows (Ehrlich and Ehrlich 1990). While coastal and island inundation fears may be well justified, many high risk areas already face serious ecological problems, recurring natural disasters, and high levels of forced migration.

With a rapidly urbanizing world, major industrial accidents will likely become more frequent, forcing emergency evacuations of urban populations. The flights of hundreds of thousands from the nuclear disaster of Chernobyl and the toxic gas release at Bhopal are the most glaring examples of life-threatening evacuations caused by industrial mismanagement. Industrial centers, which are not always in urban areas, often exhibit the vivid scars of ecological degradation, directly from the industrial activity or indirectly from poorly planned migrant settlements. As economic conditions change, large numbers of ecomigrants move into or out of degraded industrial environments. Areas undergoing a sudden influx of migrants also experience serious infrastructural strains, in some cases resulting in life-threatening conditions. The proliferation of very crowded squatter settlements means that more people are vulnerable to flash floods and fires.

While horrific industrial disasters grab headlines, many more people are affected by the mundane consequences of degraded urban environments. Rapid urbanization carries a profound ecological impact, with overburdened infrastructure and high levels of air and water pollution that contribute to hundreds of thousands of premature deaths annually. As third world cities grow, many will become very crowded; living conditions for a growing share residing in slums and squatter settlements are already in decline. If these residents choose to leave behind the economic opportunities of the polluted metropolis (meager though they might be) for rural areas, they may find cleaner air and water (though many rural areas also have contaminated water supplies), but no jobs.

Ecomigrants, like all migrants, are pulled and pushed in different directions along paths strewn with physical, economic, and bureaucratic obstacles (Lee 1966; Wood 1995). They can be "pushed" out of areas with deteriorating environmental conditions or natural disasters, but they can also be "pulled" into other areas by the perceived opportunities of abundant resources and the relatively high incomes associated with resource extraction jobs; their arrival helps create "boom cities" in resource frontier regions (Wood 1986). Their increased mobility, though, usually does not resolve underlying and intertwined dilemmas; using the umbrella analogy, each new one they move under has similar structural defects.

The traditional ecomigrations of the nomad and shifting cultivator are being replaced by more "modern" ones in the third and first worlds: perhaps the largest ecomigration is that to and from third world cities and resource frontiers; perhaps the most significant ecomigration in the first world is that of retired persons migrating, either seasonally or permanently, to the Sun Belt. While the latter have a much greater choice of destinations and are driven more by comfort needs than basic survival than the former, both groups of ecomigrants are clearly environment-guided (rather than determined).

Although the distribution of the world's poor does not fit neatly within the boundaries of fragile or "threatened" environments, poverty and environmental degradation have been shown to be closely linked (Kates and Haarman 1992; Myers and Kent 1995). Poor people are especially vulnerable when they lose access to or face degraded "common property" resources, which then pushes them deeper into poverty and can force some to flee (Blaikie and Brookfield 1987). Though prospects vary with region, soil condition, and crop, agricultural productivity and average farm sizes in some regions are failing to keep up with the basic needs of growing populations (Brown, Kane, and Roodman 1994). While the Green Revolution's high yielding varieties of grain helped boost substantially crop yields (which meant more cheap food for urban markets), it also increased dependence on chemical fertilizers, pesticides, and mechanization, transformed village economies, and increased rural unemployment. The latter two consequences have helped spur massive rural to urban migration. As growing numbers of landless and near landless peasants become vulnerable to recurring natural disasters and chronic food shortages, ecomigration pressures will increase.

Discussions over the future of transnational ecomigrations will be increasingly tied to debates over environmental stress, resource scarcity, national security, and military conflict in key regions (Homer-Dixon 1994; Hugo 1995). Declining financial and food aid suggest that hundreds of millions of young people will be forced to endure even higher levels of destitution, malnutrition, and violence, as well as chronic political and economic instability (Kaplan 1994). While many will wish to leave areas of increasing environmental scarcity, few will be able to go far as immigration departments and border patrols clamp down on illegal border crossers. The lack of quick fixes to ecomigration problems demand, at the very least, a better understanding of their causal factors, processes, and consequences.

Resource-Based Ecomigrations: Regional Perspectives

Each ecomigration is a complicated process that can only be understood within the context of socioeconomic, cultural, political, and environmental linkages between places of origin and destination. With this caveat, the emphasis here is to provide brief glimpses of the range of resource-based ecomigrations through illustrative regional examples.

Interregional Linkages

Recent European and North American concerns about uncontrolled immigration reflect the latest twist in a long history of ecomigrations among world regions. Colonization, transnational ecological and economic linkages, and population redistribution often underlie current immigration dilemmas (Castles and Miller 1993). The migration of over 50 million Europeans during the past three hundred years, for example, "opened up" vast areas for farming, ranching, resource extraction, and trade. European migrants were "pulled" by popular but ultimately false perceptions of fertile tropical soils and "pushed" by fears of recurring famines in Europe (Crosby 1986). They helped redistribute globally plants and domesticated animals, altering the landscapes of almost all inhabited regions. Colonial plantations also relocated millions of Africans and Asians to almost all corners of the world. Imported laborers, as indentured servants, slaves, prisoners, or "free" persons, were used to radically reconstruct local landscapes and revolutionize local economies. When postcolonial plantations become unprofitable (perhaps for ecological as well as economic factors) or less labor intensive, plantation workers can become ecomigrants, seeking work within or outside their countries.

African Pastoralists

Efforts to improve economic productivity in Africa's large tropical savanna region requires careful study of pastoral lifestyles and mobility patterns, which are based on seasonally fluctuating ecosystems (Solburg and Young 1992). In Mali, for example, while the overall level of migration did not rise during the 1983–85 drought, the percentage of women and children did increase sharply as did a shift toward more circular patterns (Findley 1994). Unless declining economic conditions are turned around and political stability established, the plight of African ecomigrants will never cease. Constructive assistance, though, requires a recognition of intricate seasonal land use patterns and communal management, and then locally focused, flexible, and environmentally sound development strategies. Numerous government-sponsored population relocation schemes, ostensibly funded to help such poor people, have failed because ecological constraints—such as soil quality, water availability, and/or unique local agroecosystems—were neglected during critical planning stages.

China's Floating Population

China now has a rapidly growing "floating population" of 80 million, over which Beijing has relatively little control. Despite rustication programs and continuing efforts to demolish congested urban neighborhoods of recent in-migrants, rural Chinese continue to move to cities, especially those along the coast which have experienced very high rates of economic growth (Mufson 1995). This pull of urban-based economic opportunities, though, must also be balanced by grimmer prospects for the over 65 percent of the population that live in rural areas, where per capita farm size continues to decline. Conversion of farmland to nonfarm uses, widespread soil degradation, and depletion of aquifers, in conjunction with rising urban incomes, has created a dynamic migration pattern as well as concerns over the availability and affordability of basic staples (Brown 1994). The specter of hungry, unruly migrants has led to questions about China's long-term "environmental security" and its global impacts.

Amazonian Resources

Ecomigrants moving into resource frontiers, such as the Amazon, often find themselves competing fiercely to rapidly extract a nonrenewable resource that, once depleted, will leave them unemployed again and in search of new areas to relocate (Godfrey 1990). The Amazon's frontier regions, despite generally poor soil fertility, are being exploited at the expense of indigenous shifting cultivators and complex forest ecosystems. Governments in the region have traditionally subsidized settlement of the Amazon, resulting in the migration of millions to its "underpopulated" peripheries. Exploitation of tropical forests, however, has not proven to be an effective, long-term regional development strategy, a release valve for population pressures, or a means of curbing ecological degradation in other subnational regions (Wood 1990). While governments have tried recently to curb "uncontrolled" deforestation, they face growing populations who still view the Amazon as a common resource they can exploit to pull them out of poverty.

Haiti's Decline

Haiti represents a nation full of tattered umbrellas. Haiti's alarming levels of land degradation, exacerbated by decades of misguided agrarian policies, is intertwined with desperate living conditions in rural areas and is a major factor in rural to urban migration and even emigration from Haiti's shores (Catanese 1990–91). Haiti's over six million people have endured successive generations of intensifying poverty, soil erosion, deforestation, and shrinking average farm sizes, leaving many peasant families unable to meet bare subsistence levels. Since the 1800s, Haitians have tried to escape certain poverty by seeking work on sugar cane plantations in neighboring countries, often under very harsh conditions. Recent labor immigration restrictions, continued rapid population growth in Haiti, declining crop yields, and very high unemployment rates are intensifying pressure on Haiti's already destitute rural economy and heavily degraded landscape. For many Haitians, repeated eco-emigrations to other Caribbean islands as well as to the United States are a desperate gamble to escape grim ecological and economic conditions.

Government Reactions

Haitian ecomigrants represent to some a frightful future of third world ecological ruin threatening first world stability. Fears of weakened "national security" and unemployment have dominated political debates about vigorous government reactions to international migration trends, particularly in western Europe (Castles and Miller 1993; Martine 1995). Although international migration flows in the future will likely be most influenced by disparities in population growth and economic opportunities between poor and rich regions (and cultural linkages based on colonial ties and current political relations), ecological factors may also play a growing role in determining emigration trends and immigration policies. But nationalistic "closed door" responses to the plight of ecomigrants in poor countries, such as those Haiti or Mexico, will likely worsen "push" factors rather than easing them, especially if they are accompanied by a reduction in foreign assistance.

Governments, acting either domestically or internationally, generally have not been successful in turning off migration to areas where higher incomes can be earned. Indeed, governments often encourage labor migration to these areas in the hope of increasing foreign exchange earnings from export crops or tourism. Such "development" schemes may lead to forcible relocation of locals who oppose or are in the way of the government's plans. Similarly, government-sponsored development projects—often subsidized by international funding agencies—have directly uprooted millions of peasants. In India, for example, dams and irrigation projects have reportedly uprooted over 20 million people since 1947 (Maloney 1990–91). Futile governmental attempts to halt unwanted migration flows, particularly from rural to urban areas, have also generated strong resentment by those constrained (Skeldon 1990). Some governments, such as China and the Soviet Union, attempted to regulate migration through local residency permits and ration cards; but as they shift toward market-based economies, central governmental controls over mobility are either being lifted or effectively ignored.

With only a murky understanding of "green" economics, government finance ministries tend to undervalue the natural resources they exploit in the name of national economic development (Repetto 1990; World Bank 1995). As competitive trade and investment pressures within the global economy increase, governments may jeopardize or ignore sound resource management policies in favor of short-term upswings in macroeconomic indicators (such as increasing foreign exchange earnings through wholesale timber exports). When government planners treat these nonrenewable natural resources as a relatively "free" good, they set the stage for poorly planned resource exploitation and, indirectly, ecomigration. Ironically, some of these same economic growth-promoting policies may actually stimulate, at least in the short term, international emigration (Martin and Taylor 1995). If governments in wealthier countries wish to curb pressures on their international borders, they may need to look more closely at the resource management policies in those countries that serve as major labor exporters.

Green Walls?

Xenophobic fears of a potential "flood" of foreigners into Europe have led governments in western Europe, North America, and Australia to enact new laws designed to curb immigration, ostensibly because of the threat to public security, regional economic stability, and quality of life (Papademetriou and Hamilton 1995). Yet Western governments have yet to systematically "manage migration pressures" as part of their "central economic, political, and security objectives" (Meissner 1992). Current anti-immigrant rhetoric are more intertwined with nationalist movements than the product of any long term strategy to achieve national economic development goals.

Reactions to legal and illegal immigrants from poor countries may be also influenced by less obvious environmental and cultural factors. Immigrants, in refashioning their umbrellas, modify their new environments and can physically change the appearance of their new communities. Often they have been forced into creating ethnic ghettoes, which create their own distinct urban environments. These imported "foreign" environments are most apparent in the more homogeneous western and northern European countries, where violence against "foreign" looking and acting immigrant communities has led to emotional political debates over immigration and cultural assimilation.

While the social and environmental sciences could provide a foundation for better understanding the environmental impacts of immigration into the United States and other industrialized countries, thus far the critical elements of accurate data on trends, an appropriate scale of analysis, and an interdisciplinary methodology for analyzing immigration-environment interactions are lacking (Hugo 1995; Kraly 1995). Even if these large hurdles could be met, necessarily complex and statistically valid assessments of local and regional environmental consequences of immigrant influxes in North America and western Europe would be likely ignored or oversimplified in politically charged debates.

The use of environmental concerns to justify immigration restrictions plays more on perceptions than realities, especially in North America. In the third world one of the biggest sources of violent conflict between migrants and natives is over access to arable land. In North America, where many small farms are being abandoned and where natives show little interest in low wage farm labor, that argument clearly does not hold. Some of this debate suffers from a confusion of scale because national immigration data does not correlate with a corresponding national environmental data set. Very different processes are at work in generating these numbers. While some fragile environments within the United States (particularly in coastal, high mountain, and desert areas) are suffering from an influx of people, there is no evidence that these are mostly immigrants; more likely, they are relatively well-off "natives" (i.e., descendants of previous immigrants) seeking to retire or engage in recreational activities. Immigrants usually end up in urban areas, taking over neighborhoods abandoned by other ethnic groups whose younger generations are dispersing to the suburbs. Anti-immigrationists have not shown much interest in the less-than-pristine environments of these old urban neighborhoods.

The environmental anti-immigrant argument for North America is also ironic because previous waves of immigrants, largely voluntary from Europe and Asia and forcibly from Africa, have already altered much of the continent's land cover—in some places several times. However it might be measured, current rates of immigration, as an independent variable, cannot have more than minimal overall impacts on environmental quality, either in Europe or North America. Again, governmental policies concerning natural resource use, particularly those affecting agriculture, have had much more influence on environmental quality. Unless it can be shown that immigrants have a disproportionate environmental impact, national immigration policy debates should focus on other consequences of a sustained influx (Kraly 1995).

Conclusion

A recent drought in northern Mexico underscores some of the overlapping realms of ecomigration pressures discussed in this essay (Robberson 1995). At the global level, 1995 was another El Niño year, with its characteristic weather aberrations of severe regional floods and droughts. While the U.S. Midwest suffered through floods, northern Mexico experienced a drought that withered crops and killed cows. At the same time, a request from Mexico to divert 26 billion gallons of water from a shared natural resource, the Rio Grande, was turned down because of claims by Texas that it also needed the water. Underlying recurring droughts are ecological problems that should be of regional concern, including land degradation that, according to the Mexico's National Commission for Arid Zones, affects 20 million Mexicans in twenty-two states. As Mexico's population rises from about 95 million in 1996 to 119 million in 2010 (Population Reference Bureau 1996), how will their demands for arable, fertile land and clean water be met?

Mexico's long-term demographic and ecological trends, along with structural changes in its agricultural sector, will likely push millions of peasants out of rural Mexico over the next two decades (Natural Heritage Institute 1997). Those that have left or are leaving jobs in Mexican farms and ranches for Mexico's rapidly growing and increasingly polluted cities may find few jobs that can support their families. They then face a harsh choice: head back to desolate villages empty handed or try to seek work illegally across Mexico's northern border. The latter option by potential ecomigrants is one the United States is attempting to dissuade with increased funding and personnel for border guards and immigration enforcement. These border control measures, though, might be strengthened with long-term, bilateral assistance directed at employment generation and resource conservation in rural Mexico.

Ecomigrants, whether Mexican, Haitian, Brazilian, Nepali, or Ethiopian, carry similarly frayed umbrellas: declining access to arable land; decreasing farm productivity; less livable urban environments; recurring "natural" and "man-made" disasters; degraded resources (especially soil and water); weak off-farm employment prospects; and increasingly restricted international migration. Population growth, projected increases in per capita energy consumption, and higher greenhouse gas emissions will have both local and global ecological impacts over the next few decades that many governments will be unable to control (McKibbon 1998). As ecological degradation and poverty continue in many vulnerable regions and as governments continue to deal ineffectively with causal factors, the number of ecomigrants will likely increase. As with other impoverished migrants, ecomigrants do not need political rhetoric but pragmatic, environmentally sound economic assistance to counter the effects of ill-conceived government policies that have encouraged hasty natural resource exploitation and lasting resource depletion and degradation. Until such fundamental resource management failures are turned around, ecomigrants will have no choice but to keep moving.

References

Blaikie, Piers, and Harold Brookfield. 1987. *Land Degradation and Society*. London: Metheun Press.

Brown, Lawrence. 1991. *Place, Migration, and Development in the Third World*. London and New York: Routledge, Ltd.

Brown, Lester, Hal Kane and David M. Roodman. 1994. *Vital Signs 1994*. New York: W. W. Norton.

Burton, Ian, Robert W. Kates, and Gilbert F. White. 1993. *The Environment as Hazard*, 2nd ed. New York: The Guilford Press.

Castles, Stephen, and Mark Miller. 1993. *The Age of Migration*. New York: The Guilford Press.

Catanese, Anthony. 1990–91. "Haiti's Refugees: Political, Economic, and Environmental" (Latin America, 1990–91/No. 17); Field Staff Reports. Universities Field Staff International and the Natural Heritage Institute.

Clarke, John, P. Curson, S. Kayastha, and P. Nag, eds. 1989. *Population and Disaster*. Oxford: Basil Blackwell in association with the International Geographical Union Commission on Population Geography.

Connelly, Mathew, and Paul Kennedy. 1994. "Must It Be THE REST Against THE WEST?" *The Atlantic Monthly* (December): 61–84.

Crosby, Alfred. 1986. *Ecological Imperialism: The Biological Expansion of Europe, 900–1900*. Cambridge: Cambridge University Press.

Cutter, Susan. 1995. "The Forgotten Casualties: Women, Children, and Environmental Change." *Global Environmental Change: Human and Policy Dimensions* 5, 3: 181–94.

Doos, Bo R. 1997. "Can Large Scale Environmental Migrations be Predicted?" *Global Environmental Change* 7, 1 (April): 41–62.

Ehrlich, Paul, and A. H. Ehrlich. 1990. *The Population Explosion*. New York: Simon and Schuster.

El-Hinnawi, Essam. 1985. *Environmental Refugees*. Nairobi: United Nations Environmental Programme.

Findley, Sally. 1994. "Does Drought Increase Migration? A Study of Migration from Rural Mali during the 1983–1985 Drought." *International Migration Review* 28: 539–53.

Godfrey, Brian. 1990. "Boom Towns of the Amazon." *The Geographical Review* 80, 2: 103–17.

Goodland, Robert, ed. 1990. *Race to Save the Tropics—Ecology and Economics for a Sustainable Future*. Washington, D.C. and Covelo, Cal.: Island Press.

Homer-Dixon, Thomas. 1994. "Environmental Scarcities and Violent Conflict: Evidence From Cases." *International Security* 19, 1: 5–40.

Hugo, Graeme. 1995. "Environmental Concerns and International Migration." Paper prepared for International Conference on Ethics, Migration, and

Global Stewardship, Center for Migration Studies, Georgetown University, 13–15 September.

Jacobsen, Karen. 1994. *The Impact of Refugees on the Environment: A Review of the Evidence.* Washington D.C.: Refugee Policy Group.

Jacobson, Jodi. 1988. *Environmental Refugees: A Yardstick of Habitability, 1988.* Worldwatch Paper 86; Washington D.C.: Worldwatch Institute.

———. 1989. *"Abandoning Homelands": State of the World 1989.* Washington D.C.: Worldwatch Institute.

Kaplan, Robert. 1994. "The Coming Anarchy." *The Atlantic Monthly* (February).

Kasperson, Roger. 1994. "Global Environmental Hazards: Political Issues in Societal Responses." *Reordering the World: Geopolitical Perspectives on the 21st Century,* edited by G. Demko and W. Wood. Boulder, Colo.: Westview Press.

Kates, Robert, and Viola Haarman. 1992. "Where the Poor Live, Are the Assumptions Correct?" *Environment* 34, 4: 5–11, 25–28.

Kraly, Ellen. 1995. "U.S. Immigration and the Environment: Scientific Research and Analytic Issues." Washington, D.C.: U.S. Commission on Immigration Reform Research Paper.

Kritz, Mary. 1995. "Population Growth and International Migration: Is There a Link?" Paper prepared for Migration Policy in Global Perspective Conference at the New School, September, New York City.

Lee, Everet. 1966. "A Theory of Migration." *Demography* 3: 47–57.

Leonard, H. Jeffrey, and contributors. 1989. *Environment and the Poor: Development Strategies for a Common Agenda. U.S.-Third World Policy Perspectives,* No. 11. Overseas Development Council, New Brunswick and Oxford: Transaction Books.

Maloney, Clarence. 1990–91. "Environmental and Project Displacement of Population in India—Part I: Development and Deracination," (Asia 1990– 91/ No. 14), Field Staff Reports.

Martin, Philip, and J. Edward Taylor. 1995. *Managing Migration: The Role of Economic Policies.* Paper prepared for the Migration Policy in Global Perspective conference at the New School for Social Research, 8 September 1995.

Martine, George. 1995. *Population, Environment and International Security.* Research monograph, Center for Population and Development Studies, Harvard University.

McGregor, JoAnn. 1993. "Refugees and the Environment," in *Geography and Refugees—Patterns and Processes of Change,* edited by R. Black and V. Robinson. London and New York: Belhaven.

McKibbon, Bill. 1998. "A Special Moment in History." *The Atlantic Monthly,* May, 55–78.

Meissner, Doris. 1992. "Managing Migrations." *Foreign Policy* 86: 66–83.

Mufson, Steven. 1995. "Beijing's Migrant Masses." *The Washington Post,* 27 November A14.

Myers, Norman, and Jennifer Kent. 1995. *Environmental Exodus—An Emergent Crisis in the Global Arena.* Washington D.C.: Climate Institute.

Natural Heritage Institute. 1997. *Environmental Degradation and Migration—the U.S./Mexico Case Study.* Research paper for the U.S. Commission on Immigration Reform, December.

Papademetriou, Demetrios, and Kimberly Hamilton. 1995. *Managing Uncertainty: Regulating Immigration Flows in Advanced Industrial Countries.* Washington D.C.: Carnegie Endowment for International Peace.

Peterson, William. 1975. *Population*. New York: Macmillan Publishing Co.

Population Reference Bureau. 1996. *World Population Data Sheet*. Washington, D.C.

Refuge, Canada's Periodical on Refugees. 12, 1 (June) 1992 (published by York University's Centre for Refugee Studies).

Repetto, Robert. 1990. "Deforestation in the Tropics." *Scientific American* 262, 4: 36–42.

Robberson, Tod. 1995. "Mexico in Mid Crisis." *The Washington Post*, 29 May, A17.

Sawyer, Kathy. 1995. "Asian Fossils Suggest Early Migration." *The Washington Post*, 16 November, A3.

Skeldon, Ronald. 1990. *Population Mobility in Developing Countries*. London and New York: Belhaven Press.

Solburg, Otto, and Michael Young. 1992. "Toward a Sustainable and Equitable Future for Savannas." *Environment* 34, 3: 6–15, 32–35.

Suhrke, Astri. 1992. "Pressure Points: Environmental Degradation, Migration and Conflict." Paper prepared for a conference on environmental conflict at the Brookings Institute, 11–12 May 1992.

United Nations High Commissioner for Refugees, International Organization for Migration, and Refugee Policy Group. 1996. *Environmentally Induced Population Displacements and Environmental Impacts Resulting from Mass Migrations*. Proceedings of an International Symposium in Geneva, 21–24 April 1996. Published by the International Organization for Migration.

Wood, William. 1986. "Intermediate Cities on a Resource Frontier." *The Geographical Review* 76, 2: 149–59.

———. 1990. "Tropical Deforestation—Balancing Regional Demands and Global Environmental Concerns." *Global Environmental Change* (December): 23–41.

———. 1994. "Forced Migration: Local Conflicts and International Dilemmas." *Annals of the Association of American Geographers* 84, 4: 607–34.

———. 1995. "Hazardous Journeys: Ecomigrants in the 1990s." *Global Change: How Vulnerable Are North and South Communities?* edited by Dennis Conway and James C. White. Indiana Center on Global Change and World Peace.

World Bank. 1992. *World Development Report 1992: Development and the Environment*. Washington, D.C.: World Bank

———. 1995. *Monitoring Environmental Progress: A Report on Work in Progress*. Draft report. Washington, D.C.: World Bank.

– *Chapter 3* –

CONFLICT AND FORCED MIGRATION: A QUANTITATIVE REVIEW, 1964–1995

Susanne Schmeidl

Introduction

International responses to refugee flows in the post–Cold War period increasingly include calls to go beyond providing protection and assistance to the displaced by addressing the "root causes" of forced migration. However, consideration of whether a more proactive approach is feasible and what it would entail calls for an adequate understanding of the "root causes" themselves. Accordingly, the present chapter seeks to contribute to the ongoing international policy debate by providing a systematic quantitative analysis of the causes of worldwide refugee migrations in recent decades. The analysis begins with a general overview of the changing patterns of refugee populations by countries of origin, which are then linked to the structures of conflict in these countries. Overall, the causes of refugee migration are found to be similar across regions, with minor variations. A key question is whether post–Cold War struggles are merely a version of "old" conflicts, modified by new international circumstances, or whether the end of the Cold War induced a shift in the pattern of refugee migrations, possibly reflecting the emergence of new types of conflict.

The Approach

The quantitative methodology used here seeks to identify the structural causes of refugee migration by way of a pooled time-series analysis across countries and time. In distinction from the approach commonly used in the refugee literature, the analysis is not limited to countries that actually experience refugee migration, but compares these to countries that do not, so as to facilitate the identification of factors associated with forced displacement. By synthesizing causes, quantitative analysis yields an overview of extensive historical materials. Table 3.2 (see the appendix at the end of this chapter) presents the results of such an analysis for twenty years (1971–90; N=2,180 cases; see Schmeidl 1995, 1997). Pooled time-series analysis tests for patterns (or causes) of mass displacement across cases and over time. Due to the lack of information on annual refugee flows, the analysis uses change in stock as a substitute; this is modeled by including the dependent variable lagged by one year (t-1) among the independent variables (see Finkel 1995). Thus, refugee stock is included twice in the equation, once as dependent variable at time t, and once as independent variable at times t-1. It should be noted that substitution is imperfect mainly because the data includes other demographic changes in refugee camps (births and deaths) in addition to new in-migrations.

The dependent variable of refugee stock was constructed by combining two sources: the United Nations High Commissioner for Refugees (UNHCR) and the U.S. Committee for Refugees (USCR). Both have tried to systematically report annual refugee estimates over the past three decades. Table 3.1 (see appendix) provides a list of all countries that were reported to have part of their population in exile and/or internally displaced during the indicated period.

The use of these estimates—the best ones available—for an analysis of refugee migrations entails certain limitations. All numbers are "guesstimates" at best, mostly provided by aid organizations and host governments, which are often systematically biased towards the overreporting of camp figures. On the other hand, it is likely that self-settling refugees who do not claim assistance are underreported. Moreover, the estimates include only persons considered to be refugees under the 1951 Refugee Convention and the broader definitions implied by the 1969 OAU Convention and the 1984 Latin American Declaracion de Cartagena. This leaves out persons displaced by environmental events (often referred to as "environmental refugees") and those who were forcibly displaced from a foreign country but returned home (e.g., guest workers from Kuwait during the Gulf War, or French settlers from Algeria in the process of decolonization). Similarly, refugee stocks do not include persons who exercise their "right to return" (notably persons of German descent who moved from East and Central Europe to Germany, or Russian Jews moving to Israel). Finally, persons who entered a country as refugees are no longer counted if they cease being refugees, for example by becoming citizens. Another limitation is that refugees who obtained asylum in Western industrialized countries are excluded from the count as well.[1] Figures for the internally displaced are even less precise than those for refugees, largely because most of them are not assisted or protected by international organizations, and hence are uncounted. Thus, these refugee estimates provide a general understanding rather than precise census-type population data.

While quantitative methodology can establish certain structural commonalties, no one model is able to explain all refugee migrations equally well. "Outlier" analysis provides a test for a number of countries (and/or cases) that deviate from the general pattern, indicated here by more than two standard deviations from zero for several years. Outliers were identified by removing the residuals from the final model and standardizing them with their standard deviation. Covering different periods, they included Afghanistan, Ethiopia, Rwanda, Mozambique, Sudan, and El Salvador. All produced some of the largest and most prolonged refugee situations in the period under consideration. Removing these outliers from the actual analysis produced some changes (see Model 2 in Table 3.2 in the appendix); this should caution us regarding the ability of quantitative methodology to explain all forms of refugee migrations equally.

Trends in Forced Migration

The Cold War and After

In the two decades prior to 1990, the data show seventy-four countries with population segments in exile and thirty-five countries with internal displacement. In the period 1990–95, there were seventy countries with populations in exile and fifty-one countries with internal displacement. Of the countries with internal displacement in the two time periods, only four and three, respectively, did not also produce international refugees. In these exceptional cases, either the violence was very narrowly targeted, so that it could be escaped without going abroad (Tanzania and Syria),[2] or there were obstacles that made exit more difficult (e.g., Cyprus being an island). For the two periods as a whole (1964–95), in forty-five of the fifty-two countries characterized by concurrent internal and international displacement, the international movement preceded the internal. In each of the seven exceptions, flight across international borders was initially deterred by either real or perceived obstacles to exit (e.g., East Timor an island with only one internal border; Peru bounded by the Andean mountains); fighting in neighboring countries (Cambodia, Croatia, and Laos); or narrowly targeted violence (Russia).

This initial overview suggests the following: (1) more countries produce external refugees than internally displaced persons; (2) most countries with internal displacement also produce refugees; (3) there is rarely exact simultaneous displacement of both, and usually the start of internal displacement lags behind refugee migration for a minimum of one but often several years; and (4) refugee displacement became more globalized in the post–Cold War era, meaning that more countries (both in terms of number and diversity) than ever before were affected by forced migration, including the nondeveloping countries of the North (in the case of the Yugoslav breakup literally at the doorsteps of western Europe).

Some other patterns emerge in Figures 3.1 to 3.4, showing the trend of international and internal displacement over time from 1964 to the present. Refugee numbers declined in the early 1970s, after which they grew constantly until 1990, with the largest increases coming between 1989 and 1990. Internal displacement reveals greater fluctuation, attributable in part to the problematic nature of the estimates. However, after the early 1980s, there is also a continuous increase until 1994. More specifically, in 1970 there were about nine million refugees from twenty-five countries and five million internally displaced from five countries. Due to repatriation and settlement, the number of refugees dropped to 2.5 million (and twenty-seven countries) in 1975, while the number of internally displaced increased by over one million. However, by 1980 the number of refugees almost tripled to slightly more than six million (from thirty-eight countries) while the number of internally displaced increased by barely two million (with twice as many countries, ten instead of five). Between 1980 and 1990, the number of refugees nearly tripled again to about seventeen million refugees from fifty countries; so did the internally displaced by growing to over twenty-two million in twenty-three countries. Overall, from 1970 to 1990, the number of refugee-producing countries had literally doubled, from twenty-five to fifty, as had the refugee stock, from nine to seventeen million.

In the 1990s, the number of refugee-sending countries initially continued to increase (from fifty in 1990 to sixty-three in 1994), but the number of refugees declined; furthermore, in 1995 the number of refugee-sending countries also declined. This can be attributed to two factors: (1) the repatriation of refugees to Afghanistan, Ethiopia/Eritrea, and Mozambique; and (2) the temporary addition of new refugee-sending countries from the former Warsaw Pact region, some lasting only a few years. In contrast with refugees, the number of internally displaced increased sharply in the early 1990s, peaking at twenty-seven million in thirty-two countries in 1994, but then dropped markedly by six million the following year. The changes are accounted for largely by reduced numbers reported for Africa (including South Africa, Angola, Ethiopia, and Rwanda), as well as for Afghanistan.

Africa

While the data set does not encompass the refugee migration that accompanied the decolonization of Algeria (1954–62), it does include the final phase of the decolonization process in Africa, as most French colonies gained independence around 1960, and British colonies a few years later. As Figure 3.1 indicates, decolonization occasioned few refugees, as it involved mostly "non-settler" colonies that experienced negotiated transitions. In contrast, decolonization in settler colonies, regardless of

Figure 3.1: Refugee Migration by Region, 1964–1995

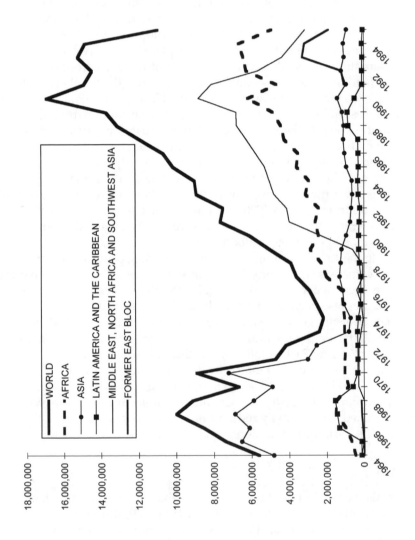

Figure 3.2: Internal Displacement by Region, 1964–1995

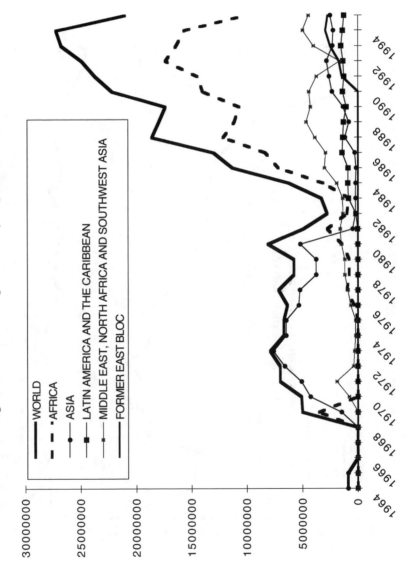

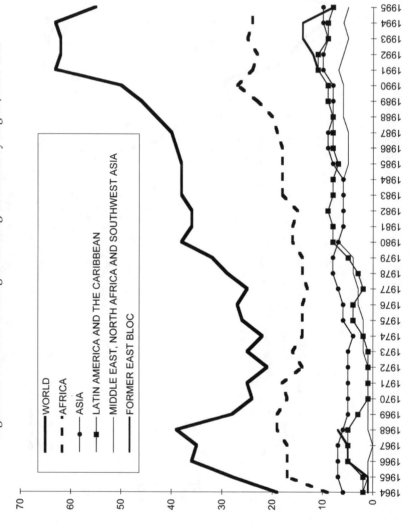

Figure 3.3: Number of Refugee-Sending Countries by Region, 1964–1995

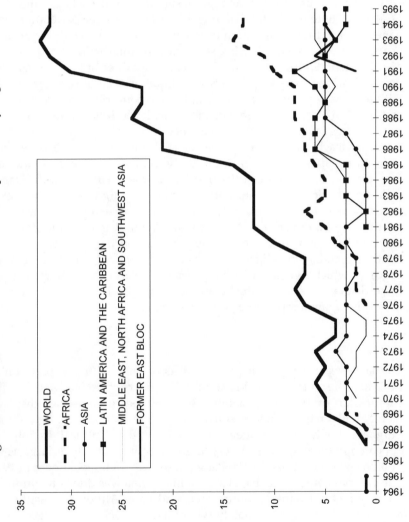

Figure 3.4: Number of Countries with Internal Displacement by Region, 1964–1995

nationality, usually entailed a prolonged violent struggle. Examples include Zimbabwe (former Southern Rhodesia) and the Portuguese colonies. Some of the longer struggles with refugee exoduses occurred in Guinea Bissau (1960–74), Angola (1961–75), and Mozambique (1964–75).

After decolonization, many African countries produced prolonged displacement as the result of brutally repressive regimes, ethnic conflict (including both communal confrontations and separatism), and external destabilization campaigns and interventions (e.g., activities of South Africa in the Southern African region, superpower activities in the Horn of Africa). There were a total of fifteen "chronic" refugee populations that were displaced for a minimum of ten and a maximum of thirty or more years, with eleven experiencing simultaneous international and internal displacement. Of these chronic situations, only three are the remnants of decolonization proper—Guinea Bissau, Equatorial Guinea, and Namibia, with refugee populations from the latter two countries ceasing to receive assistance in 1990. Although Zimbabwe achieved independence in 1980, some of those who fled abroad remained in the refugee pool until 1990. South Africa began resolving the internal and external displacements induced by apartheid in 1992. Similarly, conflicts in Mozambique and Ethiopia came to an end in the first half of the 1990s, permitting large-scale repatriations. Not counting the long-standing population in exile for Guinea Bissau, there are still seven "chronic" cases on the African continent (Angola, Burundi, Chad, Rwanda, Sudan, Uganda, and Zaire). In addition, nine new movements emerged from the late 1980s onward (Djibouti, Kenya, Liberia, Niger, Mali, Mauritania, Senegal, Sierra Leone, and Togo), of which five also involve internal displacement. The majority of these displacements are attributable to struggles by ethnic or political minorities against repressive governments.

Asia

The large-scale refugee displacement associated with the partition of India and the creation of Pakistan in 1947 is not captured in Table 3.1. The suppression of Tibetan autonomy (1956–59) led to large-scale displacements, with many refugees still remaining in exile. An undetermined number of Chinese refugees induced by the Cultural Revolution appeared in the late 1960s. A very large outflow—possibly as large as ten million—was generated by the Bangladeshi war of independence in 1971. The other major refugee displacement in the area was due to the Indochinese conflict in Vietnam, Kampuchea, and Laos. Although exact figures are not available, approximately two million Indochinese refugees were resettled in North America and Australia in the late 1970s, with another 750,000 boat people resettled in Europe in 1978–81 (Bach 1989). All three Indochinese countries experienced continuous displacement brought on by successive wars, starting with the war for independence against the French after World War II. The major external outflows were occasioned by the reunification of Vietnam in 1975, the genocidal governmental violence in Cambodia, and the Vietnamese invasion of Cambodia and the ongoing war thereafter. In all three cases, substantial internal displacement occurred prior to large-scale international flight. Burma/Myanmar has experienced refugee migration on and off since the early 1960s, with the most continuous movement resulting from regime repression, separatism, and ethnic warfare beginning in the mid-1980s.

Separatism in Sri Lanka (early 1980s–present) and in the southern Philippines (1972–87) occasioned refugee migration and internal displacement long before they began to be reported in the late 1980s. Protracted struggles for independence from Indonesia were ongoing in Irian Jaya and East Timor as of the mid-1990s. A recent conflict has emerged in Bhutan between Nepalese Hindu immigrants and the government over settlement and political rights. In sum, as of the mid-1990s, there were ten population segments that remained in exile in Asia (excluding the Middle East).

Latin America and the Caribbean

With a few exceptions, Latin America did not figure in the world of massive forced migrations until the early 1980s. Haiti experienced continuous displacement from the early 1960s onward when the Duvalier reign added brutal repression to widespread poverty, and Cuba generated refugees in the course of its revolution, followed by a continuous trickle rising to occasional peaks. In the southern cone, violence erupted following military takeovers in Chile (1973–95), Uruguay (1975–76), and Argentina (1976–83), producing substantial outflows. Authoritarian regimes in Bolivia (1966–69, 1975–76, 1980–82) and Paraguay (1966–69) also produced refugee flows. International assistance to Chilean refugees continued until recently.

In the 1980s, however, massive new refugee populations arose in Central America. These were linked to struggles for social transformation in three of the poorest and most highly stratified agrarian societies of the region: Nicaragua, El Salvador, and Guatemala. Honduras had also some displacement from the mid-1980s to the early 1990s resulting from a semi-repressive regime. In Nicaragua, the revolution of 1979 triggered an initial displacement; subsequently, the struggle between the Marxist government and the "Contra" rebels supported by the United States led to continuous refugee flows, both internal and international. Far more grave was the protracted struggle between a weak but very repressive government and Marxist rebels in El Salvador. The numbers were considerably underreported because the bulk of the outflow consisted of persons who fled to the United States, but were not recognized as refugees. While violence in Guatemala dates back to U.S. intervention in 1954, refugees did not emerge until the 1980s when terror, repression, and random killings reached their peak. In all three countries peace agreements were concluded in the first half of the 1990s, beginning with Nicaragua (1990) and ending with Guatemala (1996). Peace permitted a remarkably swift return of exiles from neighboring countries in the region; however, most of those who had fled to the United States remained there. In the early 1990s, the struggle between the government and Shining Path guerrillas in Peru produced a considerable number of internal displacements as well as a very small number of refugees. Small-scale internal and external displacement also resulted from the turf war raging between governments and drug lords in Colombia and from internal violence associated with the U.S. invasion of Panama.

The Middle East, North Africa, and Southwest Asia

The most protracted refugee population in the Middle East is Palestinians dispersed by the Arab-Israeli wars (1948 and 1969). Although this protracted regional conflict also uprooted many Jews living in Arab countries (including North Africa), most of them migrated to Israel under the "law of return" and therefore never appeared in the refugee pool. In Afghanistan, revolution, invasion, and protracted civil war produced the largest refugee migration in the post–World War II era. Although Soviet troops were withdrawn in 1987 and the Soviet-backed government was overthrown in 1992—leading to large-scale repatriation—ensuing civil war on a smaller scale has continued to uproot populations and slowed down return.

Elsewhere in the region, a variety of conflicts have produced displacements of various types and magnitudes. They include the struggle of the Polisario Front in Western Sahara (1975–present);[3] internal displacement in Cyprus following the Turkish invasion in 1973; international but especially internal displacements caused by the protracted civil war in Lebanon in the 1970s and 1980s; substantial outflows from the 1979 Iranian Islamic revolution (with some estimates reaching two to three million); large-scale internal displacements, but also harrowing stories of ships full of refugees seeking in vain international asylum from war, and unification in Yemen (1978–89). Another major refugee population in the region is Kurds. In Iraq, displacement started with a rebellion in the mid-1960s and peaked at one million in 1991 in the wake of the Gulf War; in Turkey, Kurds have been fleeing for two decades in a pattern reflecting the intensity of the struggle and the changing availability of asylum in Europe. Since 1994, the intensifying political and religious confrontation in Algeria has resulted in some fifty thousand deaths and a significant number of refugees, albeit vastly underreported because most of them enter France as authorized or unauthorized visitors.

The Soviet Bloc and Its Aftermath

Major exoduses were induced throughout the region by regime changes in the post–World War II period. Initially triggered by Communist takeovers in eastern and central Europe shortly after the war, they were followed by intermittent outflows occasioned by repression in the wake of revolt (Hungary in 1956, Czechoslovakia, 1968, Poland, 1981). A third wave is associated with the breakup of the Soviet Union and the collapse of communist regimes in the region, a well as the sudden lifting of draconian border controls. This was inaugurated by spectacular boat loads of Albanians landing in Italy, raising fears in Europe that this was a precursor of major migratory flows; however, ordinary migrations were quickly contained, and only the protracted violent conflicts in Yugoslavia and the former Soviet Union produced large-scale internal and external displacements. Much of this represented, in effect, a painful "unmixing" of populations (Zolberg 1996). As Zolberg notes, where the groups are spatially concentrated, the dynamics of separatism are likely to lead to a clean break, as in the Czechoslovak divorce and in Slovenia, unless state authorities choose to resort to force (e.g., Russia's policy in Chechnya). However, where groups are interspersed, as in Bosnia and various parts of the Caucasus, efforts to separate often precipitate conflicts that explode into violence. In this sense, Croatia was a mixed case: the degree of violence in the breakup thus became a critical factor determining displacement.

In the former Soviet Union, several successor states, notably the three Baltic republics as well as Ukraine and Belorussia, managed nonviolent breaks. In other areas, the breakaway process or subsequent conflicts within the successor state took a violent turn and generated substantial displacements. Instances include Georgia, Moldova, Tajikistan, Armenia, Uzbekistan, and Azerbaijan. Particularly intractable was the war between Azerbaijan and Armenia over the Armenian-populated enclave of Nagorno-Karabakh.

Findings from Empirical Analysis

Using the quantitative data, an attempt will be made to ascertain the relative importance of three major determinants of refugee flows. Drawn from the recent literature, they include interstate wars, intrastate conflicts, and repressive states (Ferris 1987; Gibney, Apodaca, and McCann 1994; Gordenker 1987; Hakovirta 1986; Loescher 1992; Weiner 1996; Wood 1994; Zolberg, Suhrke, and Aguayo 1989). I shall proceed from the weakest to the strongest determinant and conclude this section with a brief discussion of the contribution of economic factors to forced migration.

Interstate Wars

The association of interstate wars with refugee migration is largely based on the experience of World War II. Large-scale interstate wars have clearly contributed to some refugee migration in the period covered, including the Arab-Israel wars, the East Pakistan conflict, the Vietnam War, the invasion of Afghanistan by the Soviet Union, and, most recently, the Gulf War. In addition, interstate wars can also cause internal displacement as refugees flee from the conflict zones, which by the very nature of things tend to be in border areas. Invasions, even if designed to reduce or remedy conflict, often have the opposite effect. For example, Vietnam's invasion of Cambodia (1978–79) to drive out the Khmer Rouge regime did stop the "politicide"[4] but set off a new round of conflict that generated the first massive outflows from the country. Nigeria's intervention in the Liberian conflict by way of leading a peacekeeping force in 1994 did not bring about an immediate and decisive reduction of the conflict and attendant uprooting. Of course, the distinction between an interstate war and a foreign intervention in a civil war may be thin, as indicated by the Soviet invasion of Afghanistan. Furthermore, interstate war may occur as part of a more complex conflict, in which case its causal status in relation to a refugee flow may be hard to determine. For example, following the partition of Palestine, Palestinians in the new Israel may have been pushed out or may have decided to leave even in the absence of a war.

These ambiguities are further revealed by the quantitative analysis. The analysis used a measure of interstate war from Singer's (1994) "Correlates of War" data set; this is a dichotomous variable which measures the presence of war (1) or its absence (0). Table 3.2 shows two models: Model 1 with all 109 cases and Model 2 with the exclusion of six powerful outlier cases involving some of the largest and most protracted displacements (Afghanistan, El Salvador, Ethiopia, Mozambique, Rwanda, and Sudan). The fact that the measure is only significant in the first equation (Model 1) but not in the second (Model 2), demonstrates its inability to consistently predict refugee migration. The magnitude of any one of the large cases, for example Afghanistan or Rwanda, could have thrown it off.

The weak predictive power of interstate wars is probably due to the fact that, except for the Iraqi invasion of Kuwait, none of the others occurred independently of some other form of political violence, but took place in the broader context of conflicts with an internal dimension. Some interstate wars generated large internal displacements in addition to refugees, such as the Vietnam War (1965–75), the Vietnamese-Cambodian war (1975–79), the Ethiopian-Somalian war (1977–78), the Sino-Vietnamese war (1979 and 1985–87), and the Iran-Iraq war (1980–88). Some cause few if any refugee migration at all (e.g., the Football war between El Salvador and Honduras in 1969, the Falkland war between Argentina and the United Kingdom in 1982, the India-Pakistan war of 1962, and the conflict between Turkey and Greece over Cyprus in 1974).

The incidence of interstate wars declined in the 1990s. During the period 1969–89, there were fifty-eight wars in thirty-nine locations, of which fourteen were interstate wars; but of forty-nine wars in 1990, only three were interstate; and in 1991 (fifty-one armed conflicts), 1992 (fifty-five), and 1995 (thirty-five), there was only one interstate war (Wallensteen and Sollenberg 1996).[5] This was the war between Armenia and Azerbaijan, mentioned earlier, which thus becomes a lonely outlier. It should be noted, however, that the war evolved from an "internal" into an "interstate" one by way of changing sovereignties, which of course was the principal cause of the confrontation in the first place. However, despite this decline, Wallensteen and Sollenberg (1996) caution against an overly optimistic prognosis, since "each of the past four decades has witnessed short but intense interstate conflicts" (11).

Intrastate Conflicts

While Weiner (1996) distinguishes between ethnic and nonethnic conflicts and civil wars, this clear distinction will not be retained in the quantitative analysis because labeling a conflict as "ethnic" assumes that we understand its underlying causality. The labeling also downplays elements that are common to all conflicts, namely competition for power and resources. Ethnic and other civil conflicts often have similar roots in the exclusion of groups from the political process or in excessive inequalities among groups. In addition, some conflicts that were initially shaped by Cold War confrontations unfolded along ethnic and/or religious lines (e.g., Afghanistan).

Intrastate conflicts here encompass any sustained challenge that seeks to alter a political regime or a state's territorial domain. Although intrastate conflicts normally involve confrontations between the government and some opponents, recently attention has been drawn to conflicts that are destructured, in the sense that there is no clear government, but a power struggle among several warring parties with diffuse or localized aims, such as warlords. Opposition may be founded on demands for social change, or resistance to it. Leaving aside classic colonial independence struggles, one can distinguish between struggles based on class and those shaped by ethnic or national identities, usually concerning access to power and resource distribution in relation to ethnic boundaries. However, both types can take many forms: they can coexist and overlap, they can vary in the level of violence and persistence, and both are likely to be exacerbated by foreign interventions that boost their destructiveness and duration.

Each of the two types is more likely to occur in certain regions. Ferris (1987) argues that "[w]ith few exceptions, the Central American political game has been characterized by the concentration of wealth in the hands of a few, the almost total exclusion of indigenous groups from the political processes, and frequently brutal efforts to prevent the formation of broad-based opposition groups" (14; see also Zolberg et al. 1989). A government may not recognize protest or rebellion as a "wake-up call" to reform, but instead increase repression (Bowen 1985). In such circumstances, nonviolent protest can turn into civil wars that produce both internal displacement and refugees, as was the case in Guatemala, El Salvador, Nicaragua, and Iran. It might be noted that even in conflicts that mainly center around class formations, ethnicity may play a role, as in Guatemala with its Mayan population or Iran with regard to religious minorities.

Ethnic minorities may extend their objectives to political and territorial separation from the existing state. Secessionist claims can arise from (1) the unwillingness of the government to consider the rights of minorities; (2) economic exploitation of minorities; (3) disputes over historical claims to specific territories; and/or (4) minority ambitions beyond their current status and rights. Once disputes develop into secessionist claims, open conflict is often inevitable since secession is a direct threat to the very integrity of the state (e.g., Eritrea-Ethiopia, East Timor-Indonesia).[6]

Because of definitional ambiguities regarding ethnic conflicts vs. those based on other social formations, notably class, many data sets fail to distinguish between them. For instance, the "Correlates of War" dataset by Singer (1994) recognizes separatist conflicts but not other ethnic wars; the case list differentiates merely between intrastate and interstate conflicts. The two data sets covering the 1990s also failed to provide clear classifications, either distinguishing between conflicts over "territory" and conflict over "government" (Wallensteen and Sollenberg 1996); or distinguishing between civil war, regional civil war, interstate war, and war of independence (Smith 1997). Here, intrastate conflict has been coded as a dichotomous variable measuring its presence (1) or absence (0) as indicated by deaths.[7] A separate measure of separatist wars was dropped from the final analysis because of its lack of predictive power as demonstrated in earlier runs. The reason for this is probably the rarity of occurrence during the period 1971–90, which impairs predictive ability in large-scale analysis. However, case evidence shows that when separatist struggles did occur, they produced refugees—albeit in sharply varying numbers (e.g., Eritrea, Ogaden, and Tigre vs. Ethiopia; East Timor vs. Indonesia; Western Sahara vs. Morocco; Moro vs. the Philippines; Kurds vs. Turkey and Iraq). In order to ascertain some measure of ethnically motivated struggle, Gurr's measure of ethnic rebellion (1993a, 1993b) was used; it is coded on a six point scale in terms of the intensity of the protest, ranging from zero (none reported) to five (highest form of protest or rebellion and/or greatest number of participants).

The blurred distinction between ethnic and nonethnic internal wars showed up also in the quantitative analysis. The measure of ethnic rebellion was significant until the general measure for intrastate conflict was entered into the analysis. However, in Model 2, where the six large outliers were excluded, ethnic rebellion reappeared as the weakest, yet significant, predictor of refugee flows. In other words, and not unexpectedly, this indicates that the more general measure of intrastate conflicts has greater predictive power than the narrower ethnic conflict measure.[8] Overall, the analysis thus supports the proposition that *intrastate conflict in general and ethnic conflicts more specifically, increase the likelihood of a refugee exodus*, net of other causes. This was true even during the Cold War, when ideological alignments were usually considered more important than ethnic affiliation.

The more striking finding is *the importance of foreign intervention in intrastate conflicts*, thus confirming the insights from historical analysis. Many localized resource or territorial struggles are fueled or supported by outsiders. During the Cold War, the United States and the Soviet Union frequently exploited conflicts in the developing world for their own purposes, notably in Indochina, Central America, and Afghanistan, as did regional powers such as South Africa (Angola, Namibia) or Vietnam (Kampuchea). Intervention ranged from economic assistance to military activities. Although the empirical analysis was able to weigh the role of foreign military intervention, it could not measure more subtle forms of intervention, such as monetary assistance.

The measure of foreign military intervention was constructed as a dichotomous variable from Singer's "Correlates of War" (1994) data, based on troop commitments.[9] It was then used in interaction with intrastate conflicts and emerged as the second strongest predictor of refugee migration, even stronger than intrastate wars by themselves. Foreign interventions tend to prolong civil wars that might otherwise have ended for lack of resources; they also increase the number of refugees and prolong their exile abroad. This confirms findings first advanced in the literature on refugees by Zolberg et al. (1989). However, since the majority of interventions were by regional powers, their argument that the Cold War was a major source of the refugee crisis of the 1970s to 1980s is somewhat weakened. While it is possible that client states acted on behalf of superpowers, regional rivalries for power are just as plausible. Thus, the predictive power of foreign military intervention should not be simplified as meaning only Cold War rivalry.

While the 1990s may have shown a decline in interstate wars, there has not been a comparable decline in intrastate conflicts. "From 1990 to 1995, 70 states were involved in 93 wars which killed five and a half million people" (Smith 1997: 13). A look at the correlation between wars and refugee migration shows that in the 1990s all but three (Bhutan, Uzbekistan, Zaire) of the sixty refugee flows coincided with an intrastate conflict during some point in time. In two more cases, intrastate conflicts resulted in internal displacement (Lebanon, the Philippines). Similarly, foreign military interventions have shown no great decline. Between 1969–89, sixteen out of thirty-eight civil wars had foreign military intervention, as measured by troop commitments (Singer 1994). In 1990 and 1992 there were only two wars with outside intervention of this kind; in 1991 one; and in 1994 and 1995 none. However, 1993 had four (Wallensteen and Sollenberg 1996).

The growing number of intrastate conflicts in the 1990s is cause for grave concern. It has been suggested that contemporary civil wars produce higher death counts than in the past due to the extent to which the civilian population is drawn into the conflict—with estimates ranging to over 90 percent of casualties in some cases (Independent Commission on International Humanitarian Issues 1986, 25 as cited in Loescher 1993: 13).

Duvall and Stohl (1988) have suggested that the killing of innocent bystanders is a common tactic of repressive governments to induce terror in witnesses (such as insurgency groups, or rebels). Jongman (1990) also observed that "the magnitude of human rights violations is closely linked to the presence and scale of armed conflicts" (14).

In addition, although it is not only Cold War-type interventions that produce refugee migrations, this confrontation's poisoned legacy persists, in that the surplus of increased weapon production has flooded local markets throughout the developing and post-Communist worlds.[10] While the impact of this trade on current refugee flows is not tested in this essay, it probably increases their magnitude by prolonging and broadening intrastate conflicts and rendering them more lethal.

A recent study by Hartung (1996) shows that there is still considerable arms trade between great powers (U.S., France, U.K., China, Germany, and Russia), other European nations, regional powers, and countries at war all over the world. Focusing largely on the United States he shows that the "see-no-evil" mentality has survived into the 1990s, as indicated by suggestions that countries trade weapons even with parties to conflicts under UN arms embargo (as was possibly the case of France in the Great Lakes Region). U.S. weapons apparently still flow into refugee-producing conflicts in Afghanistan, Indonesia, Guatemala, Turkey, and Colombia. Moreover, one of the most striking features of U.S. arms sales since the end of the Cold War has been "the regularity with which U.S.-supplied weapons have ended up in the hands of U.S. adversaries," a phenomenon sometimes referred to as the "Boomerang Effect" (Hartung 1996: 20). The examples he mentions are Panama, Iraq, Somalia, and Haiti.

In addition, light weapons trade by independent contractors or smaller countries (or factions) continues to supply intrastate conflicts. Hartung summarizes findings from research on light weapons that show the very difficult nature of controlling its trade:

> 1) There are ample surplus stocks of light weaponry already existing as a sort of handover from the Cold War to keep most ethnic wars amply stocked even in the absence of new productions for export; 2) There are dozens of producers of light weaponry seeking international sales, making supply side controls problematic at best; 3) Because light weaponry is cheap and relatively easy to transport, it is difficult to monitor and control; 4) Light weaponry can move through established black market channels without being detected by government officials. (1996: 26)

Repressive States: Institutional Human Rights Violations vs. Severe Threats to Life

Persecution based on race, religion, nationality, membership in a particular social group, and/or political opinion is an integral part of the definition of "refugee" in the 1951 UN Convention. While states are typically viewed as the main perpetrator of these persecutions, the concept of "refugee" has also been interpreted to include those fleeing persecution by nonstate actors, where the state is unwilling or unable to provide protection. These interpretations have been adopted also by many scholars who focus on human rights as a source of flight. Gibney, Apodaca, and McCann (1996) found that an increasing number of refugees are associated with a general rise in violence and human rights violations in the world. Harkovirta (1986) also reports a modest to strong correlation between government repression and refugee exodus. Stanley (1987) linked the level of violence in El Salvador to increasing refugee flight to the United States. Yet it is important to define what types of human rights violations increase the likelihood of refugee flows. The studies cited above relied on general measures of violence that are associated with repressive regimes or government terror, including a wide range of government actions such as arbitrary arrests, random killings, and torture. More broadly, Loescher (1993) states that "[i]t is true that the principal sources of the current world refugee problem—Angola, Burma, Ethiopia, Iran, Iraq, Somalia, and Vietnam—are among the world's most repressive societies" (13). Similarly, Weiner (1996) argues that oppressive authoritarian and revolutionary regimes, such as in China (Cultural Revolution), Cuba (Castro), Iran (Khomeni), Cambodia (Khmer Rouge), Central and Latin America, and eastern Europe, caused refugee migration.

Arguably, a greater differentiation of form and levels of coercion would be useful. For definitional purposes, state repression is the government's or its allies' use of threat of coercion against political opponents in order to weaken resistance or opposition to government objectives (Stohl and Lopez 1984: 7). Government repression can range from the imposition of governmental sanctions, such as declarations of state emergency and restrictions on press freedom and civil actions, to physical destruction of political organizations. Strong and weak states engage in different forms of repression. Strong states can often rely on a general aura of terror, while weak states have to act in order to stay in control. For example, after a period of initial rebellions against the "Communist" governments in the East Bloc countries, extreme human rights violations against the population began to cease and a general sense of terror—combined with strict exit controls—prevented both large-scale dissent and exodus until the breakdown of those regimes in the late 1980s. Communist regimes thus were generally strong enough to control both borders and dissent, and human rights violations were largely targeted against political dissidents or took the form of denial of political freedoms and rights. Governments in the developing world, on the other hand, often lack sufficient power to instil a general fear in their populations and may therefore resort to harsh human rights violations to stay in power. The pattern of repression varies from harassment tactics (Cuba) to death squads (El Salvador), or even the genocide of opponents (Cambodia). This form of governance combined with a general inability of weak governments to fully control their borders has led to large-scale refugee migration in these countries.

For the sake of simplicity, government repression in the former East Bloc countries will be called institutional human rights violations, indicating that the physical safety of the majority of the population is not threatened, in contrast to the government repression in other parts of the world which often entails a great deal of physical violence (such as random killings, death squads, and torture). The latter has been most often associated with refugee migration in previous studies. To measure institutional human rights violations, the Freedom House index of civil liberties was used. The index ranges from countries with the fewest civil liberties (1) to those with the most (7) (Gastil 1978). The civil rights index broadly includes the freedom of forming and expressing political opinions (e.g., freedom of religion) as well as political activism.[11] In order to distinguish between regimes that are repressive and strong, and those that are repressive and weak, a measure was taken from theories of political activism (dissent) and the nature of regimes (Jenkins 1983; Tilly 1978). These writers depict the relationships among repression, activism, and regime strength as an inverted U-shape since deprived populations only rebel when there are viable options to do so. In democratic societies, neither out-migration nor political activism is constrained, thus there is (with some exceptions) no imminent necessity for violence and forced flight. On the other tail end of the inverted U are repressive regimes where dissent and migration often entail a very high cost due to real or "imaginative" punishments. Thus, political rebellion tends to occur in countries midway between democracy and extreme "state repression," where political opportunities have opened up and resistance is not too costly. This is supported by Fein's (1992) study on human rights violations that finds that there are "more murders in the middle," or "there is more internal strife in partially free states than in the unfree or free states" (10). Since "free" states lack exit controls, moreover, people can also vote with their feet by exiting (Hirschman 1970). To represent such a curvilinear relationship, a squared term of civil rights was introduced into the equation in this study.

In order to measure more severe government repression, it was decided to use the harshest and most extreme form of violence that targets specific groups for extermination. These actions are called "genocide" if a distinct ethnic group is targeted, and "politicide" if political orientation is the predominant reason for singling out parts of the population. More specifically, "genocide is defined as the promotion, execution and/or implied consent of sustained policies by governing elites or their agents, or in the case of civil war, either of the contending authorities— that result in the deaths of a substantial portion of a communal and/or politicized communal group. In politicides groups are victimized primarily because of their political opposition to the regime" (Gurr and Harff 1996: 48). Fein (1990) defines genocide as "sustained purposeful action by a perpetrator to physically destroy a collectivity directly or indirectly, through interdiction of the biological and social reproduction of group members, sustained regardless of the surrender or lack of threat offered by the victim." Fein (1993) and Jonassohn (1993) argue that most refugee migrations are caused by some kind of genocide against a particular group. Two case-lists were used here (Fein 1993 and Harff and Gurr 1989, 1995), to construct a variable that indicates the presence (1) or absence (0) of genocides/politicides. A scoring is given per country and year according to whether such an event was in progress.

The empirical analysis showed that refugees are less likely to flee from states that infringe on their political and civil rights than from states that threaten their lives. While the idea of the inverted U-shape relationship was confirmed by the direction of both sets of variables, it did not significantly predict refugee migration once genocides/politicides were controlled for. This shows that measures of extreme violence overpower measures of institutional human rights violations. Among all variables, genocide/politicide is the strongest and most consistent predictor of refugee migration. Between 1969 and 1990 there were twelve cases of genocide and twenty-two politicides in twenty-six out of sixty-nine countries with ongoing refugee migrations, and all were associated with forced displacement.

African as well as Asian states have used minorities as scapegoats during critical phases of state formation. For example, the Communist Vietnamese government targeted the Chinese minority in the period after its forceful unification of Vietnam in 1975. Other conflicts between governments and target minorities have occurred in the Philippines (the Moro) and Turkey (the Kurds).[12] Iraq, as well as Turkey, has launched multiple campaigns against the Kurds. From 1959–75, Iraq attempted to destroy Kurdish political organization and, under the cover of the Iran-Iraq war, used poison gas for genocidal purposes. In Uganda, in the early 1970s, Idi Amin attacked the Baganda and other political opponents. After refugee insurgents overthrew Amin with Tanzanian sponsorship in 1979, the new government victimized Catholic opponents in southern Uganda. Other countries with sizeable refugee populations considered to have experienced genocide/politicide include Afghanistan, China, Chile, Guatemala, Laos, and Myanmar (Burma).

According to a list developed by Harff and Gurr (1995), between 1990 and 1995 there were two clear cases of genocide and politicide each in Bosnia/Herzegovina (1992–94), Rwanda (1994), Angola (1990–94), and El Salvador (1991–93). In addition, there are two mixed cases: Sudan (1990–95) and Iraq (1990–94), in which serious civil war has been punctuated intermittently by wholesale massacres of civilians. In all six cases, forced migration occurred. In addition, Myanmar may already be another Yugoslavia, based on the government's vicious campaign to subdue many minorities, and the current level of mass murder, relocations, and rapes.

There have been some changes in the universe of repressive states in the 1990s. Weiner (1996) observes that "refugee flight from countries with authoritarian regimes that persecute dissident individuals and social classes ... have declined as a result of the reduction of authoritarian regimes" (25). Most obviously, the repressive regimes in the former East Bloc have imploded and, with the removal of repression as well as exit controls, opened the door to out-migration. Some of Africa's weak states collapsed altogether (Somalia and Liberia). As noted earlier, violence and human rights violations arising not from an identifiable government, but from random actors in a decentralized conflict, seems to have become more common. Thus, Serbian warlords were responsible for much of the ethnic cleansing in Bosnia and Herzegovina, and in southern Sudan, warlords are also increasingly involved in human rights violations and violence.

The Role of Economic Factors and Population Pressures

Refugees are defined in international law as the victims of political causes broadly understood. During the 1980s, however, in the "root cause" debate that developed in the public and scholarly discourse on refugee migration, it was argued that refugees usually come from very poor countries, hence economic causes could be considered as a "root" or primary cause of refugee migration. Yet, the data examined here shows that while refugees indeed come from poverty stricken countries, not all poor countries send refugees. This disqualifies poverty as a direct and necessary push factor of refugee migration. Nevertheless, it is intriguing that more and more scholars maintain that economic (and also ecological) problems are associated with refugee migration (CIMADE, INDOEP, and MINK 1986; Kibreab 1987; Rogge 1985; Smyser 1987; Sutter 1990; Wood 1994). If we accept that economic factors are not a direct and necessary cause of refugee migration, only two possibilities are left: (1) that poverty causes political violence that in turn pushes refugees out, or (2) that poverty interacts with political violence as a cause of refugee migration.

This analysis uses several measures that have been associated in the literature with poverty and level of economic development (rate of urbanization, infant mortality, and energy consumption).[13] None of these indicators was able to predict refugee migration directly. However, an interaction term between genocides/politicides and the log of energy consumption was significant and negative, suggesting that in areas with higher levels of economic development, refugee exodus is less likely during political conflict than in areas with lower levels of economic development. Thus, the level of economic development or poverty might be an accelerating factor. Another way of interpreting this finding is to consider poverty as a trigger for refugee migrations. During the initial phase of a conflict, people may try to await the end of the struggle; however, famine or deepening poverty robs them of their last option for survival. Some governments have used starvation as a political tool, inducing famine by destroying crops or poisoning water in order to break the will of insurgency groups. Such "scorched earth" tactics were used by Nigeria during the Biafra conflict and Ethiopia during its conflict with Eritrea.

The experience in the former Soviet Union and the Balkans highlights the importance of economic dimensions. In Yugoslavia, for example, the two most prosperous regions (Croatia and Slovenia) initiated the break-up process and were successful after initial struggle. Similarly, the relatively wealthy Estonia, Latvia, and Lithuania were the first to break away from the former Soviet Union. In other areas, however, secession and the formation of new states have been much more problematic.

While policymakers have long argued that population growth contributes to refugee migrations, the argument was most recently put forth by Weiner (1996) in the sense that the size of refugee populations is partly a function of population growth. In addition, he suggests that increasing population density creates more people at risk. Other authors (e.g., Edmonston 1992) suggest that very high population density can constitute an additional push for refugee migration. In this view, population factors serve as accelerators of refugee migration. Thus, there seem to be differing explanations on how demographic causes work—either as underlying causes or accelerators of proximate causes. Several measures from World Bank data (1994) were tried for this study—population size, population growth, and population density (1,000 people per square mile)—but the latter one worked best in the analysis. In the end, however, none of these variables could significantly predict refugee migration once political factors were controlled for. This is an important finding, which discredits arguments that imminent population pressure is a direct cause of refugee migration. Another finding is intriguing: an interaction effect between civil war and the log of population density was negative and significant, suggesting that while civil wars cause refugee migration regardless of a country's level of population density, such political violence leads to less refugee migration in countries with a higher population density. The finding can be explained in two ways: (1) in areas with high population density, people value land very much and have to consider the consequence of losing their property when fleeing abroad; and/or (2) as Crenshaw (1995) argues, population density measures social complexity, which can be associated with democracy and thus lower levels of political violence. Yet, since the interaction term ceased to be significant once six outliers were excluded from the analysis, the overall impact of population measures on refugee migration becomes indeed questionable.

Conclusion

This chapter points to several factors in the formation of refugee migration that need to be considered in assessing likely future trends. To return to our initial question as to whether the end of the Cold War induced a shift in the pattern of refugee migration, the analysis suggests that we are seeing "new" versions of "old" conflicts modified by contemporary international circumstances rather than the emergence of a completely new set of conflicts, unique to the 1990s.

First, state implosions and the formation of new states, or the restructuring of existing states, are key factors of forced exodus and these findings are consistent across time and space, although the type of implosion may differ in its form. Out-migration may be particularly large if implosions occur in strongly repressive states that were able to control their borders in the past.

Second, the persistence of genocidal violence and its consistent association with refugee migration needs to be noted. Unfortunately, we have not seen a decline in vicious mass murder during the 1990s. An important factor in this connection is the manipulation of popular fears and insecurities by chauvinistic entrepreneurs in order to gain power for their own political gain. In the former East Bloc, for instance, the power-vacuum that was created after state implosions enabled ethnic entrepreneurs to gain a stronghold. For these reasons, monitoring the emergence of political entrepreneurs may be important, although condemnation alone may not be adequate and indeed could be counterproductive as a response. A study by Harff (1998) suggests that "international declarations against the perpetrator led to increases in violence against the targeted groups" (9). Thus, there is still much to be learned about how to mediate and prevent genocidal situations that lead to large-scale refugee displacements.

Third, there is a continuing likelihood of internal struggles over power-sharing and resource distribution, particularly along ethnic demarcation. The impact of religious strife is also a central dimension of internal conflict in some areas, such as Algeria. One underlying reason for these struggles are the lack of institutional means to accommodate differences and grievances shared by parts of the populations. Some states are too weak to support differences and others are not willing to incorporate minorities. While the strengthening of democratic movements in conflict-prone areas is an important long-term solution, the continuing trade of weapons into conflict areas works in the opposite direction by contributing to protracted conflicts and refugee migration. The majority of these weapons come from "a handful of suppliers—the United States, France, Russia, the United Kingdom, China, and Germany—and [if we consider] that in the majority of conflicts just one or two suppliers accounted for more than half of the weapons imported by the government party to the dispute," there is hope for trying to control the legal weapons trade (Hartung 1996: 1). The problem of small weapons trade—which could not be tested here due to unavailability of data—however, is more intractable owing to its ability to support even small conflicts, and the difficulty in tracking and penalizing such trade.

In this connection it is important to restate a major finding of this study: military intervention (including the commitment of arms) plays a major role in the formation of refugee migration. Intrastate conflicts with foreign military intervention were the second strongest predictor of refugee migration and far more powerful than the conflicts themselves. Thus, it is important to monitor not only the conflicts, but also outsiders who may benefit from their persistence and therefore continue to support these intrastate struggles.

Finally, the significant effects of how poverty interacts with indicators of political violence constitute a first step toward disentangling the role of nonpolitical factors in causing refugee migration: they suggest that poverty can provide the final push-factor for people to leave a politically unsatisfying environment (or even mild repression). The implications for the United States in terms of likely out-migration pressures from Mexico, among other places, seem clear. Controlling the entry of illegal migrants may not prove to be the best way of preventing future mass migration from the neighbor in the South. Moreover, while Mexico is hardly a totalitarian regime, it is not a full-fledged democracy either. Thus it would fall at the top of the inverted U-shape, where the government is not strong enough to control exit, but does not provide the full freedom required for the democratic resolution of political differences.

In conclusion, while one can state with certainty that refugee flows are affected by state implosions and/or the formation of new states, genocidal violence, and internal struggles (particularly those fueled by foreign military interventions); the nature of the interaction between conflict, refugee migration, and poverty requires further investigation. While some scholars (e.g., Boswell and Dixon 1990) found that relative deprivation due to poverty leads to political conflict, others (e.g., Moaddel 1994) caution us about the validity of these findings. A possible relationship between economic hardship and refugee migration was demonstrated by Edmonston (1992) in two panel regression for the years 1986 and 1990. While it is generally assumed that economic difficulties exacerbate problems associated with state formation, and that economic development may aid in the development of democratic institutions and economic justice, the exact nature of these relationships needs further exploration.

Appendix

Table 3.1: List of Forced Migrations by Country of Origin

Continent/ Country	International	Internal
A. Africa (N=35)	(N=34)	(N=21)
Angola	1964–95	1976–95
Burundi	1967–1995	1993–95
Cameroon	1968–71 and 1983–90, 1995	—
Central African Republic	1983–95	—
Chad	1970–95	1982–89
Congo	1965–69	—
Cote d'Ivoire	1964–71	—
Djibouti	1993–95	1993
Equatorial Guinea	1973–90	—
Ethiopia/Eritrea	1967–95	1977–94
Gabon	1964–66	—
Ghana	1964–66 and 1981–95	1995
Guinea Bissau	1965–94	—
Kenya	1965–69 and 1995	1982, 1993–95
Lesotho	1972–73, 1980, 1983, 1989–90	—
Liberia	1989–95	1990–95
Malawi	1967–71 and 1982–90	—
Mali	1964–68 and 1990–95	1995
Mauritania	1989–95	—
Mozambique	1964–95	1982–95
Namibia	1969–90	—
Niger	1965–66 and 1990–95	—
Nigeria	1968–69	1969
Rwanda	1964–95	1991–95
Senegal	1988–95	—
Sierra Leone	1964–68 and 1990–95	1991–95
Somalia	1965–71 and 1987–95	1969, 1982, 1988–95
South Africa	1964–92–95	1967–68, 1985–95
Sudan	1965–95	1986–95
Tanzania	—	1980–81
Togo	1971 and 1991–95	1993–94
Uganda	1973–95	1981–91
Zambia	1967–81	—
Zaire	1965–66 and 1969–95	1992–95
Zimbabwe	1965–90	1980–81

Table 3.1: List of Forced Migrations by Country of Origin *(continued)*

Continent/ Country	International	Internal
B. Asia (N=15)	(N=15)	(N=10)
Bangladesh	1964–73, 1978–80, 1986–95	—
Bhutan	1991–95	—
Cambodia (Kampuchea)	1974–95	1970–95
China	1964–77 and 1983–87	—
Tibet	1964–95	—
India	1964–77	1973, 1987–95
Indonesia	1978–95	1969,1980–81
East Timor	1984–90	1980–81
Irian Jaya	1978–95	—
Laos	1975–95	1969–81
Myanmar (Burma)	1965–73, 1977–79, 1985–95	1988–95
North Korea	1964–67	—
Philippines	1972–87	1988–95
Papau New Guinea	1994–95	1968
Sri Lanka	1985–95	1986–95
Vietnam	1964–71 and 1975–95	1964–65,1969–77

C. Latin America and the Caribbean

(N=15)	(N=14)	(N=9)
Argentinia	1980–82	—
Bolivia	1966–69, 1975–76, 1980–82	—
Chile	1966–68 and 1973–95	1986–88
Colombia	1983–84 and 1989–95	1990–95
Cuba	1964–68 and 1979–95	—
El Salvador	1979–95	1981–92
Guatemala	1980–95	1983–95
Haiti	1964–95	1991–93
Honduras	—	1986–91
Nicaragua	1978–95	1983–91
Panama	1991–92	1991
Paraguay	1966–69	—
Peru	1992–95	1986–95
Surinam	1986–92	—
Uruguay	1975–76 and 1982–90	—

(continued)

Table 3.1: List of Forced Migrations by Country of Origin *(continued)*

Continent/ Country	International	Internal
D. Middle East, North Africa and Southwest Asia		
(N=14)	(N=12)	(N=9)
Afghanistan	1979–95	1985–95
Algeria	1994–95	—
Cyprus	—	1973–95
Iran	1980–95	1981–89, 1993
Iraq (Kurds)	1965–66 and 1973–95	1976–80, 1986–95
Kuwait	1990–91	—
Lebanon	1976–84	1976–95
Morocco	1964	—
Pakistan	1969–74, 1980 and 1988–92	1971
South Yemen (Democratic)	1978–89	1994
Syria	—	1970–73, 1986, 1995
Tunisia	1964 and 1968	—
Turkey	1991–95	1991–95
Western Sahara	1975–95	—
E. Former East Bloc		
(N=19)	(N=19)	(N=9)
Albania	1966–68 and 1991–92	—
Czechoslovakia	1968	—
Czech Republic	1994	—
Bulgaria	1966–68 and 1991–92	—
Hungary	1993–94	—
Poland	1968 and 1991–94	—
Romania	1966–68 and 1991–94	—
USSR (former)	1964–68	1991
Armenia	1991–95	—
Azerbaijan	1991–95	1992–95
Georgia	1991–95	1992–95
Moldova	1991–92	1992–94
Russian Federation	1995	1994–95
Tajikistan	1991–95	1992–94
Uzbekistan	1991–95	—
Yugoslavia (former)	1966–68 and 1991–95	1991
Bosnia	1992–95	1992–95
Croatia	1993–94	1992–95
Macedonia	1993–94	—
Slovenia	1993–94	—
Serbia	1995	—

Table 3.1: List of Forced Migrations by Country of Origin *(continued)*

Note: The dates in this table vary depending on when the start and end-date of a refugee migration was reported for each individual country, with one exception: certain movements may have begun prior to 1964 or are still continuous past 1995.

Table 3.2: Pooled Time-Series Analysis of Effects of Explanatory Variables and Interaction Terms on Change in Refugee Stock, 1971–1990

	Model 1 (N=109)		Model 2, Excluding Six Outlier (N=103)	
	b	ß	b	ß
Refugee Stock (lagged one year)	.914[c]	.891	.579[c]	.761
Root Causes:				
Logged energy consumption/capita (lagged two years)	26	.000	-28	-.000
Logged population density	-63	-.000	114	.001
Proximate Events:				
Civil rights	30	.000	642	-.001
Civil rights squared	-4	-.000	-99	-.012
Genocides/politicides	56,418[c]	.042	44,257[c]	.097
Ethnic rebellion (lagged one year)	36	.000	2,025[c]	.028
Civil wars	29,117[b]	.025	20,840[a]	.053
Intervention in civil war (lagged one year)	-980	-.000	727	.001
Civil wars[a]—intervention in civil war	59,113[b]	.029	41,877[b]	.061
Interstate wars	8,090[c]	.004	3,408	.006
Interaction Terms:				
Genocide/politicide[a] energy consumption	-20,035[c]	-.033	-13,156[b]	-.066
Civil war[a] population density	-13,286[b]	-.019	-7,268	-.032
Constant		74		721
Constant Rho	.19031		.31720	
Buse's R[b]	.8004		.5235	

[a]$p<.05$
[b]$p<.01$
[c]$p<.001$ (all using a two-tailed test)

Notes

This essay was originally prepared for the Pew "Migration Policy in Global Perspective" Project at the International Center for Migration, Ethnicity and Citizenship, New School for Social Research. The research was supported by a Postdoctoral Fellowship from the Centre for Refugee Studies, York University; a Graduate School Presidential Fellowship from The Ohio State University; a National Science Foundation Grant (SES–9113829); and funding from the Mershon Center for International Security, The Ohio State University. I would like to thank J. Craig Jenkins and Stéphane Baldi, but in particular Astri Suhrke and Ari Zolberg for their helpful commentary on this essay.

1. This is due to complicated asylum procedures that make the estimation of refugees difficult. In addition, the sources used have very unreliable information from those countries. However, this entails a reduction of only 5 to 10 percent of the actual refugee numbers (Hein 1993, UNHCR 1993). In the 1990s, the two sources used reported refugees from the former Yugoslavia and Soviet Union who sought asylum in the West, but still excluded refugees from other parts of the world who reside in western industrialized countries.
2. The short-term displacement of 1980–81 in Tanzania was due to a border conflict with Uganda that uprooted residents in the disputed territory (U.S. Committee for Refugees 1982). In Syria, the struggle with Lebanon and pro- vs. anti-Syrian forces led to the displacement of Palestinian refugees only.
3. Since 1992 a UN monitoring force of soldiers and police is monitoring a cease-fire and in 1998 the UN brokered a national referendum to determine the fate of Western Sahara.
4. The term has come into use as a parallel to genocide, but targeting a political rather than an ethnic group (see Gurr and Harff 1996: 48).
5. In 1993 and 1994 no interstate wars were reported at all.
6. Secessionist claims, however, can also be dealt with peacefully. In countries with strong democratic institutions, the population can decide such matters by constitutional procedures (e.g., Canada-Quebec).
7. A war is only counted if "sufficient deaths" occurred, defined as reaching a threshold of 1,000 battle fatalities (Singer and Small 1982: 55).
8. There may also be slight incompatibilities between Singer's and Gurr's classifications, but these could be sorted out by way of case studies.
9. The "Correlates of War" data set only counts as external military interventions those which "reached serious proportions (at least 1,000 troops committed [to combat] or 100 battle deaths)" (Singer and Small 1972: 234).
10. Although so far there is no systematic way of tracking the flow of small arms, a number of studies have documented its impact (Human Rights Watch Arms Project 1994; British American Security Information Council's Project on Light Weapons [see Dyer and Goldring 1996; Husbands 1995]).
11. This was the reason for its inclusion over the political rights index that more narrowly captures the rights of the population to participate in government activities through the selection of representatives (voting). In addition, both indexes were highly correlated with one another, which provides problems for quantitative analysis. The civil rights index proved to be of a higher predictive power and thus was retained.

12. Since quantitative analysis is able to test the effect of certain variables net of all other effects, it is possible that countries can experience both intrastate conflict and gross human rights violations without confounding the effect of either variable.

13. I excluded monetary measures of economic development such as Gross National Product or Gross Domestic Product since they have often been considered as biased (lacking information on distribution and unsuited to proper comparative analysis). Energy consumption measures the kilograms of oil equivalent per capita; the less energy consumption the poorer the country and the longer this low energy consumption continues over time, the more persistent poverty is. Due to its skewed distribution, I logged this variable. Accepting the argument of modernization theories that urbanization means advanced development, I also included the percentage of urban population. The assumption here is that urbanization signifies development and the more urbanization exists the higher a country's development. Infant mortality (per 1,000 live births) is often considered to measure social development of a country. By definition it shows how well the general population has access to health care and indirectly how good the nutrition level is. Thus, the lower the infant mortality, the higher the social level of development (or the better the access to health care and proper nutrition). All three variables were taken from a computerized version of the World Bank data (1994).

References

Bach, Robert. 1989. "Third Country Resettlement." In *Refugees and International Relations,* edited by Gil Loescher and Laila Monahan. New York: Oxford University Press.

Boswell, Terry, and William J. Dixon. 1990. "Dependency and Rebellion: A Cross-National Analysis." *American Sociological Review* 55, 4:540–559.

Bowen, G. 1985. "The Political Economy of State Terrorism: Barrier to Human Rights in Guatemala." In *Human Rights and Third World Development,* edited by G. W. Shepherd, Jr. and V. Nanda. Westport, CT: Greenwood Press.

CIMADE, INODEP, and MINK. 1986. *Africa's Refugee Crisis: What's to Be Done?* London: Zed Books Ltd.

Crenshaw, Edward. 1995. "Democracy and Demographic Inheritance: The Influence of Modernity and Proto-Modernity on Political and Civil Rights, 1965 to 1980." American Sociological Review 60, 5:702–19.

Duvall, R., and M. Stohl. 1988. "Governance by Terror." In *The Politics of Terrorism,* edited by M. Stohl. New York: Marcel Dekker.

Dyer, Susannah L., and Natalie J. Goldring. 1996. "Controlling Global Light Weapons Transfers: Working Toward Policy Options." Paper presented at the Annual Meetings of the International Studies Association, San Diego, CA, 16–20 April.

Edmonston, Barry. 1992. "Why Refugees Flee: An Analysis of Refugee Emigration Data." Paper presented at the Annual Meeting of the Social Science History Association, Chicago, 5–8 November.

Fein, Helen. 1990. *Genocide: A Sociological Perspective.* Special Edition of *Current Sociology* 38,1.

———. 1992. "Free to be and Freedom: Life Integrity Violations and Liberal Democracy in 145 States, 1987." Paper prepared for the Conference on "Human Rights in a New World Order." Prague, Czechoslovakia.

———. 1993. "Accounting for Genocide after 1945: Theories and some Findings." *International Journal on Group Rights* 1:79–106.

Ferris, Elizabeth G. 1987. *The Central American Refugees.* New York: Praeger Publishers.

Finkel, Steven E. 1995. *Causal Analysis with Panel Data.* Thousand Oaks, CA: A Sage University Paper.

Gastil, Raymond. 1978–91. *Freedom in the World: Political Rights and Civil Liberties.* New York: Freedom House.

Gibney, Mark, Terri Apodaca, and Jay McCann. 1994. "Refugee Flows, the Internally Displaced and Political Violence: An Exploratory Analysis." Paper presented at the IRAP Conference in Oxford, England.

———. 1996. "Refugee Flows, the Internally Displaced and Political Violence: 1980–1993." In *Whither Refugee? The Refugee Crisis: Problems and Solutions,* edited Alex P. Schmid. Leiden: PIOOM.

Gordenker, Leon. 1987. *Refugees in International Politics.* Beckenham, Kent: Croom Helm Ltd, Provident House, Burrell Row.

Gurr, Ted Robert. 1993a. *Minorities at Risk: Data Files.* College Park, MD: Center for International Development and Conflict Management, University of Maryland.

———. 1993b. *Minorities at Risk: A Global View of Ethnopolitical Conflict.* Washington, D.C.: United States Institute of Peace Press.

Gurr, Ted Robert, and Barbara Harff. 1996. *Early Warning of Communal Conflicts and Genocide: Linking Empirical Research to International Responses.* Tokyo: United Nations University Press.

Hakovirta, Harto. 1986. *Third World Conflicts and Refugeeism: Dimensions, Dynamics and Trends of the World Refugee Problem.* Helsinki: The Finnish Society of Sciences.

Harff, Barbara. 1998. "Early Warning of Humanitarian Crises: Sequential Models and the Role of Accelerators." In *Preventive Measures: Building Risk Assessment and Crisis Early Warning Systems,* edited by John L. Davies and Ted Robert Gurr. Lanham, Md.: Rowman and Littlefield Publishers, Inc.

Harff, Barbara, and Ted R. Gurr. 1989. "Victims of the State: Genocides, Politicides and Group Repression since 1945." *International Review of Victimology* 1: 23–41.

———. 1995. "Victims of the State: Genocides, Politicides and Group Repression from 1945–1995." PIOOM Newsletter 7, 1: 24–39.

Hartung, William. 1996. "Arms Trade as a Tool for Conflict Prevention: Patterns of Weapons Deliveries to Regions of Conflict, 1985–1994." Paper presented at the Annual Meetings of the International Studies Association, San Diego, California.

Hein, Jeremy. 1993. "Refugees, Immigrants, and the State." *Annual Review of Sociology* 19: 43–59.

Hirschman, A. 1970. *Exit, Voice and Loyalty.* Princeton, N.J.: Princeton University Press.

Human Rights Watch Arms Project. 1994. *Arming Rwanda: The Arms Trade and Human Rights Abuses in the Rwandan War*. New York: Human Rights Watch Arms Project.

Husbands, Joe. 1995. "Controlling Transfers of Light Arms: Linkages to Conflict Process and Conflict Resolution Strategies." In *Lethal Commerce: The Global Trade in Small Arms and Light Weapons*. Cambridge, Mass.: American Academy of Arts and Sciences.

Jenkins, J. Craig. 1983. "Resource Mobilization Theory and the Study of Social Movements." *Annual Review of Sociology* 9: 527–53.

Jonassohn, Kurt. 1993. "Prevention without Prediction." *Holocaust and Genocide Studies* 7, 1: 1–13.

Jongman, Berto. 1990. "The Most Unfortunate Nations in the World: A Brief Survey of Various Databases." *PIOOM Newsletter* 2, 2: 14–17.

Kibreab, Gaim. 1987. *Refugees and Development in Africa: The Case of Eritrea*. Trenton, N.J.: The Red Sea Press.

Loescher, Gil. 1992. *Refugee Movements and International Security*. Adelphi Papers 268. London: International Institute for Strategic Studies.

———. 1993. *Beyond Charity: International Cooperation and the Global Refugee Crisis*. New York: Oxford University Press.

Loescher, Gil, and John A. Scanlan. 1986. *Calculated Kindness: Refugees and America's Half-Open Door, 1945 to the Present*. New York: The Free Press.

Moaddel, Mansor. 1994. "A Cross-National Analysis of Political Conflict." *American Sociological Review* 59, 2: 276–304.

Rogge, John R. 1985. *Too Many, Too Long: Sudan's Twenty-Year Refugee Dilemma*. Totowa, N.J.: Rowman and Allanheld Publishers.

Schmeidl, Susanne. 1995. *From Root Cause Assessment to Preventive Diplomacy: The Possibilities and Limitations of the Early Warning of Forced Migration*. Ph.D. diss., The Ohio State University.

———. 1997. "Exploring the Causes of Forced Migration: A Pooled Time Series Analysis, 1971–1990." *Social Science Quarterly* 78, 2:184–309.

Singer, J. David. 1994. *Correlates of War Project: Data Files*. The University of Michigan.

Singer, J. David, and Melvin Small. 1982. *Resort to Arms*. Beverly Hills, CA: Sage.

Singer, J. David, and Michael D. Wallace, eds. 1979. *To Augur Well: Early Warning Indicators in World Politics*. London: Sage.

Smith, Dan. 1997. *The State of War and Peace Atlas*. New York: Penguin.

Smyser, W. R. 1987. *Refugees: Extended Exile*. New York: Praeger Publishers.

Stanley, William D. 1987. "Economic Migrants or Refugees From Violence? A Time-Series Analysis of Salvadoran Migration to the United States." *Latin American Research Review* 22, 1: 132–55.

Stohl, Michael, and George Lopez. 1984. *The State as Terrorist*. Westport, CT: Greenwood.

Sutter, Valerie O'Connor. 1990. *The Indochinese Refugee Dilemma*. Baton Rouge: Louisiana State University Press.

Tilly, Charles. 1978. *From Mobilization to Revolution*. Reading: Addison-Wesley.

United Nations High Commissioner for Refugees. 1969–95. *Report on UNHCR Assistance Activities and Proposed Voluntary Funds, Programmes and Budget*. Geneva, Switzerland: Executive Committee of the High Commissioner's Programme.

————. 1984. *Declaracion de Cartagena: Coloquio Sobre La Proteccion Internacional de los Refugiados en America Central, Mexico y Panama: Problemos Juridicos y Humanitarios.* Cartagena, Colombia 19–22 November.

————. 1993. *The State of the World's Refugees: The Challenge of Protection.* New York: Penguin Group.

————. 1993–95. *Populations of Concern to UNHCR: A Statistical Overview.* Office of the United Nations High Commissioner for Refugees: Food and Statistical Unit, Division of Programmes and Operational Support.

U.S. Committee for Refugees. 1969–74. *World Refugee Report.* Washington, D.C.: U.S. Committee for Refugees.

————. 1977–78. *World Refugee Survey Report.* Washington, D.C.: U.S. Committee for Refugees.

————. 1980–present. *World Refugee Survey.* New York: Hudson Press.

U.S. Department of State. 1980–94. *World Refugee Report.* Washington, D.C.: U.S. Department of State.

Wallensteen, P., and M. Sollenberg. 1996. "The End of International War? Armed Conflict 1989–95." In *States in Armed Conflict 1995,* edited by M. Sollenberg. Uppsala University, Department of Peace and Conflict Research.

Weiner, Myron. 1996. "Bad Neighbors, Bad Neighborhoods: An Inquiry in the Causes of Refugee Flows." *International Security* 21, 1: 5–42.

Wood, William B. 1994. "Forced Migration: Local Conflicts and International Dilemmas." *Annals of the Association of American Geographers* 84, 4: 607–34.

World Bank. 1994. *Computerized Version of the World Tables and World Development Report.* Washington D.C., World Bank.

Zolberg, Aristide. 1996. "The Un-Mixing of Peoples in the Post-Communist World." New York: International Center for Migration, Ethnicity and Citizenship (ICMEC), Occasional Paper No. 4.

Zolberg, Aristide, Astri Suhrke, and Sergio Aguayo. 1989. *Escape from Violence: Conflict and the Refugee Crisis in the Developing World.* New York: Oxford University Press.

– *Chapter 4* –

MANAGING MIGRATION: THE ROLE OF ECONOMIC POLICIES

~~

Philip L. Martin and J. Edward Taylor

> The scale and diversity of today's migration are beyond any previous experience. Responses to the questions they raise will help to determine the course of the 21st century. (United Nations 1993: 6)

This chapter summarizes recent patterns of international migration for employment, explains why people cross borders for economic reasons, and reviews the likely effects of trade, investment, and aid policies adopted by immigration countries to reduce what is termed "unwanted immigration." The unwanted adjective emphasizes that much of the economically motivated migration to the United States is not necessarily illegal. It includes foreigners who arrive as students or tourists and request asylum, and unauthorized family members of legal residents who, when discovered, are granted a Temporary Protected Status.

The major message of this essay is that there are solutions for unwanted immigration, but no quick fix. Economic and job growth reduce emigration pressures, but they take time to have migration-dampening effects. The key conclusion is that the trade and investment policies that hasten economic and job growth must be maintained even in the face of the sometimes perverse short-term effect of having emigration increase temporarily when a country puts itself on the road to long-term growth.

Several assumptions underlie the argument. First, it is assumed that immigration into the industrial democracies will continue through front, side, and back doors, and migration policies can affect the number, characteristics, and expulsion/integration prospects of immigrants. Second, it is assumed that this inevitable migration should be managed, and primarily in the interest of the immigration country. Third, it is assumed that economic policies can play important direct and indirect roles in managing migration.

Immigration countries have three major economic instruments available to indirectly reduce unwanted migration: trade, investment, and aid. There is also a fourth policy—political and military intervention—that is discussed briefly to put the economic instruments in perspective. Trade policies affect the competitiveness of both emigration and immigration country products and also affect employment in their export and import sectors. Foreign investment can provide the funds, technology, and management expertise that can increase the number of jobs in emigration countries. Aid can enable emigration countries to undertake economic and investment policies that would otherwise be unattainable.

The policy with the best track record to accelerate so-called stay-at-home growth is free trade, followed by policies to promote private foreign investment in emigration countries. However, as trade and investment bring economies closer together, they may also temporarily increase migration, especially if the economies being integrated have income gaps of five or more, that is, average per capita income in one country is four or five times higher than in the other; if there are established migration networks between them; and if supply-push emigration pressures increase as a result of economic restructuring. Under these circumstances, there can be a migration hump, meaning that the same policies that decrease emigration pressures in the long run can increase them in the short term.

There is no quick fix to the problem of unwanted immigration. Countries should avoid the temptation to abandon the trade and investment policies that work because it sometimes takes so long for their migration-reducing effects to be felt.

A World on the Move

According to the World Bank, there were about 125 million persons living and often working outside their countries of citizenship in the mid-1990s, making this "nation of migrants" equivalent in size to the world's tenth most populous country (World Bank 1995: 65).[1] Most estimates suggest that the number of immigrants, migrant workers, refugees, and asylum seekers living outside their country of citizenship is rising by 2 to 4 million annually.

There are about 60 million immigrants, refugees and asylum seekers, and authorized and unauthorized migrant workers in the high-income industrial democracies (Widgren 1994). Many are unwanted, in the sense that their settlement was not anticipated—as with guest workers who settled in western Europe or applicants for asylum whose claims that they would face persecution at home are rejected, but who nonetheless are allowed to stay. The continued arrival and settlement of unwanted migrants led some to speculate that mass uncontrolled movements of poor people will be common in the twenty-first century. This has been portrayed as a peaceful invasion in Jean Raspail's *Camp of the Saints*, in which Indians set out for the French Riviera from Calcutta, and in the film *The March* (BBC 1993), in which desperate Africans set out for southern France while European political leaders debate how to prevent their arrival. Mass migrations encourage policymakers to think about troops on borders rather than economic policies that reduce migration pressures over decades. The logical quick fix for invasions is to use force to protect the integrity of borders. If policymakers are convinced that unpredictable waves of immigrants will become the norm, they may be encouraged to shift resources from economic policies that have been proven to reduce migration pressures over time instead of spending resources on border controls. We argue that if the industrial nations turn their backs on slow but proven strategies to reduce migration, they may invite the very mass migrations they fear. Migration should be seen as a manageable challenge, and managing migration, in turn, requires an understanding of why people migrate. Although there are as many reasons for international migration as there are migrants, researchers group the myriad factors that motivate migration into those that attract migrants to a destination area (demand-pull), those that motivate emigration (supply-push), and those that link areas of origin and destination (networks).

These three factors influence the direction and volume of economically motivated migration. All are evolving in ways that promise more rather than less international migration. However, little is known about the relative importance of demand-pull, supply-push, and network factors in particular migration flows; how these three factors change in importance as migration flows evolve; and how trade, investment, and aid policies affect these factors and thus alter migration flows.

Migrants do not move randomly around the globe. There are good reasons why more Filipinos migrate to the United States than to Japan, or why Turks tend to head for Germany while Moroccans migrate to Spain and France. Understanding the factors shaping international migration can make managing migration easier today, and reduce migration pressures in the future.

Managing Migration

Three basic migration facts seem important to bear in mind:

- most people never cross national borders to live or work in another country;[2]
- at least half of all migrant workers move from one developing country to another, usually from a poorer to a richer developing nation;

• a diverse group of countries—from Italy and Spain to Korea—have successfully made the transition from being net exporters to net importers of labor.

Given large and widening economic differences between nations, the surprise may be how *little*, not how much, international migration for employment occurs. The world's population in 2000 was 6 billion, and almost 4 billion people are in the fifteen to sixty-four age group from which the world's 3 billion workers are drawn. The world's population and its potential work force are increasing by about 90 million persons annually.

Neither people nor incomes are distributed equally around the globe. The World Bank divides the countries on which it collects data into twenty-two "high-income" and about 110 middle- and low-income countries. High-income countries—the United States and Canada, western European nations from Sweden to Spain, and Asian countries such as Japan, Singapore, and Australia—include 15 percent of the world's population, but they accounted for over almost 80 percent of the world's $30 trillion GDP in 2000.[3] The average income in these rich countries was over $23,000 annually in 1993, versus an average $1,100 in low- and middle-income countries.[4]

These data suggest that an average person from one of the poorer 110 countries could increase his or her income ten or twenty times merely by moving into one of the twenty-two richest countries. Many young people *are* responding to the chance to "go abroad" for opportunity. But most of them travel only a short distance, so that the most typical international migration for employment is a move from one developing country to another, as from Indonesia (per capita GDP of $740 in 1993) to Malaysia ($3,140), or Colombia ($1,400) to Venezuela ($2,840). Seen in this light, migration is a manageable challenge. Managing migration, in turn, requires an understanding of three major factors that influence economically motivated international migration:

• demand-pull factors that draw migrants into another country,
• supply-push factors that encourage migrants to leave their own countries,
• networks of friends and relatives already settled in destination countries who serve as sources of information about jobs and opportunities, provide money to finance the trip, and serve as anchor communities for newcomers.[5]

The relative importance of each factor differs from one migration stream to another, and the weight of each factor can change over time. A common pattern is for demand-pull foreign worker recruitment to set migration for employment in motion, and for supply-push and network factors to become more important as a migration stream matures. Policymakers sometimes fail to appreciate the changing importance of these factors.

Countries that begin guest worker programs often stop recruitment and expect migration to stop when demand-pull recruitment stops. But the major migration motivator may have shifted from demand-pull recruitment to supply-push or network factors, so that migration continues even if recruitment is stopped.

Demand-Pull

Most labor migrations begin inside the industrial countries, as employers there, with or without explicit government approval, recruit and employ migrant workers. During the early years of such labor migrations, demand-pull factors often dominate, so that in Germany during the 1960s, the annual influx of migrant workers could be explained almost entirely by fluctuations in the German unemployment rate—migrants came when unemployment was low, and left when unemployment rose (Böhning 1984; Stalker 1994). The belief that the foreign worker tap could be turned on and off as needed gave European governments a false assurance that they could regulate with precision migrant worker flows (Martin 1980).

However, in what has become a familiar story, demand-pull, supply-push, and network factors evolved to produce one of the "principles" of migration for employment: there is nothing more permanent than temporary workers (Miller and Martin 1982). European guest workers were really probationary immigrants who, at the behest of their employers, could have their initial one-year work permits renewed for two or three more years. With renewal came the right to unify one's family, and a trickle of migrants and their families settled. Migrant workers can make a place for themselves in labor markets, whether as farm workers and janitors in Germany and the U.S., or as factory and construction workers in Malaysia. This supply-creates-its-own-demand effect of unskilled immigrants helps to explain why migrant workers continued to arrive in western Europe, the United States, and Japan despite historically high unemployment rates, especially in the early 1990s (Cornelius et al. 1994).

When labor-recruitment countries debate whether to stop the legally sanctioned recruitment of foreign workers, employers sometimes argue that, without such workers, their businesses and the economy would grind to a halt. This is rarely true in a literal sense, simply because foreign workers are typically just 5 to 10 percent of the labor force. What the subset of employers who employ most of the migrants mean is that adjusting to the sudden removal of migrants would be costly.[6]

But foreign workers are rarely removed suddenly, and sometimes their removal reduces rather than raises costs to consumers. One concrete example of the effects of a fairly dramatic end to a guest worker program occurred after 1964 in California tomato fields, when the Bracero program that had brought 4.5 million Mexican farm workers to the U.S. over the previous twenty-two years was ended. Toward the end of the program, Braceros handpicked most of the tomatoes that are used to make catsup, and it was widely predicted that the tomato industry would have to follow its work force to Mexico. But what happened? The entire tomato growing and processing system changed in response to higher wages, increasing the production and lowering the price of processed tomato products and helping to fuel the fast food revolution (Martin and Olmstead 1985).

If policymakers pay too much attention to the adjustment costs that would be incurred by those who lose access to foreign workers, demand-pull recruitment may be permitted to continue. But it is rare that foreign workers are suddenly made unavailable to an industry; industries usually have time to adjust, and the question is how public policy can encourage adjustments.

It is clear that the continued availability of unskilled and flexible workers alters wage levels and trends in the prices of fixed assets such as land, so that some employers may become dependent on the continued availability of foreign workers. In labor-intensive U.S. agriculture, for example, land prices are higher than they would be if immigrant workers were not available, and land buyers are willing to pay high prices for land that reflects the profits they expect to reap if minimum wage workers are available when they are needed. Labor shortages that increase wages may reduce land prices, which helps explain why U.S. farmers have such a keen interest in maintaining access to immigrant farm workers (Martin et al. 1995)

Relatively few of the migrant workers arriving in the industrial democracies are employed in industries in which trade in place of migration is an easy option. Labor-intensive manufacturing industries such as garments and shoemaking are often dependent on migrant workers and protected from emigration-country imports, but freeing up trade in goods would directly affect only 10 to 20 percent of the migrant workers in most industrial countries, since most are employed in services. Free trade is desirable as a means to accelerate economic growth, but it will not immediately curb the demand-pull in relatively rich countries for migrant construction workers, janitors, and maids.[7]

Supply-Push

The demand-pull of jobs in industrial democracies is matched neatly by the supply-push of low wages and joblessness in the developing countries from which most migrant workers come. About five in six of the world's workers are in the world's poorer nations, and every year another 80 to 85 million workers join the 3 billion strong work force there.

This leads to an enormous job creation challenge. Developing nations from Mexico to Turkey to the Philippines must create 500,000 to 1 million new jobs annually for the youth who every year enter the work force.[8] In addition, they need to find jobs for the 20 to 40 percent of the work force that is currently unemployed or underemployed. On top of these job creation challenges, developing nations must create jobs for ex-farmers—about 44 percent of the world's workers produced food in 1994 (World Bank 1995: 9), but that percentage can and probably will be reduced to less than 10 percent during the twenty-first century—and create employment for workers who are currently not seeking work because there are too few jobs, such as urban women.

About 60 percent of the workers in the world's developing countries work in agriculture. During the twentieth century, most of today's industrial nations experienced agricultural revolutions that permitted fewer farmers to produce food, and ex-farmers and farm workers to become factory workers. In the twenty-first century, it will be the developing world's turn to experience an agricultural revolution, and this revolution is expected to release as many as 500 million farmers and farm workers from agriculture in the first several decades of the twenty-first century. If one-third of the world's farmers and farm workers are displaced over the next fifty years as projected, then the developing nations would have to create as many additional urban jobs for farmers as now exist in all high income countries.[9]

The speed of displacement from agriculture can be influenced by policy choices. Many developing nations today keep farm incomes lower than urban incomes by taxing farmers in order to subsidize urban residents, usually by requiring them to sell their cotton or coffee at below world market prices to a government agency, which in turn exports the commodity at the world price and pockets the difference. Farming thus generates for farmers only one-fourth to one-third of the average $2,000 to $5,000 annual income in countries such as Mexico and Turkey, and ex-farmers crowd booming cities from Mexico City to Ankara. Once rural residents arrive in these capital cities, it is much easier for them to migrate abroad, either by boarding an airplane and, a day or two later, arriving in Frankfurt, or by making contact with a middleman who can smuggle them into the U.S.

A second dimension of the job creation challenge is the fact that many workers in emigration nations do not seek work because they know jobs are scarce. In the industrial democracies, half of the population is typically in the work force, so that the United States, with a population of 270 million, has a work force of about 135 million. In developing nations, one-third of the population is typically in the work force, so that Mexico, with 100 million people, has a work force of about 35 million. Many of the Mexicans who are not in the work force are urban women who would seek jobs if they were available.

Supply-push emigration pressures often increase at least temporarily when a country adopts the economic policies that are needed to accelerate long-run economic growth. Several of the world's major countries of emigration, such as Mexico, pursued protectionist and state-dominated economic policies during the 1960s and 1970s. These policies typically produced poor farmers, large and inefficient manufacturing sectors, and governments dependent on tariffs for 20 to 40 percent of government revenues. When closed economies open themselves to global economic integration, farmers may become poorer, since imported food is available so cheaply. At the same time, governments that lower trade barriers have less revenue to finance the infrastructure needed to attract foreign investment, or to create or expand the social safety net. As a result, implementing the "right" economic polices after decades of misguided policies can at least temporarily increase supply-push emigration pressures.

Networks

Demand-pull and supply-push factors are like battery poles: without a link between them, they produce no migration. The major linkage that turns potential migration into actual migration are migration networks, which are defined to encompass everything that enables people to learn about opportunities abroad and take advantage of them (Massey et al. 1994).

The most important elements of networks are friends and family members abroad who can provide credible information about job opportunities there, perhaps finance the trip, and often provide shelter and employment to migrants after their arrival. In the absence of friends and family, labor brokers, smugglers, churches, and migrant organizations can play some of these information and placement functions.

Networks or linkages have been shaped and strengthened by three of the major revolutions of the past generation: the communications revolution, the transportation revolution, and the rights revolution. The *communications revolution* refers to the fact that potential migrants know far more about opportunities abroad than did turn-of-the-century migrants from southern and eastern Europe who set out for North and South America and Australia. The migrants' major source of information is countrymen already settled abroad who can tell the migrants about opportunities in Paris or Los Angeles. Information travels quickly, so that employers say that, after passing the word that more workers are needed, new employees can be expected to show up within two or three days, even if illegal entry is required to get to the work place. The industrial democracies perhaps unwittingly add to the allure of emigrating by portraying, in TV shows such as *Dallas* and *Dynasty* that are exported even to the remote corners of the globe, a life of opulence.

The *transportation revolution* is simply the fact that the cost of traveling has dropped enormously, while access to and the convenience of international travel has increased geometrically. Even the most remote peasant is less than one week away from the bright lights of New York. Once he gets to his own capital city, the international transportation system can take him anywhere within a day or two for less than the average monthly earnings of even an unskilled and seasonal worker in an industrial country, $1,000 to $2,000. The British who indentured themselves to migrate to the North American colonies in the seventeenth century, by contrast, often promised to work three to five years to repay transportation costs.

The third network revolution that turns potential into actual migration is the *rights revolution*, or the spread of individual rights and entitlements to all residents of industrial democracies. All of the industrial democracies have strengthened personal rights vis-à-vis government agencies, and most have signed treaties and conventions that commit them, for example, not to return foreigners to their countries of origin if they would face persecution there. One effect of this rights revolution is that after a migrant arrives in an industrial country, he or she can usually avoid deportation for several years, and the longer a migrant stays abroad, the more likely he or she is to eventually settle.[10]

Reducing Emigration Pressures

The number or percentage of a country's residents attempting to emigrate is sometimes termed emigration pressure; crude measures of emigration pressure suggest it is higher in, for example, the Dominican Republic than Costa Rica. Emigration pressure can be reduced, but it is mostly the policies of the emigration country that determine how fast the country grows, and thus how quickly economic and job growth reduce emigration pressures. Policies of immigration countries can, at the margin, accelerate or retard the adoption and effectiveness of "correct" economic policies, but the solutions to emigration pressure lie mostly within emigration countries.[11]

How quickly can emigration pressures be reduced? First, it should be remembered that nothing happens quickly—developing countries that change their economic polices often have a credibility gap, so that simply announcing new policies may not convince local and foreign investors that the new trade and investment policies will continue to be followed. Second, investors crave certainty, which is why they want new trade and investment regimes such as NAFTA locked into place with international agreements so they cannot easily be undone. Third, economic policies that indirectly reduce emigration pressures need time to work, and the time required for the indirect effects of economic growth to reduce emigration pressures is easy to underestimate.

Changing economic policies can create a new environment for economic growth. At the same time, there has been a revolution in how researchers think about migration decision making. Most people live in family units, and family considerations can play important roles in migration decisions, an insight that is at the core of the so-called new economics of labor migration (NELM). The "new economics" recognizes a variety of secondary reasons for migration. For example, migration may represent an effort to "keep up with the neighbors"—if migrant families have better homes and TVs, then non-migrant families may be motivated to send a migrant abroad to overcome their relative deprivation (Stark and Taylor 1989, 1991).

In other cases, migration may be motivated by missing services and markets. Many Mexican migrants to the U.S. are from farm families that depend on the rain to get a crop. Since there is no local crop insurance that provides an income if the rains fail, the U.S. labor market can serve as a means of reducing the risk of having no income when there is no rain in Mexico (Taylor 1986). In other cases, migration can overcome a local obstacle to development, as in developing nations in which banks are reluctant to lend money to farmers who own land communally rather than individually. In some cases, farmers who want to buy new machines, or experiment with new crops, migrate to obtain the capital they need to purchase these items.

Spending remittances earned abroad create local multipliers that generate additional local income and jobs. The expenditure of $1 earned in the U.S. back home in rural Mexico may create $2 or $3 of local income, as families that receive remittance incomes build or renovate their houses.

The desire to emigrate is also influenced by immigration country control policies. Mexico-U.S. migration increased after the 1994–95 devaluation of the Mexican peso. But emigration does not necessarily increase in lockstep with events such as devaluation, especially if migrants are deterred by stepped up border controls, new restrictions on their access to social services, and well-publicized efforts to prevent unauthorized migrants from obtaining U.S. jobs.

Governments trying to reduce emigration pressures have four types of control instruments at their disposal: trade, investment, aid, and intervention. Trade and investment tend to be undertaken by private actors rather than governments, and their migration-reducing effects are sometimes not noticeable for decades. Aid and intervention, on the other hand, are typically under the direct control of governments, and can have significant short-term effects.

Trade

Trade is the production of a good in one country for sale or for use in another. Trade is the closest thing to a free lunch in economics—if goods are produced where it is cheapest to make them, and then traded for other goods that can be produced cheaper in other locations, most people in both areas are better off. In this way, trade affects both the location and cost of production; trade policies affect the competitiveness of an emigration country's products, and employment in the export and import sectors of *both* sending and receiving countries.

The world's exports and imports of goods in 1998 totaled $11.5 trillion, equivalent to over one-third of the world's GDP.[12] International trade in goods has been increasing at about twice the pace of worldwide economic growth—about 6 percent per year, while worldwide economic growth averages 3 percent.[13] Most of the world's trade is between affiliates of the world's 40 thousand multinational businesses—they accounted for about two-thirds of all world trade in 1994—and half of the trade engaged in by multinationals is between affiliates of the same company.

According to economic theory, economically motivated migration should decrease in a free trade world because of factor price equalization, which is the tendency of wages to equalize as workers move from poorer to richer countries. In the terms of economic theory, this means that trade and migration are substitutes: countries that have relatively cheaper labor can export labor-intensive goods or workers. Over time, differences in the prices of goods and the wages of workers should be reduced, reducing emigration pressures.

The truth of this commonsense proposition was borne out over the past 150 years on both sides of the North Atlantic. For over a century, Europeans migrated to North America, until restrictive legislation in the 1920s almost stopped the flow. When European growth rates in the 1950s and 1960s rose above U.S. growth rates, the gaps in wages and incomes narrowed, and migration across the Atlantic slowed even when the United States reopened opportunities for migration. A similar story of narrowing wage and income gaps helps to explain why labor migration between southern European nations such as Italy and Spain and northern Europe has virtually stopped despite the right of Italians and Spaniards to live and work anywhere in the European Union.

Trade theory emphasizes what economists term comparative statics, which are before and after snapshots of the economy. Economists spend most of their time comparing comparative static equilibria, and much less processing the adjustment, or what happens during the years or decades until economically motivated migration stops (Taylor and Martin 1995).

THE MIGRATION HUMP Those who focus on the process of adjustment to freer trade find that, instead of migration decreasing immediately after an emigration country adopts a free trade policy, migration can temporarily increase. This means that, compared to a situation in which the emigration country continues to pursue often protectionist trade policies, emigration pressures can rise when a country adopts the "correct" free trade policy, producing a migration hump (Martin 1993). In Figure 4.1, the migration hump is illustrated by the shaded region A.

The migration hump is a reminder that the same free trade policies that make immigration controls less necessary in the long run may make them more necessary in the short run. Countries that maintain protectionist polices are likely to have migration flows that reflect demographic factors, while economies that restructure by deregulating, privatizing, and opening themselves up to the world economy are more likely to experience a migration hump, first more migration and then less. The migration hump reflects the fact that economic restructuring often displaces workers and promotes rural-urban migration, so that a country on the

Figure 4.1: The Migration Hump

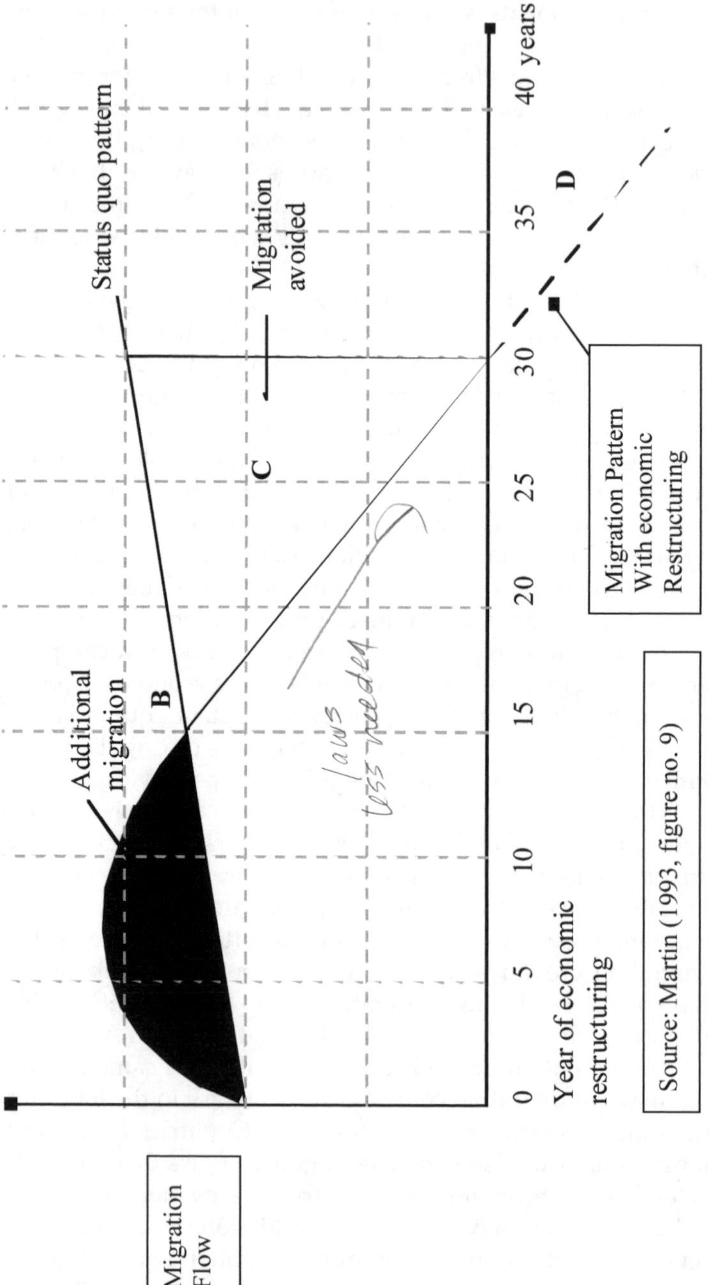

Year of economic restructuring

Status quo pattern

Migration avoided

Additional migration

B

C

D

laws needed

Migration Pattern With economic Restructuring

Source: Martin (1993, figure no. 9)

Migration Flow

40 years

move economically is often also awash with internal migrants, some of whom spill over its borders if there is already an established international migration pattern exists.

Relatively little is known about the parameters of points A-B-C-D. It would be helpful to determine the size of hump A, or how much additional migration is there during the economic takeoff phase of restructuring. It is also important to determine when point B reached—when migration flows return to their pre-hump levels? Third, it is important to know about C, the migration that did not occur because of stay-at-home development. We could also ask about a fourth parameter—the amount of migration that enables countries such as Italy, Spain, and Korea to turn from emigration to immigration countries as represented by D.

Despite the possibility of a migration hump, most of those who have carefully studied the relationship between trade and migration believe that there is no choice but to press for freer trade policies. The final report of the U.S. Commission for the Study of International Migration and Cooperative Economic Development, for example, concluded that "*expanded trade* between the sending countries and the United States *is the single most important remedy*" for unauthorized Mexico-to-U.S. migration despite the likelihood that "the economic development process itself tends in the short to medium term to stimulate migration." (1990: xv–xvi, emphasis added).

It is important to emphasize that a migration hump is not inevitable. Generally, all three conditions must be satisfied for emigration to produce a migration hump, viz., a continued or expanded demand-pull of jobs in the destination country, increased emigration pressures in the country of origin, and well-established networks that can bridge the border. Under these circumstances, increased pressure on any of the three factors motivating migration can produce a migration hump.

Foreign Investment

Economists agree that an economy can grow faster if there is investment in machinery, education, and infrastructure that makes workers more productive. An investment is a commitment of monies today to reap a return in the future. The monies for such investment can come from domestic savings, or from savers in other countries who invest abroad, i.e., foreign investment. There are many types of investments, but the investment most likely to spur economic and productivity growth is the commitment of local private savings to build factories and other enterprises in emigration countries. The "East Asian miracle" was built on domestic savings and investment; foreign investment played a critical but only supporting role in the Asian "miracle" of rapid economic growth.[14]

Immigration countries can promote two types of private investment in emigration countries: foreign direct investment (FDI) and portfolio investment. FDI is a private investment that usually results in the building of a factory or workplace in another country, and often the importation of managers and equipment. Portfolio investment, by contrast, is typically a private investment in an existing firm. The firm may use the funds raised by the sale of stock to foreign investors to modernize and expand, thus creating jobs; or it may use funds from the sale of stock to invest abroad, as several Mexican conglomerates did by buying U.S. firms.

Both FDI and portfolio investments in emigration countries have increased in recent years. Private capital flows to developing countries worldwide quadrupled between 1989 and the mid-1990s.[15] Most private investments in developing countries were portfolio investments. According to the World Bank, countries that attracted the most FDI in 1992 included China ($11.2 billion),[16] Mexico ($5.4 billion), Argentina ($4.2 billion), and Malaysia ($4.1 billion).[17] Countries attracting significant portfolio investment in 1992 included Mexico ($9 billion), Brazil ($6.6 billion), Argentina ($3.5 billion), Korea ($2.4 billion) and Venezuela ($1.8 billion).[18] There is no standard measure of a country's dependence on FDI, but one indicator, FDI as a percent of GDP, showed that FDI was equivalent to almost 7 percent of GDP in Malaysia and 1.5 percent of GDP in Mexico in the early 1990s.

Expected profits and risk drive private foreign investment, and these variables are not necessarily correlated with emigration pressure. Indeed, if FDI is measured vertically and per capita GDP is measured horizontally, countries line up along a C-shaped distribution, with Singapore ($19,900 per capita GDP in 1993) and Malaysia ($3,100), attracting FDI equivalent to 6 to 10 percent of GDP,[19] while Sweden ($24,700) exporting FDI equivalent to 6 percent of its GDP (Lucas 1995: 21).[20] Countries such as Mozambique ($90 per person per year in 1993), Pakistan ($400), or the Philippines ($850) attracted relatively little FDI in the early 1990s.

Economic theory would predict that private investment would flow from the capital-rich immigration countries to the capital-poor emigration countries. Although much foreign investment does originate in Europe and Japan, it tends to go to relatively rich developing countries that are net immigration rather than emigration areas, such as Singapore and Malaysia.[21]

Contrary to the usual analysis in which an increase in the supply of something (capital) lowers its price, there may be increasing returns to more investment, at least over a certain range, so that the availability of a pool of electronics engineers and assembly workers in a country such as Malaysia tends to make the return on an electronics investment there higher than in Bangladesh, which has much lower wages, but also fewer positive spillover effects from past investments and fewer skilled workers.[22]

The East Asian nations that have attracted much of the world's private foreign investment in the 1980s pursued a set of widely praised economic policies, but it is not clear what cause-and-effect role private investment played in the East Asian miracle. For example, both Malaysia and the Philippines invest heavily in higher education. Malaysia receives high levels of FDI, complains of skills shortages, and yet is slow to change a discriminatory higher education policy (against Chinese and Indian Malaysians) widely recognized as inefficient. The Philippines produces more doctors, nurses, and seamen than can be absorbed in the domestic economy, and counts on being able to export them to make the often private investment in education pay off.

In sum, there are no obvious links between emigration pressure and private foreign investments. FDI tends to flow to regions and toward countries that have already turned the corner toward being net immigration areas rather than emigration areas. Once a country has adopted the policies needed for faster growth, FDI can accelerate that growth.

THE CASE OF MEXICO Mexico's recent experience with private foreign investment illustrates the promises and pitfalls of relying on foreign rather than domestic savings to accelerate economic and job growth. Mexico has had major devaluations at the end of each of the last four presidencies, and Mexico near the end of 1994 was headed for a deficit in its trade balance of $20 billion, equivalent to 5 percent of its $395 billion GDP. Mexico's foreign currency reserves fell from $30 billion early in 1994 to $6 billion on 22 December 1994, as Mexico attempted to support the peso at a rate of 3.45 pesos to $1. The Zedillo government that took office on 1 December 1994 confidently predicted that the economy would grow by 4 percent in 1995, that inflation would be only 4 percent, and that the peso-dollar exchange rate would remain stable. Local and foreign investors saw that the trade deficit would not be reduced under the Zedillo plan and that the Mexican Central Bank was running out of reserves to support the peso, so they bet that Mexico would have to devalue its currency, and they converted even more pesos into dollars. On 19 December, Zapatista rebels reported falsely that they had taken over thirty-eight towns in Chiapas. On 20 December 1994, Mexico devalued the peso, and it eventually fell 45 percent, from 3.4 pesos to $1 to 6.2 pesos to $1 in September 1995.

President Clinton asked Congress to approve $40 billion in loan guarantees to preserve the confidence of foreign investors in Mexico and to avoid, inter alia, increased illegal immigration. Many in Congress wanted to make the Mexican loan guarantee conditional on Mexico explicitly cooperating with the U.S. to reduce illegal immigration; Mexican reluctance to publicly commit to immigration control was a factor in Clinton's withdrawal on 31 January 1995 of the loan guarantee package and its replacement with a package of aid that did not require Congressional approval. On 21 February 1995, the U.S. and Mexico reached agreement on a $52 billion multilateral rescue package, and on 9 March, Mexico announced new austerity measures—including a 12 percent hike in the minimum wage—that went into effect 1 April 1995. Bankruptcies and layoffs spread throughout the Mexican economy in 1995, leading to the loss of about 1 million of Mexico's 10 million formal sector jobs. After the optimism of NAFTA in 1994, there was widespread disillusionment in 1995.

What went wrong in Mexico? Unlike fast-growing Asian nations, Mexico's 1990s boom was fueled largely by foreigners' savings. An overvalued peso made imports of both capital and consumer goods cheap and imports surged, but the Mexican boom could be sustained only as long as foreigners believed that Mexico truly was the next "tiger economy." U.S. and other foreign investors lent money to Mexico, and Mexicans used these foreign savings to buy U.S. goods, including machinery for new factories as well as luxury cars. However, when the peso was devalued, the foreign savings evaporated—total foreign investment in Mexico fell an estimated 22 percent in 1994, with most of the decline coming in the last ten days of the year.

Mexico represents a case of inflated expectations gone awry. Even though migration had been the major linkage between the U.S. and Mexico for most of the twentieth century, NAFTA virtually ignored migration, as both Presidents Bush and Salinas, in their public pronouncements, implied that emigration pressures would decrease as soon as the trade agreement was signed. Both the U.S. and Mexican governments then exaggerated the positive first year data on NAFTA, so that economic problems in December 1994 came as an unexpected shock to foreign investors. In retrospect, it would have been far better to emphasize slow and gradual changes rather than to pretend that NAFTA marked a new era in which Mexico-U.S. immigration problems would fade away.

Foreign Aid

Official Development Assistance (ODA) are monies granted by one country to assist the development of another. In 1996, the OECD nations that are members of the Development Assistance Committee provided $55 billion in ODA, down from $58 billion in 1994.[23] Almost 60 percent was provided by four countries: the U.S. ($9.4 billion in 1993), Japan ($9.4 billion), Germany ($7.6 billion), and France ($7.5 billion).[24] The OPEC nations have sharply reduced their ODA—they provided $6.9 billion in 1990, with Saudi Arabia providing over two-thirds of OPEC aid, but less than $1.5 billion in 1993.

The leading recipients of ODA in 1993 included China ($3.1 billion), Egypt ($2.3 billion), Indonesia ($2 billion), and India and the Philippines ($1.5 billion each). On a per capita basis, ODA averaged $9 per person per year in recipient countries in 1993, and ranged from $242 per person in Israel to $3 or less in Korea, Mexico, and China (World Bank 1995: 196–99).

The ILO and UNHCR in 1992 undertook a major project to investigate the capacity of ODA to minimize unwanted emigration (Böhning and Schloeter-Paredes 1993). The premise of the research was that donor nations already withhold ODA unless recipient countries adopt the "right" policies in areas that range from environmental protection to respect for human rights. The ILO-UNHCR asked the this question: if donor nations wanted to use ODA to reduce unwanted emigration pressures, how should they change the volume, form, and aims of their aid policies to achieve migration-reducing goals? The experts commissioned to prepare background papers were asked to review the role that aid played in the countries and regions that sent large numbers of economic migrants and political refugees streaming across national borders in the 1970s and 1980s. They were then asked to consider the level and type of aid that would be necessary to practically eliminate economically and politically motivated migration within a generation or two, say by 2030.

The conclusions of experts consulted by the ILO and UNHCR depended on whether they were studying refugees or economic migrants. Those who focused on the conflicts that produced refugees in the 1970s emphasized how aid often intensified and sustained the conflict under review and thus led to more rather than fewer refugees. These contributors recognized that humanitarian relief in the 1990s needed to expand from two R's to four R's—in addition to *relief and resettlement*, they argued that refugee policies should be expanded to reconstruct homelands in order to encourage *repatriation*, and a new emphasis should be placed on policies that reduce the *root causes* of refugee-producing conflicts. This expansion of assistance for refugees would, of course, require more aid.

The experts dealing with the role that aid can play to reduce economically motivated emigration were even more explicit about the need for larger sums, for the need to tie aid to economic policy reforms in recipient countries, and for donor countries to recognize that their choice is not aid *or* trade but aid *and* trade. Several concluded that perhaps the single most important "aid" that industrial countries can provide to emigration nations is to themselves have free trade policies—to remain open to emigration country goods, which are often produced in labor-intensive or job-creating ways.

If the polices recommended by ILO and UNHCR experts were adopted, what migration pressures would be likely in 2030? There may be fewer refugees if the world paid more attention to extirpating the root causes of conflict that generate them, but the refugee experts were unanimous in their conviction that it is likely that refugees will continue to be in need of help. They noted that it may, however, become easier to repatriate refugees if homes and workplaces devastated by conflict are made safe and reconstructed with international assistance.

Economic development experts were both more optimistic and more pessimistic. They were more optimistic in the sense that they outlined what they considered feasible economic development scenarios to produce the growth needed to keep migrants at home. However, the economists were pessimistic that such development would in fact be launched and maintained in emigration countries from the Philippines to Tunisia to El Salvador. They cite many obstacles: not enough industrial country aid; aid that is dispersed over too many areas or projects; or aid that makes it unnecessary for the recipient country to modify economic policies that slow down job-creating growth.

There was more agreement on how to change the use of aid than on how to get more aid flowing from rich to poor countries. Most experts endorse the 1980s and 1990s change in the focus of aid, from funding mega-infrastructure projects to supporting basic human needs, such as education and health care for women and girls. Instead of simply building a dam to provide farmers with irrigation water, donors began to realize that their aid will do more to accelerate stay-at-home development if it is used to help get agricultural policies and prices right.

It seems more difficult to increase the amount of aid. After peaking at $61 billion in 1992, the OCED's ODA fell 10 percent in 1993. The UN's Social Summit in Copenhagen in March 1995 heard an appeal from the Group of seventy-seven—representing 130 developing nations—for more aid, and for the aid to be used according to a 20-20 formula. Twenty percent of the aid provided by donor countries would be earmarked for basic human needs such as schools and hospitals, and recipient countries would also commit 20 percent of their own governmental expenditures to basic human needs.

However, implementing the 20-20 formula proved to be difficult, even with the promise of less migration. The threat of immigration was used by Prime Minister Rasmussen of Denmark as a "very concrete" argument for more foreign aid: "if you don't help the third world ... then you will have these poor people in our society." He continued, "Europe has now lived through a period where thousands and thousands and thousands of refugees are coming from various parts of the world ... ordinary people now recognize ... the global situation" making "ordinary people" more receptive to the need for aid to reduce emigration pressures (*Migration News*, April 1995).

Intervention

Intervention means that an immigration country interjects itself, politically or militarily, into the affairs of an emigration country to head off emigration, as the U.S. did in 1994 in Haiti.[25] The Haiti example illustrates how easy it is to be penny-wise and pound-foolish when seeking to stem emigration pressures.

Haitians have been leaving their country in small boats for the United States for years. Beginning in 1981, Haiti allowed the U.S. Coast Guard to stop boats in Haitian and international waters to determine whether they were carrying Haitians to the United States. Under U.S. policies in effect in 1994, boats determined to be carrying Haitians to the U.S. were forced to return to Haiti without individuals having the opportunity to present their claims for asylum.

On 16 June 1994, the U.S. announced that henceforth Haitians picked up at sea by U.S. ships would be eligible to present to U.S. asylum officers on board, evidence that they face persecution in Haiti. As a result, over 11,627 Haitians were picked up by the U.S. Coast Guard during the next three weeks, and many hoped that they would be granted refugee status and allowed to settle in the United States. Those turned down, about 70 percent of the Haitians requesting asylum on board ships, were returned to Haiti.

On 5 July 1994, this policy changed. After that date, Haitians picked up at sea were sent to the U.S. base at Guantánamo Bay, Cuba, to make their case for asylum. If they were deemed in need of safe haven, they were kept in safe haven camps, but not taken to the U.S. This safe-haven-outside-the-U.S. policy dramatically reduced the number of Haitians picked up by the Coast Guard. During the week of 16 July 1994, not a single Haitian was picked up at sea, compared to the 1,340 people the previous weekend.[26] By mid-July 1994, there were 16,500 Haitians at Guantánamo, and a few hundred began to trickle back to Haiti after they learned that, even if they could prove they needed safe haven, they would not be going to the U.S. The U.S. decided in September 1994 to intervene in Haiti to prevent more Haitians from heading to the U.S. in small boats. On 31 July 1994, the UN Security Council approved the use of force to restore President Aristide to power. On 18 September 1994, with American planes in the air, Haitian leaders resigned, and the U.S. invasion of Haiti was called off.

The U.S. intervention in Haiti proved to be costly. Some 21 thousand Haitians were picked up at sea by U.S. ships between January and August 1994. At the time American troops landed in September 1994, some 14 thousand Haitians were being held in Guantánamo, at a cost to the U.S. of $200 million. The occupation of Haiti cost the U.S. about $140 million per month, or $700 million between September 1994 and February 1995, according to the testimony of Deputy Secretary of State Strobe Talbot before the House International Relations Committee on 24 February 1995. This means that, in about five months, the U.S. spent the equivalent of about half of Haiti's GDP, which was about $1.5 billion in 1994.[27]

What lessons has the U.S. learned from Haiti? The neighboring Dominican Republic, which also has about 7 million people and a per capita GDP of $1,000, perhaps five times that of Haiti, may also suffer a political-economic crisis that would result in more U.S.-bound migrants. Like most other Caribbean nations, the Dominican Republic imports far more than it exports, and it finances its trade deficit with remittances from Dominicans in the U.S.—in 1992, the Dominican Republic exported goods worth about $570 million, and imported goods worth $2.2 billion. According to the World Bank, in 1992 the Dominican Republic attracted no private investments that were not guaranteed by a government agency, versus $500 million in Hungary, a slightly larger country. Finally, the Dominican Republic received about $2 million in ODA in 1993, down from $143 million in 1989.

These data suggest that policymakers are not convinced that encouraging trade, investment, and aid can have measurable consequences within the time horizons for which they expect measurable results.[28] As external private and public assistance diminish, the U.S. in this case seems more prepared to spend money to cope with migrants after they exit than to invest to the prevention of emigration.

Toward International Cooperation?

Migration is probably the most important international economic phenomenon that is *not* coordinated by an international organization. Unlike defense or economic policies, which are coordinated in international organizations from NATO to the OECD and the WTO, immigration policy has remained largely country-specific (Weiner 1993).

International organizations are likely to find migration on their agendas in the future. The migrants living in the industrial countries send at least $75 billion in remittances to their countries of origin, one and one-half times the level of Official Development Assistance (Russell and Teitelbaum 1992). From Algeria to Yugoslavia, labor is the most important export of many nations, and remittances are often the quickest and surest source of foreign exchange in countries suffering from or recovering from civil war.

Many emigration countries try channel remittances to accelerate development. However, there has been relatively little research on how to channel remittances to reduce emigration pressures effectively (Abadan-Unat et al. 1976; Penninx 1982), especially in comparison to the vast literature that evaluates the use of development assistance funds.

As international organizations begin to deal with migration, a logical question is whether it makes sense to promote international coordination in trade, investment, and aid policies that are designed to reduce emigration pressures. Trade, investment, and aid play minor roles in relations with many major immigration countries, as even a quick glance at a listing of the top ten countries of immigration to the U.S. in the 1970s and 1980s reveals. The top ten countries of immigrants to the U.S. in the 1980s were home to about 55 percent of the decade's immigrants, but they accounted for only 20 percent of U.S. imports and 22 percent of U.S. exports in 1993. These countries had only 5 percent of the U.S. direct investment abroad in 1993, and received about 2 percent of U.S. foreign aid.

Conclusions

Trade, investment, and aid policies that seek to stimulate economic growth and reduce emigration pressures remind one why economics is sometimes called the dismal science—it is very hard to help emigration countries and leave no emigration-increasing side effects. Freer trade may increase imports before exports rise, producing a currency crisis, devaluation, recession, and emigration, as in Mexico in 1995. Multinationals tend to use more imported components, so that breaking up local monopolies and attracting direct foreign investment can increase imports, the use of capital-intensive production techniques, and exports, without increasing the number of jobs. Finally, aid in the form of infrastructure can have the perverse effect of stimulating emigration, as when better roads meant to help farmers to market their crops also permits cheap imported food to reach even the countryside, destroying jobs and stimulating emigration.

This sobering picture should not deter immigration countries from adopting, and persuading emigration countries to adopt, the economic policies that have the proven ability to speed up economic growth. Immigration countries should be comforted by how little—not how much—wage and job gaps must be narrowed to deter migration. Experience suggests that, after wage gaps are narrowed to four or five, and more rapid economic and job growth in the emigration area creates the widespread expectation that economic differences will continue to narrow, economically motivated migration practically ceases.

Emigration pressures diminish as economic differences narrow. There are two ways in which differences between countries can be narrowed: migration alone, in a world without free trade, or migration and trade in an open economy. Although migration will eventually diminish in both cases, there is an important difference between reducing migration pressures in a closed and an open world economy. In a closed economy, economic differences can be narrowed as wages fall in the immigration country, a sure recipe for an anti-immigrant backlash. In an open economy, by contrast, economic differences can be narrowed as wages rise faster in the emigration country. It is far better to have both countries on the up escalator, with one escalator rising faster, than to have both escalators stopped, and migration from one to the other pushing wages down.

Notes

1. The number of persons temporarily outside their country of citizenship for tourism or business reasons has risen even faster than the number of settled persons in the nation of migrants. According to the World Tourism Organization, there were 455 million tourist entries in 1991, up from 288 million in 1980. About 61 percent of the tourist arrivals were in Europe, followed by 16 percent in North America, and 6 percent in the Asia/Pacific region.
2. There is also a considerable amount of internal migration, especially that associated with rural-urban migration, in a country such as China. There are an estimated 100 million internal migrants within China. If China were a series of independent countries, the world's nation of migrants might double in size.
3. According to the 1994 World Development Report, the 828 million people in the "high income countries" that, when ranked by GDP per capita, begin with Ireland's $12,000 and end with Switzerland's $36,000, include 15 percent of

the world's population and account for 78 percent of the world's GDP (World Bank 1994: 163–67).

4. According to World Bank calculations, the gap between average incomes in the richest and poorest countries was about eleven to one in 1870, thirty-eight to one in 1960, and fifty-two to one in 1985 (World Bank 1995: 9).

5. Both historically and today middlemen recruiters and transporters have been involved in the migration process. Today, these understudied middlemen— who might be considered as arbitrageurs of differences between international labor markets—play an role in facilitating illegal labor migration, extracting a fee from migrant workers or their employers equivalent to 25 to 100 percent of what the migrant will earn in his first year abroad.

6. There are about 13 million foreign-born workers among the 130 million persons in the U.S. labor force. In only three major occupations—those with 1 million or more employees—is the majority the work force arguably foreign-born: janitors (3 million), farm workers (2 to 3 million), and maids (1 million). The percentage of illegal workers among these immigrant workers is estimated to be less than 30 percent, so, at most, up to 30 percent of the workers in these most-migrant dependent occupations could be removed by aggressive enforcement of immigration laws.

7. Some industrial countries are engaged in a debate over whether the best way to discourage their employers from preferring to employ unauthorized workers is to step up border and interior enforcement so that such workers are not available, whether it is better to enforce labor laws so that migrant workers are not "exploited," or whether both immigration and labor law enforcement is needed. Generally, pro-migrant groups favor placing the emphasis on labor law enforcement, while restrictionist groups favor border and interior immigration enforcement. Over the past several years, a new element has entered the debate over immigration control. In both North America and western Europe, the argument is that some immigrants come to obtain social welfare program benefits, from education to health care to cash assistance, prompting a move in the U.S. Congress to make non-U.S. citizens ineligible for such benefits and to more carefully screen illegal aliens out of benefit programs. Such arguments are made most often by those who advocate reducing social welfare programs for citizens and migrants alike.

8. The youthful age structure in developing nations guarantees a continuing influx of teens. In the United States, for example, about 20 percent of the population is younger than fifteen. In Mexico, almost 40 percent of the population is younger than fifteen.

9. In 1995, there were about 382 million workers in the high-income countries (World Bank 1995: 2, 9).

10. Industrial democracies could detain migrants, but at an enormous cost. The average cost of detaining a prisoner in the U.S. is $20,000 to $25,000 annually. If a government wants to have migrants readily available to be deported, it must pay high detention costs. However, if migrants are allowed to live and work freely while their cases are considered, then the humanitarian right to due process can turn into a backdoor guest worker program.

11. There is no consensus definition of emigration pressure. Emigration pressure is often defined as the number or proportion of people wishing to leave a country temporarily or permanently during a given time period. Beginning from a situation with no migration, personal factors (marriage, schooling, etc.),

family decisions, such as to keep rural Mexican girls close to home as maids in cities, and to send boys to the U.S. to do farm work, or economic or political changes external to the individual or family can encourage migration.

12. World trade in commercial services such as transport, banking, and insurance totaled $1 trillion in 1992, up 12 percent from 1991, and equivalent to about 20 percent goods trade. The U.S., France, Italy, Germany, and Britain are the leading exporters, and Germany, the U.S., and Japan are the biggest importers of services. The U.S. has the world's biggest surplus in services ($55 billion in 1992) and the biggest deficit in goods trade ($106 billion in 1992).

13. There are fears that rapid economic growth in developing nations will displace jobs and production in the industrial nations. However, a recent OECD report argues that economic growth that expands the middle class in nations such as China, India, and Indonesia, countries that have a combined population of 2.25 billion and a middle class of 100 million, could see their middle classes expand to 700 million by 2010, almost as many people as are in the industrial countries today (*New York Times*, 26 May 1995: C2).

14. In 1995, many Asian nations had savings rates equivalent to about 30 percent of GDP, versus 4 percent in the U.S. For example, in Singapore savings are equivalent to 54 percent of GDP, in Korea, 37 percent, and in Indonesia, 33 percent.

15. There are several definitions and estimates of foreign investment. Forbes reports that FDI in 1994 totaled $205 billion, with $80 billion or 40 percent going to LDCs, including $30 billion of FDI in China and $8 billion in Mexico in 1994 (10 April 1995: 41).

16. The 55 million overseas Chinese play a special role in foreign investment in China—an estimated 80 percent of the foreign investment in China is made by so-called overseas Chinese. In mid-1994, it was estimated that foreign investments in China included $40 billion from Hong Kong, $8 billion from southeast Asia, and $5 billion from Taiwan (*Far Eastern Economic Review*, 14 July 1994: 47).

17. Overseas Chinese play an important role in foreign investment throughout southeast Asia. The estimated 23 million ethnic Chinese are 5 percent of the region's population and, although heterogeneous like the 23 million Hispanics in the U.S., the Chinese wield far more economic power in Asia.

18. Preliminary FDI data for 1994 indicate that total FDI reached $204 billion, up 5 percent from 1993's $193 billion. However, the amount of FDI in the U.S. doubled to $41 billion, so that the U.S. replaced China ($34 billion in FDI in 1994) as the world's major recipient of FDI—the U.S. attracted 20 percent of all FDI in 1995. U.S. investors made $56 billion in foreign investments in 1994 (*Wall Street Journal*, 15 March 1995: A2).

19. Capital inflows rose from 3 percent of GDP in 1989 to 21 percent of GDP in 1993. In 1989–90, over half of the capital inflows were in the form of FDI; more recently, Malaysian companies have been able to attract foreign funds by borrowing through Malaysian banks. Malaysia requires most employers and workers to contribute to an Employee Provident Fund, which then provides pensions to retired workers. The EPF in Malaysia holds 20 percent of the country's financial assets.

20. Between 1950 and 1993, both the U.S. and Japan invested fourteen times more abroad than they received in FDI, while western European nations invested ten times more abroad than they received in FDI. However, in recent years, the U.S. has become a net recipient of FDI—in 1994, for example, foreigners invested $57 billion in the U.S., versus $2 billion in Japan.

21. The UN Division of Transnational Corporations, in an April 1995 report, criticized the incentives offered by over 100 countries to attract FDI. According to the report, tax and other incentives offered to attract FDI in recent years amounted to $110,000 per job to attract a BMW plant to South Carolina, $57,000 per job to locate a Mercedes-Benz Swatchmobile factory in France, and $30,000 per job to land a South Korean electronics factory in Britain (*Wall Street Journal*, 14 April 1995: A2).

22. As rules for trading goods become standardized, there is increasing pressure to standardize rules for FDI, so that a foreign investor has the same right to e.g., hire local workers, or to repatriate profits, in many countries. There is today a system of bidding wars for FDI.

23. Four of the twenty-one OECD countries providing aid reached the UN target of contributing 0.7 percent of GDP in 1994—Norway, Denmark, Sweden, and the Netherlands. OECD nations collectively provided aid equivalent to 0.3 percent of their GDP in 1993, down from 0.4 percent in 1983.

24. Italy provided $3 billion in ODA in 1993; the U.K. $2.9 billion;, and Canada $2.4 billion.

25. The cost of intervention is usually high in both economic and humanitarian terms. The Gulf War cost the allies about $61 billion in 1991, or more than worldwide ODA in that year.

26. The decline was attributed to a number of factors, including choppy seas and soccer's World Cup, and word reaching the interior of Haiti that refugees intercepted at sea would no longer be able to settle in the U.S.

27. The World Bank does not report economic data for Haiti. In 1994, Haiti had about 7 million people and a per capita GDP estimated at $100 to $400 per person per year. The $1.5 billion estimate is based on a per capita GDP of $200 per person per year.

28. Aid sometimes fails to prevent the need for costly intervention. The U.S. provided Somalia with $390 million in aid over three decades, but still spent $2 billion to intervene over sixteen months.

References

Abadan-Unat, Nermin, Rusan Keles, Rinus Penninx, Herman van Renselaar, Leo van Vlezen, and Leyla Yenisey. 1976. *Migration and Development: A Study of the Effects of International Labor Migration on Bogaziliyan District*. Ankara: Ajams-Turk Press.

Abowd, John M., and Richard B. Freeman, eds. 1991. *Immigration, Trade and the Labor Market*. Chicago: University of Chicago Press for the National Bureau of Economic Research.

Appleyard, Reginald. 1989. "Migration and Development: Myths and Reality." *International Migration Review* 23, 3: 486–99.

Böhning, W. R. 1972. *The Migration of Workers in the United Kingdom and the European Community*. Oxford University Press for the Institute of Race Relations.

———. 1984. *Studies in International Labor Migration*. London: Macmillan.

Böhning, W. R., and M. Schloeter-Paredes. 1993. *Economic Haven or Political Refugees: Can Aid Reduce the Need for Migration?* Geneva: Proceedings of a May 1992 ILO-UNHCR Conference.

Castles, Stephen, and Mark Miller. 1993. *The Age of Migration*. New York: Guilford Press.

Cornelius, Wayne, Philip Martin, and James Hollifield, eds. 1994. *Controlling Immigration: A Global Perspective*. Stanford, Cal.: Stanford University Press.

Freeman, Gary. 1994. "Can Liberal States Control Unwanted Migration?" *Annals of the American Academy of Political and Social Science* 534 (July).

Freeman, Gary, and James Jupp, eds. 1992. *Nations of Immigrants: Australia, the United States, and International Migration*. New York: Oxford University Press.

Goonerate, Wilbert, Philip Martin, and Hidehiko Sazanami, eds. 1994. *Regional Development Impacts of Labour Migration in Asia*. UNCRD Research Report Series No. 2. United Nations Centre for Regional Development, Nayoga, Japan.

Hiemenz, U., and K. W. Schatz. 1979. *Trade in Place of Migration: An Employment-Oriented Study with Special References to the Federal Republic of the Federal Republic of Germany, Spain and Turkey*. Geneva: International Labour Office.

Hollifield, James. 1992. *Immigrants, Markets, and States: The Political Economy of Immigration in Postwar Europe and the U.S*. Cambridge, Mass.: Harvard.

Hönekopp, Elmar. 1991. *East/West Migration: Recent Developments in the Changing Course of International Migration*. Paris: OECD.

———. 1992. "Auswirkungen eines EG-Beitritts der Türkei auf Demographie und Arbeitsmarkt in der EG und in Deutschland." Mimeo (February).

Koener, Heiko. 1990. *Internationale Mobilitaet der Arbeit. Eine Empirische und theoretische Analyse der internationalen Wirtschaftsmigration im 19. und 20. Jahrhundert*. Darmstadt: Wissenschaftliche Buchgesellschaft

Layard, Richard, Oliver Blanchard, Rudiger Dornbusch, and Paul Krugman. 1992. *East West Migration: The Alternatives*. Cambridge, Mass.: MIT Press.

Lucas, R E. B. 1987. "Emigration to South Africa's Mines." *American Economic Review* 77, 3: 313–30.

Martin, Philip. 1980. *Guestworker Programs: Lessons from Europe*. Washington, D.C.: U.S. Department of Labor, International Labor Affairs Bureau.

———. 1991. *The Unfinished Story: Turkish Labor Migration to Western Europe*. Geneva: International Labour Office.

———. 1993. *Trade and Migration: NAFTA and Agriculture*. Washington, D.C.: Institute for International Economics.

Martin, Philip, and Alan Olmstead. 1985. "The Agricultural Mechanization Controversy." *Science* 227, 4687 (8 February): 601–6.

Martin, Philip, and Elizabeth Midgley. 1994. "Immigration to the United States: Journey to an Uncertain Destination." *Population Reference Bureau Population Bulletin* 49, 2 (September).

Massey, Douglas, Rafael Alarcon, Jorge Durand, and Humberto Gonzales. 1987. *Return to Aztlan: The Social Process of International Migration from Western Mexico*. Berkeley: University of California Press.

Massey, Douglas S., Joaquín Arango, Graeme Hugo, Ali Kouaouci, Adela Pellegrino, and J. Edward Taylor. 1993. "Theories of International Migration: A Review and Appraisal." *Population and Development Review* 19, 3 (September).

Miller, Mark, and Philip Martin. 1982. *Administering Foreign Worker Programs*. Lexington, Mass.: Lexington Books.

Mundell, R. A. 1957. "International Trade and Factor Mobility." *American Economic Review* 47: 321–35.

Organisation for Economic Co-operation and Development (OECD). 1978. *Migration, Growth and Development*. OECD: Paris.

Penninx, Rinus. 1982. "A Critical Review of Theory and Practice: The Case of Turkey." *International Migration Review* 16: 781–818.

Piore, Michael J. 1979. *Birds of Passage: Migrant Labor and Industrial Societies*. New York: Cambridge University Press.

Reder, Melvin W. 1963. "The Economic Consequences of Increased Immigration." *Review of Economics and Statistics* 45: 221–30.

Russell, Sharon Stanton, and Michael Teitelbaum. 1992. *International Migration and International Trade*. Washington, D.C.: World Bank.

Sassen, Saskia. 1995. "The De Facto Transnationalizing of Immigration Policy." Mimeo.

Schiller, Günter, et al. 1976. *Ausländische Arbeitnehmer, and Arbeitsmärkte Nürnberg*. IAB-BA, Beitr AB7.

Stahl, Charles W. 1982. "Labor Emigration and Economic Development." *International Migration Review* 16, 4: 869–99.

Stalker, Peter. 1994. *The Work of Strangers: A Survey of International Labour Migration*. Geneva: International Labour Office.

Stark, Oded, and J. Edward Taylor. 1989. "Relative Deprivation and International Migration." *Demography* 26: 1–14.

———. 1991. "Migration Incentives, Migration Types: The Role of Relative Deprivation." *The Economic Journal* 101: 1163–78.

Straubhaar, Thomas. 1988. *On the Economics of International Labor Migration*. Bern: Haupt.

———. 1992. "Allocational and Distributional Aspects of Future Immigration to Western Europe." *International Migration Review* 26, 2 (Summer): 462–83.

Taylor, J. Edward. 1986. "Differential Migration, Networks, Information and Risk." In *Migration Theory, Human Capital and Development*, edited by O. Stark. Greenwich, Conn.: JAI Press.

———. 1992. "Remittances and Inequality Reconsidered: Direct, Indirect, and Intertemporal Effects." *Journal of Policy Modeling* 14: 187–208.

Todaro, Michael. 1969. "A Model of Labor Migration and Urban Unemployment in Less Developed Countries." *American Economic Review* 59: 138–48.

United Nations. 1993. *The State of World Population*. New York.

United Nations Division of Transnational Corporations. 1995. *Incentives and Direct Foreign Investment*. Geneva: UNDTC.

U.S. Commission for the Study of International Migration and Cooperative Economic Development. 1990. *Unauthorized Migration: An Economic Development Response*. Washington, D.C.

Weiner, Myron, ed. 1993. *International Migration and Security*. Boulder, Colo.: Westview Press.

Widgren, Jonas. 1994. *The Key to Europe: a Comparative Analysis of Entry and Asylum Policies in Western Countries*. Vienna: ICMPD.

World Bank. 1995. *Workers in an Integrating World*. Washington, D.C.: World Development Report.

Zolberg, Aristide, Astri Suhrke, and Sergio Aguayo. 1989. *Escape from Violence: Conflict and the Refugee Crisis in the Developing World*. New York: Oxford University Press.

Zolberg, Aristide. 1989. "The Next Waves: Migration Theory for a Changing World." *International Migration Review* 23, 3 (Fall).

– *Chapter 5* –

CURRENT DILEMMAS AND FUTURE PROSPECTS OF THE INTER-AMERICAN MIGRATION SYSTEM

Robert C. Smith

"how can he have such a basic name" -R

Introduction

America has experienced a larger influx of immigration between the mid-1980s and the present than during any period except the early decades of this century. Not surprisingly, it has also witnessed the reemergence of debates on immigration whose vociferousness resonates with those of the 1910s to 1920s. These debates pivot on different understandings of several key issues: the "root causes" of migration and the efficacy of state intervention to control immigration, the relationship of migration and development, fear of the "declining quality" of immigrants and the ability of the U.S. to assimilate new immigrants, and the fiscal and other costs of immigration.[1] This chapter focuses mainly on the first two of these issues, and does so in two ways. First, I argue that we can usefully understand migration and evaluate policy by using the concept of the "inter-American migration system." Second, and secondarily, I briefly critique and summarize the "catastrophic" position on immigration, which predicts calamitous results if immediate and drastic measures are not taken to control immigration.

I describe the inter-American migration system as a "loosely hinged" system. This conceptualization of "system" owes less to the architectural metaphors of Parson's structural-functionalism than it does to the physics metaphors of Wolf's "open system," whose shape emerges from the contingent interplay of various levels and kinds of forces (Schnieder 1995: 4; Wolf 1982). It also attempts to take up Tilly's (1985) plea for concrete, historically grounded analysis that takes account of the timing and sequence of events. In this chapter, I argue that the inter-American migration system encompassing Mexico, Central America, and the Caribbean emerged over time through the interaction of (1) government policies creating the conditions favoring migration, including those focused on economic development, immigration control regulation, and foreign policy; (2) changes in local, national, and global economies and population trends creating incentives to migrate; and(3) the internal logic by which migration becomes a semiautonomous process once it has become established through immigrant social networks. Such a framework offers advantages over the classic but more static framework identifying forces that "push" and "pull" migrants, by enabling us to analyze how these forces affect each other and evolve, currently and historically.

This systemic, historical analysis also offers insights into other issues, such as the capacity of the state to control immigration once it has become self-perpetuating. While I disagree with Massey and colleagues (1998, 1987) that the state cannot do anything to control immigration, I agree that it most likely will not take the measures necessary to achieve its stated objectives, keeping immigration control largely at the level of symbolic politics (Zolberg and Smith 1996; see especially Andreas 1997; Calavita 1996; Edelman 1964; Zolberg 1998). Similarly, while I agree with Freeman (1994) and Miller (1994) that measures to control immigration cannot be said to have failed because they have not seriously been tried, the next task is then to explain why bona fide efforts have not been made. This chapter takes this discussion of state capacity further by including in the analytical framework the reciprocal, systemic influence of foreign policy on U.S.-bound immigration and immigration policies, and sending states emerging interests in developing domestic diasporas and lobby groups. This chapter also uses concrete cases to divine different relationships between migration and development in Mexico, and within its regions, and in Central America, and the Caribbean. This deeper more systemic understanding of inter-American migration should help us in making better policies, and to more realistically assess the potential consequences of policies while they are being discussed.

This chapter is organized into three sections. The first briefly critiques the catastrophic view of immigration. The second section outlines the basic elements of the inter-American migration system, analyzing it in three subsections: one on Mexico, another on the Caribbean and Central America, and the third on transnationalization and the interactive relationship between domestic and foreign politics. The third main section assesses the likely challenges the U.S. will face regarding migration and refugee flows in Mexico, Central America, and the Caribbean; and to discuss some recent or current debates in American policies designed to address immigration, assessing their probable impacts and humanitarian implications. These policies include all those relevant to the making and functioning of the inter-American migration system: American immigration, refugee and asylum policy, as well as U.S. foreign policy, including economic development and integration policies, security, and ideological Cold War policies.

Population Growth, State Capacity, and Unauthorized Immigration

"Must It Be the West against the Rest?" asks the cover of the December 1994 *Atlantic Monthly* magazine picturing a casually dressed, middle-aged white man standing next to a backyard barbecue, while a horde (literally) of dark faces peers over the picket fence behind him. This image neatly captures the two main elements of the catastrophic argument, repeated in various forms in the popular media and scholarly literature: that uncontrolled population growth and political instability in the Southern Hemisphere (or "the South") will overwhelm America and the West, and that the U.S. and the West have lost control of their borders and have less capacity to control immigration than in the past. While sometimes treated as a "straw man" in academic circles, this view has gained currency in the popular media and has been advanced by some prestigious academics and policy experts and hence merits a response here. Moreover, the catastrophic view does raise issues of real concern for U.S. policy that I attempt to give more complete consideration in this chapter.

Both elements of the catastrophic positions are flawed, but for different reasons. The first draws incorrect conclusions about immigration based on accurate demographic data. The second too readily accepts as fact political rhetoric that consistently high levels of immigration mean it is "out of control" and cannot be controlled, without analyzing the reasons for or efforts to improve current state capacity to control immigration nor entertaining seriously the counterfactual regarding what immigration levels would be like without these controls (see Brubaker 1994; Freeman 1994).

The first position depends on our accepting a direct and proportional relationship between population growth and migration from the Third World to the First World. In *Preparing for the Twenty-First Century* (1993), Paul Kennedy argues that low fertility in the industrialized countries and high fertility in the developing ones will cause increasing rates of immigration in the future. However, as discussed in Mary Kritz's contribution to this volume, this argument cannot explain a number of aspects of migration, including why there is more migration between developing countries than there is between industrialized and developed countries. Sounding a similar theme to Kennedy's but focusing on Mexico, David Simcox and Leon Bouvier imaginatively ask readers to compare Mexico City in 1950 with what it is today to illustrate the population pressures in Mexico (Simcox and Bouvier 1986; see also Bouvier 1992). In 1950, a visitor

> would have found a languid and uncrowded country of 27 million. If our visitor returned today [1992], she would find a teeming country of 85 million [with] ... nearly half the population less than 15 years old and 60 percent under [age] 25. Surging growth and growing youthfulness have fed Mexico's soaring emigration in recent decades. Given the projected rise in population the prospects are for even greater emigration pressures in the future. (Bouvier 1992: 47)

Bouvier and Simcox show how birth rates can go down at the same time as the total population goes up, as has happened in Latin America for the last thirty-five years. Reasons for this apparent inverse relation include decreasing death rates for infants and longer lives for adults. Hence, they argue that Mexico's decrease in population growth from 44.5 births per thousand people between 1945 and 1949 to 33.9 births per thousand between 1980 to 1985 is too late. The Mexican and Central American population "bulge" is growing because the 1950 to 1970 boomers are having children. Hence, even while they are having fewer children, there are so many of them that the population will continue to increase through the first decade or more of the next century. They could refine their argument by saying that the problem is not the number of births, but rather that the entrance of between 700,000 and 800,000 new job seekers into the Mexican labor force annually through the 1980s and 1990s, compounding the problem each year (Garcia y Griego 1989, and personal communication, 1996). The implication is that the U.S. will be swamped with undocumented immigrants from the South.

Yet more than decade after Simcox and Bouvier (1986) made their initial prediction, the U.S. is not being swamped by undocumented immigrants. In fact, more legal immigrants are added to the U.S. population each year—about 800,000—than undocumented immigrants, who, according to the most reliable estimates, add only about 200,000 to 300,000 per year (Fix and Passel 1994; Passel 1995; see also Massey and Singer 1995; Warren 1995; Espenshade 1993). Moreover, the cumulative number of undocumented immigrants has not skyrocketed over the last fifteen years, as Bouvier and Simcox's analysis predicts. Estimates have ranged from 3.5 million to 2.5 million in April 1980, to 3.5 million to 5.0 million in June 1986, to October 1992 levels of between 2.7 million and 3.2 million (Warren 1995). Adding to the total the more than 3 million people who legalized their status through the "amnesty" provisions of the 1986 Immigration Reform and Control Act and via related family reunification, the contribution of undocumented immigrants to the U.S. population would rise to 5.7 to 6.2 million in 1992—much less than Simcox and Bouvier's analysis would lead us to expect.

One major reason why the U.S. has not been swamped is that for every 100 undocumented people who illegally cross the U.S.-Mexico border, between eighty-six and eighty-two return home (Bustamante, Corona, and Santibanez 1995; Massey and Singer 1995). The convergence of Mexican and American estimates, despite very different data sets and estimation techniques, lends credibility to their analyses. Massey and Singer (1995) further estimate that over the course of the twenty-five-year period ending in 1990 there was a net influx of approximately 5.2 million, well below what Simcox and Bouvier, and Kennedy's analysis would predict. A change during the 1990s in the nature of Mexico-U.S. migration from sojourner to a settler model (Cornelius 1991; Durand et al. 1999) is increasing the percentage of undocumented people who stay in the U.S.

for the longer term or permanently, but the number has crept only back to the 5 million range.

This theory of a proportional relationship between increase in population growth and in migration fails on other grounds as well. First, it fails to seriously consider what would levels of immigration have been in the absence of the controls that we have. By failing to ask this question, it accepts the political rhetoric about industrialized democracies' loss of control over immigration. Some versions of this argument view the state as having completely lost control and implicitly measure immigration against a standard of no undocumented immigration, a goal that would require police powers unacceptable to most Americans. Other versions see an increasing gap between the goals and outcomes of immigration control policies, leading to public discontent (Cornelius et al. 1994; Hollifield 1992). These accounts take little notice of the effectiveness of many of the immigration controls we already have. For example, the "remote control" strategy of tighter visa restrictions at the point of origin on all international air travel to the U.S. discourages much illegal entry (Zolberg and Smith 1996: 84) that would have occurred if population pressure were the main driving force behind migration. And, as will be argued later, the lack of such capacity is not accidental, but is in fact systemic, in that attempts to improve the American state's capacity to control unauthorized immigration are in large part the result of efforts of those groups in society that benefit from the presence of a "cheap multinational work force" (Brubaker 1994; Calavita 1992; Garcia y Griego 1981; Russell 1996: 101; Zolberg 1990; Zolberg and Smith 1996). Hence, Freeman (1994) argues that measures like employer sanctions in the U.S. cannot be said to have failed because they have not really been tried yet. In this context, even the U.S. government has admitted in the past that its prospects for controlling immigration are "dim" (GAO 1980).

However, the U.S. and the industrialized states have as a group recently begun to attempt to improve the capacity of their states to prevent unauthorized entry, employment or overstaying (Brubaker 1994; Cornelius et al. 1994; Freeman 1994; Zolberg and Smith 1996). In the U.S., these measures include increasing the budget for the INS, and implementing new entrant-tracking technology at the border (INS 1996; author interviews with INS agents, 1995, 1996). These measures are discussed more extensively in the last section of the essay.

The equation between population growth and migration also fails to appreciate the link between prior American involvement in an area of the world and immigration from it: Why would the Philippines be the second largest source of legal immigrants after Mexico, if not for its long involvement with the U.S. as a colony and then close ally? Why would we have such large Southeast Asian populations, and relatively smaller populations from countries that are also quite populous and are closer to the U.S., such as Brazil? Clearly, current immigrant and refugee populations reflect prior policies, including foreign policy.

In summary, the United States is in fact much more successful at controlling and deterring potential unauthorized immigration than current political rhetoric would lead us to believe. Moreover, it is developing increased capacity to control it. However, the capacity to control unauthorized immigration is not absolute and engenders fiscal and human rights trade-offs that must be factored into policy decisions. The genesis of these trade-offs can be seen in the following analysis of the inter-American migration system.

Migration between the U.S. and Mexico, Central America and the Caribbean

The analysis of a "migration system" enables us to understand how migration begins, how and why it continues, and why there are limits on the extent to which a democratic state can hope to absolutely control it. The "inter-American migration system" emerged from the conjunction of three broadly related sets of processes: (1) the integration of local and national markets into the global economy; (2) the inherent tendency of migration to become self-perpetuating once established, partly aided by population growth; and (3) the effects of politics surrounding immigration, and of state policies regarding immigration, development, population, and foreign and economic policies.

While migration from the South to the North can usefully be conceived of as one system, important distinctions can be made between Mexico-U.S. migration and Caribbean/Central American-U.S. migration. Mexico-U.S. migration is largely the result of the confluence of domestic political forces in the U.S.—particularly the weight of employer lobbies— and long-term economic and demographic trends in Mexico. In contrast, in the Caribbean and Central American cases, U.S. foreign policy and preponderant economic and political influence have played a larger role in helping to cause out-migration and in determining the nature of the flow. If, following Torres-Rivas (1985: 12), we define refugees as "all persons ... forced to leave their habitual homes and workplaces due to political violence," and economic migrants as those seeking to take advantage of better economic opportunities abroad, the Central American flows have been much closer to the refugee pole of the "political-refugee v. economic migrant" continuum than has most Mexican migration. Cuba and Haiti are two Caribbean flows that are politically determined to a significant degree.

Mexico-U.S. Migration

In the Mexico-U.S. case, arguably the most important factor in increasing migration to the U.S. was the Bracero Program, a labor importation program begun to meet a wartime demand for labor that was extended largely through the political weight of southwestern growers and their representatives in Congress.[2] The Bracero Program was initially imposed by a wartime American government that wanted a secure supply of labor for growers who wanted to continue to employ their undocumented workers without state regulation. Growers soon found the program to be advantageous, however, and succeeded in having it extended through the early 1960s; the labor shortages that developed during the Korean War also helped prolong its duration. More than 4.6 million Mexican workers came to the U.S. through the Bracero Program, thus establishing a social infrastructure for future undocumented migration (Calavita 1992; Garcia y Griego 1981; Massey et al. 1987; Portes and Bach 1985). When the Mexican economy experienced economic shocks in the mid-1970s and then an extended crisis through the 1980s and 1990s, this social infrastructure was already in place to facilitate the entry of undocumented migrants.

This social infrastructure consists of migrant networks that lower the costs of migration by providing information and references for jobs, aid upon arrival, and other benefits (see especially Massey et al. 1987). Over time, entire villages and regions in Mexico became involved in migration, and experienced a process that has been called "nortenizacion" (Alarcon 1992), through which local life in Mexico becomes oriented toward "el norte" (the U.S.) and is lived in a migrant culture and economy. The central states of the El Bajio region are among the oldest sending regions—including the states of Guanajato, Michoacan, Zacatecas, Jalisco, San Luis Potosi—though more recently many other states such as Oaxaca, Puebla, and Guerrero and Mexico City have become important senders as well. These local and regional economies come to depend on dollars remitted from the U.S. and can even be conceived of as "remittance economies" (Smith 1995, 1998). Estimates for total remittances to Mexico range from $2 billion to $4 billion U.S. dollars (Banco de Mexico 1991; Durand et al. 1996; Lozano Ascencio 1993). Remittances also have important developmental effects in Mexico. Durand and his colleagues (1996) estimate that 10 percent of income and 3 percent of GDP in Mexico is accounted for by migrant remittances and the economic activity they generate.

The development of this social infrastructure was facilitated by the duality of American immigration policy. Starting with the 1921 and 1924 reforms and continuing in various forms to the present, the U.S. has maintained a "front gate-back door" policy (Zolberg 1990). The establishment in the 1920s of quotas based on national origin—and underpinned by eugenical theories of the superiority of "nordic" over "slavic," "latin," and other "stocks"—led to the limiting of immigration from southern and eastern Europe. However, while Mexicans were seen to be of inferior stock, similar to southern Europeans, agricultural employers in the Southwest succeeded in preventing Western Hemisphere entrants numbers from being limited by quota. They also prevented strict enforcement of immigration laws and border controls, but encouraged qualitative restrictions on the permanent immigration of Mexicans. They encouraged the entrance of temporary labor while discouraging permanent settlement. Hence, while the front door of permanent settlement was closed, the back door of undocumented entry or temporary work was open (Calavita 1992; Garcia y Griego 1981, 1997; Zolberg 1990). While quotas were imposed on the Western Hemisphere in 1965, the back door was kept open in other ways.

A graphic illustration of the "back door" policy and the power of southwestern growers to influence legislation that facilitated migration was the "Texas Proviso" of the 1952 McCarran-Walter Act, which stipulated that it was a crime to aid, harbor, or abet an undocumented person, but specifically defined employment not to constitute aiding, harboring, or abetting. Hence, while an immigrant committed a crime in taking employment without work authorization, the employer committed no crime in hiring him (Bustamante et al. 1992). The Texas Proviso was repealed in the 1986 Immigration Reform and Control Act (IRCA), when sanctions for employers who knowingly hired undocumented immigrants were established. However, weak enforcement of employer sanctions has not made them a credible threat to employers or deterrent to immigrants. Moreover, in exchange for acceding to employer sanctions, the growers lobby secured a provision in the law stipulating a warrant was needed for INS officers to enter fields looking for the undocumented. And farm workers got the easiest terms for legalizing their status in the 1986 law's "amnesty" provision. Further, the law provided for Replacement Agricultural Workers (RAW) if labor shortages were to emerge later. Many link these weak enforcement measures to the pressure of interest groups, especially employers, who feared loss of access to immigrant labor, but also Latinos, who feared discrimination against those who look or sound "foreign." In other cases, the Border Patrol's funding has been cut in response to complaints from employer organizations that work was being disrupted (Calavita 1992). I will discuss current measures to control immigration at the end of this chapter.

A crucial though frequently overlooked aspect of the U.S. law that facilitated the emergence of the inter-American migration system is the family reunification provision of the 1965 law, which enables immigrants and permanent residents to bring in immediate family members outside of any numerical country cap. As illustrated by Reimers (1985), this provision has made possible the "migration chain" through which one person can sponsor relatives, who in turn sponsor others, resulting in greater settlement than would otherwise have been the case. Although especially important in boosting legal immigration from Mexico, this provision facilitates immigration from elsewhere as well (Massey, Donato, and Liang 1990; Massey, Goldring, and Durand 1994). While often criticized for facilitating migration, the humanitarian principle of family reunification enjoys great support among most Americans.

The above analysis has focused mainly on "pull" factors in the U.S. that created a demand for labor or on "facilitating" factors that kept it going once it began. There are at least three important "push" factors. The initial potential for migration stems from the 1848 War between Mexico and the U.S., which left "Mexicans" living in the U.S., who still had links with Mexico. More important in causing large-scale migration was the Mexican Revolution (1910–21), and the residual Cristero Rebellion (1926–29) which took place in the central western states of Michoacan, Guanajato, Zacatecas, and Jalisco. Some scholars estimate that 1.5 million people, or 10 percent of Mexico's population, migrated to the U.S. during and just after the Revolution (Cross and Sandos 1981). These wars displaced massive numbers of immigrants (who would probably be eligible for temporary protected status today). A second cause has been population growth, and more particularly growth in the labor force since the 1980s, coupled with Mexico's inability to create enough good jobs, though this has not been as singularly important a cause as the catastrophic view would have it.

A third cause has been Mexican development policy itself and the nature of Mexico's links with the global and U.S. economies. Under both its Import Substituting Industrialization (ISI) phase from the 1940s to 1982, and in its liberalization phase since 1982, Mexican economic policies have led to increased push pressures. The capital intensive nature of ISI led to "growth without jobs" (Cornelius and Martin 1993; Martin 1993)—that is, it sustained an economic growth rates of 6 percent per year from the 1950s through the 1970s without generating commensurate levels of employment, especially not in rural areas (Alba 1978). The liberalization and structural adjustment programs of the 1980s and 1990s have placed the burdens of adjustment disproportionately on the poor and middle class (Friedman et al. 1995; Lustig 1993, 1995). Within a context where so many have access to migration networks to the U.S.—one scholar estimates that up to one-third make such a trip and one-half have relatives who do in their lifetimes (Camp 1993)—such conditions are readily converted into migration push pressures. That migration can be understood to have been facilitated under both development policies suggests that at least part of its cause lies with Mexico's larger economic and political relationship to the world economy, and the U.S. in particular (Grindle 1988; Portes and Bach 1985; Portes and Walton 1981; Sassen 1988). For example, Mexico's debt servicing in the 1980s impeded the kind of structural adjustment and economic development that the U.S. and world financial organizations were encouraging—Mexico transferred between 6 and 7 percent of its GDP out of the country via debt servicing in the 1980s (Cordera Campos and Gonzalez Tiburcio 1991)—thus impeding economic recovery. Yet because Mexican migration has so many causes—it is overdetermined—it is hard to determine which factors caused particular effects. The North American Free Trade Agreement (NAFTA) has been touted as a solution to the issue of migration, though, for a variety of reasons to be discussed later, this seems highly unlikely for at least the next generation.

Central American and Caribbean Migration

The Caribbean and Central American segments of the inter-American migration system differ from that between Mexico and the U.S. To a greater degree than in Mexico, migration within the Caribbean was established before the onset of large-scale migration to the U.S. and other metropoles beginning in the 1940s (Marshall 1987), providing a set of practices that could be adapted. In the Central American case, the economic and political determinants of migration to the U.S. are especially difficult to disentangle. Important causes can be found in both the social inequality that fostered the revolutionary and counterrevolutionary conflicts of the 1970s and 1980s that pushed refugees and migrants north, and the presence of established Central American communities in the U.S. that provided a place to go when the violence became pervasive in the 1980s (Aguayo and Weiss Fagen 1988; Hamilton and Stoltz Chincilla 1991). Moreover, while the preponderant influence of the U.S. cannot be cited as the only or main cause of U.S.-bound migration, there are significant ways that U.S. foreign policy helped cause migration and contributed to the creation of the current inter-American migration system.

To better understand the more political nature of migration and refugee flows from Central America, one can start by observing that there was not much migration from there to the U.S. prior to 1979 (Diaz-Briquets 1989; Schoultz 1992). However, in the next several years, civil strife in El Salvador, Guatemala, and Nicaragua would create massive flows of refugees and migrant from these countries, first to neighboring countries, then to Mexico, and then to the U.S. From relatively tiny presences before the 1980s, Schoultz estimated that by 1984 there were between "750,000 and 1.3 million Central Americans living in the U.S., legally and (mostly) illegally. This represents 3 to 6 percent of the population of Central America, and in the case of El Salvador, at least 10 percent of the country's citizens." What caused this sudden and massive outflow, and how did it grow?

We can begin to answer this question by looking at the case of El Salvador, which illustrates particular dimensions of the inter-American migration system. The potential for high rates of migration from El Salvador (and Central America in general) to the U.S. was created by extremely high population pressure, an unequal distribution of land organized on a oligarchic, plantation model maintained after the rest of Latin America had switched to an ISI model, and repressive, often U.S.-backed, governments that defended this order (Hamilton and Stoltz Chincilla 1991). These conditions fostered periodic rebellions, often resulting in massacres, such as that in 1932 when between 10,000 and 20,000 rebels were killed by the military. During the 1970s the opposition created the Frente Farabundo Marti para la Liberacion Nacional (FMLN) and the Frente Democratico Revolucionario (FDR), its armed and political fronts, respectively. The Reagan administration viewed the rebels in terms of the Cold War, and provided support for the Salvadoran regime and its military.

The key to the sudden exodus in 1980 through 1985 was the considerable violence that characterized the conflict, leading to some 500,000 internally displaced, and more than one million refugees in Mexico and the United States (Hamilton and Stoltz Chinchilla 1991; Schoultz 1992). More than 200,000 were displaced in the first wave of political violence in 1980 to 1982, when the Salvadoran military attempted to deprive the guerrillas of support through brutal sweeps of the countryside; concurrently, they organized death squads in urban areas to eliminate rebel organizers and suspected supporters. In 1983 through 1984, the guerrillas increased pressure on the largely noncommitted civilian populace to join them, and launched a campaign to eliminate government supporters. They also attempted to destroy the economy and force a settlement of the conflict. The Salvadoran military was at the same time receiving extensive aid from the U.S. Special Forces, including intelligence and helicopter gunships, and infrared technology that made it impracticable for guerrillas to mass their forces, even at night. Pervasive violence and extensive antipersonnel mines made much of El Salvador too dangerous to inhabit, rendered agriculture impossible, occasioning both internal and international migration (Aguayo and Weiss Fagen 1988; Torres-Rivas 1985).

By 1985, between 20 and 35 percent of the total population was uprooted, with between 5 and 6 percent of the population living in the United States (Diaz-Briquets 1989: 41). The massive scale of the migration cannot be attributed simply to the desire of peasants to avoid being caught in the crossfire. Rather, it was flight from a systematic terror campaign, attributable to the implementation of a counterinsurgency aimed at "definitively breaking up the logistic base, social support and the possible sympathy of the civilian population" (Torres-Rivas 1985: 15), and to the rebels own terror strategy, which some experts estimate accounted for 20 percent of the deaths in the conflict. The government's strategy led to the notorious massacres at El Mozote and dozens of other villages. In 1989, following a nationwide FMLN military offensive, the rebels and the government and military began negotiating peace, and in 1992 signed a comprehensive peace accord, leading to the establishment of electoral governance. This settlement and its importance for migration are discussed further in the third section of the essay.

This brief review of the Salvadoran case illustrates an important aspect of the migration-inducing dynamics that developed in Central America during the Cold War. American foreign policy contributed to the migration flow, especially via the key role of the U.S. Special Forces, but the rebels' violent strategies in response also contributed to making the situation impossible for many Salvadorans. Salvadorans fleeing generalized violence were ultimately granted recognition as a hybrid category between formal refugees (who must show individual persecution) and economic migrants, first by the Cartagena Declaration by Latin American states in 1984, and later by the granting of Temporary Protected Status (TPS) by the United States in the 1990s. This status allows one to stay in the U.S. for a limited but extendable period until conditions in the home country improve (Aleinikoff 1994). While a justified humanitarian gesture, it also left large numbers of immigrants in ambiguous legal status in the early 1990s (Russell 1995: 202).

Guatemala and Nicaragua have histories similar to El Salvador's with respect to migration (Hamilton and Chinchilla 1991, 1995; Repak 1995; Zolberg et al. 1989). Given this analysis of the political causes of Central American migration and refugee flows and the inter-American migration system, we must explicitly state *that removal of the original causes is not a sufficient condition for the reversal of the flows from Central America because the system has a logic of its own.* One reason is that while the military conflict no longer rages, its effects in terms of land mines, disorganized economies, unprofessional police, and civil tension still remain.

Perhaps more importantly, dynamics at both the individual and societal levels tend to perpetuate migration once it has become established. These dynamics make it more likely that immigrants will stay in the U.S. On the level of the migrants themselves, many have been here long enough that their children are in school and they have established their lives here.

On a societal level, remittances from the U.S. have become an increasingly important element of the sending countries economies in Central America and the Caribbean. For example, remittances account for 15–25 percent of El Salvador's GDP (Hamilton and Stoltz Chinchilla 1995; M. P. Smith 1996). This figure makes it seem less anomalous that the Salvadoran government sends consular personal to help Salvadorans file asylum claims in the U.S., claiming that they will face persecution should they return home (Mahler 1996). Remittances are increasing in importance as a source of foreign exchange. In relation to the value of exports, remittances to El Salvador have increased from around 20 percent in 1980 to more than 100 percent in 1992; for the Dominican Republic, from about 5 percent in 1980 to around 70 percent in 1993; for Colombia, from around 3 percent in 1980 to around 9 percent in 1993; for Guatemala, from less than 1 percent in 1980 to more than 10 percent in 1993; and in Mexico, from around 4 percent in 1980 to around 11 percent in 1993 (de la Garza, Orozco, and Barona 1997; World Bank 1995). Neither these migrants nor their governments wish to see these remittances stop, and a reasonable argument can be made that it is in the U.S.'s long-term interest that they continue.

Transnationalization and the Interactive Relationship of Domestic and Foreign Politics

The high level of interdependence has led to increasingly interactive relations between domestic and foreign or international politics.[3] This is so both for the U.S. and for the sending states, especially those whose societies and economies have become most thoroughly integrated with the U.S. via migration.

The link between many refugee or migrant flows to the U.S. and U.S. involvement with the source countries mentioned above deserves further consideration. Flows from the major sending areas of Central America, the Caribbean, Southeast Asia, and the Philippines can all be linked to significant U.S. involvement, including military involvement in these areas. Moreover, through the 1980s, anticommunism was a constant criterion in admitting immigrants and refugees, be they from Cuba, Nicaragua, the former Soviet Union, or Poland. Also in the 1980s, there was a politicization of refugee policy by both the right and the left (Dominguez 1992; Schoultz 1992). The Reagan administration granted asylum or refugee status to those from Nicaragua and its Sandinista government much more readily than those from, for example, Guatemala, whose authoritarian government was seen to be an ally of the United States (Russell 1995). The U.S. left engaged in civil disobedience through the Sanctuary movement, breaking U.S. law to aid those fleeing Central American conflicts (Schoultz 1992).

Cuba is a clear case where foreign policy concerns determined immigration and refugee policy and had effects on migration. The U.S. attempted to embarrass Castro by accepting large numbers of Cubans refugees and defectors escaping Communism. The dictator turned the tables on America in the Mariel boatlift of 1980 by allowing many Cuban "undesirables," including prison inmates, to leave pell-mell for U.S. shores. Even overtly less "political" and more "economic" migrations have connections with U.S. policy. Migration from the Dominican Republic had been limited by the Dominican dictator Trujillo until his assassination in 1961. Migration was moderately increased when the U.S. suddenly increased the number of visas to give politically active, middle-class Dominicans an escape from the country's political instability prior to and following the U.S. intervention there in 1965, after the election of a leftist president and a military coup. In this way, the U.S. sought to provide an alternative to political action at home (Mitchell 1992a: 98–100, 1992b). This use of migration as a literal "safety valve," combined with the negative effects on employment of U.S. sugar quotas in later years (discussed later; see McCoy 1991), contributed to Dominican migration to the U.S.

The creation of ethnic lobbying groups are another aspect of the inter-American migration system. The Cubans are the most obvious and successful case in the Western Hemisphere, though the Jewish-Israeli lobby is still stronger (Newland 1995). Cubans in the U.S. lobbied for and got strong anti-Castro policies, and acquired an influence in U.S. foreign policy well beyond their numbers because of the consonance of their anti-communism and that of the U.S. Other domestic communities organizing in the U.S. lobbies by themselves or in relation to their home states include the Vietnamese (Newland 1995), Colombians (Sanchez 1997), Dominicans (Graham 1995), and Mexicans (Guarnizo 1998; Smith 1998a,

1998b, 1998d). The influence that these groups will ultimately have is not only a consequence of their own organizing, but also the confluence of their interests with U.S. foreign policy interests, their electoral strength, and other factors (de la Garza 1996).

A final U.S. domestic effect is the *increasing sensitivity of U.S. foreign policy to its potential effects on immigration and refugee flows.* Whereas immigration, asylum, and refugee policies had traditionally been influenced by America's foreign policy goals—especially anti-communism—in the 1980s and 1990s we saw the emergence of foreign policy designed with an eye to controlling the domestic and other political implications of refugee and asylee flows (Dominguez 1992; Stepick 1992). For example, the U.S. fear that political violence and instability in Haiti would lead to an overwhelming flood of "boat people" led or contributed first to policy changes that hastened the end of the Duvalier regime (Stepick 1992), and next, to U.S. intervention in Haiti that restored democratic elections. Such was stated directly by President Clinton in justifying the impending U.S. invasion of Haiti in September 1994: "If we don't act, they [Haitian refugees] could become the next wave of refugees at our door" (cited in Newland 1995: 202). Another part of the calculus in favor of intervention was the high domestic political costs of a surge of "boat people" descending upon a key electoral state,[4] or of the ugly image of the U.S. Coast Guard interdicting them at sea, and opposition to this policy by such groups as the Black Congressional Caucus and TransAfrica (Newland 1995; Russell 1995; Zolberg 1995). In this way, Clinton turned a potential domestic political disaster into a foreign policy success.

Sending states are also experiencing the reciprocal influence of domestic politics and foreign policy, though in different ways due to the dependent nature of their integration with the U.S. Increasing numbers of sending states have taken steps to cultivate and deepen relations with their emigrant populations in the U.S., to create diasporas and lobbies on the Israel-American Jewish model. These steps include constitutional changes to allow dual nationality (Mexico), dual citizenship (the Dominican Republic), provision for a representative in that nation's congress of its nationals living abroad (Colombia, discussions in Mexico and the Dominican Republic), or voting in presidential elections for nationals from abroad (Colombia, Mexico, the Dominican Republic). Equally important are their new outreach efforts and strategies, which stress to their nationals in the U.S. the importance of acquiring U.S. citizenship because it will enable them to vote in U.S. elections and defend their own interests in the U.S.

In the Mexican case, this position became important in the wake of Governor Pete Wilson's virulent attacks on immigrants and the passage the anti-immigrant measure, Proposition 187, in 1994. The Mexican government also wants to keep and even increase remittances from the U.S. (Goldring 1997; Guarnizo 1998; Smith 1996, 1998a, 1998b). These motivations are similar to many other cases. The Colombian government wanted to improve its image in the U.S. by lobbying through its emigrants there (Sanchez 1996). The Guatemalan and Salvadoran governments have taken similar positions with their emigrants in the U.S. in the hopes of keeping the remittances flowing and gaining better political position, and have successfully lobbied for changes in U.S. policy giving Salvadorans and Guatemalans special treatment. An important motivation for El Salvador and Guatemala's policy changes was the desire to integrate into NAFTA (see especially Mahler 1996; Popkin 1998). It has also produced the ironic situation of the Salvadoran government paying for services in the U.S. to help Salvadorans there apply for asylum. The similarity of these measures across cases suggests that they stem from systemic effects such as their dependent economic integration with the U.S.

A final similarity is that each sending state used changes in its policies toward its emigrants to gain advantage and legitimacy in its own domestic politics. The Program for Mexican Communities Abroad was created in part to take back political ground ceded to the Mexican opposition in the U.S., and to legitimize itself at home by manifesting concern for its emigrants abroad (Goldring 1997; Guarnizo 1998; Smith 1996, 1998a, 1998b). The Salvadoran government created parallel institutions among the emigrant community to attempt to counteract the preponderance of support for the leftist opposition among the diaspora, while the Guatemalan government attempted to gain support at home through its activities abroad (Popkin 1998). That domestic American political considerations about immigration now influence American foreign policy, that sending state foreign policy concerns influence their policies toward their emigrants, and that their "emigrant policies" yield them domestic political gain—all these realities are evidence of what can be described as the transnationalization of political life in the Americas, and are important parts of the emerging inter-American migration system.

Actual or Potential Challenges for U.S. Policy

Having laid out the elements of the inter-American migration system, we are now in a position to assess some of the migration and refugee challenges facing the U.S. and evaluate the likely effects of a variety of policies or proposals addressing these challenges.

Mexico

Under current conditions, the most important determinant of future migration from Mexico is past migration. Hence we should anticipate continued high levels of immigration from Mexico, especially from areas where migrant social networks and a culture and economy of migration have been established. These regions include not only the traditional sending states in the western central region of Mexico—Zacatecas, Guanajato,

Michoacan, Jalisco—but also more recent sending areas, including the states of Oaxaca, Puebla, Guerrero, and Mexico City itself (Cornelius 1991). This being said, the two sections below consider economic and political factors that may affect migration from Mexico and policies proposed to address it.

ECONOMIC DEVELOPMENT AND MIGRATION: NAFTA AND MAQUILADORAS AS "SOLUTIONS" TO "ROOT CAUSES" The North American Free Trade Agreement (NAFTA), and to a lesser extent *maquiladoras* (border assembly plants), have both been touted as solutions to the "root causes" of Mexican migration to the U.S. Former Mexican President Salinas promoted NAFTA by arguing that Mexico could export tomatoes or tomato pickers, and the Bush and then Clinton administrations supported this view, arguing that NAFTA and the economic development it would spur would remove the "root causes" of migration in the long term. While there may be some truth to such statements in the long run, they distort or misunderstand both the relationship of migration to economic development and to trade liberalization, and the limits of the potential impact on migration of NAFTA and maquiladoras.

The most optimistic estimates of NAFTA's job producing potential are around 60,000 jobs per year in the first decade (Martin 1993), while there will be between 700,000 to 800,000 new workers annually entering Mexico's labor force until the year 2010, when demographic pressures will decrease (Garcia y Griego 1989). This limited job creation potential also contrasts with the estimated 3 million immigrants from Mexico to the U.S. between 1981 and 1995, which amounted to about 20 percent of Mexico's net population growth in the period (Martin and Taylor 1995: 1).

Moreover, there is considerable evidence to support the notion that economic development migration *induces* migration (national and international), and that uneven development, as is likely to take place in Mexico, is especially likely to do so (e.g., Massey 1991; Massey et al. 1987; Portes and Walton 1981; Sassen 1988, 1991, 1996). A main reason economic development causes migration is because mechanization and industrialization decrease the ratio of capital to labor, as fewer workers can do the work of many, and increasing numbers become redundant. Moreover, evidence suggests that trade liberalization—which is what NAFTA is between Mexico and the U.S.—leads to increases in migration, and the lower the income of the sending country relative to the receiving country, the larger the effect (Schiff 1994). Indeed, a critical period in the development of migration from Mexico was during the 1960s and 1970s, when Mexico's economy grew around 6 percent annually.

NAFTA is part of a broader process of economic integration between Mexico and the U.S., which is likely in the foreseeable future to exacerbate Mexico's uneven development. Regarding NAFTA, an important question is where investments will be made. They are most likely areas with good physical infrastructure, skilled workforces, and access to either export or domestic markets. Yet many migrant sending areas lack precisely these attributes. Paralleling what happened in the U.S.—where for example, western Appalachia remained very poor despite development in the New South—backward regions in Mexico will continue to supply labor to other parts of Mexico or the U.S. and will be juxtaposed with increasingly modern and prosperous regions. The extremely marginalized Mixteca region in the states of Puebla, Oaxaca, and Guerrero (Presidencia de la Republica 1983) is a relatively new sending area that is unlikely to get much NAFTA investment. Migrant sending areas that do have such conditions will likely get some new investment, whether linked to NAFTA or not. Indeed, migrants themselves are more likely to invest in such regions (Massey et al. 1987; Massey and Durand 1992). However, such investment is not likely to substantially reduce migration because of its self-perpetuating dynamic.

Hence, the best strategy for inhibiting emigration is to invest in areas that have good infrastructure, skilled workforce, and good market access, *but no strong tradition of migration*. The effectiveness of such a strategy would also depend on the establishment of backward linkages with the rest of the economy and the offering of adequate wages and working conditions superior to those found, for example, among *maquilas* (e.g., maquiladoras) at the border. The lack of such linkages has made maquilas a weak development strategy and a weak alternative to migration. Cornelius (1990) found that three-fourths of potential migrants in sending villages were considering going to the U.S., while only one-fourth contemplated a move within Mexico, and only 7 percent move to the border where most maquilas are located. Most maquila workers have little hope of advancement through internal career ladders or of making more money in the future (Salzinger 1996).

Moreover, evidence suggests that maquila employment at the border may be linked to increasing U.S.-bound migration. Whereas studies done in the early and late 1980s (Carillo 1990; Seligson and Williams 1980) found that only 15 percent of maquila workers said that they planned to go to the U.S., Pinal Calvillo's 1995 survey of five hundred maquila workers found that 49.5 percent planned to do so, and that two-thirds of this group had previously worked in the U.S. One important cause of this change is the increasing number of males and internal migrants working in maquiladoras. One strategy to deal with this trend might be to locate future maquiladoras deeper in Mexico's interior, where it would arguably do less to induce international migration and would also be more likely to increase linkages with the rest of the economy (Cordera Campos and Gonzalez Tiburcio 1991).

There is evidence to suggest that NAFTA itself could contribute to increased migration to the U.S. via two paths. First, NAFTA includes provisions for the elimination of corn subsidies in Mexico. Corn is a staple of the Mexican diet, and is used to make tortillas. Studies analyzing the migration effects of rural displacement as corn prices fall in Mexico estimate that between 600,000 and 800,000 farmers—about 15 percent of the economically active population in agriculture—would ultimately migrate to the U.S. (de Janry et al. 1994: 6; Heppel and Torres 1995: 16; Hinojosa-Ojeda and Robinson 1992). Even those who argue this displacement would be less because most corn production is for consumption and not sale concede that between 28 percent and 43 percent of corn producers in various states would be put at risk of economic loss and migration by the elimination of subsidies (de Janry et al. 1994).

It has been suggested that displaced corn producers might move into the rapidly growing export fruit and vegetable industry in Mexico, which has grown greatly and is likely to receive substantial investment with NAFTA. However, Zabin and Hughes (1995) found that working in export agriculture in northern Mexico facilitated the development of social networks into American agriculture for Oaxacan migrants, who subsequently went to California and Oregon. As one employer put it: "We're a school for el Norte ... after two or three years outside their pueblo, they go to the United States" (1995: 413). While not all export agriculture is likely to lead to migration, such investment in the northern states or others with network links to the U.S. is likely to do so.

Finally, inhibiting migration would require several decades of sustained economic growth to narrow the wage gap with the U.S. and reverse pessimism among Mexican youth regarding their futures in Mexico. As Weintraub (1989) points out, a growth rate as high as 5 percent per year would only yield an increased income of about $75 for the average Mexican, an amount unlikely to keep them in Mexico but which perhaps might help fund a trip to the U.S. Doing a comparative analysis with the western European experience, Martin and Cornelius (1993) argue that there is a "hope factor" that inhibits migration when wages between the countries of destination and origin reach a factor of 4:1 or 5:1. In this case, would-be migrants stay at home because they have a reasonable hope things will improve. This situation was achieved in Italy, in part through massive developmental grants from the rest of the European community. Comparable grants from the U.S. to Mexico would equal about 15 billion per year, an unlikely event at best (Martin and Taylor 1995). Moreover, Gregory (1991: 96) argues that on the basis of pre-NAFTA calculations, it would take ninety-three years for Mexico's per capita income to reach half that of the U.S. The current ratio of legal minimum wages in Mexico and the U.S. is 13:1 or 14:1.

All this is not to say that we should not have NAFTA—especially if the side agreements on labor and the environment are enforced, and eventually incorporated into NAFTA itself—or that we should not encourage investment in Mexico. To the contrary, fixed investments in Mexico are more stable than highly mobile investment capital. This analysis is a plea for a more realistic set of expectations regarding the effects of such a policy on migration. While we should pursue economic integration with Mexico as we have been doing, we should not create unrealistic expectations regarding its limited ability to reduce the desire to migrate.

POTENTIAL MIGRANT OR REFUGEE CREATING DEVELOPMENTS IN
MEXICO: POLITICAL OR ECONOMIC INSTABILITY Mexico faces a situation
of political and economic uncertainty that poses challenges to U.S. policy.
Moreover, as in the case of with Central America and the Caribbean, the
relationship between foreign policy goals and immigration policy goals is
not always clear and can sometimes be conflictual. Below, I discuss how
these issues might contribute to economic instability, migratory pressures
or refugee flight.

Mexico's economic system has experienced profound change on a
neo-liberal model that has made certain sectors of the economy more
competitive in the global market, and which its authors believed would
produce prosperity for all. While the strategy for economic development
is clear—integration with the U.S. and opening to the world economy—
the prospects for real development for most Mexicans are dim. Indeed,
the government's own figures show that more than half the population—
some 50 million Mexicans in 1997—had incomes one could describe as
living in poverty, and some 25 percent of the population lived in
"extreme poverty" (Censo INEGI 1995; Cuarto Informe 1998; Dussel
Peters 1998). One must note, however, that while another course might
have had fewer negative redistributive effects, it is not clear concretely
what such a course would have been or how it would have been able to
overcome Mexico's dependent debt and development position.

Mexico's political system is experiencing a more successful if incomplete transition, the result of various factors. First, the PRI is still internally riven between those who want to promote democratic reforms and
those who do not, and between those who have benefited from neoliberal
reform and those who have not. Second, strong, organized democratic
opposition has emerged in Mexico for the first time in the PRI's seventy-
year history, leaving a situation in which the PRI's power has eroded but
new rules of the game are still in play and have not been fully institutionalized. Third, the PRI has suffered several important "defections,"
including that of Ricardo Monreal, elected governor of Zacatecas in 1998
as an independent with heavy support from the PRI. Monreal won by
taking a large piece of the Zacatecas PRI machine with him out of the
party, though he has maintained a good relationship with the PRI and
was described to me by a high ranking PRD member as the "PRI incon-
forme"(non-conforming PRI).

The systemic change is dramatic. From a near total PRI monopoly
ten years ago, in June 1997 the opposition governed seven of thirty-two
state governorships, seventeen of thirty-two state municipal capitals,
sixty-four of the 100 most important cities, and 44 percent of the 2,418
municipios (counties), the basic political and administrative unit in Mexico (Amparo Casar and de la Madrid 1998: 43). By some estimates, more
than half of all Mexicans live in an entity governed by the opposition.
The PAN party has been the strongest opposition, and its presidential
candidate, Vicente Fox, was leading in the polls earlier this year. Fox has,

surprisingly, stayed more or less even with the PRI's official candidate, Labastida, even as the PRI mobilizes its electoral machine. The PRD and Cuahutemoc Cardenas will also continue to be important factors in the election. Domestic and international NGOs have made important contributions to this democratization, as have the foreign and domestic media (Dresser 1996). Perhaps most important on the domestic political scene for this transition has been the influence of the IFE (Instituto Federal Electoral), which has been able to foster increasing levels of transparency in elections through the 1990s, which have done much to create the space for the democratic contestation taking place in the 2000 elections. One can compare the greater number of allegations of fraud and recall movements in the 1994 elections with the lesser number in 1999.

Still, serious issues remain. While federal elections and Mexico City elections have been more transparent than in the past, those in rural areas controlled by the PRI are much less transparent. These areas are also losing population, which will ultimately decrease their electoral importance (Imaz 1999). Moreover, the human rights of dissident organizers or opposition candidates are still violated, particularly in places where local or regional caciques power is being contested. Reports of the influence of drug traffickers in 1997–98 in the Mexican government complicate the picture (Guillermoprieto 1996; Olsen 1997). In the Zapatistas (EZLN), and the People's Revolutionary Army (or ERP) there is the emergence of the first serious guerrilla movements since the 1970s (Corro 1997). Regarding immigrants, the PRI's rejection of and failure during the summer 1999 to implement the constitutionally approved right to vote from abroad is disappointing. Much progress has been made, but there is much still to be done.

In this context, the U.S. faces three main challenges. First, U.S. policies should aim to promote economic development and stability in Mexico, while acknowledging that there are limits to the extent that the U.S. can or should attempt to influence Mexican policies. One example of a prudent intervention was U.S. actions in the Mexican peso crisis of Winter 1994–95, which helped avert a deepening or prolongation of the crisis that could have increased migration pressures. Moreover, economic recession in Mexico hurts important sectors of the U.S. economy and worsens the effects of integration with Mexico. A recent study argues that NAFTA has had net positive impacts in terms of job creation in the U.S. for two (1994 and 1996) of its three years in large part because many Mexican exports are in fact made with American exported intermediate inputs. The net U.S. job loss in 1995 was due mainly to the 1995 peso crisis, which decreased the demand for U.S. imports to be used in Mexican exports (Hinojosa-Ojeda et al. 1996: 61).

However, the U.S. has no unambiguous path here, and each path has its own limits and risks. With analyses coming from very different perspectives, the Council on Foreign Relations (1997) and Jorge Castaneda (1996a, 1996b) argue that such bailouts create a "moral hazard": that is, they insulate investors against risks incurred in the market and encourage not only irresponsible management of Mexico's economy but also the cycle of vast overspending in presidential election years (Castaneda 1996a, 1996b; Enriquez 1997). However, the risk of moral hazard must be weighed against the potentially greater consequences of peso instability for economic instability and U.S.-bound migration. In this context, the creation of an "Emergency Financing Mechanism" proposed by the Clinton administration should be seriously considered for Mexico and other countries crucial to American interests. More generalized coordination, or at least communication in each country's macro-economic policies, should also be considered.

Secondly, the U.S. needs to entertain the possibility that local or regional political instability in Mexico could encourage migrant or refugee flows to the U.S. Mexico's attempts to democratize its political system through such measures as recent electoral reform, bump up against the reality of profoundly undemocratic local political and social structures. Indeed, local and regional political bosses and traditional hard-line PRI officials have come to play an increasingly important role in politics as President Zedillo has decentralized power (see, for example, Dresser 1996, 1994; Fox 1996; Kaufman and Trejo 1996). Luis Hernandez Navarro, the editor of the Mexico City newspaper *La Jornada*, writes that "While some believed that the breakdown of PRI rule would promote greater democratization and decentralization in Mexico, the result has actually been a feudalization of power and a dramatic rise in political violence" (1998: 8). He sees an enduring conflict between "a set of political institutions based on top-down corporatist and clientelist relations on the one hand, and an increasingly mature civil society, on the other." A related danger is that the Mexican military could increasingly be used by the elite to quell social conflict and mobilization, as the PRI loses hegemonic control, as per Ronfeldt's (1975) speculation, and as appears to be happening in Chiapas and Oaxaca (Aubry and Inda 1998; Hernandez Navarro 1998; Stahler-Shok 1998).

Two other potentially dangerous and related developments are the increasing influence of drug traffickers and the increasing role of Mexico's military in fighting them and performing other law enforcement functions. One indication of the potential influence of drug cartels is that they reportedly spend up to 60 percent of their $10 billion annual proceeds on corruption, according to Francisco Molina Ruiz, an ex-director of the National Institute to Combat Drugs (Gutierrez 1997; Olson 1997); others speculate that illicit drugs now account for 10 percent of Mexico's GDP. As early as the late 1980s, some observers argued that drug traffickers had established de facto control in certain areas in some Mexican states, or that the military had preempted the civilians as the supreme authority in such regions (Bolis 1985; cited in Camp 1992: 92; Craig 1989). Efforts to fight drugs have escalated since President Zedillo took office in 1994; he had the Mexican Constitution changed to enable military officers to fill top police positions, which they now do in two-thirds of Mexico's states (Olson 1997). Mexican observers warn that this policy exposes the military to corruption and increases the chance that they will become involved in human rights abuses.[5] The virtual "purchase" of General Gonzalez Rebollo, the Mexican drug "czar," by drug traffickers makes such concerns even more compelling. Others argue that drug traffickers have gained an alarming degree of influence within the local, state, and even federal governments, with some speculating that the PRI used drug money to finance its electoral machine when the electoral process became more transparent (Castaneda 1996a, 1996b; Guillermoprieto 1996).[6]

The links between these developments and actual or potential migration and refugee flows are indirect, but merit consideration. The greatest immediate danger with "poli-narcos" in Mexico is not that they will directly challenge the state for control over territory as in Colombia or Peru. Rather, the danger is that they may be able to use money and violence to establish de facto partial or shared control over certain territories and organs of the state, particularly the counter-narcotics forces, army, or special judicial police. The state would thus be "colonized" by the poli-narcos, undermining its sovereignty. The result could be a Colombia-like environment (see Hernandez Navarro 1998: 10) with the constant threat of violence, and risk of eventual challenges to state authority.

Migration is implicated in two ways. First, in areas where there is already a tradition of migration, such a situation could greatly increase it; in areas without such a tradition, high levels of violence might induce people to relocate or flee. Second, in areas where "narcos" have gained local political and economic power, migrants have become directly involved in carrying drugs across the border as *camillos* (camels), in growing marijuana or poppy in Mexico, in manufacturing meta-amphetamines in Mexico and the U.S., and even "transferred" in their jobs from tending marijuana fields in Mexico to tending them in the U.S. (Malkin 1998). Here, the dynamics and irony of the interdependence of the inter-American migration system are quite sharp: America's drug habit has helped foster drug production in Mexico, and that illicit industry is now imbricating itself into Mexican migration streams and being "imported" into the U.S.

Civil conflict is another possible stimulator of migration, including armed groups such as the Zapatistas in Chiapas or the People's Revolutionary Army in Guerrero, Oaxaca, and Puebla. While these conflicts seem to be localized and contained, and while most people who fled the fighting in 1994 were only temporarily displaced (Luevano et al. 1995), tensions in the area are getting worse. The massacre in the municipio of Acteal, Chiapas of forty-seven peasants in December 1997 by pro-PRI paramilitary forces that the police did nothing to stop reflects the growing division between pro-PRI and pro-Zapatista groups in Chiapas (Hernandez Navarro 1998; Stahler-Shok 1998; Aubry and Inda 1998). The potential links with migration to the U.S. are indirect, beginning with significant push forces in Chiapas: extremely unequal distribution of wealth made worse by neoliberal reforms, political repression, and close-knit rural communities (Harvey 1994). What has been lacking is a link between Chiapas and U.S. labor markets. Preliminary evidence for such a link comes in the increasing—though still very small—numbers of Chiapanecos that began to show up in surveys of agricultural workers in 1993, 1994, and 1995.[7] There is the potential here for the fast development of migration networks if the situation in Chiapas continues to deteriorate.

In sum, democracy and human rights in Mexico present challenges to the U.S., including their implications for migration. For many years, democracy and human rights in Mexico have not been top priorities in American foreign policy. If America's southern neighbor did not present an immediate threat of instability, its domestic political situation was treated as an internal matter. However, the U.S. cannot afford to ignore these issues anymore, both for moral reasons and because the democracy and human rights movements have changed Mexican politics significantly (see Dresser 1996). Moreover, economic and political stability in Mexico—two important determinants of migration pressures—will increasingly depend on Mexico's successfully democratizing its political processes, and addressing its urgent social inequality and human rights abuses (See Americas Watch 1990). The U.S. government, international organizations, and groups in American and Mexican civil society must facilitate Mexico's attempts to democratize and indirectly advise it to do so. Moreover, both the U.S. and Mexico must be careful that in their desire to fight the drug trade that they do not cast a blind eye to human and constitutional rights.

Central America and the Caribbean

PEACE, POLITICAL PROCESSES, AND MIGRATION   The political causes of migration and refugee flight in Central America are less severe than they have been since at least before the 1980s. In El Salvador, the peace process has been successful in consolidating democratic institutions since the Peace Accords were signed in 1992. The war has ended, and the FMLN has evolved into an opposition political party contesting elections—and not battles—with the government and its ARENA party. In Guatemala, the government and rebels have recently signed a number of agreements ending the thirty-six-year civil war, including a controversial amnesty agreement that some believe offers virtual impunity to human rights abusers among both government troops and the Guatemalan National Revolutionary Unity (URNG) guerrillas so long as these abuses were committed in connection to the conflict. Still, the agreements are a step toward peace, as is the disbanding in December 1996 of the civilian patrols, which also had questionable human rights records (Popkin 1996). Guerrilla and army units have actually begun the process of decommissioning and "reinserting" themselves back into civilian life (Rohter 1997).

Perhaps most importantly, the end of the Cold War has removed a major cause, if not of the conflicts themselves, then of their escalation and prolongation (Bergerman 1997; Weiss Fagen 1997). Rather than being funneled into the region in support of ideologically opposed combatants, outside support is in the 1990s more likely to be funneled into projects consolidating peace or promoting economic or political development. Indeed, one observer argues that Latin America stands uniquely positioned for democratization and peace in the 1990s, presenting an opportunity and challenge to the U.S. (Farer 1996).

These changes suggest that migration from Central America now lies closer the "economic migrant" pole than the "political refugee" pole on that continuum, though to characterize it as completely one or the other would be to pull it out of its historical context. The most important immediate change is that the reality of Central American-U.S. migration will increasingly be determined by the internal dynamics of settlement in the migration process itself and the processes affecting it, and have somewhat less to do with the political causes of migration as they manifest themselves in Central America through the 1980s. However, this is not to say that the United States need not worry about peace in the region and its potential effects on migration. Indeed, were the peace to break down again and systemic violence to reach former levels, the exodus would be even greater because the immigrant social network pathways to the U.S. are already in place. Hence, aside from compelling moral and foreign policy concerns, the United States interest in deterring unauthorized immigration gives it good reason to do all it can to ensure peace in Central America.

One important way to do this is to support the international organizations that were crucial in creating the peace. The United Nations (UN) was especially important in El Salvador; the Organization of American States and other NGOs were also important. The UN's effectiveness was due in part to the trust engendered by its pre-peace programs. It built on this trust to facilitate negotiations and concrete steps toward peace. The institutional learning of the UN and other agencies in El Salvador benefited their work in Haiti, Guatemala, and elsewhere (Bergerman 1997; Weiss Fagen 1996). In addition to pursuing its interests directly, the United States would spend its money and use its power wisely if it facilitated such institutional development. Such steps might do more to reduce unauthorized migration than many others, and surely cost less than U.S. interventions during the 1980s. Moreover, when the U.S. lags in supporting the United Nations or like institutions, it detracts from work that might ease future migration pressures.

Another issue of particular importance in the post-peace period is the training and professionalization of a civilian police force that replaced the notorious security forces that were unaccountable to civilian authority under the old regime. The U.S. has done well in working with Salvadoran government in training an almost entirely new police force, though too many of these "new" police had or have links with past human rights abuses, and at one point hundreds of former members of the Special Investigative Unit and the Anti-Narcotics Unit were hired, though many later resigned. The U.S. and the international community need to ensure that the Salvadoran elite do not reconvert the police force into a private army (Stanley 1996; see also Farer 1996). Professionalization and stabilization of the judicial system is also important. These recommendations apply for Haiti, and Guatemala and the rest of Central America as well (Call 1995).

ASSESSING POLICY ALTERNATIVES   As with Mexico, economic development in the Caribbean and Central America is often proposed as the solution to the "root causes" of migration. While true on some level, the expectation that policies such as the Caribbean Basin Initiative (CBI) or the establishment of maquiladoras and export zones in these regions will stem migration is misplaced and unrealistic. Moreover, NAFTA may put these regions at a competitive disadvantage relative to Mexico regarding the terms on which they relate to their major export market, the U.S.

Why policies like the CBI have less potential to deter migration is clear from looking at their initial effects. The CBI excludes most of those goods in which Central America or the Caribbean nations have a comparative advantage. Moreover, U.S. legislation only permits imports of goods that are assembled in export zones, a practice that does not foster linkages with producer or other sectors of the economy crucial to fostering a sustainable export development strategy. For example, Guatemalan maquiladoras must use cloth produced and cut in the U.S., which is then assembled in Guatemala and exported to the U.S. Only the value added through labor in Guatemala is subject to tariff. Such a development device cannot foster sustainable development, though it does provide jobs for people who would probably not otherwise have them (Farley 1996; Peterson 1994).

The Caribbean sugar cane industry is an even more pointed example. Sugar producers in the U.S. have a powerful lobby and have been able not only to increase tariffs for Caribbean sugar, but also to continue U.S. government programs importing labor from the Caribbean to cut the cane that is grown in the U.S., mostly in Florida. Indeed, McCoy's (1991) analysis of the effects of tariffs indicates that U.S. exclusionary trade policy on sugar was responsible for the loss of substantial exports and jobs in Caribbean sugar producing nations, and suggests that these losses were large enough to serve as push forces for further out-migration to the U.S.

Maquiladoras are often said to provide promise for economic development in the region that might make migration unnecessary. Some even speculate that Central American maquiladoras could lead to export-led development on the "Asian tiger" model of South Korea, Taiwan, and other NICs, with Central America as the next Near East. This is highly unlikely for several reasons. As discussed earlier, economic development often increases migration, especially if the development is uneven, as is usually the case with export zones. Moreover, Central American maquiladoras face greater competition now than did Asian NICs in their time, though they also have lower labor costs and less organized workers than many Asian NICs (Broad and Cavanagh 1988; Farley 1996; Peterson 1994). Finally, the comparison between Asian and Central American states is specious. The Asian model involves a developmental (though also authoritarian) state, which takes a lead in promoting economic development and guiding the economy, subsidizing and developing promising export industries and ensuring relatively equal distribution of the fruits of economic gain (e.g., Amsden 1985 on Taiwan).

Central American states are not developmental, but rather are increasingly neoliberal, with decreasing social expenditures, private sector driven investment with minimal state involvement, repressive policies toward labor, and very low minimum wages. They also retain their burdensome legacies of large expenditures for military and police forces (e.g., Spence et al. 1997). Hence, maquiladoras in the current context are likely to increase profits for foreign companies (or celebrities) investing there and for local elites who own or have interests in such businesses, but are unlikely to serve as engines for economic growth that will stem migration.

The effects of NAFTA on the Caribbean has been an issue of increasing concern of late. Drawing on World bank reports by Alexander Yeats (1997), the press and Caribbean trade groups argue that NAFTA has had negative effects on Caribbean trade with the U.S. because it gives preferences to Mexico (Rohter 1997). Yeats, drawing on a World Bank working paper (1997), analyzes the effects of Mercosur (a regional trade agreement including Brazil, Argentina, Uruguay, and Paraguay established in 1991) on member countries trade patterns. He concludes that a main effect has been a shift toward "uncompetitive capital-intensive intra-block trade" in which Mercosur consumers pay higher prices for lower quality goods than would have been the case without Mercosur. Effects on migration were not considered.

Yeats's paper offers compelling reason for more research, especially if it inquires directly into the effects of NAFTA on the Caribbean. His work suggests that Regional Trade Agreements (RTAs) like NAFTA do not create jobs and investment, but rather promote job relocation by changing incentives, often with negative consequences. Yet we should be careful not to take Yeats' findings further than he does or than the data can bear. He carefully limits his argument, explicitly excluding from his evaluation of Mercosur the benefits from enhancing political cooperation, lending credibility to reform strategies, or dynamic gains from trade. These are all arguably important elements of North American integration. Were NAFTA found to have an adverse effect on the Central America and the Caribbean, this would not make eliminating NAFTA the only conceivable response. Rather, NAFTA could be extended to include Central America and the Caribbean, a move likely to also promote enhanced political relations between the U.S. and these regions. Secondly, if worldwide trade barriers continue to come down through such arrangements as the Uruguay Round, the effects of increased free trade might greatly outweigh the effects of RTAs like NAFTA.[8] All this points to the need for more empirical research, and the need to be attentive to the possibility of NAFTA's causing adverse effects in the Caribbean.

Conclusion: Implications for Policy and Theory

This chapter began by evoking the image of a "loosely hinged system" to describe the migration system that evolved out of the interaction of economic integration, the domestic and foreign policies of sending and receiving states, and the self-perpetuating nature of the migration process itself. We have reviewed how push and pull forces have developed in Mexico, Central America, and the Caribbean, and in the U.S., and how the effects of domestic and foreign policies and interest groups have combined to create a powerful tendency toward continued high levels of immigration to the U.S. We now discuss some of the theoretical and policy implications of the inter-American migration system for concrete proposals or policies, and broader policy priorities. This chapter has attempted to make a case for the importance of considering causal sequence in systematically analyzing the potential impacts of policy and determining what "causes" and "is causing" migration and what policy to pursue. For example, the Bracero Program facilitated undocumented immigration by strengthening social networks between 1942–64; these networks then made it harder to combat unauthorized immigration later, and helped create a compelling U.S. interest in legalizing its growing undocumented population. Employer sanctions have not worked for many reasons, two of which are that they are greatly underfunded and that many people perceive the employment of undocumented workers to be necessary and largely cost free. A third example is the indirect expulsive effects of U.S. foreign policy in Central America, which contributed to the emergence of a sizeable undocumented Central American population, movements to legalize their status, dependence on their remittances by their countries of origin, and ultimately to a compelling U.S. interest in their being able to stay here and continue to remit money back home. Hence, previous U.S. foreign policy contributed to changed foreign and domestic policy interests that will probably allow these Central Americans to stay. These examples underline the importance of situating events in their historical contexts to understand how events or policies are likely to affect each other in the future.

This chapter also disagrees with the position that unauthorized migration cannot be controlled at all by the state (e.g., Massey et al. 1998) and with those that argue that the problem is simply a lack of political will or underdeveloped state capacity (Freeman 1994; Miller 1994). While these arguments both explain part of the reality, they leave important aspects of the problem unexamined. The lack of political will or state capacity argument fails to recognize that the ability of a democratic state to control undocumented immigration is affected by civil liberties, human rights, practical and financial considerations on the one hand, and the social dimensions of the problem on the other (see Zolberg 1998; Zolberg and Smith 1996). The argument that the state cannot do much to control migration fails to acknowledge what the state is already doing, or how much higher levels might be without these controls, or how the state has in the past been able to control most movement—by for example, militarizing the border, as in Operation Wetback in 1950–51. While such a move today would be seen to have unacceptably high foreign and domestic policy costs that would far outweigh the benefit in terms of stopping migration, it is within the U.S. state's capacity to do this. In evaluating state capacity to control movement, we must consider the often unanticipated consequences of such policies, especially in controlling undocumented immigration.

A central theme in policy debates on immigration in the 1990s in the United States and Europe was undocumented immigration. One response in both places has been to been to increase state capacity to deter or to stop unauthorized immigration (Cornelius et al. 1994). In the U.S., the number of Border Patrol Agents has more than doubled, the INS budget has increased greatly, and the U.S. has built a twelve-foot-high steel wall across a dozen miles of the San Diego sector, traditionally the busiest in the country. Most recently, the U.S. has embarked on an ambitious project called the IDENT system, which will attempt to fingerprint and photograph everyone caught trying to illegally enter the U.S. by crossing its border with Mexico, and put that information into a database. Moreover, it will prosecute selected repeated crossers who, for example, are regularly caught in groups, as this may indicate that they are smugglers. The technology for this project has been successfully tested in smaller locations in Texas, and plans are currently underway to implement it along the whole border (interviews with INS agents by author 1995 and 1996; INS 1986, 1989, 1996). The IDENT system is one of the most comprehensive and insightful attempts to change the routine nature of border crossing by significantly raising the costs of illegal entry.

However, as with the economic development policies discussed earlier, these policies should be watched with reasonable expectations, for two reasons. First, they will do nothing to control the 52 percent of undocumented immigrants that the INS estimates enter the U.S. legally and overstay their visas. Of these, approximately 20 percent are from Mexico, while slightly higher percentages are from Europe and Asia. Secondly, earlier research shows that immigrants who have been detained in attempting to cross into the U.S. are almost never deterred (Koussoudji 1992; Massey and Espinosa 1997; Massey and Singer 1995; Massey et al. 1987). Rather, they attempt repeated crossings until they make it, but then stay even longer in the U.S. because they have incurred more debt in crossing and delayed the start of their earning period in the U.S. Hence, the IDENT system, even if perfectly enforced, would likely meet with the unintended consequence of prolonging an undocumented border crosser's stay. And if the risks for crossing were indeed raised to include a possibility of jail time, or significantly greater monetary cost, the likely consequence would not be to discourage most long-term crossers, but rather to discourage return migration and encourage more long-term settlement and family reunification.

This outcome is even more likely if the IDENT system is enforced at the same time that employer sanctions—the previous "magic policy bullet" for stopping migration—are not: if the real risk lies at the border, undocumented immigrants are most likely to respond by spending less time there and reorganizing their lives and migration habits accordingly. Just as the "amnesty" provisions of the 1986 Immigration Reform and Control Act led to increases in undocumented entry as relatives and friends of newly legalized workers entered and reunited with their families (Massey and Espinoza 1997; Donato, Durand, and Massey 1992), IDENT may have significant unintended consequences.

That the law has these particular unintended consequences reflects the reality of the inter-American migration system. Employer sanctions have been difficult to enforce in the U.S. both because the law relieves employers of responsibility for the authenticity of the documents shown for employment, and because of the woefully inadequate funding for such enforcement. For example, while there are 6.5 million employers in the United States, the Department of Labor can carry out only 30,000 to 40,000 checks of I-9 forms, the document an employer must fill to certify work authorization (see discussion in Zolberg and Smith 1996: 49). These conditions in turn are due to the lobbying of employers, who want access to cheap immigrant labor, and civil liberties and ethnic lobbying groups, who invoke the increasing due process rights of immigrants in democratic states to limit the state's ability to control immigration (Calavita 1992; Freeman 1994; Hollifield 1992; Zolberg 1990). Moreover, American resistance to a verifiable ID card for employment makes enforcing sanctions even harder. Yet even in France, where such an ID card has long been required and supported, sanctions are hard to enforce, in part because even enforcement agents see unauthorized employment as a victimless crime, and hence are hesitant to enforce sanctions even when they catch employers in violation (Marie 1994).

Operation Hold the Line at the U.S.-Mexico border works at least in some aspects as intended. Begun in Texas in September 1993 and still in effect, the program concentrates enforcement at the border by massing Border Patrol agents and resources on the border itself, thus attempting to deter illegal entry and representing a significant change in strategy. Its successes have been to reduce petty crime (the victims of which were mostly other undocumented aliens, see Wolf 1987), and to improve relations between the Border Patrol and local Latino communities by moving

the site of enforcement out of their neighborhoods and back to the border.[9] It has also decreased the number of unauthorized "commuters,"
who cross the border to sell wares in El Paso's streets or to work as
maids. However, its deterrent effect on long-term migrants has decreased over time, and its main effect now seems to be to have moved
the place they cross away from El Paso itself, out into the surrounding
desert (Bean et al. 1994). As with IDENT, if the costs of crossing are
raised permanently, the likely effect for many immigrants will be to
increase the length of stay of undocumented immigrants, or to accelerate family reunification.

Another consequence of the new policy has been a significant
increase in the numbers of deaths of border crossers at the U.S.-Mexico
border and an increase in other dangers, and particularly for women the
risk of rape (Hagan and Hernandez 1998). The Border Patrol's humane
response has been to train its personnel in first aid and to carry Gatoraid
and ice packs in order to help save more of the people it finds. More
needs to be done to ensure that the human costs of this policy are sharply
limited. Especially if the long-term deterrent effects of Hold the Line are
small, the policy should be reviewed. Decreasing slightly the numbers of
undocumented workers hardly seems worth the cost of an increase in
deaths at the border.

In conclusion, four broad points are in order. First, we must have
realistic expectations about immigration and the likely effects of policies
addressing it. That the U.S. is likely to have continued high levels of
immigration for the foreseeable future does not mean that immigration to
the U.S. is "out of control." Rather, it means that given the limits that
Americans are likely to put on enforcement, and the systemic causes of
migration, we should adjust our expectations regarding the extent to
which the U.S. can completely control unauthorized immigration. This
analysis of inter-American migration stresses that most policies will have
unintended consequences, many of which we can anticipate if we think
more systemically. Finally, we should consider the extent to which
attempts to control it so completely are worth the added financial, human, or civil liberties costs especially if the returns are marginally
decreasing numbers of undocumented immigrants, and if without such
measures the numbers are not greatly increasing. We must question the
net "value added" for such policies.

Second, a new look at the developmental potential of remittances in
home countries and in the U.S. is in order. Given the tremendous and
growing importance of remittances in the economies of sending states
(Alarcon et al. 1998; de la Garza et al. 1997), and their often positive
developmental consequences (Durand et al. 1996), designing ways to
encourage their productive investment seems a wise move. Creating an
inter-American financial institution with offices in the U.S. and in
affected areas of sending countries through which immigrants could
remit their savings more safely and cheaply than through messenger or

wire services might be one step. Another could be creating programs or conditions for investment in productive activities in the home country, by for example, state or international investment in infrastructure on the European Union model, or creating new links with the U.S. or regional markets. Moreover, given the volume of remittances and the location of most migrants in poor, minority neighborhoods, ways could be found to make this money work both for Latinos in the U.S. and for home countries (de la Garza et al. 1997).

Third, U.S. policy should make democracy, respect for the rule of law, and just economic development priorities in its foreign policy in Latin America, for principled and pragmatic reasons. The kinds of institutions that govern Latin America and develop its economy have had and will continue to have important impacts on migration pressures in the region. One important way that the U.S. can promote democratization and political stability in the region is to use its position as the most powerful country in the hemisphere to *make aid and access to U.S. markets conditional on human rights progress.* This move is likely to get the attention of Central American and Mexican elites in a globalizing market (Farer 1996). However, the U.S. would be wise to act as much as possible through international institutions, especially in Central America. While in the past the U.S. has been able to practice its foreign policy with a "big stick" in the Caribbean and Central America, the results of such policies today are uncertain, and may help create "feet" or "boat people." With respect to Mexico, too, the U.S. should take prudent steps to ensure that respect for law, democracy, and human rights are policy priorities. Failure to do so may eventually "show up" in the form of increasing unauthorized migration to the U.S.

Finally, the U.S. needs to pay more attention to the model of economic integration it pursues with respect to Central America and the Caribbean. Neo-liberal integration, like NAFTA, is likely to promote more out-migration in the short to medium term. But the European experience shows that another model can work. As discussed above, integration of less developed countries into the European Union happens over a period of time and is preceded by large infusions of aid (decreasing over time) to the less developed countries to improve infrastructures and change the structures of their economies (Martin and Taylor 1995: 7). Such policies enabled the European Union to integrate Italy in the 1960s without the feared mass exodus to other countries despite the presence of well-established migrant networks; Italy is now a country of immigration (Zolberg and Smith 1996). Ireland's integration experience in the 1990s is similar. This comparison must take note of important differences between the two cases, especially the greater developmental distance between the U.S. and Mexico than between the north and south of Europe, and a lack of other migration options for Mexicans and Central and South Americans today that the southern Europeans had, specifically migration to the Americas. While wholesale adoption of the European model may not be feasible for the U.S., the success of this other model and the predictable increase in migration pressures that NAFTA-like integration will cause make compelling the case for an alternative model of integration. Politically, the closer engagement that integration entails could have very positive impacts on the democracy, human rights, and the rule of law, and ultimately help decrease migration pressures.

Notes

The second section of this chapter draws extensively on Zolberg and Smith (1996). I wish to thank Aristide Zolberg, Peter Benda, and Christopher Mitchell, the members of the Pew Working Group on Migration, and an anonymous reviewer for their helpful comments on an earlier version of this chapter. My thanks to The Pew Charitable Trusts for its support in this project. This chapter also draws on research commissioned by the U.S. State Department, Bureau of Population, Refugees and Migration, May 1996; and research supported by the Social Science Research Council and the Rockefeller Foundation; the William and Flora Hewlett Foundation and the Institute for Latin American and Iberian Studies at Columbia University; the Tinker Foundation and El Colegio de la Frontera Norte; and the International Center for Migration, Ethnicity and Citizenship at the New School for Social Research.

1. The "declining quality" of recent immigrants is the argument of George Borjas (1994, 1996). The most persuasive answer to Borjas I have seen is Dowell Myers (1998). On migration and development, see work by Papademetriou and Martin (1991), Ethier (1986), and Durand et al. (1996). A good summary of most aspects of the debates on immigration, including the assimilation of new immigrants, is contained in Isbister (1996). Calavita (1996) has an insightful discussion of why the fiscal costs of immigration have been used to frame anti-immigrant sentiment today, as opposed to their previous framing as strikebreakers or anarchists.

2. The World War II program was actually the second Bracero Program, with a previous one begun during World War I that ran from 1917–20. See Kiser and Kiser (1978).

3. For more extensive treatments on the relationship between U.S. foreign policy and immigration, readers are directed to an insightful book on the topic, Teitelbaum and Weiner's *Threatened Peoples, Threatened Borders: World Immigration and U.S. Policy* (1995); to Myron Weiner's *International Migration and Security* (1993); and to the work of Charles Keely (e.g., in Teitelbaum and Weiner [1995]).

4. Many speculate that Clinton's hard line on Haitian boat people was related to the negative consequences that the Cuban "Marielitos" riots had had for him in Arkansas in the early 1980s when running for reelection as governor.

5. This is the opinion of Jorge Chabat, Director of the International Studies Division of the Economic Research and Instruction Center (CIDE), as expressed in the article by Corro (1997). One should note that Chabat does *not* recommend

that the military not become involved in such areas if there is clear danger. Rather, he recommends that institutions to guarantee human rights be strengthened or created. For thoughtful discussions about national security in Mexico, see the book edited by Bruce Bagley and Sergio Aguayo Quezada *Mexico: In Search of Security* (1993), a translation from the Spanish version published in 1990. On the Mexican military in general, see Camp (1992), Pineya (1989), Ronfeldt (1975, 1984), and Wager (1994). Potentially the most important aspect of the increased military involvement in anti-drugs efforts is that it could change the long tradition of Mexican noninvolvement in political and civic life (with important exceptions in keeping rural order, in industrial disputes, and in Tlalteloco in 1968; see Camp 1992 and Ronfeldt 1975). While the Mexican military has been involved in anti-drugs campaigns since at least the mid-1940s (Wager 1994), its efforts and U.S. pressure increased in the late 1970s and through the 1980s, but have escalated again since President Zedillo took office in 1994. Zedillo changed the Mexican Constitution to enable military officials to fulfill top police positions, which they now do in two-thirds of Mexico's states (Olson 1997). Government officials argue that this is necessary because drug traffickers are armed with military caliber weapons against which the police are ill-equipped and ill-trained to fight. Mexican observers warn that this policy exposes the military to corruption and increases the chances they will become involved in human rights abuses, especially given the extensive influence of drug cartels.

6. Paternostro (1995) reports that as far back as 1988, a cousin of Juan Garcia Abrego (leader of one of the three drug cartels) was put in the U.S. Witness Protection Program after testifying that he had personally paid off Mexico's deputy Attorney General, Javier Coello Trejo, not to investigate drug activity. Moreover, the special counter-narcotics advisor to the Mexican Attorney General in 1993 and 1994 resigned his post in protest to what he saw as a lack of interest on the Attorney General's part in investigating drug corruption in the government or in prosecuting drug cases. Other evidence of corruption includes shoot-outs between federal judicial police protecting drug shipments and local police trying to capture them, as reported in the magazine *Proceso*, and in Castaneda (1996a, 1996b) and Guillermoprieto (1996). Moreover, recently declassified material from the U.S. National Security Archives indicates that the U.S. has been aware of narco-corruption at high levels in Mexico for some time (Puig 1997). Most shocking are recent allegations in *Proceso*, a leading Mexican magazine that is critical of the government, of high-level corruption and links between drug traffickers and Raul Salinas, the former president's brother, with the assassinations of the PRI's second ranking official, Mario Ruiz Massieu, and the 1994 PRI presidential candidate, Luis Donaldo Colosio (Marin 1997a, 1997b; see also Dillon 1997). Some observers allege that the PRI may have turned to drug traffickers to finance its electoral machine as the electoral process became more transparent (Castaneda 1996a, 1996b; Guillermoprieto 1996). Whatever the reality, this is an area of increasing concern for the U.S.

7. The Chiapanecos I interviewed were working and traveling in the same migrant streams with Guatemalans, leading me to speculate that the Chiapanecos came with the help of Guatemalan migrants or former refugees coming through the area who may have received assistance in Chiapas (on Mexico's border with Guatemala) as refugees themselves during the 1980s. Regarding the ERP, the potential for migration here is less, though this group

presents a more potent threat to civil peace in Mexico because of its greater organization and links with guerrilla groups of the 1970s (Corro 1997).

8. Such was predicted to be the case for NAFTA's effects on East Asian exports, which in 1994 were estimated to be a loss of up to $700 million, a figure that represented just 1 percent of the gains they stood to make through the implementation of the Uruguay Round of trade agreements (Primo Braga, Safidi and Yeats 1994).

9. Enforcement at El Paso High School, where Latino students were allegedly asked for immigration documents, is reported to have especially irked the local community. Support for Operation Hold the Line is suggested by the fact that local community members hung a "Viva Silvestre!" poster in El Paso, referring to Silvestre Reyes the chief of the El Paso Border Patrol who initiated Operation Hold the Line. De la Garza attributes this support to the feeling on the part of the community that Reyes strategy acknowledged that they were directly affected by enforcement, and that Reyes attempted to improve that situation by moving the site of enforcement out of their neighborhood (de la Garza 1996).

References

Aguayo, Sergio, and Patricia Weiss Fagen. 1988. *Central American Refugees in Mexico and the United States*. Washington D.C.: Hemispheric Migration Project, Center for Immigration Policy and Refugee Assistance, Georgetown University.

Alarcon, Diana. 1994. *Changes in the Distribution of Income in Mexico and Trade Liberalization*. Tijuana: El Colegio de la Frontera Norte.

Alarcon, Rafael. 1992. "Nortenizacion: Self-Perpetuating Migration from a Mexican Town." In *U.S.-Mexican Relations: Labor Market Interdependence*, edited by J. Bustamante, C. Reynolds and R. Hinojosa-Ojeda. Stanford: Stanford University Press.

Alarcon, Rafael, David Runsten, and Raul Hinojosa-Ojeda. 1998. "Migrant Remittance Transfer Mechanisms Between Los Angeles and Jalisco, Mexico." *Research Report Series # 7*. North American Integration and Development Center, University of California, Los Angeles.

Alba, Francisco. 1978. "Mexico's International Migration as a Manifestation of its Development Pattern." *International Migration Review* 12, 4.

———. 1989. "The Mexican Demographic Situation." In *Mexican and Central American Population and U.S. Immigration Policy*, edited by F. Bean, S. Weintraub, and J. Schmandt. Austin: University of Texas at Austin Center for Mexican American Studies.

Aleinikoff, Alex. 1994. "United States Refugee Law and Policy: Past, Present and Future." In *International Migration, Refugee Flows, and Human Rights in North America: The Impact of Trade and Restructuring*, edited by Allan B. Simmons. Staten Island, N.Y.: Center for Migration Studies.

Ambriz, Agustin. 1997. "Informe militar sobre el general Gutierrez Rebollo: otros oficiales del Ejercito, agentes y comandantes del INCD y de la PGR, complices de Amado Carillo." *Proceso* 1060 (23 February).

Americas Watch. 1990. *Human Rights in Mexico: A Policy of Impunity*. New York: Americas Watch.

Amparo Casar, Maria, and Ricardo Raphael de la Madrid. 1998. "Las elecciones y el Reparto del Poder." *NEXOS* 247 (July).

Amsden, Alice. 1985. "The State and Taiwan's Economic Development." In *Bringing the State Back In*, edited by Peter Evans, Dietrich Rueschemeyer, and Theda Skocpol. New York and London: Cambridge University Press.

Andreas, Peter. 1997. "Policing the Clandestine Side of Economic Integration." In *The City and The World: New York's Global Future*, edited by Margaret Crahan and Alberto Vourvoulias-Bush. New York: Council on Foreign Relations Press.

Aubry, Andres, and Angelica Inda. 1998. "Who are the Paramilitaries?" In *North American Congress on Latin America: Report on the Americas* 31, 5.

Bach, Robert. 1978. "Undocumented Migration and the American State." *International Migration Review*.

Bagley, Bruce, and Sergio Aguayo Quezada. 1993. *Mexico: In Search of Security*. New Brunswick, N.J.: Transactions Publishers (translation from a Spanish language version published in 1990).

Basch, Linda, Nina Glick-Schiller, and C. Blanc-Stanton, eds. 1994. *Nations Unbound*. Gordon and Breach Publishers.

Bean, F. R. Chanoe, R. Cushing, R. de la Garza, G. Freeman, C. Haynes, and D. Spenner. 1994. *Illegal Mexican Migration and the United States/Mexican Border: The Effects of Operation Hold the Line*. Austin: Population Research Center, University of Texas.

Bean, Frank, Jurgen Schmandt, and Sidney Weintraub, eds. 1994. *Mexican and Central American Population and U.S. Immigration Policy*. Austin: University of Texas at Austin Center for Mexican American Studies.

Bergerman, Susan. 1997. "The Evolution of Compliance: Domestic Politics, Transnational Networks and United Nations Peacebuilding." Doctoral Dissertation, Columbia University.

Bolis, Guillermo. 1990. *Friends or Strangers: The Impact of Immigrants on the American Economy*. New York: Basic Books.

———. 1996. "The New Economics of Immigration." *Atlantic Monthly* (November).

———. 1999. *Heaven's Door: Immigration Policy and the American Economy*. Princeton, N.J.: Princeton University Press.

Bolis, Guillermo M. 1985. "Los militares en Mexico (1965–85)." *Revista Mexicana de Sociologia* 47 (January–February).

Bouvier, Leon F. 1992. *Peaceful Invasions: Immigration and Changing America*. Washington: Center for Immigration Studies.

Broad, Robin, and John Cavanagh. 1988. "No More NICs." *Foreign Policy* 72 (Fall).

Brubaker, Rogers. 1994. "Are Immigration Control Efforts Really Failing?" In *Controlling Immigration: A Global Perspective*, edited by W. Cornelius, P. Martin, and J. Hollifield. Stanford: Stanford University Press.

Brubaker, W. Rogers, ed. 1989. *Immigration and the Politics of Citizenship in Europe and North America*. Washington D.C.: German Marshall Fund of the United States and University Press of America.

Bustamante, Jorge A. 1994. "Migration and Immigrants: Research and Policies." SOPEMI report from Mexico.

Bustamante, Jorge A., Rodolfo Corona, and Jorge Santibanez. 1995. *Encuesta Sobre La Migracion en le Frontera Norte*. Tijuana: El Colegio de la Frontera Norte.

Bustamante, Jorge, C. Reynolds, and R. Hinojosa-Ojeda, eds. 1992. *U.S.-Mexican Relations: Labor Market Interdependence*. Stanford: Stanford University Press.

Calavita, Kitty. 1992. *Inside the State: The Bracero Program and the INS*. New York: Routledge.

———. 1996. "The New Politics of Immigration: 'Balanced Budget Conservatism' and the Symbolism of Proposition 187." *Social Problems* 43, 3: 285–306.

Call, Charles T. 1995. *Demilitarizing Public Order: The International Community, Police Reform and Human Rights in Central America and Haiti*. Washington: The Washington Office on Latin America.

Camp, Roderic Ai. 1992. *Generals in the Palacio: The Military in Modern Mexico*. New York: Oxford University Press.

———. 1993. *Politics in Mexico*. New York: Oxford University Press.

Carillo, M. 1990. *The Impact of Maquiladoras on Migration in Mexico*. Washington D.C.: Commission for the Study of International Migration and Cooperative Economic Development in Mexico.

Casillas, Rodolfo. 1995. "Central American Migration to Mexico in the Era of NAFTA." *Pew Monograph Series #1*, edited by Stewart Lawrence. Washington D.C.: Georgetown University.

Castaneda, Jorge. 1996a. *The Mexican Shock: Its Meaning for the United States*. New York: New Press.

———. 1996b. "Mexico's Circle of Misery." *Foreign Affairs* (July / August).

Castillo, Manuel Angel. 1995. "Immigration in Mexico: A Policy Brief." *Pew Monograph Series #1*, edited by Stewart Lawrence. Washington D.C.: Georgetown University.

Connelly, Matthew, and Paul Kennedy. 1994. "Must It be the West against the Rest?" *Atlantic Monthly* (December).

Cordera Campos, Rolando, and Enrique Gonzalez Tiburcio. 1991. "Crisis and Transition in the Mexican Economy." In *Social Responses to Mexico's Economic Crisis of the 1980s*, edited by Mercedes Gonzalez de la Rocha and Agustin Escobar Latapi. La Jolla: Center for U.S.-Mexico Studies.

Cornelius, Wayne. 1991. "Los Migrantes de la Crisis: The Changing Profile of Mexican Migration to the United States." In *Social Responses to Mexico's Economic Crisis of the 1980*, edited by Mercedes Gonzalez de la Rocha and Agustin Escobar Latapi. La Jolla: Center for U.S.-Mexico Studies.

———. 1992. "From Sojourners to Settlers." In *U.S.-Mexican Relations: Labor Market Interdependence*, edited by J. Bustamante, C. Reynolds, and R. Hinojosa-Ojeda. Stanford: Stanford University Press.

Cornelius, Wayne, and Philip Martin. 1993. *Trade and Migration: NAFTA*. La Jolla: Center for U.S. Mexico Studies.

Cornelius, Wayne A., Philip L. Martin, and James Hollifield. 1994. *Controlling Immigration: A Global Perspective*. Stanford: Stanford University Press.

Corona Vaquez, Rodolfo. 1995. "Cambios en la Migracion de Indocumentados a Estado Unidos en los Ultimos Anos." Manuscript.

Corro, Salvador. 1997. "Al minimizar al EPR, Zedillo incurre en los mismos errores cometidos con el EZLN: Carlos Montemayor." *Proceso* 1057 (2 February).

Council on Foreign Relations. 1996. *Lessons of the Mexican Peso Crisis*. Report of an Independent Task Force. New York: Council on Foreign Relations.

Craig, Richard B. 1989. "Mexican Narcotics Traffic: Binational Security Implications." In *The Latin American Narcotics Trade and U.S. National Security*, edited by Donald Mabry. Westport, Conn.: Greenwood Press.

Cross, Harry, and James Sandos. 1981. *Across the Border: Rural Development in Mexico and Recent Migration to the United States*. Berkeley: University of California Press.

de Janry, Alain, Elisabeth Saduolet, and Gustavo Gordillo de Anda. 1994. "NAFTA and Mexico's Corn Producers." Draft paper.

de la Garza, Rodolfo O. 1980. "Chicanos and U.S. Foreign Policy: The Future of Chicano-Mexican Relations." *Western Political Quarterly* 33, 4.

———. 1982. "Chicano-Mexican Relations: A Framework for Research." *Social Science Quarterly* 63, 2.

———. 1985. "Mobilizing the Mexican Immigrant: The Role of Mexican American Organizations." *Western Political Quarterly* 38, 4.

———. 1996. "Foreign Policy Comes Home: The Domestic Consequences of the Program for Mexican Communities Abroad." Draft paper.

de la Garza, Rodolfo O., and Carlos Vargas. 1992. "The Mexican Origin Population as a Political Force in the Borderlands." In *Changing Boundaries in the Americas*, edited by Herzog. La Jolla: Center for U.S.-Mexico Studies.

de la Garza, Rodolfo O., Manuel Orozco, and Miguel Barona. 1997. "Binational Impact of Latino Remittances" *Policy Brief*, Tomas Rivera Center, Claremont, Cal., and Austin, Texas. March.

Diaz-Briquets, Sergio. 1989. "The Central American Demographic Situation: Trends and Implications." In *Mexican and Central American Population and U.S. Immigration Policy*, edited by F. Bean, S. Weintraub, and J. Schmandt. Austin: University of Texas at Austin Center for Mexican American Studies.

Dillon, Sam. 1997. "Officer Says He Took Bags of Cash to Mexico Anti-Drug Chief." *New York Times*, 13 March.

Dominguez, Jorge I. 1992. "Cooperating with the Enemy? U.S. Immigration Policies Toward Cuba." In *Western Hemisphere Immigration and U.S. Foreign Policy*, edited by C. Mitchell. University Park, Penn.: Penn. State University.

———. 1993. "Immigration as Foreign Policy in U.S.-Latin American Relations." In *Immigration and U.S. Foreign Policy*, edited by Tucker, Keely, and Wrigley. Boulder, Colo.: Westview Press.

Donato, K., J. Durand, and D. Massey. 1992. "Stemming the Tide? Assessing the Deterrent Effects of the Immigration Reform and Control Act." *Demography* 29.

Dresser, Denise. 1991. *Neopopulist Solutions to Neoliberal Problems: Mexico's National Solidarity Program*. San Diego: Center for U.S.-Mexico Studies, University of California, San Diego.

———. 1994. "Bringing the Poor Back In: National Solidarity as a Strategy of Regime Legitimation." In *Transforming State-Society Relations in Mexico: The National Solidarity Strategy*, edited by W. Cornelius, A. Craig, and J. Fox. La Jolla: Center for U.S.-Mexico Studies.

———. 1996. "Treading Lightly and Without a Stick: International Actors and the Promotion of Democracy in Mexico." In *Beyond Sovereignty: Defending Democracy in the Americas*, edited by Tom Farer. Baltimore: Johns Hopkins University Press.

Durand, Jorge, and Douglas Massey. 1992. "Mexican Migration to the United States: A Critical Review." *Latin American Research Review* 27, 2: 3–43.

Durand, Jorge, Emilio Parrado, and Douglas Massey. 1996. "Migradollars and Development: A Reconsideration of the Mexican Case." *International Migration Review* 30, 114.

Dussel Peters, Enrique. 1998. "Recent Structural Changes in Mexico's Economy: A Preliminary Analysis of Some Sources of Mexican Migration to the United States." In *Crossings: Mexican Migration in Interdisciplinary Perspectives*, edited by Marcelo Suarez-Orozco. Cambridge, Mass.: Harvard University Press.

Edelman, Murray. 1964. *The Symbolic Uses of Politics*. Chicago: University of Chicago Press.

Enriquez, Juan. 1997. "Mexico's Cycle of Failure." Op-Ed page, *New York Times*, 11 March.

Espenshade, Thomas. 1993. "Using INS Border Apprehension Data to Measure the Flow of Undocumented Migrants Crossing the Mexico-U.S. Frontier." *International Migration Review* 24, 2.

Estrada, Richard. 1995. "The Dynamics of Assimilation in the United States." In *Identities in North America*, edited R. Earle and J. Wirth. Stanford: Stanford University Press.

Ethier, Wilfred. 1986. "International Trade Theory and International Migrations." *Research in Human Development* 4.

Farer, Tom. 1996. "Collectively Defending Democracy in the Hemisphere: Introduction and Overview." In *Beyond Sovereignty: Defending Democracy in the Americas*, edited by Tom Farer. Baltimore: Johns Hopkins University Press.

———, ed. 1996. *Beyond Sovereignty: Defending Democracy in the Americas*. Baltimore: Johns Hopkins University Press.

Farley, Kathleen A. 1996. "A Study of Non-Traditional Exports and Sustainable Development in Guatemala." Masters Thesis, Economics, University of Wisconsin, Madison.

Fix, Michael. 1991. *The Paper Curtain: Employer Sanctions, Implementation, Impact, and Reform*. Washington D.C.: Urban Institute.

Fix, Michael, and J. Passel. 1994. *Immigration and Immigrants: Setting the Record Straight*. Washington D.C.: The Urban Institute.

Fox, Jonathan. 1996. "The Difficult Transition from Clientelism to Citizenship: Lessons from Mexico." *World Politics* 46, 2.

Freeman, Gary. 1994. "Can Liberal States Control Unwanted Immigration?" In *The Annals of the Academy of Political and Social Science*, edited by Mark Miller. Philadelphia, Penn.: Sage. Vol. 534.

Friedmann, S., N. Lustig, and A. Legovini. 1995. "Mexico: Social Spending and Food Subsidies during the Adjustment in the 1980s." In *Coping with Austerity*, edited by N. Lustig. Washington: Brookings Institution.

Garcia y Griego, Manuel. 1981. *The Importation of Mexican Contract Laborers to the U.S., 1941–64*. La Jolla: Center for U.S. Mexico Studies.

———. 1989. "The Mexican Labor Supply, 1990–2010." In *Mexican Migration to the United States: Origins, Consequences, and Policy Options*, edited by Wayne A. Cornelius and Jorge A. Bustamante. La Jolla, Cal.: Center for U.S. Mexican Studies, University of California San Diego.

———. 1996. Personal communication.

———. 1997. *Managing Migration: The U.S., Mexico and the Bracero Program.* Book manuscript.

Goldring, Luin. 1990. *Development and Migration: A Comparative Analysis of Two Mexican Migrant Circuits.* Commission for the Study of International Migration and Cooperative Economic Development, No. 37, May.

———. 1996. "Blurring Borders: Reflections on Transnational Community." In *Research in Community Sociology,* edited by D. Chekki.

———. 1997. "El estado mexicano y las organizaciones transmigrantes: Reconfiguranod a nacion, ciudadania, y relaciones entre estado y sociedad civil?" Paper presented at XIX Coloquio at El Colegio de Michoacan, Zamora, Michoacan, Mexico, 22–24 October.

Gonzalez de la Rocha, Mercedes, and Agustin Escobar Latapi. 1991. *Social Responses to Mexico's Economic Crisis of the 1980s.* La Jolla: Center for U.S.-Mexico Studies.

Gonzalez-Gutierrez, Carlos. 1993. "The Mexican Diaspora in California: The Limits and Possibilities of the Mexican Government." In *The California-Mexico Connection,* edited by K Burgess and A. Lowenthal. Berkeley: University of California Press.

Graham, Pamela. 1995. "Nationality and Political Participation within the Context of Dominican Transnational Migration." Papers presented at the Latin American Studies Association Meeting and at a Conference on *Caribbean Circuits* at Yale University, September.

Gregory, Peter. 1991. "The Determinants of International Migration and Policy Options for Influencing the Size of Population Flows." In *Determinants of Emigration from Mexico, Central America and the Caribbean,* edited by S. Diaz-Briquets and S. Weintraub. Boulder Colo.: Westview Press.

Grindle, Merilee. 1988. *Searching for Rural Development.* Ithaca: Cornell University Press.

Guarnizo, Luis. 1994. "Los Dominicanyorks: The Making of a Binational Society." In *Annals of the Academy of Political and Social Science.* Sage: Philadelphia, Penn.

———. 1996. "What is New About Transnationalism?: Comparing the Dominican and Mexican Cases." Paper presented at the American Ethnological Society, Puerto Rico.

———. 1997. "De migrantes asalariados a empresarios transnacionales: la economia etnica mexicana en Los Angeles y la transnacionalizacion de la migracion." *Revista de Ciencias Sociales,* Centro De Investigaciones Sociales, Universidad de Puerto Rico, Recinto de Rio Piedras.

———. 1998. "The Rise of Transnational Social Formations: Mexican and Dominican State Responses to Transnational Migration." *Political Power and Social Theory* (Summer).

Guillermoprieto, Alma. 1996. "Mexico: Murder Without Justice." *New York Review of Books,* 3 October.

Hagan, J., and R. Hernandez. 1998. "Death at the Border." *International Migration Review.*

Hagan, Jacqueline, and S. Gonzalez Baker. 1993. "Implementing the U.S. Legalization Program: The Influence of Immigration Policy Reform." *International Migration Review* 27: 513–37.

Hamilton, Nora, and Norma Stoltz Chinchilla. 1991. "Central American Migration: A Framework for Analysis." *Latin American Research Review* 26, 1.

————. 1995. "Social and Economic Aspects of Central American Migration and Return." *Monograph #1.* Center for Multicultural and Transnational Studies, University of Southern California.

Hansen, Roger D. 1971. *The Politics of Mexican Development.* Baltimore: The Johns Hopkins Press.

Harvey, Neil. 1994. *Rebellion in Chiapas.* Transformation of Rural Mexico, Paper #5. La Jolla: Center for U.S. Mexico Studies.

Heppel, Monica, and Luis Torres. 1995. *Mexican Migration and NAFTA: Policy Brief.* Washington D.C.: Inter-American Institute on Migration and Labor.

Hernandez Navarro, Luis. 1998. "The Escalation of the War in Chiapas." *North American Congress on Latin America: Report on the Americas* 31, 5.

Heyman, Josiah. 1995. "Putting Power Into the Anthropology of Bureaucracy: The Immigration and Naturalization Service at the U.S.-Mexico Border." *Current Anthropology* 36.

Hinojosa-Ojeda, Raul, and Sherman Robinson. 1992. "Labor Issues in a North American Free Trade Area." In *North American Free Trade: Assessing the Impact,* edited by N. Lustig, B. Bosworth and R. Lawrence. Washington D.C.: The Brookings Institution.

Hinojosa-Ojeda, Raul, Curt Dowds, Robert McCleery, Sherman Robinson, David Runsten, Craig Wolff, and Goetz Wolff. 1996. *North American Integration Three Years After NAFTA: A Framework for Tracking, Modeling and Internet Accessing the National and Regional Labor Market Impacts.* Report of the Center for North American Integration and Development, University of California, Los Angeles.

Hollifield, James. 1992. *Immigrants, Markets and States: The Political Economy of Postwar Europe.* Cambridge, Mass.: Harvard University Press.

Huerta, Mario Carillo. 1990. *The Impact of Maquiladoras on Migration Working Paper #51.* Washington: U.S. Commission for the Study of International Migration and Cooperative Economic Development.

Immigration and Naturalization Service. 1986. "Develop the Methodology to Measure the Effectiveness of the Border Patrol." Strategic Plan prepared by INS Analyst Karen Hess.

————. 1989. "Apprehension Recidivism in the San Diego Sector. Western Region." U.S. Border Patrol, 29 November.

————. 1996. Status Report on Border Patrol Staffing Models, 28 August.

Isbister, John. 1996. *The Immigration Debate: Remaking America.* West Hartford, Conn.: Kumarian Press.

Jarque, Carlos. 1993. "Informe de la Pobreza en Mexico: 1984–92." Mexico, DF: INEGI.

Kaufman, Robert, and Guillermo Trejo. 1996. "Regionalism, Regime Transformation, and Pronasol: The Politics of the National Solidarity Program in Four Mexican States." *Papers on Latin America.* Institute for Latin American and Iberian Studies, Columbia University.

Kearney, Michael. 1991. "Borders and Boundaries of State and Self at the End of Empire." *Journal of Historical Sociology* 4 (March).

————. 1995. "The Local and the Global: The Anthropology of Globalization and Transnationalism." *Annual Review of Anthropology* 24.

Keely, Charles. 1989. "Population and Immigration Policy: State and Federal Roles." In *Mexican and Central American Population and U.S. Immigration*

Policy, edited by Bean, Frank, Jurgen Schmandt, and Sidney Weintraub. Austin: University of Texas at Austin Center for Mexican American Studies.

———. 1995. "The Effects of International Migration on U.S. Foreign Policy." In *Threatened Peoples, Threatened Borders: World Migration and U.S. Policy*. New York: Norton and Norton.

Keely, Charles, and W. Anderson. 1989. "Remittances from Labor Migration: Evaluation, Performance and Implications." *International Migration Review* 23.

Kennedy, Paul. 1993. *Preparing for the Twenty-First Century*. New York and London: Harper Collins.

Kiser, George, and Martha Kiser, eds. 1978. *Mexican Immigrants in the United States*. Albuquerque: University of New Mexico Press.

Koussoudji, Sherrie. 1992. "Playing Cat and Mouse at the U.S.-Mexico Border." *Demography* 29: 159–180.

Krissman, Fred. 1994. "Comparing the Impacts Upon Mexican Based Bi-National Migrants of Incorporation into Network Based Institutions in California." Paper presented at LASA, Atlanta, Ga.

Kritz, Mary, L. Lean Lim, and H. Zlotnick. 1992. *International Migration Systems: A Global Perspective*. New York: Oxford University Press.

Lozano Ascencio, E. 1993. *Bringing It Back Home: Remittances to Mexico from Migrant Workers in the United States*. Monograph Series, #37. La Jolla: Center for U.S.-Mexico Studies, University of California at San Diego.

Luevano, Alejandro, Rocio Lombera, and Rafael Reygadas. 1995. "Los Desplazados y Afectados por el conflicto militar en Chiapas y los esfuerzos civiles por la paz." Draft paper. Mexico, DF: Academia Mexicana de Derechos Humanos.

Lustig, Nora. 1992. *Mexico: The Remaking of an Economy*. Washington: The Brookings Institution.

———, ed. 1995. *Coping with Austerity*. Washington: The Brookings Institution.

Mahler, Sarah. 1996. "Transnational Migration and Gender: Some Unanswered Questions with Observations from the Salvadoran Case." Paper presented at the American Ethnological Society, Puerto Rico.

Maingot, Anthony. 1996. "Haiti: Sovereign Consent versus State-Centric Sovereignty." In *Beyond Sovereignty: Defending Democracy in the Americas*, edited by Farer, Tom. Baltimore: Johns Hopkins University Press.

Malkin, Victoria. 1998. "Narcotrafficking, Migration and Gender in Rural Mexico: A Case Study of the Tierra Caliente, Michoacan, Mexico." Paper presented at University of Manchester, Conference on "Transnational Communities," 16 May.

Marie, Claude-Valentin. 1994. "From the Campaign against Illegal Immigration to the Campaign against Illegal Work." In *The Annals of the Academy of Political and Social Science*, edited by Mark Miller. Philadelphia, Penn.: Sage.

Marin, Carlos. 1997a. "Testimonios Obtenidos por la Departamento de Justicia: Raul Salinas Lozano, sus hijos Carlos, Raul y Adriana. los hermanos Ruiz Massieu y Colosio, ligados a los principales capos." *Proceso* 1059 (16 February).

———. 1997b. "La defensa de Mario Ruiz Massieu sorprendida por la monstruosidad del nuevo juicio: Juan Collado." *Proceso* 1059 (16 February).

Marshall, Dawn. 1987. "A History of West Indian Migrations: Overseas Opportunities and Safety Valve Policies." In *The Caribbean Exodus*, edited by Barry Levine. New York: Praeger Press.

Martin, Philip L. 1993. *Trade and Migration: NAFTA and Agriculture*. Washington D.C.: Institute for International Economics.

Martin, Philip, and M. Miller. 1982. *Administering Foreign Worker Programs*. Lexington Mass.: Lexington Books.

Martin, Philip, and J. Edward Taylor. 1995. "The Mexican Crisis and Mexico-U.S. Migration." Draft paper.

Massey, Douglas. 1991. "Economic Development and International Migration in Comparative Perspective." In *Determinants of Emigration from Mexico, Central America and the Caribbean,* edited by S. Diaz-Briquets and S. Weintraub. Boulder Co: Westview Press.

———. 1995. "The New Immigration and Ethnicity in the United States." *Population and Development Review* 21, 3: 631–52.

Massey, Douglas, Rafael Alarcon, Jorge Durand, and Humberto Gonzalez. 1987. *Return to Aztlan: The Social Process of Transnational Migration from Western Mexico*. Berkeley: University of California Press.

Massey, Douglas, K. Donato, and Zai Liang. 1990. "Effects of the Immigration Reform and Control Act of 1986: Preliminary Data from Mexico." In *Undocumented Migration to the United States: IRCA and the Experience of the 1980s,* edited by F. Bean, B. Edmonston, and J. Passel. Washington: Urban Institute Press.

Massey, Douglas, and Jorge Durand. 1992. "Mexican Migration to the United States: A Critical Review" *Latin American Research Review* 27, 2: 3–43.

Massey, Douglas, Luin Goldring, and Jorge Durand. 1994. "Continuities in Transnational Migration: An Analysis of Nineteen Mexican Communities." *American Journal of Sociology* 99.

Massey, Douglas, and Audrey Singer. 1995. "New Estimates of Undocumented Mexican Migration and the Probability of Apprehension." *Demography* 32, 2.

Massey, Douglas, and Kristin Espinosa. 1997. "What's Driving Mexico-U.S. Migration? A Theoretical, Empirical and Policy Analysis." *American Journal of Sociology* 102, 4: 939–99.

Massey, Douglas, Joaquín Arango, Graeme Hugo, Ali Kouaouci, Adela Pellegrino, and J. Edward Taylor. 1998. *Worlds in Motion: Understanding International Migration at the End of the Millennium*. New York: Oxford University Press.

McCoy, Terry. 1991. "The U.S. Sugar Industry and Caribbean Migration." Washington, D.C.: Binational Commission on Immigration.

Miller, Mark. 1981. *Foreign Workers in Western Europe: An Emerging Political Force*. New York: Praeger.

———. 1994. "Towards Understanding State Capacity to Prevent Unwanted Migration: Employer Sanctions Enforcement in France, 1975–1990." *West European Politics* 17, 2.

———. 1995. "Employer Sanctions in Western Europe." *U.S. Commission on Immigration Reform*.

Mitchell, Christopher. 1992a. "U.S. Foreign Policy and Dominican Migration to the United States." In *Western Hemisphere Immigration and U.S. Foreign Policy,* edited by C. Mitchell. University Park: Pennsylvania State University Press.

———, ed. 1992b. *Western Hemisphere Immigration and U.S. Foreign Policy*. University Park: Pennsylvania State University Press.

Newland, Kathleen. 1995. "The Impact of U.S. Refugee Policies on U.S. Foreign Policy: A Case of the Tail Wagging the Dog?" In *Threatened Peoples, Threatened Borders: World Migration and U.S. Policy*. New York: Norton and Norton.

Olson, Eric. 1997. "Mexico Drug Fighting Questionable." *Miami Herald*, Op-ed page, 28 February.

Oppenheimer, Andres. 1996. *Bordering on Chaos: Guerrillas, Stockbrokers, Politicians and Mexico's Road to Prosperity*. Little Brown.

Papademetriou, Demetrios, and P. Martin. 1991. *The Unsettled Relationship: Labor Migration and Economic Development*. New York: Greenwood Press.

Passel, Jeffrey. 1995. "Illegal Immigration: How Big a Problem?" Paper presented at the Conference on Latin American Migration: The Foreign Policy Dimension. Washington D.C.: Medidien House.

Paternostro, Silvana. 1995. "Mexico as Narco-Democracy." *World Policy Journal*.

Perotti, R. "Employer Sanctions and the Limits of Negotiation." In *The Annals of the Academy of Political and Social Science* 534, edited by Mark Miller. Philadelphia, Penn.: Sage.

Peterson, Kurt. 1994. "The Maquila Revolution in Guatemala." In *Global Production: The Apparel Industry in the Pacific Rim*, edited by Edna Bonocich, Lucie Cheng, Norma Chinchilla, Nora Hamilton, and Phil Ong. Philadelphia: Temple University Press.

Pinal Calvillo, Sylvia. 1995. "La Industria Maquiladora y la Migracion en Mexico." *Pew Monograph Series*, edited by Stewart Lawrence. Washington D.C.: Georgetown University.

Pineya, Jose Luis. 1985. *Ejercito y Sociedad en Mexico: Pasado y Presente*. Puebla: Universidad Autonoma de Puebla.

Piore, Michael. 1992. "Comment on Hinojosa-Ojeda and Robinson." In Hinojosa.

Popkin, Eric. 1998. "The Economic, Political and Socio-cultural Dimensions of Salvadoran and Guatemalan Transnationalism in Los Angeles." Paper presented at a conference on States and Diasporas, organized by Robert Smith, at Casa Italiana at Columbia University, 8–9 May.

Popkin, Margaret L. 1996. *Civil Patrols and Their Legacy: Overcoming Militarization and Polarization in the Guatemalan Countryside*. Washington: Robert F. Kennedy Center for Human Rights.

Portes, Alejandro. 1979. "Illegal Immigration and the International System: Lessons from Recent Legal Immigrants from Mexico." *Social Problems*, 26.

Portes, Alejandro, and J. Walton. 1981. *Labor Class and the International System*. New York: Academic Press.

Portes, Alejandro, and Robert Bach. 1985. *Latin Journey: Cuban and Mexican Immigrants in the United States*. Berkeley: University of California Press.

Portes, A., and A. Stepick. 1993. *City on the Edge The Transformation of Miami*. Berkeley: University of California Press.

Presidencia de la Republica. 1982. *Geografia de la Marginalizacion en Mexico*. Coordinacion General del Plan Nacional de Zonas Deprimidas y Grupos Marginados Mexico, D.F.

Primo Braga, Carlos A., Raed Safedi, and Alexander Yeats. 1994. "NAFTA's Implications for East Asian Exports." *Policy Research Working Paper 1351*, The World Bank.

Reimers, David. 1985. *Still the Golden Door? The Third World Comes to America*. New York: Columbia University Press.

Repak, Terry A. 1995. *Waiting on Washington: Central American Workers in the Nation's Capital.* Philadelphia: Temple University Press.

Rickets, Erol. 1987. "U.S. Investment and Immigration from the Caribbean." *Social Problems* 34: 374–87.

Robert, Bryan. 1997. "Immigration: The Contradictions of Citizenship and Transnationalism." Paper prepared for UCLA Social Theory Seminar.

Rohter, Larry. 1997. "Guatemala Foes Now Train for Peace." *New York Times,* Tuesday, March 11.

Ronfeldt, David. 1975. "The Mexican Army and Political Order Since 1940." RAND Corporation. Reprinted in *The Modern Mexican Military: A Reassessment,* edited by Ronfeldt. 1984. La Jolla: Center for U.S.-Mexican Studies, University of California, San Diego.

Russell, Sharon Stanton. 1995. "Migration Patterns of U.S. Foreign Policy Interest." In *Threatened Peoples, Threatened Borders: World Migration and U.S. Policy.* New York: Norton and Norton.

———. 1997. Book review of *Controlling Immigration: A Global Perspective,* edited by Cornelius et al., 1994, in *Journal of American Ethnic History.*

Salzinger, Leslie. 1996. "An Ethnographic Comparison of Four Maquiladoras." Talk, Columbia University, Spring.

Sanchez, Arturo Ignacio. 1997. "Transnational Political Agency and Identity Formation Among Colombian Immigrants." Paper presented at Conference "Transnational Communities and the Political Economy of New York City in the 1990s." New School for Social Research.

Sassen, Saskia. 1988. *The Mobility of Capital and Labor.* New York and London: Oxford University Press.

———. 1991. *The Global City: New York, London, Tokyo.* Princeton: Princeton University Press.

———. 1996. *Losing Control? Sovereignty in an Age of Globalization. The 1995 Columbia University Leonard Hastings Schoff Memorial Lectures.* New York: Columbia University Press.

Schiff, Maurice. 1994. "How Trade, Aid and Remittances Affect International Migration." *Policy Research Working Papers,* The World Bank.

Schnieder, Jane. 1995. "Introduction: The Analytic Strategies of Eric R. Wolf." In *Articulating Hidden Histories: Exploring the Influence of Eric R. Wolf.* Berkeley, California: University of California Press.

Schoultz, Lars. 1992. "Central America and the Politicization of U.S. Immigration Policy." In *Western Hemisphere Immigration and U.S. Foreign Policy,* edited by Christopher Mitchell. University Park: Pennsylvania State Press.

Schuck, P. and Rogers Smith. 1985. *Citizenship Without Consent: Illegal Aliens in the American Polity.* New Haven, Conn.: Yale University Press.

Seligson, Mitchell, and Edward Williams. 1981. *Maquiladoras and Migration: A Study of the Workers in the Mexican-United States Border Industrialization Program.* Austin: University of Texas, Mexico-U.S. Border Research Program.

Simcox, David, and Leon Bouvier. 1986. *The Mexican Time Bomb.* Washington: Center for Immigration Studies.

Smith, Michael Peter. 1996. "Transnational Salvadoran Migration." American Ethnological Association Meetings, Puerto Rico.

Smith, Robert C. 1993. "De-Territorialized Nation Building: Transnational Migrants and the Re-Imagination of Political Community by Sending States." Seminar on Migration, the State and International Migration, *Occa-*

sional Papers Series, New York University, Center for Latin American and Caribbean Studies, Spring.

——. 1995. "Los Ausentes Siempre Presentes: The Imagination, Making and Politics of a Transnational Community." Ph.D. diss., Political Science Dept. Columbia University.

——. 1996. "Domestic Politics Abroad, Diasporic Politics at Home: The Mexican Global Nation, Neoliberalism, and the Program for Mexican Communities Abroad." Paper presented at the American Sociological Association Meetings and American Political Science Association Meetings, August.

——. 1997. "Transnational Migration, Assimilation, and Political Community." In *The City and the World*, edited by M. Crahan and A. Vourvoulias-Bush. New York: Council on Foreign Relations Press.

——. 1998a. "Transnational Localities: Community, Technology and the Politics of Membership within the Context of Mexico-U.S. Migration." In *Transnationalism from Below: Journal of Comparative Urban and Community Research*, edited by M. P. Smith and Luis E. Guarnizo, Vol. 6.

——. 1998b. "Transnational Public Spheres and Changing Conceptions of Citizenship, Membership and Nation: Insights from the Mexican and Italian Cases." Paper presented at the University of Manchester, England, Conference on Transnational Communities, 15–16 May.

——. 1998c. "Thick and Thin Membership within a Transnational Public Sphere: Domestic Politics Abroad, Diasporic Politics and Home, and the Program for Mexican Communities Abroad." Draft paper.

——. 1998d. "Reflections on the State, Migration, and the Durability and Newness of Transnational Life: Comparative Insights from the Mexican and Italian Cases." *Soziale Welt*, Sonderband 12. Nomos, Germany.

Soysal, Y. N. 1994. *Limits to Citizenship: Migrants and Postnational Membership in Europe*. University of Chicago Press.

Spence, Jack, David Dye, Miek Lanchin, Geoff Thale, with George Vickers. 1997. *Chapultepec: Five Years Later: El Salvador's Political Reality and Uncertain Future*. Cambridge, Mass.: Hemispheric Initiatives.

Stahler-Shok, Richard. 1998. "The Lessons of Acteal." *North American Congress on Latin America: Report on the Americas* 31, 5.

Stanley, William. 1996. *Protectors of Perpetrators? The Institutional Crisis of the Salvadoran Civilian Police*, edited by George Vickers and Jack Spence. A Joint Report of the Washington Office on Latin America and Hemispheric Initiatives

Stepick, Alex. 1992. "Unintended Consequences: Rejecting Haitian Boat People and Destabilizing Duvalier." In *Western Hemisphere Immigration and U.S. Foreign Policy*, editor C. Mitchell. University Park: Pennsylvania State University.

Teitelbaum, Michael, and Myron Weiner, eds. 1995. *Threatened People, Threatened Borders: World Immigration Policy*. New York: Norton and Norton.

Tello, Carlos. 1991. "Combatting Poverty in Mexico." In *Social Responses to Mexico's Economic Crisis of the 1980s*, edited by Mercedes Gonzalez de la Rocha and Agustin Escobar Latapi. La Jolla: Center for U.S.-Mexico Studies.

Thomas, Robert. 1985. *Citizenship, Gender and Work*. Berkeley: University of California Press.

Tilly, Charles. 1985. *Big Structures, Large Processes, and Huge Comparisons*. New York: Russell Sage Foundation.

Torres-Rivas, Edelberto. 1985. "Report on the Condition of Central American Refugees and Migrants." *Hemispheric Migration Project*. Washington D.C.: Center for Immigration Policy and Refugee Assistance, Georgetown University.

Wager, Stephen. 1994. *The Mexican Military Approaches the 21st Century: Coping with a New World Order*. Carlisle Barracks, Penn.: Strategic Studies Institute, U.S. Army War College.

Warren, Robert. 1995. "Estimates of the Undocumented Immigrant Population Residing in the United States. by County of Origin and State of Residence, October, 1992." Paper presented to the Annual Meeting of the Population Association of America, San Francisco. April.

Weiner, Myron. 1993. *International Migration and Security*. Boulder, Colo.: Westview Press.

Weintraub, Sidney. 1989. "Implications of Mexican Demographic Developments for the United States." In *Mexican and Central American Population and U.S. Immigration Policy*, edited by F. Bean, S. Weintraub, J. Schmandt. Austin: University of Texas at Austin Center for Mexican American Studies.

———. 1990. "The Maquiladora Industry in Mexico: Its Transitional Role." *Commission for the Study of International Migration and Cooperative Economic Development*.

———. 1992. "North American Free Trade and the European Situation Compared." *International Migration Review* 26, 9.

Weiss Fagen, Patricia. 19996. "El Salvador: Lesson in Peace Consolidation." In *Beyond Sovereignty: Defending Democracy in the Americas*, edited by Tom Farer. Baltimore: Johns Hopkins University Press.

Wolf, Daniel. 1987. *Undocumented Aliens and Crime*. La Jolla: Center for U.S.-Mexico Studies, University of California San Diego.

Wolf, Eric R. 1982. *Europe and the People Without History*. Berkeley: University of California Press.

World Bank. 1995. *World Data*. Washington: The World Bank (CD-ROM).

Yeats, Alexander. 1997. "Does Mercosur's Trade Performance Raise Concerns About the Effects of Regional Trade Arrangements?" *Policy Research Working Paper 1729*. The World Bank.

Zabin, Carol, and Allie Hughes. 1995. "Economic Integration and Labor Flows: Stage Migration in Farm Labor Markets in Mexico and the United States." *International Migration Review* 29, 2.

Zimmerman, Warren. 1995. "Migrants and Refugees: A Threat to Security." In *Threatened Peoples, Threatened Borders: World Migration and U.S. Policy*. New York: Norton and Norton.

Zolberg, Aristide R. 1983. "Contemporary Transnational Migration in Historical Perspective: Patterns and Dilemmas." In *U.S. Immigration and Refugee Policy*, edited by Mary Kritz. Lexington, Mass.: Lexington Books.

———. 1989. "The Next Wave: Migration Theory for a Changing World." *International Migration Review* 23, 3. Staten Island, N.Y.: Center for Migration Studies.

———. 1990 "Reforming the Back Door: The Immigration Reform and Control Act of 1986 in Historical Perspective." In *Immigration Reconsidered*, edited by Virginia Yans-McLaughlin. New York: Oxford University Press.

———. 1991. "Bounded States in a Global Market: The Uses of International Migrations." In *Social Theory for a Changing Society*, edited by Pierre

Bourdieu and James Coleman. Boulder: Westview Press/Russell Sage Foundation.

———. 1992. "International Migration and International Economic Regimes: Bretton Woods and After." In *International Migration Systems: A Global Perspective*, edited by Mary Kritz, L. Lean Lim, and Hania Zlotnick. New York; Oxford University Press.

———. 1995. "From Invitation to Interdiction: U.S. Foreign Policy and Immigration Since 1945." In *Threatened Peoples, Threatened Borders: World Migration and U.S. Policy*. New York: Norton and Norton.

———. 1999. "Matters of State: Theorizing Immigration Policy." In *The Handbook of International Migration: The American Experience*. New York: The Russell Sage Foundation.

Zolberg, Aristide R., Astri Suhrke, and Sergio Aguayo. 1989. *Escape From Violence: Conflict and the Refugee Crisis in the Developing World*. New York: Oxford University Press.

Zolberg, Aristide R., and Robert C. Smith. 1996. *Migration Systems in Comparative Perspective: An Analysis of the Inter-American Migration System with Comparative Reference to the Mediterranean-European System*. Report to the U.S. Department of State, Bureau of Population, Refugees and Migration, through the International Center for Migration, Ethnicity and Citizenship at the New School for Social Research.

PART TWO

IMPLICATIONS FOR U.S. POLICY

– Chapter 6 –

PROTECTION AND HUMANITARIAN ACTION IN THE POST–COLD WAR ERA

～～

Gil Loescher

Since the end of the Cold War, a number of humanitarian crises have erupted in scale and intensity. In 1993 alone, "complex emergencies" (crises caused by the combination of civil and political conflicts and natural disasters usually complicated by the breakdown of state authority) affected some 59 million people across the world (UN 1994).

Unlike in the recent past, when conflicts were linked to liberation struggles against colonial domination, external aggression, or superpower rivalry (Zolberg et al. 1989); the majority of these are intrastate conflicts, and many are extremely violent, involve serious violations of human rights, and often result in the targeting and expulsion of entire civilian populations.[1] According to the earlier chapter in this volume by Schmeidl, political violence such as genocide and politicide and civil wars are the most accurate predictors of refugee migration. Recent conflicts in Northern Iraq, Somalia, former Yugoslavia, and Rwanda, for example, have involved protracted humanitarian operations and have each resulted in the displacement of more than a million people. For each of these well-known refugee crises, several other difficult and complex refugee problems can be found somewhere on the globe. For example, returnees resulting from "ethnic cleansing" in the former Soviet Union and the Balkans occasion difficulties for receivers, particularly when they do not come under the refugee regime. Overall, according to the United Nations High Commissioner for Refugees (UNHCR), there are some 12 million refugees and an estimated 23 million internally displaced persons today.

Today's wars are also lasting longer than before as new power structures and parallel economies are created within war societies, making the settlement of conflicts extremely difficult (Duffield 1994).[2] According to Peter Walker of the Federation of Red Cross and Red Crescent Societies, the average humanitarian relief operation today lasts for three to five years (Walker 1996). During the conflict in the former Yugoslavia, for example, UNHCR committed approximately one-quarter of its staff and one-third of its total resources worldwide to providing assistance and protection to nearly four million people.[3] UNHCR risks not only overextending itself because of its involvement in vicious and intractable conflicts, but also exhausting the political interest of donor governments in continuing to fund such protracted operations, even in high profile situations like Bosnia.

Changing International Environment for Humanitarian Action

Humanitarian action itself has undergone considerable change during recent years. Traditionally, the refugee regime approached the refugee problem in a manner which could be characterized as reactive, exile-oriented, and refugee-specific.[4] The UNHCR, for example, primarily worked with people after they had fled across borders to neighboring countries where they required protection and assistance. UNHCR staff concentrated their activities on assisting refugees in camps and negotiating with host and donor governments for support. The Office focused exclusively on the consequences of refugee flows rather than on the causes and paid little or no attention to preventing or averting refugee movements. It placed primary responsibility for solving refugee problems on states that received refugees rather than on states that caused refugees to flee. Hence, UNHCR emphasized local settlement and third country resettlement over repatriation.

In the post–Cold War period, by contrast, refugee crises are seen as matters affecting the security of both sending and receiving states (Loescher 1992). As states have come to view refugee movements as potential threats to international and regional security, UN member states have been willing in some instances to invoke an expanded interpretation of the phrase "threat to peace" in the UN Charter to intervene in internal conflicts involving humanitarian concerns. In recent years, the UN Security Council has thus repeatedly authorized humanitarian interventions both to stave off further conflict and to prevent massive outflows of war-affected populations, and NATO and other regional organizations have become involved in many of the conflicts which generate flows of refugees and internally displaced persons. At the same time, governments have increasingly called upon UNHCR to operate on both sides of borders where there is conflict, to ease tensions, and to assist and protect civilians during fighting and immediately afterwards.

As UNHCR has become deeply enmeshed in complex political situations, an increasing proportion of the agency's operations occur within countries of origin, in zones of active conflict, and often in close association with UN mandated peacekeeping forces. While carrying out these new activities, UNHCR has extended its services to a much wider range of people who are in need of assistance including returnees, internally displaced people, war-affected populations, the victims of mass expulsions, and unsuccessful asylum-seekers as well as refugees. Indeed, in the former Yugoslavia, UNHCR moved away from its usual preoccupation with categorizing refugees as distinct from other civilians suffering the consequences of armed conflict. With the urging and financial support of donors, UNHCR extended assistance to all the casualties of the former Yugoslavia's wars regardless of their physical location or legal standing. "War affected populations," that is people who had not been uprooted but needed humanitarian assistance and protection, comprised a substantial proportion of UNHCR's beneficiary population during the height of that conflict, and the bulk of UNHCR's total budget for the former Yugoslavia was allocated to this group (UNHCR 1995; see Weiss 1996). Worldwide, refugees now constitute less than 50 percent of UNHCR's beneficiaries.[5] Consequently, UNHCR has in many senses expanded from a refugee organization into a more broadly based humanitarian agency.

The changing international environment and the expansion in the categories of people "of concern" to UNHCR signals fundamental changes in the international refugee regime. In contrast to the largely "reactive" Cold War period, the international community now places a greater emphasis on policies that aim to address the underlying causes of the refugee problem in the countries of origin. Governments no longer stress the "right to leave" but now emphasize the "right to remain" and the "right to return." The fundamental principle of this new orientation is that it is the responsibility of governments to ensure that their citizens live in humane and secure conditions with their human rights respected, so that they do not become refugees in the first place, or so that they can safely return home. Another principle is the perception that the international community can avert or ameliorate refugee movements if action is taken to reduce or remove the threats which force people to flee their own country and seek asylum elsewhere. Such policies (which are still more rhetorical than real) include early warning, preventive diplomacy, and ensuring respect for human rights. In an effort to halt conflicts and reduce refugee flows in the last few years, the international community has selectively but increasingly employed interventions in the form of aid, trade and investment conditionality, sanctions, coercive diplomacy, and armed intervention (Dowty and Loescher 1996).

While there have been some successes, the commitment of governments to a preventive approach to address conditions that force people to abandon their homes is still in doubt. Proactive crisis prevention policies are in fact rarely employed by states. Powerful states perceive only minimal interests in most countries involved in internal conflicts and humanitarian crises. During the post–Cold War era, refugees, for the most part, have lost their strategic value. Moreover, early warning is only effective when states are willing to act on such information. Recent experience indicates that the momentum for international intervention to prevent humanitarian crises is difficult to generate until conflict actually breaks out, and comparatively speaking, the amount allocated by donors for conflict prevention is miniscule. The bulk of resources disbursed in this area today by governments go into peacekeeping/enforcement and the militarization of humanitarian interventions.

The pitfalls of a preventive approach for the protection of refugees are also becoming evident, particularly for humanitarian agencies. In the new international political environment, UNHCR is unable to make decisions solely on the basis of international legal norms which have been the guide for its work in the past. Given the tendency of governments to limit the number of refugees through new solutions such as prevention, safe areas, and imposed return to situations where there are ongoing conflicts and human rights abuses, UNHCR has had to frequently choose between adhering to its mandate and principles, which some UNHCR officials feel would decrease its influence and marginalize the Office, or adopting politically pragmatic approaches aimed at securing the "best bargain" for refugees under the circumstances. Policies are assessed by whether there is a reasonable likelihood that desirable humanitarian objectives can be achieved. As a result, the international community, including UNHCR, has pursued policies that are often less than ideal. For example, in late 1996 UNHCR departed from its long-standing opposition to forced repatriation of refugees by supporting the expulsion of more than 300,000 Rwandans from camps in Tanzania. The UNHCR had concluded that the refugees would be better off in Rwanda than in camps under Hutu militia control and that both the host governments and the government in Rwanda were eager to see the camps closed and the refugees returned home. But several human rights organizations criticized UNHCR for supporting forced repatriation and for abandoning its responsibility to protect refugees. Similarly, in former Yugoslavia UNHCR is under great pressure to endorse forcible returns despite the fact that ethnic cleansing continues and the establishment of interethnic boundaries in Bosnia is not yet finished.

Not surprisingly, the expansion of UNHCR's tasks and mission has caused tensions within the organization. Many UNHCR staff feel that the Office's pragmatic approaches to refugee problems dilute UNHCR's protection mandate. Many also claim that an overemphasis on a "right to remain" encourages governments to shirk their international responsibilities and undermines the cardinal principle of refugee protection, namely "the right to leave and to seek asylum."

A notable feature of multilateral responses to today's conflicts is that humanitarian assistance has become a substitute for political and military intervention. Governments are all too often content to provide support to UNHCR and to nongovernmental organizations rather than to actively engage in seeking political solutions to internal wars. In place of a more proactive approach to armed conflict and to the underlying human rights causes of refugee movements, the international community has focused on providing humanitarian relief in civil wars rather than protection, principally as a means to contain the outpouring of refugees and the destabilization of regions. Reliance on providing material assistance to war-affected populations rather than focusing on protection for their human rights is most evident in the cases of northern Iraq, Somalia, Bosnia, and Rwanda, the post–Cold War's most publicized humanitarian crises.

Scope

Intervention as a Means to Contain Refugee Movements

In recent years, most humanitarian interventions have been undertaken within the UN framework and have been justified by a flexible definition of the phrase "threats to international peace and security," thereby permitting the UN Security Council to act under Chapter VII of the UN Charter. The most explicit use of UN enforcement action to contain refugee crises during the past five years was in northern Iraq. Following the end of the 1991 Gulf War, Iraqi suppression of widespread revolt in northern Kurdish areas had created fears that the entire Kurdish population would be uprooted—a particularly grave prospect for neighboring Turkey, with its own Kurdish minority unrest. Accordingly, the Security Council noted that it was "gravely concerned by the repression of the Iraqi civilian population in many parts of Iraq, including most recently in Kurdish populated areas, which led to a massive flow of refugees toward and across international frontiers and to cross-border incursions, which threaten international peace and security" (UN Security Council Resolution 688, 5 April 1991). UN Security Council action was made possible in this case because Iraq had just lost a war and could not counter such interference. In addition, this resolution was in fact rather limited. While international forces were subsequently deployed to Kurdish areas to protect the population, and Iraqi forces withdrew from these areas under pressure, the call for humanitarian action was limited to the provision of assistance within Iraq. Moreover, Resolution 688 offered no international redress to the "repression" noted other than to express "the hope for an early dialogue" among the parties to the conflict. In sum, international assistance and protection to Kurds in Iraq was clearly intended to stem their outpouring into Turkey, but, as both Saddam Hussein's and Turkey's recent incursions into Kurdish enclaves demonstrate, the security of Kurdish populations within Iraq was and remains far from guaranteed.

Unlike in Iraq in 1991, the Security Council Resolutions calling for international action in Somalia did not invoke transborder refugee flows as justification for intervention. Moreover, there was no official government in Somalia that could resist international intervention. Security Council Resolution 751 stated that it was "the magnitude of the human suffering" in Somalia that constituted a threat to peace and security. Subsequently, the Security Council authorized a multilateral force (UNITAF) "to use all necessary means to establish as soon as possible a secure environment for humanitarian relief operations in Somalia." In retrospect, UNITAF succeeded in accomplishing its principal task of delivering humanitarian assistance to the most devastated parts of Somalia but failed miserably when it went beyond its original purpose and attempted to oust the local warlords responsible for the spiral of violence. In Somalia, few resources were devoted to disarmament of military factions, or to rebuilding civil society and the political structures whose collapse was at the root of the violence and displacement in the first place. Following the abrupt withdrawal of the international force and many aid agencies in 1993–4, local Somali groups were left to pick up where outsiders had once provided the bulk of services.

In Bosnia, the humanitarian assistance program was the basis of the multilateral response to the Balkans crises and remained virtually the sole substitute for an overall approach to the political problem there. UNPROFOR's original mission in Bosnia was to facilitate the delivery of UNHCR assistance. Moreover, UN Security Council member states determined that UNPROFOR should maintain the well-established principles of consent, impartiality, and minimal use of force in achieving this objective. While Security Council Resolution 770 of 13 August 1992 invoked the threat of "all necessary means" to ensure delivery of assistance, UNPROFOR was never equipped with sufficient force to carry out this threat (Morris 1996).

The focus of UN activity remained humanitarian relief and not protection of civilians caught in the crossfire of war. The very purpose of war in the former Yugoslavia was to consolidate and legitimize territorial control on the basis of ethnic homogeneity. While Security Council resolutions condemned concentration camps, attacks on noncombatants, and ethnic cleansing, and while the Special Rapporteur for the UN Commission on Human Rights requested the Security Council to send troops to counter human rights violations, the international community never provided UNPROFOR with adequate force or a mandate to address ethnic cleansing and other atrocities. Similarly, UN human rights monitors sent to the former Yugoslavia had extremely limited resources and mandate, and there were never enough UNHCR protection officers to stop the attacks on civilians and the expulsion of refugees. And finally, with the closure of access to asylum in nearby countries and with no international protection, Bosnians threatened with displacement were compelled to remain in their own state and at the mercy of those intent on uprooting them. Even the establishment of "safe areas" in Bosnia in the spring of 1993 was in practice more focused on humanitarian assistance than on protection. International efforts to provide local protection through such means were limited, and ethnic cleansing continued unabated.

In Rwanda in 1994 estimates of people killed in mass slaughter ranged up to one million. Estimates of Rwandese Hutu refugees were 1.5 million, with an equal number of internally displaced. In response to genocide in Rwanda, the major governments chose to do nothing. After the killings had started, the Security Council in mid-May 1994 considered a resolution which would increase the force level of the United Nations Assistance Mission for Rwanda (UNAMIR) and would expand its mandate to contribute to the security and protection of displaced persons, refugees, and civilians at risk, including the establishment and maintenance of secure humanitarian areas, and to provide security for the distribution of humanitarian assistance. The Security Council failed to implement this resolution, though it supported the French deployment of forces in southwest Rwanda in late June 1994 "to contribute to the security and protection of displaced persons, refugees and civilians at risk." In Rwanda, the early warning signs that the extremist Hutu-led government were planning a systematic program of genocide were tragically ignored by the international community (Eriksson et al. 1996). The critical issue of genocide was not addressed and no substantive measures were taken by the international community to provide protection. Possible responses, in the form of international support for regional initiatives to tackle the crisis, the application of diplomatic pressures, or support for a more rapid domestic military solution to the crisis, were not tried.

Many lives were saved in the refugee camps in countries neighboring Rwanda. However, material assistance to refugees took priority over identifying and punishing the perpetrators of genocide. The relief effort was plagued from the beginning by the manipulation and diversion of aid to the very soldiers who had engineered the genocide and fueled the exodus. Nothing was done in Zaire and Tanzania to separate the criminals from the main body of refugees or to isolate the suspects (Saulnier 1996: 18–19). Food aid in Goma, Zaire, the largest camp for Rwandan refugees who had fled their country following the 1994 massacres, was initially channeled through the Hutu leaders, the perpetrators of the massacres who had taken control over the camps after fleeing Rwanda. Relief aid in many instances did not reach the neediest beneficiaries, contributing instead to the legitimacy of the former Hutu military and *interahamwe* militia and reinforcing their control in the camps. It also helped to rebuild the Hutu extremists, who were intent on returning to power in Rwanda, and prolonged both the war and the refugee crisis. The militia prevented refugees from returning home, in effect keeping them as hostages to their struggle.

These recent high-profile relief efforts in northern Iraq, Somalia, Bosnia, and Rwanda underline dramatically the detachment of assistance and protection in many responses to humanitarian emergencies and the inadequacy of providing protection in traditional humanitarian relief programs. The international community is all too often content to provide support to UNHCR and other humanitarian organizations rather than to actively engage in seeking political solutions in intrastate wars. In each of these operations, the <u>international humanitarian system</u> <u>favored assistance over protection</u> and <u>remained largely reactive to</u> <u>events, failing to address the direct links between human rights abuses,</u> <u>violence, and humanitarian emergencies</u>. These operations also demonstrate that as long as the underlying causes of conflict are not addressed, relief risks serving as a mere palliative to human suffering, or even worse, prolonging it.

Weakening of Traditional Protection and Asylum Mechanisms in Host States

In recent years, states not only have provided assistance to contain displaced populations within their borders, but also have manifested a growing reluctance to provide refuge to the victims of persecution. Alarmed by the economic, environmental, social, and security costs of hosting mass influxes of refugees, a number of governments across the world have taken steps to exclude asylum-seekers from their territory and to ensure the rapid—and in some cases involuntary—repatriation of refugees. Consequently, asylum crises in both the North and South exist.

Given the huge sums of money spent (more than $11 billion per annum) to process the asylum claims of a small minority of the world's refugees, most northern states have concluded that preventing entry of asylum-seekers by imposing visa requirements on the nationals of refugee-producing states, fining airlines and other transportation companies for bringing refugees into the country, and even forcibly interdicting refugees at frontiers and in international waters is the best way to reduce not only the problem of abusive potential asylum claimants but also the numbers and the costs of asylum applications. More recently, decisions by the German federal constitutional court and legislation before the U.S. Congress are part of recent high-level efforts in both North America and Western Europe to restrict access to asylum procedures and protection mechanisms principally by systematically expanding the legal possibilities for exclusion of asylum-seekers. In Germany, the federal court has upheld legal provisions that bar foreigners from Germany who travel first through other countries considered safe for refugees—including all of Germany's neighbors. At the same time, European governments have reached a series of regional agreements and conventions, the so-called Schengen Agreement and Dublin Convention, which seek to control their external borders and to establish criteria for determining state jurisdiction over examinations of asylum requests and procedures for entering the European Union. In addition to more restrictive legislation, there is a growing tendency in the North to confuse the status of refugees and illegal immigrants and to lump together concerns about terrorism and the problem of asylum-seekers. The U.S. Anti-Terrorism Act, for example, contains exclusionary provisions that provide for the immediate deportation of illegal immigrants and asylum-seekers at ports of entry without judicial review.

The North's policy of preventing entry has meant that most of the world's refugees, as in the past, are confined to their region of origin in the South. Faced with mass influxes and a greater share of the world's refugee burden, many governments in the South, which in the past had generally responded humanely to the needs of millions who were forced from their homelands, are now closing their doors to new arrivals. In many countries, refugees are perceived as a threat to the physical environment or security of the host state. In 1996, boatloads of Liberian refugees were stranded at sea for weeks until neighboring states reluctantly agreed to provide them refuge. In November, UNHCR had pressed refugees in Zaire to return to Rwanda. At the end of the year, Tanzania, host to hundreds of thousands of refugees from neighboring countries, expelled 300,000 Hutu refugees and refused entry to thousands of asylum-seekers and refugees fleeing violence in Burundi and Rwanda.

Failure of Innovative Protection Policies and Tactics

As more rich countries have become increasingly reluctant to grant asylum to refugees and as many developing countries improve their administrative and military capacities to control their borders, there is a greater need to develop programs to provide international protection to displaced persons within countries of origin. In recent years, states have taken many innovative steps to deal with the problem of displacement. These include the creation of "safe areas" or "security zones" in conflict afflicted countries, the setting up of temporary holding centers or "safe havens," and the establishment of international tribunals to prosecute war criminals in the former Yugoslavia and Rwanda. But such initiatives have not clearly derived from any clearly defined or agreed international strategy. Most have been experimental in nature and hastily formulated to meet immediate needs. Indeed, in the wake of the massacres following the fall of the so-called "safe area" in Srebrenica in July 1995, the credibility of these new mechanisms has been considerably undermined. Human rights protection is still not routinely available for internally displaced persons and other war affected populations who remain within their country of origin.

Safe Zones

During the post–Cold War period, the international community has sanctioned several interventions to establish military protected zones designed to shield civilian populations against attacks. The first such safe zone or security zone was created following the end of the Gulf War when international forces were deployed to Kurdish areas to protect the population. Iraqi forces were pressured to withdraw from the same areas and a de facto autonomous Kurdish area was established that allowed Kurdish refugees to return to safe havens in Iraqi Kurdish territory. The establishment of a security zone was motivated by a desire to accommodate Turkey, an important ally of the West, by preventing a massive Kurdish influx, which was prone to destabilize Turkish Kurdistan. For a period of time, the Western policy of military presence and deterrence, diplomatic isolation, and international sanctions provided reasonable protection for the Iraqi Kurds. In recent years, the zone has only offered precarious protection and has been vulnerable to a variety of external threats, including attacks by Saddam Hussein's forces. In late 1996, the five-year effort by the United States and its allies to protect Kurds was considerably reduced when the U.S. evacuated American citizens, foreigners employed directly by the American government and members of CIA backed Iraqi opposition groups as well as several thousand employees of U.S.-based and U.S.-funded relief organizations from the autonomous safe areas. Comprehensive and sustainable physical and material security for the Iraqi Kurds clearly depends more on a political settlement involving Iraq, Turkey, Iran, and other regional actors than on the temporary and increasingly fragile protection provided by the security zone guarded by the West.

In Rwanda, the UN completely failed to protect the victims of genocide. While the killings occurred, and while it was known who were the victims and who were responsible for the massacres, the UN Security Council took a neutral stand by calling for cease-fires and by imposing an arms embargo. The killings lasted two months before the Security Council even mentioned of the word "genocide." Throughout the worst killing, the UN department of peacekeeping was paralyzed, and UN member states refused to commit troops to halt the genocide. It wasn't until very late in the conflict and after a million people were murdered that the French intervened in Operation Turquoise to establish a "secure humanitarian zone" in the southwest region of the country. While the operation stabilized the situation in southwest Rwanda and provided refuge to Hutus fleeing from the advancing RPF, the zone was also used as a protective cover by segments of the retreating Hutu government, army, and militias who were responsible for mass murder and who forced large numbers of innocent Hutus into fleeing with them to Zaire.

In Bosnia, public outrage over human rights atrocities led the UN Security Council in 1993 to declare six areas as "safe areas" to which Muslims from other parts of Bosnia could find refuge. From the beginning, however, the safe areas represented a political as well as a humanitarian instrument. In humanitarian terms, the safe areas prevented for a time the starvation and expulsion, through the threat of military force, particularly air strikes, of the besieged populations in these areas. In political terms, the safe areas preserved what was left of the territorial integrity of Bosnia, by halting the Bosnian Serbs, and by promoting a solution to the conflict under which the safe areas would remain in principle under Bosnian government control. As it became evident that the protected cities and enclaves were sanctuaries not only for civilians but also for combatants and that these areas were in fact geostrategic centers controlled by one party in the conflict under the protection of the outside world, the safe area concept became discredited. In the end, the UN pledge to protect the safe area regime remained declaratory only as UN member state governments were unwilling to protect the besieged populations. In the end, the failure of international attempts to protect so-called safe areas called into question the very definition of "safe." The Bosnian Serb conquest of Srebrenica and the consequent slaughter of thousands of the city's inhabitants in July 1995 revealed the total inadequacy of safe areas in Bosnia supposedly protected by the international community.

Safe Havens

In addition to the safe zones imposed to protect civilians in internal conflicts in Iraq, Rwanda, and Bosnia,[6] the United States established safe havens at Guantánamo Bay naval base in response to an asylum crisis in the U.S. involving Haitians and Cubans who had been interdicted at sea fleeing their own countries. Concerned that a continued flow of asylum-seekers from Haiti and Cuba would outstrip U.S. capacity to cope and that many people would lose their lives making the dangerous sea voyage to Florida, safe havens were intended to prevent boat flows from Haiti and Cuba from ever reaching the U.S. While the safe haven policy afforded protection to large numbers of asylum-seekers who fell outside the statutory definition of "refugee" and the principle of non-refoulement was largely respected, Cubans held at Guantánamo were not allowed to apply for asylum and their treatment contravened standards against the long-term detention of asylum-seekers. The programs were also costly in human, political, and financial terms and in no way contributed to eliminating the causes of departure.

International Criminal Tribunals

Another major international initiative undertaken during the past several years has been the establishment of international war crimes tribunals to investigate, indict, and try the individuals who carried out genocide and mass killings in former Yugoslavia and Rwanda. These tribunals have the potential to set an important legal precedent, namely to affirm that those who commit atrocious crimes against civilians in war risk serious punishment. By the end of 1996, however, the tribunals had not fulfilled the tasks the international community had set for them. During 1996, for example, the capture of leading war criminals in former Yugoslavia, such as Radovan Karadzig and Ratko Mladic, collided with the Western powers' more urgent interests in seeing the election proceed on schedule and in ensuring that conflict did not break out once again in Bosnia.

While the Dayton agreement commits the governments of Serbia, Croatia, and Bosnia to cooperate with the tribunal, neither Belgrade nor Zagreb have been willing to take the required step of delivering members of their own communities to the Hague. Neither have the involved states passed enabling legislation that would commit them to working with and assisting the tribunal. In Rwanda, lack of international support for the tribunal and distrust of external judicial interference by the Tutsi government in Kigali has meant that the tribunal has made very little headway, and will probably, at most, try a handful of people. The states that created the tribunal seem reluctant to take any steps which could provide it or any of the other UN human rights programs for Rwanda with any long-term institutional independence. For example, totally inadequate funding is provided for the operation of the international criminal tribunal, the international program of assistance to Rwanda's justice system, and the UN human rights field operation in Rwanda.

The conflict between the goal of achieving justice by prosecuting war criminals and the objective of ending bitter intrastate conflicts by reaching agreements among contending forces has resulted in emasculated legal proceedings in the former Yugoslavia and Rwanda. Lack of support for the tribunals damages the long-term prospect for reconciliation and peace in both countries. Lord Hartley Shawcross, Britain's chief prosecutor at Nuremberg, has written that "The tribunal will fail unless those indicted for the most serious war crimes in the former Yugoslavia are arrested and can be brought to justice. Indeed, until that happens, implementation of the Dayton peace accord will be jeopardized" (Shawcross 1996). Without a strong tribunal, it is likely that the political process in the former Yugoslavia will continue to be dominated by extremist nationalist parties and that the promise of the Dayton agreements to reverse ethnic cleansing and to create a multicultural, democratic society in Bosnia will not be realized.

Since the mass return of refugees back into Rwanda in late 1996, many Hutu perpetrators of genocidal acts against Rwanda's Tutsis have been able to re-enter the country and return to their old villages and homes and back into the lives of those whom they had terrorized only a short time before. While there exists a tension between the Tutsis' longing for justice and the need for stability for national reconstruction, the prosecution of war crimes in Rwanda needs to be pursued more effectively to foster a culture of accountability, responsibility, and truth-telling and to promote long-term peace and reconciliation. If the international community wants to prevent the killing from recurring, it should also address the issues of institution-building, development, and human rights protection within Rwanda itself. If a fair judiciary process is not restored in Rwanda and if justice is not perceived to have been accomplished, there will be no end to ethnic separation and hatred (Guest 1996).

A Need for More Systematic Temporary Protection

Prevention and other measures, such as safe zones, safe havens, and other forms of in-country protection, pose a number of difficulties and risks for refugees. While prevention can be used constructively to avert refugee movements before they begin and to meet the needs of uprooted populations once they have been able to return to their homes, these measures should not mean preventing refugee movements, but rather preventing the human rights abuses and violence which cause those refugee movements. Unfortunately, prevention has usually not been centered on seeking solutions to the refugees' predicament—to their right to live their lives free from fear. Rather it has frequently been centered on states' concerns and has come to mean erecting barriers to stop the victims of persecution from entering another country, intercepting them before they make their way to a potential country of refuge, containing displaced people within their national borders, and sending refugees back to their homeland as quickly as possible, even if conditions there have not fundamentally changed (Frelick 1993; Shawcross 1993; UNHCR 1995).

In this environment, new concepts of protection must be devised for the kinds of large-scale refugee flows many regions of the world are now experiencing. In the West, refugee movements stemming from nationality and ethnic minority tensions have already occurred in ex-Yugoslavia and the former Soviet Union, and instances of this phenomenon are likely to increase in the years ahead. Neither traditional immigration nor refugee mechanisms are well equipped to handle victims of civil wars and failed states. The challenge for states is how to develop policies that do not undermine the international refugee regime nor erode the human rights principles of democratic states yet meet their own concerns about controlling borders.

Broader recognition should be given to temporary protection as a legitimate tool of international protection and as a form of burden-sharing to cope with the displacement crises that are likely to occur in the future (Thorburn 1995). Providing temporary protection for people who flee their countries due to situations that pose a serious threat to personal safety meets the immediate needs of many forced migrants as well as responds to the concerns of states regarding uncontrolled migration. Adoption of such protection policies would enable Western governments to move from ad hoc responses toward more consistent and coherent policies.

Certain states already offer forms of temporary protection. Mass protection without individual determination of eligibility has been UNHCR practice in developing countries since the 1960s (Loescher 1993). Mechanisms for coping with large influxes of persons not meeting the Convention criteria in Europe had been developed in the 1970s, with the emergence of de facto humanitarian statuses, such as B-status, humanitarian status, and "exceptional leave to remain" (Gallagher et al. 1989).

Regional regimes also already exist to coordinate refugee crises. The international community now must move to formalize these disparate initiatives into predictable collective action based on burden sharing among governments and regions and aimed at enhancing regional and international order.

For temporary protection to be an effective instrument, however, it should not be used as a substitute for asylum for those refugees meeting the international standard of a well-founded fear of persecution. Nor should this form of protection be withdrawn precipitously in order to encourage early repatriation. For example, temporary protection for refugees from the former Yugoslavia was premised on the assumption that return would occur when it was safe to do so. Yet, despite the continuation of ethnic division and hatred in the former Yugoslavia, UNHCR is under tremendous pressure from some European governments to withdraw temporary protection status for former Yugoslavs and endorse forcible returns. In order for temporary protection to be effective, it must be part of a larger process of rehabilitation, reconstruction, and reconciliation of societies emerging from conflict situations.

Gaps in the International Protection System

Humanitarian action is not just about relief or logistics. It is first and foremost about the protection of war victims and displaced people. Yet, protection is not a central concern of the international community, and there are no clear principles for providing protection in situations of intrastate conflicts and unresolved wars. Indeed, there is a serious disjuncture between expectations of UNHCR and human rights agencies to work in this new international environment and the institutional capacity of these organizations to respond to massive human rights abuses. There are several institutional gaps in the international protection system that inhibit action on the part of the international community. In addition, the tools available to respond to human rights crises and implementation procedures to enforce international humanitarian norms remain limited and weak. The absence of an autonomous resource base and the limited mandates and competencies of international humanitarian agencies continue to hinder the international community in its response to most post–Cold War refugee crises just as they have done for the past fifty years.

Human Rights and the Refugee Regime

Human rights violations and refugee flows form a seamless web. Refugees are, by definition, victims of human rights violations. As noted in the chapter by Schmeidl, people usually become refugees because their human rights are at grave risk or they are at physical risk because of violence. Refugees cut the link between themselves and their own state, and seek the protection of another state because their own government is persecuting them or cannot be relied upon to protect them from physical danger. As recent events in Bosnia, Haiti, Rwanda, and elsewhere demonstrate, today's human rights abuses are tomorrow's refugee problems. In the words of a former U.S. Coordinator for Refugee Affairs, "refugees are human rights violations made visible" (Moore 1987). Yet despite the close connection between the refugee problem and the protection of human rights, the international community has until recently maintained a sharp distinction between the two issues.

This division was a consequence of the reactive and exile-oriented approach to the problem of refugees that characterized the international refugee regime's activities during most of the Cold War (UNHCR 1995). UNHCR had almost no effect on human rights conditions in countries of origin, mainly because it dealt with refugees only after they had fled from a country where they were persecuted and sought asylum in another state. The causes of refugee flows were considered to be a separate concern, falling outside the organization's humanitarian and non-political mandate.

Even in countries of asylum, the High Commissioner's activities on behalf of refugees have generally been limited to providing material assistance, citing violations of international law, and public condemnation for those violations. Although the office has no power to force countries to provide refugees with even minimal humanitarian treatment, the High Commissioner's major weapon is diplomatic pressure to urge states to abide by international refugee law.

International refugee law provides a set of standards against which the actions of states can be measured, and it places some pressure, especially on nations which have acceded to these international instruments, to meet the obligations they impose (Goodwin-Gill 1995; Grahl-Maden 1996; Hathaway 1991). UNHCR's strategy is to measure state actions against these standards. The reality, however, is that the obligations international refugee law impose lend themselves to a variety of interpretations. Therefore, considerable scope exists for governments to perceive their obligations in ways that suit their own national interests.

No supranational authority exists to enforce the rules of the international refugee regime. The system of international refugee protection differs from the UN human rights mechanisms (UNHCR 1996). There is no formal mechanism in international refugee law to receive individual or interstate petitions or complaints. States that are parties to the 1951 Refugee Convention have not all heeded the requirement that they provide UNHCR with information and statistical data on the implementation of the Convention. There is no system of review of country practices through the examination of state party reports or other such information that could be used to formulate recommendations for government authorities. There are also few if any safeguards built into the law itself to prevent abuse by states. It is not surprising, therefore, that many governments have in recent years circumvented several of the major provisions and have exploited areas left unregulated.

In the realm of asylum, states remain the final arbiters of refugees' fates. They retain the power to grant and to deny asylum. Furthermore, the international refugee instruments leave it up to governments to tailor refugee determination procedures to their own administrative, judicial, and constitutional provisions. States regard these procedures as part of their national sovereignty and have been unwilling to transfer this authority to UNHCR or any other intergovernmental body.

Traditionally, the UNHCR has been reluctant to become heavily involved in human rights monitoring in countries of asylum for fear of jeopardizing the welfare of the refugees under its care. In order to mount refugee relief operations, UNHCR must secure permission from countries of asylum to operate within their territories as well as raise money from donor governments to support these operations. As a result, the world's principal refugee protection agency is limited in its ability to criticize host or donor governments' policies toward refugees. UNHCR has never been as weak in its traditional protection mandate as it is today, particularly in Europe and North America, where it is afraid that criticism of these countries' asylum practices will further marginalize the Office in regional discussions on integration, consultation, and harmonization. Many UNHCR staff still take the position that they should avoid public criticism of the asylum situation in countries where the Office has operations. In many instances, therefore, UNHCR is inclined to avoid raising delicate political questions when dealing with humanitarian issues for fear of overstepping its mandate or damaging relations with sensitive governments, most of whom would consider such intrusions to be interference in their internal affairs.

In the post–Cold War period, UNHCR has also become heavily involved in situations of internal conflict where, unlike other UN agencies, its mandate encompasses not only assistance but also protection.[7] The UN High Commissioner for Refugees has referred several times in recent years to the need for "soft intervention," that is, human rights monitoring and the establishment of a humanitarian presence in internal conflicts in order to enhance the observance of human rights and international humanitarian law, thereby reducing the forcible displacement of populations. In the words of the High Commissioner for Refugees addressing the UN Commission on Human Rights in 1995, "Protection of victims, as practiced by UNHCR, is not just monitoring a set of legal standards.... Our operational conception of protection means that UNHCR officers in the field are expected, not only to observe human rights violations and report, but to act upon the information by seeking remedial action from the concerned authorities" (Ogata 1995).

Despite this call for more active human rights monitoring, UNHCR is finding it difficult in practice to ensure the protection of human rights and physical security of war-affected populations. Working in countries of origin differs substantially from UNHCR's traditional work in countries of asylum. Unlike in countries of asylum, the Office must work with opposition movements and guerrilla factions as well as with governments. In some situations, UNHCR staff works alongside UN peacekeeping forces in anarchic and unstable countries that lack viable local and national structures. Often, however, UNHCR protection officers are too few in number to fulfill an adequate protection role. In the former Yugoslavia, for example, their activities included protecting civilians against reprisals and forced displacement, relocating and evacuating civilians from conflict areas, and assisting besieged populations, such as those in former safe areas in Bosnia and in Sarajevo, who chose not to move from their homes when they were under attack. Frequently, moreover, UNHCR has found that it lacks any firm institutional and legal basis for this work. Furthermore, most staff are neither recruited nor trained to work in the crossfire of internal conflicts where soldiers and guerrillas view the internally displaced and returnees as the enemy and UN assistance as favoring one side to the disadvantage of the other. In situations like Bosnia, the Caucasus, or Tajikistan, UNHCR uses humanitarian and legal interventions similar to those used by the International Committee of the Red Cross (ICRC), but its staff lacks the special training, skills, and experience of ICRC staff members.

A major obstacle to taking a more active role in refugee protection in countries of origin derives from the international refugee regime itself. The UNHCR was designed to appear to be nonpolitical and strictly humanitarian, a strategy employed to receive permission to work in host countries and to secure funding from donor governments. UNHCR, as it is presently structured, is not mandated to intervene politically against governments or opposition groups, despite clear evidence of human rights violations. In addition, UNHCR staff frequently have a limited understanding of human rights and humanitarian law and are uncertain of how governments and opposition groups will react to their interventions using these protection norms.

In many internal wars, relief assistance operations are also vulnerable to political manipulation by the warring parties who perceive humanitarian assistance as one of several weapons of warfare. For example, food assistance is very often used as a political weapon. Adversaries sometimes divert assistance from proper recipients for military or political goals, and deny assistance to certain populations and geographical areas by blocking access to international agencies. Finally, neither UNHCR nor ICRC is present in all situations of internal conflict and forcible displacement. Sometimes governments refuse to acknowledge that a noninternational armed conflict is taking place on their territory, and some refuse to allow ICRC entry.

Humanitarian agencies such as UNHCR that need to raise more and more voluntary funds from governments, obtain better and easier access to situations from governments, win the confidence of competing actors, and promote compromise solutions in bitter internal conflicts, are frequently not well placed to stand up for humanitarian principles or to resist political considerations that affect the human rights of refugees and war-affected populations. If the international community is serious about the human rights of forcibly displaced people, they should re-examine the desirability and feasibility of expecting protection functions to be carried out effectively by agencies that are ill funded and heavily dependent upon voluntary largesse, and that are also expected to be heavily involved in field operations.

Refugees and the Human Rights Regime

The UN human rights machinery has been even more reluctant than the international refugee regime to engage in human rights protection work for refugees and other displaced people. During the Cold War, the East-West conflict and the reluctance of authoritarian states to have their human rights monitored, placed serious constraints on the Human Rights Commission and the UN Human Rights Center. Consequently, the UN human rights regime focused on developing international human rights norms and standards and on promulgating a series of human rights covenants and treaties but avoided developing serious enforcement measures.

During the 1980s, the UN Human Rights Commission and the Human Rights Center increased its range of interests and activities (Forsythe 1995). New mechanisms were created to monitor torture, disappearances, summary executions, and imprisonment, and the Human Rights Commission became more open in reporting human rights situations in specific countries. The growing range of mechanisms at the UN and regional levels for monitoring the protection of human rights should have, in theory, reduced the need for people to flee or allowed those who had fled to return home in safety or to be protected in another country. However, the tasks of Special Rapporteurs were largely limited to prosecutorial functions, and they were seldom allowed full access to the situations under study and were unlikely to provide meaningful remedies to human rights abuses. Most importantly, refugees and displaced people did not figure prominently in this expansion of human rights activities at the UN, and refugee protection issues have remained largely outside the mainstream of the UN human rights program.[8]

Despite growing recognition that the UN human rights machinery needs to become directly involved in refugee protection, the UN human rights machinery has not yet been effective in providing protection for refugees or internally displaced persons in the field. In most situations involving forced displacement, UN human rights staff are not present, and even when they are, their role is usually confined to monitoring and collection of information. UN complaints procedures, early warning capabilities, minority rights protection, and on-the-ground presence are much too weak to be expected to protect refugees now or in the near future. Moreover, many of the traditional constraints on the international human rights regime have not disappeared with the passing of the Cold War. Refugees and human rights continue to have their own separate organizational domains. The fact that refugees are the responsibility of UNHCR has tended to keep refugee issues apart from the UN human rights regime. There is, for example, no Special Rapporteur or treaty body on asylum issues nor even a proper agenda item at the UN Commission on Human Rights that deals with refugee issues. Thus, there has been a lack of coordination between UNHCR and the UN Center for Human Rights as well as with country and issue specific UN human rights monitoring mechanisms. At the international level, there have been no real attempts to address the problem of refugee protection in a comprehensive manner.

NGOs and Human Rights Protection of Refugees

Among most NGOs the refugee problem is perceived as separate from the broader issue of human rights. Many national and international agencies that work on behalf of refugees and asylum-seekers have had little contact with the broader human rights movement and remain largely unaware of UN human rights standards and mechanisms.

NGOs have long been active in conflicts but their role in humanitarian emergencies in recent years has been changing (Aall 1996). Traditionally, agencies like the International Committee for the Red Cross and other NGOs have worked with the permission of governments. But in recent decades, many NGOs have become impatient with these constraints and have begun to operate more independently. As a series of wars and natural disasters exposed millions of people to hunger and starvation during the 1980s, NGOs also assumed progressively greater responsibilities. Many of the UN agencies, hampered by their mandates and by the political interests of the Superpowers during the Cold War, were unable to offer adequate response. Consequently, donor governments channeled more official funds through NGOs to high-profile emergency relief programs.

NGOs in general have made an enormous contribution in responding to the humanitarian needs of millions of refugees and displaced persons caught up in recent civil conflicts. Yet protection has not been a central element of NGO relief programs. Although NGOs are often the first to become aware of human rights problems, certain institutional features of relief operations inhibit them from acting on such information. Many aid workers are inadequately trained in human rights issues; there exist no clear channels to convey human rights observations from the field either to higher levels of most organizations or to appropriate external parties; and most agencies fear that reporting human rights violations would jeopardize their impartiality, neutrality, and ability to provide relief work or their access to their client populations and might even endanger their staff.

Post–Cold War humanitarianism has thus overwhelmingly emphasized the delivery of relief assistance over protecting human rights. Human rights have been perceived as the preserve of human rights NGOs, such as Amnesty International or Human Rights Watch groups. Apart from ICRC, however, human rights monitoring and protection in armed conflict has been largely ignored by traditional human rights NGOs, and few human rights groups have operational capacity in the field. Until recently, most human rights bodies tended to regard the problems facing the victims of war as beyond their traditional areas of concern. When they do define their mandate more broadly, they generally limit themselves to monitoring and publishing reports. Rarely do they work in the field with refugee and relief NGOs to increase protection for forcibly displaced people (Cohen 1995).

Inadequacy of Existing Resource Base

The upsurge in conflicts and mass displacements during the 1990s has led to an enormous expansion in the amounts of humanitarian and peace-making assistance provided to the victims of these conflicts. Brian Atwood, the former director of USAID, claimed that in 1994–95 the international community spent $4 billion in humanitarian assistance and $5 billion in peacekeeping in response to the complex crises occurring across the globe (Atwood 1995). In 1994 alone, an estimated $3 billion was committed to humanitarian assistance by the UN and the ICRC. The UNHCR, the lead agency in most humanitarian disasters, has seen its budget, staffing level, and international presence expand at an unprecedented rate. The sums required for UNHCR operations have risen from around $550 million in 1990 to about $1.3 billion in 1996, and staff numbers have nearly doubled during the same period to over 5,000 worldwide.

The growing financial sums devoted to humanitarian action have eroded the traditional support given to long-term economic development. In response to ever-increasing humanitarian crises, the general proportion of development assistance provided by the industrialized countries that is spent on relief increased five-fold in the decade between the early 1980s and the early 1990s.[9] Much of this governmental assistance is now channeled through nongovernmental agencies (NGOs). For many NGOs, such as CARE or Oxfam, which traditionally considered themselves as development agencies, emergency programs now form the bulk of their work. Similarly, as Tom Weiss notes in his chapter, the World Food Program now devotes about 80 percent of its resources to emergency food relief, and UNICEF directs about 25 percent of its expenditure toward emergencies.

As resources are diverted from long-term development to relief to meet the costs of conflict, there is less available to tackle the underlying poverty and social inequalities that fuel conflict in the first place. In 1993, for the first time in almost twenty years, the amount of development aid going from the richest to the poorest nations was reduced by 6 percent, from $61 billion to $55 billion (OECD 1994). This cutback in overall aid recovered to $60 billion in 1994, but ODA as a share of GNP among the twenty-one Development Assistance Committee (DAC) countries of the Organization of Economic Cooperation and Development (OECD) continued its twenty-year downward slide, falling from 0.31 percent of GNP in 1993 to 0.30 percent of GNP in 1994.[10] In 1995, the United States, once the world leader in aid to developing nations, dropped to fourth in the amount of money it spent on development assistance after Japan, France, and Germany, and to a distant last place among donor nations in the percentage of GNP it devoted to foreign aid. The OECD reported that U.S. funds for development and humanitarian assistance—not including military aid—were cut from $8.4 billion in fiscal year 1995 to $7.3 billion in fiscal year 1996 and as a percentage of its GNP, the U.S. gave 0.1 percent (Lippman 1996).

The hope that the end of the Cold War would lead to a substantial "peace dividend" that could be channeled to aid the developing world has not materialized. While aggregate global spending on arms has dropped in recent years, cuts have been most significant in the richer countries. Despite an estimated $200 billion cut in military budgets since the end of the Cold War, less than 1 percent of this sum globally has been channeled into spending on development (Randel and German 1995). In the North, most savings gained from disarmament have gone to respond to growing domestic priorities. Many Third World governments, however, continue to divert limited resources from development to buy arms, which is stimulating an increase in the $20 billion plus annual arms trade, particularly in small arms and other light weapons (Klare 1995).

There are also no new funds available to address human rights problems that are at the root of most refugee disasters. At present, the UN human rights program is grossly understaffed and underfunded, and it still lacks the means to place human rights monitors in the field on a regular and systematic basis. The first UN High Commissioner for Human Rights, for example, was given a derisory amount of $1.4 million for the first two years of his activities. At a time when billions of dollars have been poured into emergency relief programs and peacekeeping operations, virtually no extra funds have been provided for the UN human rights regime. Despite its potential to strengthen civil society, promote democratic and pluralistic institutions and procedures and, thereby, to prevent human rights abuses and mass displacements, the UN human rights regime has never received more than 1 percent of the UN budget.

While the resources available to UNHCR and other humanitarian organizations have grown substantially in the past few years, not all refugee disasters have received adequate funds. Some crises have attracted far greater international attention and support than others. In

1995, for example, UNHCR put more money into the former Yugoslavia than it spent for all its work in Africa, a continent that was home to four times as many refugees. Some strategists now argue that in a world of diminished resources the U.S. should focus its overseas assistance on a small number of "pivotal states" whose stability is highly uncertain and whose future will profoundly affect their surrounding regions (Chase and Kennedy 1996). In effect, the post–Cold War humanitarian regime is in danger of being characterized as a system of triage where those countries that are perceived to be geopolitically important will receive aid, while the other ones will largely be considered "dispensable."

Although the level of annual UNHCR expenditures increased dramatically in the early 1990s, less than 2 percent of the Office's funding is guaranteed each year through the UN general budget, and UNHCR must raise funds for each new refugee problem. Because UNHCR relies on new donations for each new situation as it arises, its independence is restricted. Humanitarian relief agencies are severely constrained in their actions by the limits posed by donor governments' politics and by levels and patterns of funding. Politics and foreign policy priorities cause donor governments to explicitly earmark funds for some refugee groups over others and to exert direct or indirect pressure to guide their use.

Not only relief aid but also postconflict reconstruction assistance remains strongly influenced by narrow considerations of self-interest and political gain of donor governments. Without compelling strategic and ideological motivations, funding for refugee operations are in danger of being cut back in favor of the domestic priorities of the industrialized states. Indeed, the increasing number of humanitarian emergencies during the past five years has coincided with falling foreign aid budgets in many of the important donor states, particularly the United States and Great Britain. The major powers are reluctant to provide funds for humanitarian programs when internal conflicts in aid-recipient countries continue unabated. Thus, despite the clear link in situations involving displacement and regional security, such as in Rwanda and the former Yugoslavia, there is weak donor interest in funding a comprehensive strategy for dealing with postconflict economic and political transitions in these countries. Consequently, donor states are failing to honor pledges for rehabilitation and reconstruction. In Rwanda, despite large-scale massacres, the international community has made no serious efforts to provide protection and to secure and enforce a peace in the region, largely viewing internal and regional insecurity in the Great Lakes region of Africa as marginal to global geopolitical concerns. By mid-1996, UNHCR had received only a tiny fraction of the $288 million it had appealed for toward meeting the cost of providing protection to Rwandan refugees. Even in the Balkans, which is central to the geopolitical interests of the major donors, only one-fifth of the reconstruction aid pledged at the Dayton peace accords was fulfilled by June 1996. Yet Rwanda and the former Yugoslavia have demonstrated that it is dangerous and irresponsible to dismiss these conflicts, and the threat of new ones, as purely internal or regional affairs. Ultimately, they represent a major threat to international security for the neighboring countries as well as for the international community at large.

Inadequacy of Existing Mandates and International Humanitarian Law

While there is a clear mandate for the protection and provision of humanitarian assistance to refugees, existing political, diplomatic, economic and legal mechanisms are not sufficiently developed to cope with the increasingly complex and volatile population movements of the post–Cold War period. In particular, there are no specific international organizations mandated to protect and assist the internally displaced (Deng 1993). At the same time, the political issues involved, particularly state sovereignty and nonintervention in domestic affairs, make the issue of the internally displaced one of the most challenging problems confronting the international community in the 1990s.

Furthermore, a recent compilation and analysis of legal norms drawn up by the Special Representative on internally displaced persons noted that existing human rights and humanitarian laws offer internally displaced persons inadequate protection (Cohen 1996a, 1996b). They also do not adequately cover forcible displacements and relocations, humanitarian assistance and access, the right to food, and the protection of relief workers (Norwegian Refugee Council and Refugee Policy Group 1993). In particular, governments do not have to accept international humanitarian assistance or provide aid to ensure the survival of internally displaced persons. There are no provisions for personal documentation of the displaced or compensation for property lost during displacement. There exist no specific protection for women and children displaced in internal conflicts. There are also many gaps in international standards. For example, situations of public emergency and internal violence fall outside the scope of the Geneva Conventions of 1949 and Additional Protocol II of 1977. As a result, many human rights provisions are suspended when an emergency threatens the security of a state, leaving internally displaced people and war-affected populations without adequate protection. Humanitarian law also is not binding on insurgent forces.

Closing the Gap between Protection and Assistance

The growing number of protracted humanitarian emergencies has put an ever heavier strain on the limited resources of international assistance and on existing mechanisms of collective response. It is increasingly clear that steps to resolve refugee problems must extend beyond humanitarian action into broader realms if they are to be effective. In the future, responses to forced migration cannot proceed solely within the mandate of international humanitarian organizations and cannot be separated from other areas of international concern, in particular human rights and security issues (see Loescher 1993).

The overall response of the international community still remains compartmentalized with political, security, and humanitarian issues mostly being discussed in different forums, each with their own institutional arrangements and independent policy approaches. Despite recent initiatives to incorporate human rights objectives and missions into peacekeeping and peace enforcement operations, there still exist too little strategic integration of approaches and too little effective coordination in the field. The Weiss chapter in this volume argues for improved modalities for cooperation, particularly because humanitarian problems are multidimensional in nature and because the number of international actors involved in such operations are great. Yet most intergovernmental organizations resist coordination and fight to preserve their autonomy.

UNHCR, however, can no longer resolve the problems of refugees, returnees, and internally displaced people single-handedly and needs to build bridges between itself and organizations dealing with issues such as human rights and peacekeeping and peacemaking. The Office has noted that this new approach to refugee problems involves an increase in the range of actors in the search for solutions, an increase in the range of issues the refugee regime seeks to address, and an increase in the range of people it is designed to benefit (UNHCR 1995). Tom Weiss emphasizes in his chapter that discussions regarding more effective division of labor among humanitarians is now part of ongoing intergovernmental discussions. Effective international responses to humanitarian disasters require not only the consolidation of the emergency functions of UN organizations as proposed by former Secretary of State Warren Christopher but also the integration of protection and assistance activities by these agencies.

Empowerment of the International Human Rights Regime

One of the greatest challenges confronting international organizations in the years to come will be to link the task of refugee protection to the broader defense of human rights. If the international community hopes to respond more effectively to the global problem of refugees and internal displacement, it must strengthen its capacity to monitor developments in human rights issues and to intercede on behalf of forced migrants. Governments must guarantee a meaningful funding base to the specialized human rights bodies and withdraw the financial and political constraints on human rights action.

The creation of the Office of the UN High Commissioner for Human Rights (OHCHR) in 1993 brought higher profile to human rights within the UN system and stepped up monitoring of protection concerns in major crises. As part of a UN-wide effort to give a higher priority to the integration of human rights into the various activities and programs of the UN, the High Commissioner has participated actively in dialogue with other UN agencies. Mary Robinson is a member of each of the four Executive Committees through which the UN system's work in humanitarian affairs, peace and security, economic and social affairs, and development is orchestrated. Despite considerable improvements, interagency coordination and the institutional division of labor regarding human rights within the UN remain problematic.

In recent years, there has also been an increase in the presence of the UN Human Rights Office staff in the field, especially as part of UN peacekeeping and peace enforcement missions. The number of OHCHR field presences has grown from one in 1992 to twenty-two in 1999. There have also been increased activities by special rapporteurs appointed by the UN Human Rights Commission to document human rights violations in certain countries and to report back to the Commission. Nevertheless, as in the past, major weaknesses continue to exist in the UN human rights system. UN human rights work depends on the cooperation of countries that can refuse entry to human rights officials and special rapporteurs and can often stonewall any new initiatives. OHCHR field presence is still limited to capital cities and primarily focuses as much on technical cooperation as on monitoring. Moreover, OHCHR staff members still have limited capacity and expertise in displacement, and OHCHR still receives only about 1 percent of the annual UN budget for its operating expenses. This is a paltry amount considering the challenges facing the Office.

A key to strengthening UN capacity to monitor human rights in the future is enhancing its capacity to undertake a protection role in the field that involves a radical change of focus for the UN High Commissioner for Human Rights. To be effective, human rights monitoring requires good planning, specialized professional expertise, clear lines of authority, and significant financial resources. At the same time, UN human rights machinery and UN agencies should continue to expand their advisory services and technical assistance programs by offering services such as training judges, strengthening electoral commissions, establishing ombudsmen, training prison staff, and advising governments on constitutions and legislation regarding national minorities and human rights.

UN member states should also support the newly created permanent international criminal tribunal. Such a mechanism is a potentially important and effective innovation toward achieving the objectives of both justice and peace in situations in which there have been intrastate conflict, genocide, human rights abuses, and forcible displacement. Institutions and individuals who are responsible for the human rights abuses that provoke forced population displacements must know they cannot act with impunity. An international tribunal can create consistent expectations of accountability for violations of human rights. As such, it would serve as a deterrent as well as a vehicle of truth-telling, reconciliation, and interethnic healing in societies torn by violent conflict and mass killings.

Addressing the Growing Problem of Internal Displacement

In future years, the problem of internal displacement and the plight of war-affected populations will acquire increasing humanitarian and strategic importance for the international community. The internally displaced generally find themselves in more difficult and dangerous circumstances than refugees, primarily because they remain under the jurisdiction of the state that is unable or unwilling to protect them (Cohen and Deng 1998a, 1998b). At the same time, given the continuing intrastate violence in many parts of the world, coupled with the growing readiness of states in both the North and the South to avert or obstruct mass refugee outflows from such situations by closing their doors to asylum-seekers and insisting on the early repatriation of refugee populations, the number of people forcibly displaced and trapped within their own country can be expected to increase. Moreover, despite the new degree of caution that exists concerning humanitarian intervention, there is growing recognition among both governments and the public that the domestic affairs of states can also be a subject of legitimate international concern (Dowty and Loescher 1999: 199–222). Thus, in addition to the problem of refugees, more attention will have to be given to the question of how to provide in-country protection and assistance to internally displaced people (IDPs).

A critical weakness of the international humanitarian system is that at present there is no special international organization to protect and assist the estimated 23 million IDPs worldwide. While there is a clear mandate for protecting refugees and the provision of humanitarian assistance, there is a lack of clarity within existing international instruments regarding the allocation of responsibilities and mechanisms for addressing the immediate needs of IDPs. One of the major gaps in the international response system for the internally displaced is a lack of predictable response. No UN agency can be counted on to respond automatically when there is a crisis involving massive internal displacement. Agencies choose the situations in which they will become involved in light of their mandates, resources, and interests. The selectivity and conditionality of their response often result in limited and inconsistent coverage for the internally displaced, leaving large numbers with little or no protection and assistance. The 1999 Kosovo emergency is a case in point. UNHCR and other international agencies were heavily involved in assisting refugees who fled the country, whereas practically no international attention was directed to the victims of ethnic cleansing and the internally displaced within the country.[11]

In the absence of a single organization within the UN system for the internally displaced, reliance has been placed on a system-wide approach, coordinated by the Department of Humanitarian Affairs from 1991 to 1998, and by the Office for the Coordination of Humanitarian Affairs (OCHA) since 1998. This collaborative approach has often been constrained by delays, duplication of effort and programs, neglect of protection issues, and insufficient support for reintegration and postconflict development efforts. Resident coordinators who have been assigned to coordinate assistance to internally displaced populations frequently have had no operational capacity, little experience in dealing with the internally displaced, and minimal understanding of protection concerns. In his program for reform of the UN in July 1997, the UN Secretary-General Kofi Annan recognized the challenge of providing protection, assistance and reintegration, and development support for internally displaced, and cited this area as an example of a humanitarian issue that falls between the gaps of existing mandates of the different agencies.[12] In January 2000, Richard Holbrooke, the U.S. Ambassador to the UN, highlighted again for the Security Council the glaring need for an international body to be responsible for the internally displaced.

There is also no adequate body of international law to regulate their treatment by governments and international organizations. The 1949 Geneva Conventions and their Additional Protocols of 1977 make allowance for protection of civilians in internal conflicts, but they were formulated when conventional war was the norm and when the task of disseminating the rules was easier. When the UN Secretary-General's Special Representative for Internally Displaced Persons made a compilation of legal norms applicable to the internally displaced in 1996, he found a significant number of gaps in existing human rights and humanitarian law. Two years later, Francis Deng submitted a set of thirty Guiding Principles, which addressed the specific needs of the internally displaced by identifying rights and guarantees relevant to their protection (Deng 1998). The Guiding Principles address all phases of displacement including protection from arbitrary displacement, protection during displacement, principles relating to humanitarian assistance, and protection during resettlement and reintegration.[13] Governments at the UN Human Rights Commission unanimously adopted a resolution acknowledging the Principles and encouraged Deng to utilize them in future efforts, including his dialogue with governments.

In discussing the Guiding Principles, the UN Human Rights Commission also noted the need to develop an institutional framework for the internally displaced. Governments signaled their clear preference for interagency coordination rather than the establishment of a new agency for addressing the assistance and protection needs of the internally displaced. UN Resolution 1998/50[14] encouraged the UN High Commissioner for Human Rights, UNHCR, the Emergency Relief Coordinator, OCHA, United Nations Development Program, UNICEF, the World Food Program, the World Health Organization, the International Organization for Migration, ICRC, and others to develop "frameworks of cooperation" to promote protection, assistance, and development for internally displaced persons by appointing focal points within their organizations for these matters. Despite these activities, it is still the case that there exists only a weak and incoherent arrangement at the international level for the internally displaced.

A Protection Role for Human Rights NGOs

Until the time when the capacity of the UN human rights regime is developed and supported, NGOs, especially human rights NGOs, will have to assume a larger share of responsibility for protection. Protection of refugees and other displaced people requires a readiness on the part of human rights agencies to act on observed human rights abuses. In order to accomplish this, human rights NGOs need to establish a continuous presence in regions experiencing conflict. Refugee Watch organizations should be established within each refugee-producing region to monitor the protection needs of refugees, asylum-seekers, and the internally displaced. Creating such organizations could provide a basis for consciousness-raising regarding humanitarian norms and democratic principles within regions, and it could enable local organizations to assume responsibility for monitoring, intervening, and managing humanitarian programs without major external involvement or infringements of concepts of national sovereignty.

Relief NGOs, likewise, have an essential protection role to play.[15] Many NGOs believe that human rights work would compromise their neutrality and their access and ability to work in intrastate conflicts. Nevertheless, many NGOs today are far more willing and able to address protection issues than they have been in the past. Their presence in most civil war situations makes them important sources of information on human rights abuses, refugee movements, and emergency food needs. This information is crucial for human rights monitoring, early warning of conflicts and refugee crises, and preventive diplomacy. Bill DeMars has argued that humanitarian organizations that operate in conflict situations should institutionalize procedures to manage and report information on human rights abuses by their own personnel in the field (DeMars 1995). Efforts should also be made to improve both the channels of communication and the readiness to act on human rights information at high political levels. At a minimum, NGOs should train their staff on protection techniques to be used in the field—both as concerted human rights efforts and as part of normal relief efforts (Maynard 1996).

Moreover, Kimberly Maynard has noted that because NGOs also have a central role in securing humanitarian access to the civilian victims of conflicts and are often in close contact with both governments and opposition movements, they can play a significant role in conflict resolution, mediation, and reconciliation (Maynard 1996). The presence of NGOs within communities at war and their ability to move among civilian populations and armed forces are characteristics not shared by UN agencies and donor governments. Thus, NGOs are well placed to engage in a new comprehensive form of humanitarian action, encompassing assistance and protection, mediation, and conflict resolution.

Refugees, UN Peacekeeping, and Outside Military Forces

The emergencies of the post–Cold War era have also highlighted the fact that protection for refugees requires a more effective interface between humanitarian relief and political and security considerations. As part of the international community's increasing focus on preventive action, there is now greater emphasis on dealing with the problem of displacement in the country of origin. UN agencies and UN peacekeeping forces now routinely provide assistance to victims of ethnic conflict as close to their homes as possible, create havens or secure areas where displaced persons can get help in relative safety, deploy troops to prevent the expulsions of civilians in some areas, and protect relief workers who are caught in the crossfire between opposing sides. In addition to greater pressures to provide in-country assistance and protection, there is greater emphasis on repatriation, which involves organizing the return moves, providing logistical assistance for the actual move, setting up on-site reception centers at the resettlement locations, and furnishing help in reintegrating refugees. Many refugees are returning home before all the problems that caused them to flee, including violence and persecution, have been resolved. There is the danger that premature returns will result in considerable human rights violations.

Under these circumstances, UN and outside military forces frequently work alongside relief agencies to meet humanitarian exigencies in conflict zones. The military brings logistics skills and resources that can meet the immediate needs of civilian populations at risk in humanitarian emergencies, including such activities as protecting relief shipments, creating safety zones, prepositioning supplies, and relocating or evacuating civilians (Gordenker and Weiss 1991). While recent experiences have demonstrated that the military has unrivaled access to a range of material and logistical resources in transportation, communications, and medical services that are simply not available to UNHCR and other humanitarian organizations, relief operations in Iraq, Somalia, Bosnia, and Rwanda have also underscored some of the difficulties of military-civilian cooperation in providing relief in situations of continuing conflict. The objectives and working methods of military and human organizations are different, and, in some cases, contradictory. Military staff are often unfamiliar with the mandates and priorities of relief organizations, lack knowledge of and specific training in human rights norms and international humanitarian law, and demonstrate little appreciation or understanding of local customs and institutions. Military forces rarely, if ever, have a purely humanitarian agenda, and they are generally unwilling to work under external direction, even in operations conducted under UN auspices.

Recent experiences in Bosnia also demonstrate that the provision of military security for relief operations can compromise the neutrality of humanitarian aid agencies, and can even threaten the delivery of humanitarian assistance. In the former Yugoslavia, UNHCR, in the past,

had difficulty in carrying out its mandate as a result of its close association both with the UN military forces on the ground and more generally
with the punitive and economic actions taken by the UN Security Council. UN troops, mandated to ensure humanitarian access to civilian populations, were not given sufficient means and political backing to carry
out their tasks. As a consequence, not only UNPROFOR, but also
UNHCR, was criticized both for not providing adequate protection to
civilians in their own communities and for not being able to rescue them
when their lives were threatened (Minear et al. 1994). In addition, sanctions imposed by the UN Security Council on the Federal Republic of
Yugoslavia caused great hardship on civilians and undermined the credibility of UNHCR to act impartially in a civil war context.

Military and humanitarian intervention can also sometimes have an
adverse impact on the resolution of conflicts. In the struggle to provide
aid to the displaced and other war victims, the resolution of the root
causes of the conflict can easily become sidetracked. In Bosnia, inadequate humanitarian and military action, combined with selective sanctions and ineffective diplomatic initiatives, impeded more robust political
and military pressures for most of the conflict. Thus, in future relief operations, it is likely that if humanitarian action is not accompanied by the
necessary political will or action to resolve interethnic conflicts, military
forces and relief agencies will become bogged down in long-standing,
protracted humanitarian operations. In extending its role in conflict situations, UNHCR should insist that the UN's political bodies and UN
member states be actively involved in seeking political solutions. There
should also be a clear understanding of the protection responsibilities of
UN peacekeeping troops in humanitarian emergencies, and these forces
should be provided the training to make this role effective. Otherwise
humanitarian action will continue to be a substitute for conflict resolution
and will undermine protection.

Coincidence of Political Objectives with Idealism

The current inclination on the part of states across the globe to erect new
barriers to deter population movements will not make the refugee problem go away, nor will it ensure a stable political base for international
relations. Much as we may prefer to focus our attention closer to home,
the persistence of refugee problems makes it impossible for states to
ignore conditions that create forced migration. In the longer term, states
must recognize that lasting solutions to the problem of displaced people
requires a new level of cooperation between countries of the North and
the South. The international community can and should insist that countries of refugee origin protect their citizens by refraining from actions that
are likely to cause people to become refugees and by accepting the return
of their people without prejudice. However, a sole emphasis on the

responsibility of the countries of refugee origin and on prevention of refugee movements risks overshadowing the responsibilities of all governments toward asylum-seekers and refugees. Governments everywhere have the responsibility to refrain from imposing or contributing to refugee-generating conditions. This means that asylum states, particularly those in the North, have international obligations too, including the support of human rights, the provision of asylum, restrictions on arms sales to refugee-producing states, and the provision of financial and political support to promote equitable and sustainable development in countries and regions of refugee origin.

It is also important to note that in confronting the protection problems of the forcibly displaced it may be extremely difficult to apply strict moral principles. In such situations, there are often conflicting objectives, such as the goal of achieving justice in Rwanda versus the objective of ending a civil war and achieving stability in Rwanda by accommodating the interests of contending forces. There also exist a variety of means (some of which may seem more just than others) for achieving a desired end, such as reconciliation and reintegration of Serbs, Croats, and Muslims in Bosnia versus partition of Bosnian territory and the separation of peoples. Finally, just as there is no certain way to prevent refugee flows, there is no certain way to protect the human rights of refugees. Not every repressive government can be reformed nor can every civil war be ended. Human rights initiatives can involve states in other countries' domestic affairs, and contribute to internal unrest that can lead to new refugee crises. If at all possible, the United States and other countries should tackle directly the human rights abuses and violence that cause refugee flight, so that people will not feel compelled to flee their homes. But in situations where policies addressing root causes have failed, and policies of humanitarian intervention and "safe area" creation have proved ineffective or inoperable, states should be prepared to support refugee flight and to offer asylum and different types of external protection to victims of persecution and violence. Under such conditions, in the words of Atle Grahl-Madsen, "asylum in a foreign country becomes the ultimate human right" (quoted in Zucker and Zucker 1996).

In the contemporary international political context, generating support for new international initiatives may very well be difficult to accomplish. The political, financial, and organizational impediments already mentioned place significant constraints on new political initiatives. Nevertheless, there are reasons of state as well as of humanitarian concern to offer protection to refugees and internally displaced persons and to seek solutions to these problems. In the realms of human rights and forced displacement, international and regional stability and idealism often coincide. Policymakers need to build on this coincidence of factors to achieve the political will necessary both to address these problems and to develop the institutional capacity to respond more effectively to future humanitarian crises.

Notes

1. As the Stockholm International Peace Research Institute noted in its 1996 yearbook, all 30 major conflicts currently underway, from Afghanistan and Algeria to Tajikistan and Turkey, are primarily internal. The distinction between interstate and intrastate war is never simple, however. The conflicts between Hutu and Tutsi in Rwanda and Burundi spilled over into Zaire and Tanzania and threatened to destabilize those countries. Moreover, as noted in the chapter by Schmeidl and Suhrke, the globalization of refugee flows is accentuated by the external supply of money, weapons and even knowledge about war strategies.

2. Within war societies, new power structures and elites arise. Those possessing power and resources are almost invariably opposed to the settlement of crises as such initiatives endanger and erode their power basis.

3. Author's interviews with UNHCR staff in Geneva 1994–96.

4. Ibid.

5. It is for this reason that UNHCR has in recent years spoken of "people of concern to the Office" rather than of refugees alone.

6. In Sri Lanka, the UNHCR offered protection for displaced persons within the country by establishing Open Relief Centers.

7. As noted in the chapter by David Forsythe, resolving refugee problems depends on a range of human rights activities, including establishing civil societies and pluralistic political systems, reinforcing legal and government structures, and empowering local grass roots organizations. However, neither ensuring good governance nor respect for human rights is a core concern or function of humanitarian or development agencies. Neither the UN Department of Humanitarian Affairs (DHA) nor the UN Development Program (UNDP) has a protection mandate. While UNDP has a democratization project, both DHA and UNDP are primarily concerned with assistance. DHA has virtually no staff presence in the field on a permanent basis. As official coordinator for UN assistance in humanitarian emergencies, DHA organizes inter-agency teams to make in-country visits and assessments of humanitarian needs. Despite the fact that protection problems are often paramount in humanitarian operations, rarely, if ever, are human rights personnel included on such teams. And although some agencies may be the first to become aware of protection problems in countries where they have programs, it has not been their practice to address these problems. Even UNDP, which has staff present worldwide through their UNDP Resident Representatives, views itself as principally having a development, not a protection, focus.

   The major exception to the near universal neglect within the UN system of protection issues is the UNHCR, whose core concern is protection of refugees. Indeed, it is UNHCR's mandate to protect the human rights of refugees which gives the organization its distinctive and unique character. But even UNHCR is severely limited by organizational constraints. Despite the close connection between the refugee problem and the protection of human rights, the international community has until recently maintained a sharp distinction between the two issues.

8. The major exception to this neglect of refugee issues was the 1981 study of root causes undertaken by Sadruddin Aga Khan.

9. In 1992, emergency relief as a proportion of global overseas development assistance (ODA) rose dramatically, from around 3 percent to 8 percent. Since then, this trend has continued. In 1994, emergency relief amounted to 10 percent of ODA. Figures reported by OECD (DAC) 1994.
10. In GNP terms, Norway with 1.05 percent is the largest donor and the United States (before recent cuts announced by Congress) is at the very bottom with 0.15 percent.
11. For a critique of UNHCR's operation in Kosovo, including its neglect of internally displaced there during the conflict, see: United Kingdom, House of Commons, International Development Committee, *Kosovo: The Humanitarian Crisis*, 15 May 1999. See also: UNHCR, Evaluation and Policy Research Unit, *The Kosovo Refugee Crisis* (Geneva: EPAU/2000/001, February 2000).
12. UN Secretary-General's Report to the General Assembly, July 1997 (A/51/950, para. 186).
13. For an analysis, see Bagshaw 1998.
14. UN Doc. E/CN/1998/50, 1998.
15. I am indebted to William DeMars for drawing my attention to the important human rights roles that relief NGOs could play in internal conflicts.

References

Aall, Pamela R. 1996. *NGOs and Conflict Management*. Washington, D.C.: U.S. Institute of Peace.

Atwood, Brian. 1995. Address to the national Association of State Universities and Land Grant Colleges Annual Conference (12 November).

Bagshaw, Simon. 1998. "Internally Displaced Persons at the Fifty-Fourth Session of the United nations Commission on Human Rights 16 March–24 April 1998." *International Journal of Refugee Law* 10, 3: 548–556.

Cels, Johan. 1989. "De-Facto Refugees." In *Refugees and International Relations*, edited by Gil Loescher and Laila Monahan. Oxford: Oxford University Press.

Chase, Hill, and Paul Kennedy. 1996. "Pivotal States and U.S. Strategy." *Foreign Affairs* 75.

Christopher, Warren. 1995. "Readying the United nations for the Twenty-First Century: Some UN-21 Proposals for Consideration." New York: U.S. Mission to the United Nations.

Cohen, Roberta. 1995. *Refugees and Human Rights*. Washington, D.C.: Refugee Policy Group.

———. 1996a. "Protecting the Internally Displaced." *World Refugee Survey 1996*: 20–27.

———. 1996b. *IDPs: An Extended Role for UNHCR*. Discussion Paper for UNHCR workshop, Geneva: UNHCR (November): 6.

Cohen, Roberta, and Francis Deng. 1998a. *The Forsaken People: Case Studies of the Internally Displaced*. Washington, D.C.: Brookings Institution Press.

———. 1998b. *Masses in Flight: The Global Crisis of Internal Displacement*. Washington, D.C.: Brookings Institution Press.

DeMars, William. 1995. "Early Warning and International Humanitarian Action After the Cold War." *Journal of Refugee Studies* 8.

Deng, Francis. 1993. *Protecting the Dispossessed: A Challenge for the International Community* Washington, D.C.: The Brookings Institution.
———. 1998. "30 Guiding Principles." *International Journal of Refugee Law* 10, 3: 563–572.
Dowty, Alan, and Gil Loescher. 1996. "Refugee Movements as Grounds for International Action." *International Security* 22, 43–71.
———. 1999. "Changing Norms in International Responses to Domestic Disorder." In *Globalization and Global Governance*, edited by Raimo Vayrynen. New York: Rowman and Littlefield.
Duffield, Mark. 1994. "The Political Economy of Internal War: Asset Transfer, Complex Emergencies and International Aid" and other chapters. In *War and Hunger: Rethinking International Responses to Complex Emergencies*, edited by Joanna Macrae and Anthony Zwi. London: Zed Books.
Eriksson, John, et al. 1996. *The International Response to Conflict and Genocide: Lessons from the Rwanda Experience, Synthesis Report*. Copenhagen: Joint OECD/DAC Evaluation of Rwanda Operation.
Forsythe, David. 1995 "The UN and Human Rights at Fifty: An Incremental but Incomplete Revolution." *Global Governance* 1: 297–318.
Frelick, Bill. 1993. "Preventing Refugee Flows: Protection or Peril?" *World Refugee Survey 1993*. Washington, D.C.: U.S. Committee for Refugees.
Gallagher, Dennis, Susan Forbes-Martin, and Patricia Weiss-Fagen. 1989. "Temporary Safe Haven: The Need for North American-European Responses." In *Refugees and International Relations*, edited by Gil Loescher and Laila Monahan. Oxford: Oxford University Press.
Goodwin-Gill, Guy. 1995. *The Refugee in International Law*. Oxford: Clarendon Press.
Gordenker, Leon, and Thomas Weiss, eds. 1991. *Soldiers, Peacekeepers and Disasters*. Basingstoke: MacMillan.
Grahl-Madsen, Atle. 1966. *The Status of Refugees in International Law*. Leyden: The Netherlands: Sijthoff.
Guest, Iain. 1996. *Rwanda's Refugee Crisis—the Outlines of a New Approach*. Geneva: World Council of Churches and UNHCR.
Hathaway, James. 1991. *The Law of Refugee Status*. Toronto: Butterworths.
Henkin, Alice, ed. 1995. *Honoring Human Rights and Keeping the Peace: Lessons from El Salvador, Cambodia and Haiti*. Washington, D.C.: The Aspen Institute.
Klare, Michael. 1995. "The Global Trade in Light Weapons in the International System in the Post–Cold War Era," In *Lethal Commerce: The Global Trade in Small Arms and Light Weapons*, edited by J. Boutwell, M. Klare, and L. Reed. Cambridge, Mass.: American Academy of Arts and Sciences.
Lawyers Committee for Human Rights. 1995. *Haiti: Learning the Hard Way: The UN/OAS Human Rights Monitoring Operation in Haiti 1993–94*. New York: Lawyers Committee.
———. 1996. *Improvising History: A Critical Evaluation of the UN Observer Mission in El Salvador*. New York: Lawyers Committee.
Lippman, Thomas. 1996. "U.S. Loses Rank in Global Giving." *The Washington Post* 18 June.
Loescher, Gil. 1992. *Refugee Movements and International Security*. London: International Institute for Strategic Studies, Adelphi Paper 267.
———. 1993. *Beyond Charity: International Cooperation and the Global Refugee Crisis*. New York: Oxford University Press.

Maynard, Kimberly. 1996. *International Aid in Complex Emergencies: Reintegration of Communities in Conflict.* Ph.D. dissertation. Cincinnati, Ohio: The Graduate School of the Union Institute.

Minear, Larry, and Associates. 1994. *Humanitarian Action in the Former Yugoslavia: The UN's Role 1991–1993.* Providence: Thomas Watson Institute for International Studies, Brown University, Occasional Paper 18.

Moore, Jonathan. 1987. "Refugees and Foreign Policy: Immediate Needs and Durable Solutions." Lecture at John F. Kennedy School (6 April), Harvard University, quoted in Louise Druke, *Preventive Action* (Frankfurt: Peter Lang, 1990): 217.

Morris, Eric. 1996. *The Role of Peacekeeping Forces in Humanitarian Operations.* Tokyo: Conference on International Peacekeeping (February): 4.

Norwegian Refugee Council and Refugee Policy Group. 1993. *Human Rights Protection for Internally Displaced Persons.* Washington, D.C.: Refugee Policy Group.

OECD. 1994. *Development Cooperation: Report of the Development Assistance Committee 1994.* Paris: Organization for Economic Cooperation and Development.

Ogata, Sadako. 1995. Address to UN Commission on Human Rights. Geneva: UNHCR (March).

Randel, J., and T. German, eds. 1995. *The Reality of Aid 95: An Independent Review of International Aid.* London: Earthscan.

Saulnier, Françoise. 1996. "The Human Shield Strategy." *The World Today* 51 (January): 18–19.

Shacknove, Andrew. 1993. "From Asylum to Containment." *International Journal of Refugee Law* 5.

Shawcross, Hartley. 1996. "Order NATO to Round Up Suspects Indicted for War Crimes." *International Herald Tribune* (23 May).

Thorburn, Joanne. 1995. "Transcending Boundaries: Temporary Protection and Burden-sharing in Europe." *International Journal of Refugee Law* 7: 459–480.

United Nations. 1994. *Strengthening of the Coordination of Humanitarian Emergency Assistance of the United Nations,* Report of the Secretary-General, A48/536 New York: United Nations.

UNHCR. 1993–95. *Populations of Concern to UNHCR: A Statistical Overview.* Geneva: UNHCR.

———. 1995. *The State of the World's Refugees 1995: In Search of Solutions.* Oxford: Oxford University Press.

———. 1996. *UNHCR and Human Rights.* Geneva: UNHCR discussion paper.

United States Permanent Mission to the United Nations. 1995 "Readying the United Nations for the Twenty-First Century: Some UN-21 Proposals for Consideration." New York: U.S. Mission to the United Nations (July).

Walker, Peter. 1996. "Challenges for an Operating Agency in the Next Five Years." Geneva: international conference, *Geneva and the Challenge of Humanitarian Action of the 1990s.* 16 February.

Weiss, Tom. 1996. "Reinventing UNHCR: Enterprising Humanitarians in the Former Yugoslavia 1991–1995." *Global Governance.*

Zolberg, Aristide, Astri Suhrke, and Sergio Aguayo. 1989. *Escape from Violence: Conflict and Refugee Crises in the Developing World.* New York: Oxford University Press.

Zucker, Norman, and Naomi Zucker. 1996. *Desperate Crossings: Seeking Refuge in America.* Armonk, New York: M. E. Sharpe.

– Chapter 7 –

REFORMING THE INTERNATIONAL HUMANITARIAN DELIVERY SYSTEM FOR WARS

Thomas G. Weiss

Euphoria at the end of the Cold War was short lived. The optimism of November 1989 about new operating assumptions for world politics after the fall of the Berlin Wall seems like ancient history. Scholars and politicians awakened with a hangover from George Bush's "new world order" and Bill Clinton's "assertive multilateralism." More sober views, even if no new slogans, dominate Washington's conventional wisdom (Christopher 1995b; Dole 1995; Helms 1996; Independent Task Force 1996; Maynes and Williamson 1996; Ruggie 1996).

Democratization and liberalization have spread, as David Forsythe argues in these pages, but so too has the plague of micronationalism, fragmentation, and massive suffering for those who have fled, and those who remain, in today's civil war zones. The demise of East-West tensions did not result in the peaceful triumph of Western liberal democracy and capitalism and Francis Fukuyama's much-heralded "end of history" (Fukuyama 1992). Rather, this latest installment in inaccurate forecasting actually ushered in a painful epoch with record numbers of refugees, internally displaced persons (IDPs), and other victims.

The onset of the post–Cold War era initially witnessed a reinvigorated United Nations (UN). There remain inveterate optimists and visionaries (Commission on Global Governance 1995; Evans 1993; Independent Task Force 1996; South Centre 1996). However, bullishness after the Gulf War has become pessimism following UN shortcomings or outright failures in Bosnia, Croatia, Somalia, Haiti,[1] and Rwanda, along with less visible ones in Angola, Afghanistan, and the Sudan. Somalia was the turning point, when Pollyannaish notions about intervening militarily to halt aggression or thugs and to help sustain civilians trapped in war zones or fleeing from them were replaced by more realistic estimates about the limits of such undertakings (Farer 1996; Weiss 1995b).

The number and scope of what Leslie Gelb has dubbed "wars of national debilitation" (Gelb 1994: 5) can thwart and even immobilize analysts. Nonetheless, I am led to ask whether it is not possible to ensure the rights of civilians suffering from the violence and displacement caused by armed conflicts. This essay can hardly be sanguine—neither for responses by the international humanitarian system nor the United States[2]—but it responds partially in the affirmative.

The bad news is that the glass is less than half full—much waste and ineffectiveness exist. The good news is that there are feasible and specific ways to improve the performance of military, UN, and nongovernmental humanitarians who help to mitigate suffering in war zones.

What Is Happening?

There are three striking characteristics of post–Cold War humanitarian crises: the predominance of civil wars; the growing demand for UN soldiers; and the devolution of responsibilities by the UN for security and services to regional and nongovernmental organizations (Weiss 1995c). The result has been an ever-increasing number of involuntary migrants, both refugees and internally displaced persons (IDPs), as well as those war victims who choose not to leave their homes in war zones. The fact that one out of every 115 citizens of the world are displaced by war, and probably an equal number have remained behind but whose lives are totally disrupted, is one of many tragic human statistics from contemporary armed conflicts (International Federation of Red Cross and Red Crescent Societies 1997; UNHCR 1997; U.S. Committee for Refugees 1997).

The most significant feature of international responses in the last five years has been the growing willingness to address, rather than ignore, emergencies within the borders of war-torn states. Eighty-two armed conflicts broke out in the first half decade following the collapse of the Berlin Wall, and seventy-nine were intrastate wars; in fact, two of the three remaining ones (Nagorno-Karabakh and Bosnia) also could legitimately be categorized as civil wars (UNDP 1994). Lawyers point out that the language of Charter article 2 (7) remains intact. But humanitarian imperatives have led governmental, intergovernmental (IGOs), and nongovernmental organizations (NGOs) to modify the interpretation of this article and effectively to redefine when it is possible "to intervene in matters which are essentially within the domestic jurisdiction of any state." Sometimes there is no sovereign in failed or collapsed states, as in Somalia (Helman and Ratner 1993; Zartman 1995), and sometimes sovereignty is overridden in the name of higher norms in cases, as the Kurds in northern Iraq (Chopra and Weiss 1992; Lyons and Mastanduno 1995). In any event, the two dominant norms of world politics during the Cold War—namely that borders were sacrosanct and that secession was unthinkable—no longer generate as much enthusiasm as they once did even among states (Ayoob 1993, 1995; Holsti 1996; Jackson 1990; Migdal 1988; Rice 1988).

The second characteristic relates to the growth in demand for UN soldiers. The dramatic increase in activities by the United Nations in the first half of the 1990s spawned a cottage industry to analyze peacekeeping (Berdal 1993; Diehl 1993; Durch 1993 and 1996; Mackinlay 1994; Ratner 1995), including former UN Secretary-General Boutros-Ghali's 1992 and 1995 "agendas" (Boutros-Ghali 1995b).[3] After stable levels of about 10,000 troops in the early post–Cold War period, the number of UN troops jumped rapidly. In the last few years, 70,000 to 80,000 blue-helmeted soldiers have been authorized by the UN's annualized "military" (peacekeeping) budget that approached $4 billion in 1995. Accumulated total arrears in the same year hovered around $3.5 billion—that is, almost equal this budget and about three times the regular United Nations budget. The secretary-general lamented that "the difficult financial situation ... is increasingly proving to be the most serious obstacle to the effective management of the organization" (Boutros-Ghali 1995c: para. 22). Both the numbers of soldiers and the budget dropped dramatically in 1996, by two-thirds, pointing to financial and professional problems and "strategic overstretch" by the UN of the type that Paul Kennedy attributes to empires but that also seems applicable to an overextended world organization (Kennedy 1987).

As such, the third characteristic in some ways arises from the first two and is the most salient for this essay—namely subcontracting for military services to both regional organizations or major states, on the one hand, and for humanitarian delivery services to international NGOs, on the other (Weiss 1998b). The pursuit of the Gulf War and the creation of safe havens for Kurds were clear and successful illustrations of military subcontracting, as were the Implementation Force (IFOR) and Stabilization Force (SFOR) in the Former Yugoslavia; a more controversial and less successful example was Somalia. A surge of three Security Council decisions between late June and late July 1994 indicated the growing relevance of military intervention by major powers in regions of their traditional interests: a Russian scheme to deploy its troops in Georgia to end the three-year-old civil war; the French intervention in Rwanda to help stave off genocidal conflict; and the U.S. plan to spearhead a military invasion to reverse the military coup in Haiti. The decision in Budapest in December 1994 by the Conference (now Organization) on Security and Cooperation in Europe (OSCE) to authorize troops from the Commonwealth of Independent States (CIS) after a cease-fire in Nagorno-Karabakh was another illustration, as were earlier efforts by Nigeria and other countries of the Economic Community of West African States (ECOWAS) in Liberia.

Military and civilian observers agree that the results from these arrangements have been anything except uniformly positive. Yet, the evident gap between international capacities and increasing demands for help could be filled by regional powers, or even hegemons, that operating under international scrutiny and with international approval, try to hold interveners accountable for their actions.

A second element of the subcontracting phenomenon relates to the growing contribution of international NGOs to the mitigation of suffering by refugees, IDPs, returnees, or war victims (Weiss 1996b).[4] This is part of a larger development, namely the burgeoning of nongovernmental organizations in all sectors that have injected new and unexpected voices into international discourse (Salamon and Anheier 1994; Schneider 1988; Weiss and Gordenker 1996). Over the last two decades, but especially since the end of the Cold War, human rights advocates, gender activists, developmentalists, and groups of indigenous peoples have become more vocal and operational in many contexts that were once thought to be the exclusive preserve of governments (Spiro 1995; Wapner 1995). As the role of the state dwindles and is reappraised and while analysts and policymakers alike seek alternatives to help solve problems, NGOs emerge as a critical actors—private in form but public in purpose.

Delivery of services is the mainstay of most of their budgets and the basis for enthusiastic support from a wide range of donors. As part of a privatization of both development and relief, several contributors to this volume indicate that bilateral and intergovernmental organizations are relying upon NGOs more and more. The last twenty years have witnessed exponential growth, so much so that now the total transferred through NGOs outweighs that disbursed by the UN system, excluding the Washington-based financial institutions of the World Bank and the International Monetary Fund (IMF) (Smillie 1995). Many NGOs run development programs; but they have become increasingly active in migration and disaster relief, which in total financial terms is becoming their most important activity.

Operational NGOs are central to comprehensive international responses to civil wars in the post–Cold War world. In 1995, at least 13 percent of total public development aid—some $10–$12 billion and probably much more since neither food aid nor military help figures in statistics—was disbursed by NGOs, an ever-growing share (approaching half) of which was emergency relief (Randel and German 1997). There has been a sixfold increase in emergency spending over the last decade. In short, NGO humanitarian relief has become a big business. How much of rising expenditures is due to inefficiencies and increasing administrative costs is, however, not clear. Having literally hundreds of subcontractors delivering similar goods and services in a disjointed and competitive marketplace during the tumult of wars means that part of the dramatic growth must be driven by NGOs themselves (Bennett 1995).

What Can Be Done?

When local capacities are overwhelmed by a complex emergency and massive human displacement occurs, or when local authorities are unwilling to help victims or even actively prevent access to them by outsiders, human solidarity and institutional mandates lead the international humanitarian system to respond. Broadly speaking, there are three challenges, which coincide with the periods before, during, and after wars. First, how can the international humanitarian system forestall manmade disasters? Prevention intuitively is attractive—"a stitch in time" resonates nicely in multilateral ears. Nonetheless, myopic decision making by governments renders bleak the prospects for meaningful action before war. Moreover, not all conflicts can or should be prevented. Second, however welcome the rhetoric of prevention, debilitating civil wars are a specific plague that will continue on the international house for the foreseeable future. Can the international humanitarian system improve responses to mitigate life-threatening suffering? As mentioned at the outset, there is indeed much room for improvement. Third, what is to be done to get a society back on its collective feet after a war has run its course? Much has been made of the continuum from relief to reconstruction to development; but the international humanitarian system has actually been moving backwards in terms of somehow getting beyond a preoccupation with crises.

The challenges before and after armed conflicts are substantial and important, but reducing involuntary migration by tackling its causes is not the emphasis here. Rather, I focus on designing better international responses to humanitarian crises and the accompanying forced migration of peoples in active war zones. The two components of better responses, emergency delivery and protection of human rights, are linked. But this essay concerns relief, an ambitious enough subject. Although my framework incorporates all the perspectives, the reader should keep in mind that elsewhere in this volume Gil Loescher focuses on protection, David Forsythe on democratization, and Elizabeth Ferris as well as Richard Bissell and Andrew Natsios on development.

Desirable and possible steps in the next half decade toward a better delivery system thus are my preoccupation in this chapter. Although this volume seeks to understand and help meet the needs of involuntary migrants (that is, by refugees and IDPs), my analysis applies as well to aiding civilians who remain in war zones. Legal distinctions emanating from categories are important for protection, but dubious for international delivery (Deng 1993; Loescher 1993).

Before Wars: Prevention of Involuntary Migration

The first challenge may be the most apparent, but also the one for which significant change is least likely. Preventive diplomacy is the latest conceptual fashion—what one honest observer called "an idea in search of a strategy" (Lund 1994: 27 and 1996). Such actions to forestall the eruption of conflict as the expanded use of fact-finding missions, human rights monitors, and early warning systems are being discussed and attempted. In addition, economic and social development are generally viewed as helpful in addressing the roots of conflict, even if the results from substantial aid and investment in the former Yugoslavia and Rwanda are hardly encouraging for those like the last UN secretary-general wishing to make a case for "preventive development" as a "necessary complement to preventive diplomacy" (Boutros-Ghali 1995a: 99). In a sense, the vast bulk of UN activities since 1945 could be considered "preventive."

In crises that involve massive involuntary migration, however, the most cost-effective yet untested preventive measure is the deployment of troops (Weiss 1996c). The only experiment to date, the symbolic deployment of a detachment of UN blue helmets to Macedonia, is widely heralded as a success, incorrectly in my view because the international bluff has not been called. To be a successful deterrent, such soldiers must be backed by contingency plans and reserve firepower for immediate retaliation against aggressors. This would amount to advance authorization for Chapter VII in the event that a preventive force was challenged. Such backup would be no easy matter to assemble, politically or operationally. Acknowledging, for example, that the combined forces of the Yugoslav People's Army (JNA) and the Bosnian Serbs would have been very hard to intimidate, without automatic backup, the currency of UN action will be devalued to such an extent that preventive action should not have been attempted in the first place.

The rub is obvious: prevention is cost-effective in the long run but cost-intensive in the short run. Both pundits and professors indicate that democratically elected governments can rarely imagine action whose time horizon extends beyond the next public opinion poll, and certainly not beyond the next electoral campaign. Moreover, economic nonsense may make political sense. There are few political risks with devoting large humanitarian resources after the fact, but there are considerable ones involved in deploying troops with possible casualties and the potential for getting mired in a protracted war. In addition, some war and violence may be necessary and just—the liberation of Rwanda by the Rwandan Patriotic Front following the 1994 genocide, or of the refugee camps in Zaire by Tutsi rebels in 1996 come to mind.

However, the growing preoccupation with saving funds could make a difference. In the former Yugoslavia, the "long run" lasted almost four years, whereas in Rwanda it was reduced to a matter of weeks. The argument that an earlier use of force would have been more economical in the former Yugoslavia runs up against the inability of governments to look very far into the future, and of their consequent tendency to magnify the disadvantages for immediate expenditures and to discount those in the future. In Rwanda, the costs of at least 500,000 dead, over four million displaced persons, and a ruined economy were borne almost immediately by the same governments that had refused to respond militarily only a few weeks earlier. The United States and the European Union ended up providing an estimated minimum of $1.4 billion in emergency aid in 1994.

If savings are essential, and if the West is viscerally and ethically unable to ignore massive tragedies with their accompanying involuntary migration and economic disruption, even in far away and geopolitically insignificant countries, there is the possibility that preventive military action may in some cases become more plausible. In spite of some 150,000 deaths in the three years beginning in October 1993, dithering reactions to Burundi's ethnic cauldron indicated that international discourse has changed. Still, the willingness to deploy troops in a preventive fashion lags far behind the rhetoric. Stephen Stedman has caricatured prevention as a contemporary version of "alchemy" (Stedman 1995). Were we suddenly to move closer to the modern era, we would still discover no magic formula. Although eminent persons disagree (Carnegie Commission 1997), spending analytical energy on improvements in the international humanitarian delivery system to counter suffering has a higher return than time in a chemistry lab.

During Wars: Reforming the International Humanitarian Delivery System

A significant number of observers argue that the international humanitarian system has acquitted itself reasonably well in Rwanda and Bosnia in light of the magnitude of involuntary displacement and suffering—a "silver lining," if there ever was one, to complex emergencies clouding the humanitarian horizon. Prescriptive thoughts about improving the international humanitarian system are linked to improvements for the military, the United Nations system, and international nongovernmental organizations (Minear and Weiss 1995a, 1995b; Weiss and Collins 1996). These ameliorations are the preoccupation in this chapter. Two points mentioned at the outset should be repeated here. First, the analysis applies to refugees, IDPs, and returnees as well as to victims who have never left a war zone (Farer 1995). Second, I concentrate on emergency relief and leave the protection of victims' rights to Gil Loescher, while being aware that most UN and NGOs could do much more to incorporate protection into their field activities (Henkin 1995; Human Rights Watch 1993, 1994; LaRose-Edwards 1995).

① MILITARY HUMANITARIANS The military performs two functions in the humanitarian arena—providing a secure environment as well as supporting the work of humanitarian agencies and carrying out relief activities themselves (Weiss 1995a, 1999). Regular military involvement in UN humanitarian efforts in war zones is a phenomenon of the post–Cold War era, but the use of military forces for such purposes is not new, the earliest recorded instances predate Alexander the Great (Cuny 1991). They continued in Europe through the Napoleonic Wars and into the twentieth century. Sometimes assistance was seen as a humane gesture to the vanquished, but it was invariably mixed with the desire to help secure loyalty from newly subject populations. Variations of this theme were played by colonial armies who orchestrated assistance to the civil authority.

A quantum expansion of the military into the humanitarian arena took place after World War II. The task of occupying Germany and Japan, as well as reconstructing as quickly as possible Europe's economic base, required new types of personnel within the armed forces: administrators, planners, developmentalists, and logisticians. At the time, there were relatively few international NGOs, and the UN's humanitarian delivery mechanisms were just starting.

In the last half century, military assistance in natural disasters has become a normal extension of civil defense. Armed forces often possess an abundance of precisely those resources that are in the shortest supply when disaster strikes: transport, fuel, communications, commodities, building equipment, medicines, and large stockpiles of off-the-shelf provisions. In addition, the military's vaunted "can-do" mentality and rapid response capabilities as well as its hierarchical discipline are useful within the chaos of acute tragedies. The same capacities that are relevant for help in a domestic disaster can also be applied to international tragedies.

The evaporation of much of the raison d'être for military spending at first led Western publics to insist upon downsizing military establishments. The successful allied mobilization for the Gulf War and the subsequent use of "military humanitarianism" (Weiss and Campbell 1991) in northern Iraq—along with substantial if sometimes less popular versions in Somalia, Bosnia, Rwanda, and Haiti—have provided a means for militaries to fend off pressures to reduce their infrastructure and personnel. Proposals and conferences sponsored by the Canadian, Dutch, and Danish militaries provide evidence that this is not simply a concern for the largest powers.[5]

The advantages of using the armed forces in war zones are twofold: their logistics cornucopia and their capacity to secure access when it is impossible or dangerous because belligerents do not consent to international action. Establishing a bottom line for either of the two basic humanitarian functions of the military requires subjectivity (Weiss 1997, 1999).

Evaluating the downside to military logistics consists largely of looking at a particular military operation while asking and then answering, "What is it worth?" The military is normally the most costly option, but

in certain situations they may be the only one. Moreover, defense departments sometimes foot the bill, and then the high costs are not directly
deducted from civilian efforts but are genuine add-ons. As demonstrated
when several military establishments responded unilaterally and multilaterally to the crisis of a million refugees in Goma in 1994, an effective
humanitarian response often requires the manpower, resources, and
rapid deployment capacity available only to the military (Joint Evaluation 1996; Minear and Guillot 1996; Prunier 1995). An assessment of costs
and benefits depends, essentially, on the existence of alternatives to the
military and, if none, then on the value attached to saving individual
human lives by the contributors of such assistance and by domestic pressure groups who make themselves heard. Civilian humanitarian organizations are learning to live with this reality and adopting procedures with
stand-by arrangements for staff, equipment, and supplies.

Guaranteeing access is more controversial and directly related to the
military's ability to overwhelm an enemy with superior force, even if
such a capacity is only a threat and not fully employed. Overriding sovereignty has always been a feature of world politics, but the normal justification has been national interests of the intervener. The frequency of
a humanitarian rationale motivating Security Council decisions for "humanitarian intervention" in the first half of the 1990s has been exceptional (Famsbotham and Woodhouse 1996; Harriss 1995; Heiberg 1994;
Mayall 1996; Pieterse 1998; Reed and Kaysen 1993; Roberts 1993 and
1996; Winter 1995).

Humanitarian organizations seek to determine the costs and benefits
of cooperation with the military when belligerents deny access. This is
considerably more problematic than evaluating logistics not only because
of the uncertainties surrounding the political willingness to stay the
course but also because the resort to military force destroys the impartiality, neutrality, and consent that have traditionally underpinned international succor. In spite of a widespread tendency among both analysts
and practitioners to lump them into a single category, military-civilian
humanitarianism—or the coming together of military forces and civilian
aid agencies to deal with the human suffering from complex emergencies—has actually taken a variety of forms. Without going into the distinct variations over the last half decade, there now exists a widespread
backlash in spite of successful efforts in northern Iraq and Haiti as well
as, arguably, partially successful ones in Somalia and Rwanda and even
less successful ones in Bosnia. The growing conventional wisdom among
publics, parliaments, pundits, and politicians is that humanitarian intervention is infeasible and unsustainable. While benevolence is never adequate, the provision of military support seems to have caused more
problems than it has solved.

If coercion to guarantee access occurs at all, humanitarian interventions in the near future will have to compensate for the military inade-
quacies of the United Nations. Experience suggests that UN decisions

should trigger interventions to be subcontracted to coalitions of the willing or to major states. Regional powers (for instance, Nigeria within West Africa, and Russia within the erstwhile Soviet republics) could take the lead combined with larger regional (that is, the Economic Community of West African States and the Commonwealth of Independent States) or global coalitions. Perhaps only when regional powers cannot or will not take such a lead should more global powers (for example, France in Rwanda, or the U.S. in Somalia) be expected to do so. However, blocking humanitarian intervention, which some powers are willing to conduct when other are reluctant to get involved (for example, the U.S. vis-à-vis Rwanda between early April and late June 1994), should be ruled out.

The strategy for the conduct of the Gulf War and especially the creation of safe havens in northern Iraq suggest how this procedure can work for the benefit of displaced persons and other victims. The host of criticism about inappropriate procedures and lack of proportionality have a hollow ring in light of the absence of alternatives. Without putting too fine a point on it, the United Nations is incapable of undertaking combat operations. The capacity to plan, support, and command peacekeeping, let alone peace-enforcement missions, is scarcely greater now than during the Cold War; and this situation will not change in the foreseeable future. Although modest improvements are feasible and sanguine views sometimes prevail (Paris 1997), states will not empower the United Nations with the wherewithal to contradict Michael Mandelbaum's judgment that "[t]he UN itself can no more conduct military operations on a large scale on its own than a trade association of hospitals can conduct heart surgery" (Mandelbaum 1994: 11).

The multilateral capacity for conflict management, and the concomitant repercussions for humanitarian action, will no doubt depend in the future upon ad hoc coalitions, regional organizations, and even hegemons. Bill Maynes dubbed this "benign realpolitik," which amounts to a revival of spheres of influence with UN oversight (Maynes 1993–94). The Security Council is experimenting with a type of great-power control over decision making and enforcement, which the United Nations had originally been founded to end, but which is increasingly pertinent in light of the inherent difficulties of multilateral mobilization and management of military force (Mearsheimer 1994–95).

Former Secretary-General Boutros-Ghali called for "a new division of labour between the United Nations and regional organizations, under which the regional organization carries the main burden but a small United Nations operation supports it and verifies that it is functioning in a manner consistent with positions adopted by the Security Council" (Boutros-Ghali 1995b: para. 86). Elsewhere in justifying UN monitoring of Nigeria and ECOWAS in Liberia as well as Russia and the CIS in Tajikistan and Georgia, he had this to say: "Finding the right division of labour between the United Nations and regional organizations is not easy. But such cooperation brings greater legitimacy and support to international efforts. It eases the material and financial burden of the United Nations. It allows for comparative advantage" (UN Department of Public Information 1995: 2). An observer might well ask, What's new about rationalization? Was the secretary-general not grasping at straws in justifying a gunboat diplomacy for the 1990s? Is this not simply realpolitik rather than a "partnership" (Henrikson 1996)? Boutros-Ghali was aware of the dangers: "Authorization to serve as a surrogate might strengthen a particular power's sphere of influence and damage the United Nations' standing as an organization intended to coordinate security across regional blocs" (Boutros-Ghali 1996: 95).

The difference could be that major powers or their coalitions act on their own behalf as well as on behalf of the Security Council—thus, they should be held accountable for their actions by the wider community of states authorizing outside interventions (Bettati 1996). While major powers inevitably flex their military muscles when it is in their perceived interests to do so, they do not necessarily agree in advance to subject themselves to international law and outside monitoring of their behavior. The political and economic advantages attached to a blue imprimatur from the Security Council provide some leverage for the community of states to foster accountability from would-be subcontractors.

In this context, what do we mean by "accountability" (Chopra and Weiss 1995; Jonson and Archer 1996)? First and foremost, it means the ability to ensure that the mandate reflects collective norms and interests at least as much as the national interests of the subcontractor. The greatest problem of any international regime is the presence or absence of enforcement measures to assure compliance. There are few means to ensure lawful behavior in general, and here we seek to influence the comportment of a powerful state or coalition during an intended or an on-going military operation. Yet, embarrassment should not be underestimated as a factor when states are asked to justify their behavior in front of allies or national electorates.

The Security Council is in a position to refuse approval or funds without three essential components of a bargain, which should be struck before an operation is blessed. The first is an effective monitoring mechanism in the field. In order to answer "Quis custodiet ipsos custodies?" UN monitors within the command structure of a subcontractor's military units are a minimum requirement, perhaps accompanied by an independent political directorate acting on behalf of the Security Council. There also should be meaningful restrictions governing the conduct by a subcontractor's soldiers—they would be expected to adhere to the specifics of the Geneva Conventions and Additional Protocols, to respect proportionality in the use of force, and to allow totally free access by the media in order to help monitor situations in the field.

The final element consists of costs associated with noncompliance. If after agreeing to respect internationally imposed restrictions, a subcontractor's forces diverge from agreed standards, the Security Council can really only hope to function as a whistle-blower and remove the blue fig leaf. This is admittedly a feeble capacity, but it could at least serve to prevent the co-optation of international organizations into national service. In addition to diplomatic embarrassment, such a withdrawal mixed with condemnation could also inhibit or prohibit trade or flows of assistance to the faulty subcontractor. This is likely to be more consequential for poorer potential subcontractors (for example, Russia, Nigeria, or India), but wealthier potential ones (for example, the U.S., Britain, or France) are democratic countries whose domestic political processes probably make public international embarrassments more of a threat to their governments. In any case, such operations should be kept on a relatively short leash. The problems of continuity notwithstanding, mandates should be obligatorily reviewed and approved every three to six months so that an embarrassed subcontractor among the permanent five could not simply use a veto to extend a United Nations cover for an unacceptable on-going operation.

(2) UN HUMANITARIANS The second set of prescriptions relates to the civilian side of the United Nations system. It would be gratuitous to denigrate the courage and dedication of individuals assisting victims, just as it would be incorrect to assume that all overlap and redundancy among UN institutions is wasteful. At the same time, humanitarian action has been marred by needless duplication and competition. Complaints are hardly new, but they are becoming more frequent and strident. In the undiplomatic prose of former U.S. Ambassador Jonathan Moore: "The UN's thoroughly fragmented and feudal nature is a big liability for critical programmes in the field" (Moore 1996: 29).

Effective international responses to human tragedies require a clearer division of labor. The United Nations, for better and for worse, is the logical candidate to assume leadership on behalf of war victims, whether they flee a war zone or decide to remain in one. Everyone is for "coordination." But no one wishes to be coordinated when it implies going beyond the mere exchange of information, the usual meaning, to encompass the sacrifice of organizational autonomy in the interests of a team effort and a single, coherent strategy on behalf of refugees, IDPs, and war victims. Excessive organizational autonomy and turf-consciousness, and perhaps creative redundancy, are easier to tolerate in normal development efforts; but there is no room in civil wars where UN or UN-blessed military forces are present under Chapter VII of the UN Charter.

As a lifetime student of international bureaucracies, I am aware of the apparent naïveté in the following suggestion: It is essential to consolidate UN organizations, or unnecessary and unacceptable waste will impede effective multilateral humanitarian delivery in civil wars. Andrew Natsios has written convincingly that "Organizational autonomy and complexity are the enemies of speed and strategic coherence" (Natsios 1996: 88)—precisely what is required in complex humanitarian emergencies. The necessity to rationalize and refocus organizational mandates has become obvious not only to reduce overlap and improve performance, but also to fill-in such glaring gaps as the one for internally displaced persons. In spite of difficulties in overhauling intergovernmental machinery, Raimo Väyrynen is not alone in coming to the conclusion that "the world community needs a new, long-term, and comprehensive doctrine of humanitarian intervention and a new multifaceted international mechanism to carry it out" (Väyrynen 1995: 29).

Moreover, this notion has moved into the mainstream of intergovernmental discussions. This is not to imply that governments themselves are efficient and sincere—indeed, there are crocodile tears in many bilateral emergency agencies where waste is also present. The call from governments for "UN coordination" is duplicitous in light of their own unwillingness to do less national flag-waving. Yet, there is a crying need for a single intergovernmental body to set priorities, raise and distribute funds, and coordinate inputs for complex emergencies in which outside military forces are present. Former Secretary of State Warren Christopher's "non-paper" at the July 1995 session of ECOSOC proposed considering "whether and how to consolidate the emergency functions of the UN High Commissioner for Refugees (UNHCR), the World Food Programme (WFP), the UN Children's Fund (UNICEF), and the Department of Humanitarian Affairs (DHA) into a single agency" (Christopher 1995a, 1995b). This was also one key option, albeit controversial, put forward by the unprecedented multinational, multi-donor evaluation effort in Rwanda (Joint Evaluation 1996: vol. 3, 159–61).

In fact, there have been a growing number of similar proposals for centralization from seasoned practitioners in recent years (Childers and Urquhart 1994; Evans 1993; Ingram 1993). The juridical status of these main actors makes their consolidation easier to conceive for three reasons: they are all part of the United Nations itself, they are not specialized agencies with budgets independent of the General Assembly, and their executive heads are appointed by the UN secretary-general. The discussion has moved out of the limelight because there had been no world-class crisis since 1994. The subject undoubtedly will return after the next massive flight of involuntary migrants accompanied by a less-than-optimum UN performance. In fact, an important opportunity for change was missed with the lackluster reform of 1997 (Annan 1997) because the result was a "shell game" (Weiss 1998a) rather than a substantial restructuring.

In addition to cost-savings, there is another reason to consolidate the UN's institutional capacities when military enforcement has been subcontracted, as proposed earlier. The staff of most UN organizations and the vast majority of NGOs are ill-equipped to function efficaciously when bullets are flying. They are uncomfortable about their association with enforcement, which by definition contradicts the principles of impartiality and neutrality. In spite of politicized responses in Somalia, Bosnia, and Rwanda, the fiction of the applicability of these traditional principles is still very much in evidence (de Waal 1997; de Waal and

Omaar 1995; Ignatieff 1997; Omaar and de Waal 1994; Pasic and Weiss 1997; Rieff 1994–95; Walzer 1995). A consolidated institution would perhaps help them to comprehend "the delusion of impartial intervention" (Betts 1994).

Like the military forces deployed for humanitarian enforcement actions, this proposed civilian delivery unit should form an integral part of a unified command that would report directly to the Security Council and not to the secretary-general. The troops authorized by the council and staff from the new humanitarian unit together would comprise a core of soldiers and civilians in possession of expertise and body armor—a "HUMPROFOR," or Humanitarian Protection Force.

Governments viscerally oppose new administrative entities, particularly for what is perceived as a bloated international bureaucracy. But one should be created for emergency aid where the international response includes Chapter VII economic or military coercion. This specialized cadre would be a truly "international" ICRC; but unlike the Swiss NGO, it would be willing and able to act in tandem with partial enforcement actions. Perhaps more in harm's way even than soldiers, these volunteers should not be part of the common UN staff system because they would have to be appropriately insured and compensated.

Resources and capable relief specialists should be recruited specifically for this new unit, although some could also be siphoned from existing humanitarian agencies provided that they left their former institutional cultures, either UN or nongovernmental, and baggage behind (J. Q. Wilson 1989). Under this arrangement, the UN's regular humanitarian personnel themselves would be absent, and the budgets of UN organizations reduced accordingly. If a peacekeeping operation changed to enforcement, regular civilian personnel would withdraw. In serious armed conflicts that do not merit Chapter VII or in which the UN simply does not wish to get involved militarily—recent examples include Afghanistan, Liberia, Sudan, and Guatemala—the new unit would still be better placed than the emergency units of UN organizations; but this new unit would not have a monopoly.

During a HUMPROFOR operation, the ICRC would continue its work with prisoners of war and its own humanitarian efforts throughout the crisis. It would be expected to distance itself, as it always has, from warring parties who do not wish to cooperate. It would be unlikely for the work of the ICRC and the new unit to clash, compete, or contradict. NGOs and the ICRC cannot be kept from a war zone, unless they have no funds or are bound by the conditions in donor contracts. If HUMPROFOR existed, governments could channel the bulk of their funds through it and place conditionality clauses in NGO and UN contracts that would remove them from the field once Chapter VII went into effect. In short, the NGO population per se would decline until Chapter VII ceased, although staff could be seconded to the new centralized unit provided that they agreed to respect the standard operating procedures.

This new unit's members would no doubt be more comfortable than the staffs of most UN organizations and international NGOs are with the inevitable consequences on vulnerable civilians of coercion as part of a comprehensive political strategy. Assistance would go to refugees and internally displaced persons without regard to their precise juridical status. There would be a coherent strategy on the side of victims. The new unit might well have a substantial number of, or even be dominated by, retired military personnel who would understand the necessity to subordinate themselves and work side-by-side with the military within a hierarchical and disciplined structure. They should in any case be experienced with the armed forces and able to bridge the military-civilian cultural divide that routinely impedes effectiveness in many war zones.

Attaching this unit to the Security Council would insulate the office of the UN's executive head from Chapter VII's finger-pointing and call to arms. The strength of the office of the secretary-general is its impartiality, which is derived from its lack of vested interests. Former Assistant Secretary-General Giandomenico Picco has persuasively argued that "[t]ransforming the institution of the Secretary General into a pale imitation of a state" in order "to manage the use of force may well be a suicidal embrace" (Picco 1994: 15).

Under this proposed schema, the UN secretary-general would be kept available for tasks such as mediation and administering failed states—which would demand strict impartiality along with political acumen (Menkhaus 1996). The new humanitarian entity, attached to the Security Council, would be a humanitarian adaptation of the precedent set by Rolf Ekeus. As executive chairman of the UN Special Commission (UNSCOM) on Disarmament and Arms Control in Iraq, he was appointed by and reports to the council rather than to the secretary-general. As part of the Chapter VII enforcement governing the terms of the cease-fire after the Gulf War, Ekeus and later Richard Butler were the Security Council's emissaries. The UN secretary-general remains a potential interlocutor for even a pariah regime or its successor.

Moreover, organizing such an integrated approach within active conflict arenas would help insulate purely humanitarian help and reduce politicization outside of war zones. UN and NGO humanitarian agencies should devote their limited human and financial resources to what they do better, namely emergency aid without combat troops, or after natural disasters or cease-fires, as well as reconstruction and development. In non-hot war settings (that is, in natural disasters, postconflict rehabilitation, or chronic emergencies), intergovernmental and nongovernmental agencies with both relief and development portfolios can move rapidly from one set of tasks to another.

The politicization of humanitarian action—or the perception of its politicization, which has the same impact—in Bosnia, Somalia, and Rwanda has altered civilian humanitarian orthodoxy. London's International Institute for Strategic Studies put forward possible new guidelines that were based on an internal UNHCR memorandum about humanitarian action when outside military forces are involved. The new bottom line was the recommendation that civilian humanitarians "should not embark on humanitarian operations where, over time, impartiality and neutrality are certain to be compromised"; and "[i]f impartiality and neutrality are compromised, an ongoing humanitarian operation should be reconsidered, scaled down or terminated" (International Institute for Strategic Studies 1995: 2). Even the ICRC is increasingly preoccupied by this subject (International Committee of the Red Cross 1997; Palwankar 1994).

This argument would have been anathema only a few years ago, when humanitarians viscerally responded to every tragedy, when the humanitarian imperative was unquestioned. But the conclusion of a comprehensive evaluation of humanitarian conflict management in Somalia prescribed "tough love"—the heretical notion that the international community should have left when it became obvious that looting, corruption, and extortion of assistance effectively was, as it has elsewhere, fueling the war (de Waal 1997; Ignatieff 1997; Maren 1997). Although it may seem callous to walk away from suffering, it may also prove to be humane: "[I]t would likely have led either to improved protection allowing the continuation of aid or to an opportunity, with departure from Somalia, to channel scarce aid resources to other countries' emergencies" (Sommer 1994: 116).

Short of the creation of this new capacity, restructuring might conceivably bring a more coherent and efficient UN presence. Without consolidation—and inertia is always the best bet in predicting the near future for international organization—then it would be better to revert to an earlier (that is, pre-1992 and pre-DHA) practice of naming a "lead agency" to spearhead the UN's humanitarian activities.

In the Balkans (Minear et al. 1994), as it had in northern Iraq (Minear et al. 1993) and as UNICEF had in Operation Lifeline Sudan (Deng and Minear 1992; Minear et al. 1991), UNHCR played this role. It was the first relief organization to arrive on the scene after the Serbo-Croatian war of June 1991: and with the full confidence of donors, the secretary-general called upon UNHCR to become the lead agency. And Mrs. Sadako Ogata became, in her own self-deprecating words, "the desk officer for the former Yugoslavia." A year later its total annual budget had doubled as a result of the infusion of some $500 million for over 2.5 million beneficiaries, only a small percentage of whom were refugees but the vast majority of whom were either internally displaced persons or war victims who had not moved at all. Eighty-five percent of UNHCR's beneficiaries fell outside of the organization's mandate and the terms of the 1951 Convention. In fact, before repatriation efforts began as a result of the Dayton agreements, not a single of the 2 million beneficiaries in Bosnia was a refugee (UNHCR 1994, 1995, 1996; Weiss and Pasic 1997, 1999).

For all the shortcomings and criticism (Weiss 1996a), UNHCR's performance in this role in the former Yugoslavia was preferable to its having a task of comparable complexity in Rwanda but without the authority to lead a coalition of UN agencies because DHA was supposedly in charge. The confusion and lack of synchronization with political and military activities inside and outside of Rwanda's borders can at least be partially attributed to the fact that the UN's main humanitarian organization on the ground did not have the authority to do what it could and should have under the trying conditions of genocide.

One other possibility merits discussion, namely trying to transform into the coordination unit that it was supposed to be what in January 1998 became the UN Office for the Coordination of Humanitarian Affairs (OCHA), what previously had been the UN Department of Humanitarian Affairs (DHA).[6] Its creation in 1992 reflected a generalized and long-standing dissatisfaction with the orchestration of activities through the UN system, which had become even more obvious after numerous operational problems in the Persian Gulf (Minear and Weiss 1992–93). In December 1991 the General Assembly authorized the secretary-general to appoint a humanitarian coordinator and created the Department of Humanitarian Affairs. However, DHA has made no appreciable difference in leadership or performance within the former Yugoslavia (Minear et al. 1994) or Somalia (Chopra et al. 1995), although information-sharing was improved in Rwanda in 1994 (Brauman 1994; Destexhe 1994; Donini and Niland 1994; Omaar and de Waal 1994). This is hardly surprising when the coordinator has no real budgetary authority and does not outrank the heads of the autonomous agencies that he is supposed to coordinate. According to the late Erskine Childers and Brian Urquhart:

> The real "division of labour" that needs concentrated effort is between a unified UN-system emergency machinery and the volunteer NGOs upon which it must in any case in the end depend. That need remains seriously neglected in the continued jockeying and jostling of the UN-system organizations vis-à-vis each other and the intrinsically weak new DHA 'Coordinator.' (Childers and Urquhart 1994: 114)

One solution could be the incorporation of OCHA's key diplomatic and information-sharing functions into the headquarters and field network of the United Nations Development Programme (UNDP). These networks could be used better than in the past to gather information. Moreover, the fusion could overcome the awkward and unacceptable situation in many war-torn countries in which there have been multiple poles of authority for the UN's civilian humanitarian presence—including the Special Representative of the UN secretary-general, OCHA's Emergency Coordinator, and the UNDP's Resident Representative acting as UN Resident Coordinator.

In light of the growing number of complex emergencies and its own inability to make a difference, UNDP established an Office of Humanitarian Programmes in 1994. However, the development background and culture of the organization impede its effective coordination of UN humanitarian agencies and set up predictable competition with more seasoned institutions that see UNDP for the moment as something of an operational newcomer in this arena. Simply folding OCHA staff into UNDP could conceivably result in combining the two weakest and least operational emergency capacities of the UN system.

Nonetheless, the consolidation—if combined with sensible recruitment and promotion policies, although this is a big "if"—could provide a better system-wide vehicle that would combine connections at the highest levels between the political and military sides of UN activities and the UNDP's field network. Not incidentally, this consolidation could also pave the way for a smoother transition from emergency to reconstruction, and eventually to the development that concerns Elizabeth Ferris elsewhere in this book. The merger of OCHA and UNDP would involve the United Nations proper; and thus the UN secretary-general, as the world organization's chief administrative officer could implement this effort by executive decision, without constitutional changes.

If no meaningful consolidation occurs, it is worth repeating the desirability of returning to the standard operating procedures prior to 1992. The UN secretary-general would nominate a "lead agency," as he did with UNICEF in the Sudan or UNHCR in Iraq or the former Yugoslavia, rather than having OCHA (and hence nobody) in charge. Although the subject of consolidation has become less visible in the absence of a major new war with accompanying displacements and suffering, this issue undoubtedly will again become topical when Burundi, Zaire, or Kosovo erupts.

NGO HUMANITARIANS The final suggestion relates to accelerating an ongoing trend for additional devolution of resources for international NGOs to deliver aid to those displaced by violence and their compatriots who choose to stay behind and try to survive in war zones. In recent civil wars, NGOs have made significant contributions (Aall 1996; Smock 1996). The surprised prose of one longtime multilateralist, who recently went to work for CARE-Canada, captures this reality: "I was woefully ignorant of many of the realities of UN actions.... [I]n a crisis, much operational capacity rests in the hands of nongovernmental organizations" (Gordon 1995: 159). Although some NGOs fly in and out only for emergencies— Médecins Sans Frontières (MSF) is the most prominent example—what commends NGOs is their working relations with community groups. These contacts, along with their commitment to staying on and their relatively low costs (on average, their salary and benefits are considerably less than those of international civil servants), explain why the United Nations and other donors are likely to continue expanding resources made available directly to private agencies. Although it is beyond the scope of the present chapter, they should also strengthen incentives for international NGOs to make better use of local counterparts (de Waal 1997).

Nongovernmental organizations have earned a reputation for being more flexible, forthcoming, and responsive than other members of the international humanitarian system. Whether an international NGO is small or large, focused or far-flung, its activities tend to concentrate on the practical needs of ordinary people. NGOs endeavor to customize their activities for the grassroots, which can be legitimately distinguished for the most part from the "wholesale" assistance provided by donor governments and the UN system.

External NGOs also bring weaknesses. Their energy may lend frenzy and confusion. Careful planning and evaluation are rarer than they should be. The desire to get on with the next emergency contributes to a lack of reflectiveness and an inattention to institutional learning. Well-known impatience with bureaucratic constraints often reflects a naïveté about the highly political contexts in which NGOs increasingly operate, and about the ramifications of activities. Some NGOs guard their independence so closely that they miss evident opportunities to combine forces with like-minded institutions.

As a quid pro quo for channeling more resources through NGOs and providing them with better access to decision making, donors should insist upon more formal cooperation between NGOs and the United Nations, on the one hand, and more self-regulation among NGOs themselves, on the other. Perhaps the thorniest decisions for international NGOs will revolve around the need for enhanced coordination under UN auspices. Andrew Natsios has summarized the best-case scenario: "The marriage of convenience between NGOs and the UN system in relief responses over time may become comfortable enough that ad hoc arrangements will work, even if a passionate love affair never occurs" (Natsios 1995: 418). Another advantage of linking NGOs with the United Nations is that the world organization's legitimacy could be enhanced by its association with what are widely viewed as popular, effective, and representative organizations. This could only help build a wider basis of support for the UN and multilateralism more generally.

The task of coordination, sizable in most natural disasters and even normal development activities, is still more challenging in war zones where duplication and turf-battles are more than simply wasteful—they cost lives. Aid practitioners favor coordination and donors insist upon it. But few agencies—and here the fierce drive for autonomy of virtually all NGOs should be noted—wish to be coordinated when this requires going beyond sharing information and abandoning institutional autonomy in favor of a centralized and coherent strategy. Many are reluctant to pay the costs, which include human and financial resources devoted to such efforts, as well as lost autonomy and fundraising opportunities. NGOs are, according to one knowledgeable observer, "even more loathe to co-ordinate themselves, let alone be co-ordinated by somebody else, than UN bodies" (Moore 1996: 36).

Coordination is particularly complicated when the international response involves the military (Beardsworth et al. 1996; Weiss 1999). Armed forces insist upon caution and a hierarchical and disciplined structure that most NGOs are reluctant to condone and sometimes actively resist. NGOs prefer to keep their distance, oftentimes reflecting preconceived notions. As one ex-military officer wrote: "There is still much work to be done through education to overcome pre-existing attitudes and prejudices" (Connaughton 1996: 71). The ICRC is the clearest about its stance; it shares information but does not allow its activities to be coordinated by the UN or anyone else, claiming its historically unique position as the custodian of the Geneva Conventions and Additional Protocols (Forsythe 1996, 1998; Hutchinson 1996).

However, the current humanitarian system has too many moving parts, especially nongovernmental ones. In 1994, for example, the National Intelligence Council estimated that "more than 16,000 NGOs were involved in responses to global humanitarian emergencies" (U.S. Permanent Mission 1994: 2), a number that undoubtedly has increased since. The multiplicity of actors can be an asset, but it is often a liability. Faced with random activity, the natural instinct of Western, and particularly American, policymakers is to move as quickly as possible to ensure greater coordination. Many observers ignore the potential downside of such efforts: significant opportunity costs; additional impediments to quick action, centralization of tasks that need to be decentralized, and politicization of assistance. We have already seen that the creation of a central mechanism such as the UN's DHA (and now OCHA) is no guarantee of success. According to former WFP Executive Director James Ingram: "The appearance of improved coordination at the center is not necessarily a factor in more effective and timely interventions in the field" (Ingram 1993: 181).

As humanitarian operations are initiated, more careful thought should be given to the nature, structures, and costs of coordination. Managers frequently are unclear about their expectations and relative priorities in the commitment of agency time and resources. According to two NGO practitioners, "The environment of a refugee camp is a bewildering alphabet soup of the UN and other entities in which coordination and cooperation are ad hoc, informal, and frequently ineffective" (Rosenblatt and Thompson 1995: 95).

These generalizations are more applicable to nongovernmental organizations than to other actors. Many are inclined to believe that "small is beautiful," to oppose calculations about critical mass, and to value intensely their independence. The more effective orchestration of NGO energy, creativity, and resources should be at the top of the international agenda.

The worsening political climate surrounding attempts to mobile additional resources might jolt nongovernmental organizations. Rather than continuing to respond impulsively, they could take the lead in trying to determine what they do best, and what they should not do at all. A clearer division of labor, common rules of procedure, and greater accountability are urgently required. Major NGOs, individually and collectively, should struggle with the design of a coordinated international delivery system with more coherence and effectiveness, but without eliminating the vitality and willingness to run risks that has often characterized NGO humanitarian action at its best (Mezzalama and Schumm 1993).

Ian Smillie, one of the most knowledgeable analysts of nongovernmental organizations, writes: "Networks, coalitions and umbrella organizations notwithstanding, one of the greatest problems facing NGOs today is the fragmentation of effort, the hundreds of look-alike organizations spawned more by charity than clarity of purpose. Fragmentation is the amateur's friend, a haven for wheel inventors" (Smillie 1995: 240). One international consortium, the International Council for Voluntary Agencies (ICVA), "wishes to generate a more active 'coordination culture'" as a result of its ongoing research effort titled "NGO Coordination in Humanitarian Assistance" (Bennett 1994: iv). Given the paucity of resources and mushrooming demands for assistance, the argument here is for more consolidation and more cooperation, rather than more autonomy.

The other component of the quid pro quo for more NGO resources would be to insist upon greater self-regulation and enhanced professionalism. Encouraging efforts have begun in a variety of settings. For example, major players like Catholic Relief Services (CRS) have drafted a code of conduct to help guide field staff, and consortiums like the Washington-based InterAction and the Geneva-based ICVA have also been urging their members to improve performance through training and moving toward a code of conduct (Minear and Weiss 1993: 83–91). Some 150 NGOs have joined the International Federation of Red Cross and Red Crescent Societies in approving a code to guide political behavior in disaster relief (International Federation of Red Cross and Red Crescent Societies 1994).

Also salient are nascent efforts among some operational agencies to regulate themselves. The notion of certifying only those NGOs satisfying prescribed standards has met with a surprising assent from participants (InterAction 1995). The multi-donor evaluation of Rwanda also recommended an "international accreditation system" (Joint Evaluation 1996: vol. 3, 161–62). In the words of George Weber, the secretary-general of the International Federation of Red Cross and Red Crescent Societies:

> With the comparatively high funding levels of the early 1990s seemingly at an end, the humanitarian organisation scene is probably in for a shake-out....
> Agencies are going to be judged not just on presence alone, but on the quality and sustainability of their work and how accountable they are for it. Those who cannot come up to standard may soon find themselves made irrelevant on the humanitarian assistance scene. (International Federation of Red Cross and Red Crescent Societies 1996: 6–7)

If NGOs were to pursue the highest professional standards for recruitment, posting, and promotions, the moral high ground, which they often claim to occupy, would be firmer and their own place in the pluralized system of global governance more authoritative.

Two additional issues should be considered in future efforts by NGOs to alter the international humanitarian system. The first emanates from the sheer size of "super" NGOs; and the second from the need to inject sufficient modesty to admit limitations.

In some ways, the challenges of coordination and monitoring are not as overwhelming as they may seem at first. In low-key emergencies (for example, in Angola and Sierra Leone), NGOs number in tens rather than hundreds. More importantly, the major families or federations of NGOs—the CAREs, the various Save-the-Childrens, MSFs, World Visions, and so on—are almost tantamount to an oligopoly. Andrew Natsios—who examines development in this volume but who has been close to NGO emergency issues at the Office of Foreign Disaster Assistance (OFDA) and World Vision Inc.—has noted that "perhaps 10 U.S. and another 10 European NGOs receive 75% of all the public funds spent by NGOs in complex emergencies" (Natsios 1995: 406–7).[7] This fact will not diminish because governments and UN agencies are better able to relate to such large conglomerations than to the atomized world of smaller nongovernmental organizations.

This concentration of power is particularly important in failed states, and even in weak ones. For instance, in the "Donors Republique of Mozambique" in the midst of civil war in the early 1990s, foreign aid accounted for 78 percent of GDP, making the country the world's most aid dependent (UN Department of Public Information 1993; K. B. Wilson 1992). After the war, World Vision Inc.—which disbursed some $80–90 million in each year from 1993–95—was the single largest donor, employer, provider of welfare services, and source of foreign exchange.

And this example is by no means isolated. The ability of many governments to provide social services—in many African countries, in a number of Asian ones, in Haiti—is poor and eroding or nonexistent. Even in Kenya, which for many years has witnessed higher growth than neighbors and by no means has a weak government, NGOs provide some 40 percent of health care (Fowler 1992). Expatriate personnel and large NGOs are increasingly assuming state-like functions that would have been unthinkable a few years ago in developing countries whose governments had committed themselves to providing such basic human needs.

There is much fondness for "privatization" among Western donors. Small and resource-poor local political authorities thus have new problems with outsiders as do local NGOs, which further exacerbates the dilemmas of dependency (Uvin 1995). International NGOs are not immune to the arrogance that comes all too naturally with differences in power of this magnitude. There is really no accountability between donors and beneficiaries; nor are there recognized professional standards. Although the need, as mentioned earlier, for a code to govern political behavior has been recognized, the market for assistance in complex emergencies is decidedly unregulated.

International "anti-trust legislation" is far-fetched, but greater self-regulation and self-questioning are certainly in order for the largest nongovernmental organizations (Donini 1996). "Accountability" and "transparency" have become dominant themes—for example, politicians and educators are being asked to meet higher standards of performance and ethics, and states also are not immune from calls for greater responsiveness (Held 1995). If social workers, school teachers, and taxi drivers are normally certified, why not aid workers? NGO humanitarians too should regulate themselves and aspire to a new professionalism, or such regulation no doubt will be imposed by others. An immediate first step is to accelerate a certification process to signify professional competence to be active in war zones. Incentives—essentially more untied resources and greater access to decision making—should elicit more cooperation than in the past for the humanitarian and development arenas (Edwards and Hulme 1996).

NGOs clearly contribute their fair share to international responses to gruesome human tragedies. Along with other humanitarians, they are expanding their activities to fill the void left by the shrinking power of weak states and the declining interests of major donors. However, they should themselves take the lead in having the courage to refuse involvement if a task is either beyond their professional competence and means, or if initial success will be ultimately counterproductive; to determine when and where their inputs would truly make a difference; and to collaborate whenever and wherever possible among themselves and with other governmental, intergovernmental, nongovernmental, and military humanitarians.

Unlike states and intergovernmental organizations whose mandates, standard operating procedures, and bureaucratic cultures make them hesitant about being drawn into internal conflicts, NGOs are less likely to make geopolitical calculations, though more likely than to react viscerally. Their raison d'être is the alleviation of suffering. Humanitarian impulses rather than geopolitics dominate. As "crisis junkies" they need to be engaged to raise money and to have credibility. It was thus difficult for NGOs not to be in Goma with Hutu refugees—their Rwanda resources would have diminished, as would and their ability to raise funds for other projects.

NGOs are frequently hostile toward, or at least skeptical about, the notion of analyzing when and where they should be active. Yet, recent experience suggests that more analytical, or perhaps less visceral, reactions are in order. Time and resources for reflection are not wasteful, despite the protestations from many NGO managers and their boards of directors to the contrary. The Belgian and French chapters of MSF, CARE-Canada, and the International Rescue Committee (IRC), for example, withdrew from the Rwandan refugee camps in Zaire early in 1995. They judged that their actions were strengthening the position of the Hutu war criminals—decreasing the immediate prospects for repatriation of refugees and the longer-term coexistence of the two ethnic groups. As Alain Destexhe, then secretary-general of the international federation of MSF and now a member of the Belgian Sénat, wrote at the time: "We can't be party to the slaughter in Rwanda ... agencies like ours are caught in a lose-lose situation; either continue being reluctant accomplices of genocidal warmongers or withdraw from the camps, leaving the refugee population to the mercy of their jailers" (Destexhe 1995: A7). Subsequent developments in late 1996 confirmed the validity of this tough-love analysis because the return of refugees to Rwanda was a prerequisite for any solution to the problem.

Bosnia provides another example of the importance of understanding the context of humanitarian action. Most NGOs, as well as other agencies, framed the issue as a stark choice between collaborating in ethnic cleansing or in genocide; and most opted for the former. Yet there was a fundamental and prior question: Did relief prolong the war and substitute for meaningful political and military engagement to address the causes of the humanitarian tragedy?

Whatever the short-term leverage over influence and resources, well-meaning but counterproductive humanitarianism is an ugly reality with operational consequences. For instance, limited resources could dictate ignoring a hopeless tragedy in one country in order to make a difference in another. NGOs should learn on occasion to just say "no." But when and where will they be willing to do so? When and where should triage apply? Answers to these potentially divisive questions are the litmus test of professionalism. They should be debated by a broad spectrum of nongovernmental organizations as their role in multilateral humanitarian action during civil wars continues to grow.

After Wars: Moving beyond Humanitarian Action

With a seemingly endless series of internal conflicts on the horizon, "donor fatigue" definitely is in the air. The general public can usually be counted upon to support emergency aid for both involuntary migrants and besieged populations who have not moved, provided that gruesome media images appear (Girardet 1995; Gowing 1997 and 1994; Minear et al. 1996; Neuman 1996; Rotberg and Weiss 1996; Strobel 1997;). However, citizens and parliamentarians are increasingly wary of development assistance, which undoubtedly will have a braking effect of sorts on emergency aid and the appearance of what the last UN secretary-general called "orphan conflicts ... deprived of international attention, concern, and effort" (Boutros-Ghali 1996: 91). This will eventually contribute to more widespread "compassion fatigue"—mobilization for the 1994 tragedy in Rwanda, for example, was not followed by a similar one to help the new Rwandan government.

In these pages, Richard Bissell and Andrew Natsios join their voices to a host of others preoccupied by the "crisis in developmentalism" (Duffield

1994; Uvin 1996). Official development assistance (ODA) is dwindling, and more and more of it is devoted to emergencies rather than to self-sustaining development (Randel and German 1997). For example, the World Food Programme was established to foster agricultural self-sufficiency, but in 1994 devoted 80 percent of its resources to emergency help; and UNICEF's emergency assistance has increased steadily to a quarter of its expenditures (Boutros-Ghali 1995c: para. 328 and 355). Some observers point out the dubious distinction between emergency and development assistance, and suggest reconceptualizing development as an integral part of humanitarian succor (Macrae and Bolton 1996).

The challenge of rebuilding war-torn societies is immense; those resulting from recent fragmentation sometimes overshadow those left over from the Cold War (Green 1995; Kühne 1996; Lake 1990). Humanitarians and the media tend to declare victory and move to the next crisis. Unfortunately, peacebuilding requires time and patience, or in the words of High Commissioner Ogata, "there is certainly no such thing as a humanitarian surgical strike" (Ogata 1996: 5). The task is nothing short of awesome. The systematic looting of physical infrastructure and the elimination of trained human resources have frequently constituted specific war aims. A task list would include transforming the security environment, strengthening local administrative capacities, reconstructing political processes, reconstructing the economy, and reknitting local social fabric (Bush 1995, 1996).

Given limited resources and virtually unlimited demands for help, the most pressing and doable task after an armed conflict would be the transformation of the security environment. This priority in postconflict peacebuilding is also where previous peacekeeping principles and recent experience (especially in Rhodesia and El Salvador, and perhaps also in Namibia and Cambodia) are pertinent. Disarmament, demobilization, and reintegration of regular and irregular troops are urgent assignments at the end or near-end of every armed conflict (Berdal 1996). They constitute a prerequisite for meaningful rehabilitation and development. And they should be the priority of multilateral efforts, building upon the new generation of multifunctional operations involving unprecedented intrusion into domestic affairs and civil administration (Chopra 1995, 1996, 1999; Weiss 1995d).

There will undoubtedly be a new role for the United Nations to play in what for lack of a better term might be dubbed "governorship" or "temporary protectorate." In spite of obvious political sensitivities, the UN secretary-general should be available for such impartial tasks as administering what have now entered into the daily operational lexicon as "failed" or "collapsed states." Proposals calling for the widespread recolonization of those countries that "are just not fit to govern themselves" are implausible (Johnson 1993: 22), not least because the former imperial powers are not interested. But the UN no doubt will be called upon selectively to pick up the pieces after humanitarian interventions and to assume temporary conservancy in some instances.

The difficulties of nation-building should not be ignored the hubris symbolized by American efforts in Vietnam or Soviet ones in Afghanistan should give pause. The denizens of postconflict countries must ultimately take responsibility for the reconstitution of viable civil societies. But they require buffers and breathing space after they themselves have been implicated in lengthy civil wars or even after short but particularly brutal ones. This is where a combination of traditional UN peacekeeping and a temporary trusteeship could be valuable, but *after* humanitarian interventions have helped protect civilians and stabilize violent situations. This task will require genuine vision and independence, which would be best served by distancing the UN secretary-general and the UN's regular humanitarian network from the use of force.

In a related and potentially crucial step, it should also be possible to associate more closely the Washington-based financial institutions with demobilization schemes. A breakthrough in this area resulted from the World Bank's efforts in financing the disarming and removal of mines and other demobilization priorities immediately after the Dayton accords. This contrasts with the earlier pattern, perhaps best illustrated by the striking disconnect between UN efforts and those of the World Bank and the IMF in El Salvador: two participants in the negotiations argued convincingly that efforts in the politico-military field were on "a collision course" with the stabilization program and other economic adjustment activities mandated by the IMF and the World Bank (de Soto and del Castillo 1994: 70). The argument is much the same for postconflict Mozambique (Alden 1995; Willett 1995). The Washington-based institutions are autonomous and, in spite of organizational diagrams in textbooks, not really part of the so-called UN system. However, their involvement is critical in moving beyond humanitarian relief in war zones.

Whatever else was meant by an "integrated approach to human security" in *An Agenda for Peace* (Boutros-Ghali 1995b: para. 16), the secretary-general intended that intergovernmental organizations working on demobilization as a prelude to sustainable development and those working on longer-run development would work in tandem rather than at cross-purposes. Institutional changes—for instance, involving the IMF and the World Bank in peace negotiations from the outset and creating a unified UN presence in postconflict countries—are required to make the most of multilateral action and to make "postconflict peacebuilding" more than a slogan.

The World Bank's original but now almost forgotten acronym (IBRD, the International Bank for Reconstruction and Development) should be no less valid for shattered societies in the 1990s than for those of Europe in the late 1940s. The mobilization of the Bretton Woods institutions side-by-side and virtually simultaneously with IFOR's deployment is critical for future development. In spite of difficulties related to creditworthiness, the World Bank appears to be moving in the direction of imaginatively being involved in the earliest phases of reconstructing war-torn countries (World Bank 1997), which is pertinent not just for the former Yugoslavia but for other war-torn societies as well. It is time to return to the drawing boards and reformulate what Dutch Minister for Development Co-operation Jan Pronk is calling a "strategy for development in conflict" (Pronk 1996).

Conclusion

Nothing in this chapter should be construed to imply that alterations proposed for the military, United Nations, and NGO components of the international humanitarian delivery system for wars will be easy. Would that it were so. However, the suggestions here are intended to be more than provocative, academic whistling in the wind.

The three characteristics of post–Cold War humanitarian crises—the prevalence of civil wars, an overstretched UN, and subcontracting to regional and nongovernmental organizations—provide the backdrop to accelerate experiments already underway that could improve international delivery in war zones. Devolving responsibilities toward coalitions of the willing have already proven successful in a number of contexts and more could be done to make such efforts accountable to the larger community of states that approves them. Although there is no consolidated UN unit for war zones, elements of such a capacity have been illustrated by UNHCR and UNICEF when acting as lead agencies, and these could be built upon. More cohesive and professional inputs from NGOs have begun to appear, and the senior staff of many such private organizations are in the forefront of calls for a "shaking-out" in the community.

Is it naive to maintain the notion that human beings are as strong as the institutions that they erect? Analysts of the international humanitarian and development systems should not in the near future be less busy than practitioners toiling to mitigate the life-threatening suffering resulting from wars. The first word of the title of this chapter, "reforming," explicitly affirms that future international responses can be better for victims than past ones. Hopefully, the present contributes modestly to that effort.

Notes

The author is grateful to David Caron and Ernst B. Haas for having offered the challenge to develop this subject at the University of California at Berkeley's Institute of International Studies under the auspices of the MacArthur Peace and Security Program. Parts of this argument appear in expanded form as "Humanitarian Action in War Zones: Recent Experience and Future Research" in *World Orders in the Making: The Case of "Humanitarian Intervention,"* edited by Jan Nederveen Pieterse (London: Macmillan, 1998), 24–79.

1. Haiti has not really endured a civil war, but is included in generalizations here. It has all the attributes—in particular, massive migration and human rights abuse—of countries that have. Moreover, it has also been the target of international actions—in particular, economic and military sanctions—that are like those in war-torn countries.
2. "Some had hoped for an elementary, partial consensus on U.S. action to help guarantee at least the right to life in the form of no mass starvation and no mass murder. Events in the 1990s in both Bosnia and Rwanda indicate much remains to be done to achieve even this minimal objective" (Forsythe 1995: 129–30).
3. Most defense ministries are arranging special training, with Canada and Ireland among others having established new centers, following those established earlier by the Nordic countries. In fact, there is now an International Association of Peacekeeping Training Centres whose inaugural meeting was held in mid-1995 at the Lester B. Pearson Canadian International Peacekeeping Training Centre in Cornwallis, Nova Scotia. Moreover, there are two journals with the same title, *International Peacekeeping*. For a discussion of these developments and the literature, see Collins and Weiss (1997).
4. The emphasis here is on external NGOs, which bring outside resources to the scene of a conflict. Local NGOs are experiencing similar growth, but they are not the focus here. Hence, "NGO" means "international NGO" unless otherwise specified.
5. See, for example, an extensive shopping list in "Table 4: Possible Uses of Military Force for Humanitarian Missions in Complex Emergencies," from *Global Humanitarian Emergencies 1995* (U.S. Mission to the United Nations 1995). See "Improving the UN's Rapid Reaction Capability: A Canadian Study" (February 1995); "A UN Rapid Deployment Brigade: The Netherlands Non-paper" (January 1995); and "A Multifunctional UN Stand-by Forces High-Readiness Brigade: Chief of Defence, Denmark" (25 January 1995). A discussion of these and other proposals is found in Dick A. Leurdijk (1995: 1–10).
6. The acronyms change with confusing rapidity, but this essay uses those in place when events occurred. In 1991, the original resolution 46/182 called for an Emergency Relief Coordinator (ERC), but the first unit was labeled the Department of Humanitarian Affairs (DHA), which existed from April 1992 through December 1997. The reform proposals and discussions between July 1997 and the General Assembly's decision in December 1997 referred to the revived Office of the Emergency Relief Coordinator (OERC). Following the recommendation of the secretary-general, General Assembly resolution 52/72 designated the Emergency Relief Coordinator as the United Nations

Humanitarian Assistance Coordinator. This decision produced the rather infelicitous acronym of OUNHAC for his office. In January 1998 and at the request of the new under-secretary-general, the Office for the Coordination of Humanitarian Affairs (OCHA) was approved by the secretary-general. The head of this office now uses two titles: under-secretary-general for humanitarian affairs and emergency relief coordinator.

7. For a list of the twenty largest NGOs, see U.S. Permanent Mission to the United Nations, 1996: 28.

References

Aall, P. R. 1996. *NGOs and Conflict Management*. Washington, D.C.: U.S. Institute of Peace. Peaceworks No. 6.

Alden, C. 1995. "Swords into Plowshares? The United Nations and Demilitarisation in Mozambique." *International Peacekeeping* 2, 2: 175–93.

Annan, K. 1997. *Renewing the United Nations: A Programme for Reform*. New York: United Nations.

Ayoob, M. 1993. "The New-Old Disorder in the Third World." In *Collective Security in a Changing World*, edited by T. G. Weiss. Boulder, Colo.: Lynne Rienner Publishers.

———. 1995. *The Third World Security Predicament: State Making, Regional Conflict, and the International System*. Boulder, Colo.: Lynne Rienner Publishers.

Beardsworth, Com. R. R., Com. R. V. Kikla, Lt. Col. P. F. Shutler, and Col., G. C. Swan. 1996. *Strengthening Coordination Mechanisms Between NGOs and the U.S. Military at the Theater/Country Level During Complex Humanitarian Emergencies*. Draft from Harvard University's National Security Program.

Bennett, J. 1994. *NGO Coordination at Field Level: A Handbook*. Oxford: Parchment Printers.

———. 1995. *Meeting Needs: NGO Coordination in Practice*. London: Earthscan.

Berdal, M. R. 1993. *Whither UN Peacekeeping?* Adelphi Paper 281. London: International Institute for Strategic Studies.

———. 1996. *Disarmament and Demobilisation After Civil Wars*, Adelphi Paper #303. Oxford: Oxford University Press.

Bettati, M. 1996. *Le Droit d'ingérence: mutation de l'ordre international*. Paris: Odile Jacob.

Betts, R. K. 1994. The Delusion of Impartial Intervention. *Foreign Affairs* 73, 6: 20–33.

Boutros-Ghali, B. 1995a. *An Agenda for Development 1995*. New York: United Nations.

———. 1995b. *An Agenda for Peace 1995*. New York: United Nations.

———. 1995c. *Report of the Secretary-General on the Work of the Organization*. Document A/50/1.

———. 1996. "Global Leadership after the Cold War." *Foreign Affairs* 75, 2: 86–98.

Brauman, R. 1994. *Devant le Mal: Rwanda, un génocide en direct*. Paris: Arléa.

Bush, K. D. 1995. "Towards a Balanced Approach to Rebuilding War-Torn Societies." *Canadian Foreign Policy* III, 3: 49–69.

———. 1996. "Rocks and Hard Places: Bad Governance, Human Rights Abuses, and Population Displacement." *Canadian Foreign Policy* IV, 1: 49–82.

Carnegie Commission on Preventing Deadly Conflict 1997. *Preventing Deadly Conflict.* New York: Carnegie Corporation.

Childers, E., with Urquhart, B. 1994. *Renewing the United Nations System.* Uppsala: Dag Hammarskjöld Foundation.

Chopra, J. 1995. "Back to the Drawing Board." *Bulletin of the Atomic Scientists* 51, 2: 29–35.

———. 1996. "The Space of Peace Maintenance." *Political Geography* 15, 3/4: 335–57.

———. 1999. *Peace Maintenance: The Evolution of International Political Authority.* London: Routledge.

Chopra, J., and T. G. Weiss. 1992. "Sovereignty Is No Longer Sacrosanct: Codifying Humanitarian Intervention." *Ethics and International Affairs* 6: 95–117.

———. 1995. "Prospects for Containing Conflict in the Former Second World." *Security Studies* 4, 3: 552–83.

Chopra, J., A. Eknes, and T. Nordbø. 1995. *Fighting for Hope in Somalia.* Oslo: Norwegian Institute for International Affairs, Peacekeeping and Multinational Operations No. 6.

Christopher, W. 1995a. "America's Leadership, America's Opportunity." *Foreign Policy* 98: 6–27.

———. 1995b. "Readying the United Nations for the Twenty-First Century: Some UN-21 Proposals for Consideration." New York: U.S. Mission to the United Nations.

Collins, C., and T. G. Weiss. 1997. *An Overview and Assessment of 1989–1996 Peace Operations Publications.* Occasional Paper #28. Providence: Watson Institute.

Connaughton, R. M. 1996. *Military Support and Protection for Humanitarian Assistance: Rwanda, April–December 1994.* Camberly, Surrey, U.K.: Strategic and Combat Studies Institute.

Cuny, F. C. 1991. "Dilemmas of Military Involvement in Humanitarian Relief." In *Soldiers, Peacekeepers and Disasters,* edited by L. Gordenker and T. G. Weiss. London: Macmillan.

Deng, F. M. 1993. *Protecting the Dispossessed: A Challenge for the International Community.* Washington, D.C.: Brookings Institution.

Deng, F. M., and L. Minear. 1992. *The Challenges of Famine Relief: Emergency Operations in the Sudan.* Washington, D.C.: Brookings Institution.

de Soto, A., and G. del Castillo. 1994. "Obstacles to Peacebuilding." *Foreign Policy* 94: 69–83.

Destexhe, A. 1994. *Rwanda: Essai sur le génocide.* Brussels: Editions Complexe.

———. 1995. "A Border without Doctors." *New York Times,* 9 February 1995, A7.

de Waal, A. 1997. *Famine Crimes: Politics and the Disaster Relief Industry in Africa.* Oxford: James Currey.

de Waal, A., and R. Omaar. 1995. "The Genocide in Rwanda and the International Response." *Current History* 94: 156–61.

Diehl, P. 1993. *International Peacekeeping.* Baltimore: Johns Hopkins University Press.

Dole, B. 1995. "Shaping America's Global Future." *Foreign Policy* 98: 29–43.

Donini, A. 1996. *UN Coordination in Complex Emergencies: Lessons from Afghanistan, Mozambique, and Rwanda*, Occasional Paper #22. Providence: Watson Institute.

Donini, A., and N. Niland. 1994. *Rwanda: Lessons Learned: A Report on the Coordination of Humanitarian Activities*. New York: United Nations.

Duffield, M. 1994. "Complex Emergencies and the Crisis in Developmentalism." *IDS Bulletin* 25, 4: 37–45.

Durch, W. J., ed. 1993. *The Evolution of UN Peacekeeping: Case Studies and Comprehensive Analysis*. New York: St. Martin's Press.

———. 1996. *UN Peacekeeping, American Policy, and the Uncivil Wars of the 1990s*. New York: St. Martin's Press.

Edwards, M., and D. Hulme, eds. 1996. *Beyond the Magic Bullet: NGO Performance and Accountability in the Post–Cold War World*. West Hartford, Conn.: Kumarian Press.

Famsbotham, O., and T. Woodhouse. 1996. *Humanitarian Intervention in Contemporary Conflict*. Cambridge: Polity Press.

Farer, T. J. 1995. "How the International System Copes with Involuntary Migration: Norms, Institutions and State Practice." *Human Rights Quarterly* 17, 2: 72–100.

———. 1996. "Intervention in Unnatural Humanitarian Emergencies: Lessons of the First Phase." *Human Rights Quarterly* 18, 1: 1–22.

Forsythe, D. P. 1995. "Human Rights and U.S. Foreign Policy: Two Levels, Two Worlds." *Political Studies* 43: 111–30.

———. 1996. "The ICRC and Humanitarian Assistance: A Policy Analysis." *International Review of the Red Cross*, 314 (September–October): 512–31.

———. 1998. "International Humanitarian Assistance: The Role of the Red Cross." *Buffalo Journal of International Law*.

Fowler, A. 1992. "Distant Obligations: Speculations on NGO Funding and the Global Market." *Review of African Political Economy* 55: 9–29.

Fukuyama, F. 1992. *The End of History and the Last Man*. New York: Free Press.

Gelb, L. H. 1994. "Quelling the Teacup Wars." *Foreign Affairs* 73, 6: 2–6.

Girardet, E., ed. 1995. *Somalia, Rwanda, and Beyond: The Role of the International Media in Wars and Humanitarian Crises*, Crosslines Special Report 1. Dublin: Crosslines Communications Ltd.

Gordon, N. 1995. NGOs in Preventive Diplomacy and Peacemaking: The Task Ahead. In *Peacemaking and Preventive Diplomacy in the New World Disorder*, edited by D. R. Black and S. J. Rolston. Halifax, Nova Scotia: Dalhousie University.

Gowing, N. 1994. *Real-Time Television Coverage of Armed Conflicts and Diplomatic Crises*. Cambridge, Harvard University Shorenstein Center.

———. 1997. *Media Coverage: Help or Hindrance in Conflict Prevention?* New York: Carnegie Commission on Preventing Deadly Conflict.

Green, R. H. 1995. "The Course of the Four Horsemen: Costs of War and its Aftermath in Sub-Saharan Africa." In *War and Hunger: Rethinking International Responses to Complex Emergencies*, edited by J. Macrae and A. Zwi. London: Zed Books.

Harriss, J., ed. 1995. *The Politics of Humanitarian Intervention*. London: Pinter.

Heiberg, M., ed. 1994. *Subduing Sovereignty: Sovereignty and the Right to Intervene*. London: Pinter.

Held, D. 1995. *Democracy and the Global Order: From the Modern State to Cosmopolitan Governance*. Palo Alto: Stanford University Press.

Helman, G. B., and S. R. Ratner. 1993. "Saving Failed States." *Foreign Policy* 89: 3–20.

Helms, J. 1996. "Saving the UN: A Challenge to the Next Secretary-General." *Foreign Affairs* 75, 5: 2–7.

Henkin, A. H., ed. 1995. *Honoring Human Rights and Keeping the Peace: Lessons from El Salvador, Cambodia, and Haiti*. Washington, D.C.: Aspen Institute.

Henrikson, A. K. 1996. "The Growth of Regionalism and the Role of the United Nations." In *Regionalism in World Politics: Regional Organizations and World Order*, edited by L. Fawcett and A. Hurrell. Oxford: Oxford University Press.

Holsti, K. J. 1996. *The State, War, and the State of War*. Cambridge: Cambridge University Press.

Human Rights Watch. 1993. *The Lost Agenda: Human Rights and UN Field Operations*. New York: Human Rights Watch.

———. 1994. *Human Rights Watch World Report 1995*. New York: Human Rights Watch.

Hutchinson, J. F. 1996. *Champions of Charity: War and the Rise of the Red Cross*. Boulder, Colo.: Westview Press.

Ignatieff, Michael. 1997. *The Warrior's Honor: Ethnic War and the Modern Conscience*. New York: Henry Holt and Company.

Independent Task Force, chaired by George Soros. 1996. *American National Interest and the United Nations*. New York: Council on Foreign Relations.

Ingram, H. O. 1993. "The Future Architecture for International Humanitarian Assistance." In *Humanitarianism Across Borders: Sustaining Civilians in Times of War*, edited by T. G. Weiss and L. Minear. Boulder, Colo.: Lynne Rienner Publishers.

InterAction and the Carnegie Endowment for International Peace. 1995. Papers for the PVO Conference on Disaster Response (17–18 September).

InterAfrica Group. 1995. "NGOs and Conflict: Three Views." *Humanitarian Monitor* 2: 30–36.

International Committee of the Red Cross. 1997. *Report on the Wolfsberg Humanitarian Forum, 8–10 June 1997*. Geneva: ICRC.

International Federation of Red Cross and Red Crescent Societies. 1994. *Code of Conduct for the International Red Cross and Red Crescent Movement and NGOs in Disaster Relief*. Geneva: IFRC.

———. 1996. *World Disasters Report 1996*. Oxford: Oxford University Press.

———. 1997. *World Disasters Report 1997*. Oxford: Oxford University Press.

International Institute for Strategic Studies. 1995. "Military Support for Humanitarian Operations." *Strategic Comments*, 2.

Jackson, R. 1990. *Quasi States: Sovereignty, International Relations and the Third World*. Cambridge: Cambridge University Press.

Johnson, P. 1993. "Colonialism's Back and Not a Moment Too Soon." *New York Times Magazine*, 18 April 1993.

Joint Evaluation of Emergency Assistance to Rwanda. 1995. *The International Response to Conflict and Genocide: Lessons from the Rwandan Experience*. Copenhagen: Joint Evaluation of Emergency Assistance to Rwanda, 5 volumes.

Jonson, L., and C. Archer, eds. 1996. *Peacekeeping and the Role of Russia in Eurasia*. Boulder, Colo.: Westview Press.

Kennedy, P. 1987. *The Rise and Fall of the Great Powers*. New York: Random House.

Kühne, W. 1996. *Winning the Peace: Concept and Lessons Learned of Post-Conflict Peacebuilding.* Ebenhausen: Stiftung und Wissenschaft.

Lake, A. J., ed. 1990. *After the Wars: Reconstruction in Afghanistan, Indochina, Central America, Southern Africa, and the Horn of Africa.* Washington, D.C.: Overseas Development Council.

La-Rose Edward, Paul. 1995. *United nations Impediments to Peace-Keeping Rapid Reaction.* Ottawa: Department of External Affairs and International Trade.

Leurdijk, D. A. 1995. "Proposals for Increasing Rapid Deployment Capacity: A Survey." *International Peacekeeping* 2, 1: 1–10.

Loescher, G. 1993. *Beyond Charity: International Cooperation and the Global Refugee Crisis.* New York: Oxford University Press.

Lund, M. S. 1994. *Preventive Diplomacy and American Foreign Policy.* Washington, D.C.: U.S. Institute of Peace Press.

———. 1996. *Preventing Violent Conflicts: A Strategy for Preventive Diplomacy.* Washington, D.C.: U.S. Institute of Peace Press.

Lyons, G. M., and M. Mastanduno, eds. 1995. *Beyond Westphalia? National Sovereignty and Intervention.* Baltimore: Johns Hopkins University Press.

Mackinlay, J. 1994. "Improving Multifunctional Forces." *Survival* 36, 3: 149–73.

Macrae, J., and J. Bolton. 1996. "Aid Trends: The State of the Humanitarian System." *World Disasters Report 1996:* 54–63.

Mandelbaum, M. 1994. "The Reluctance to Intervene." *Foreign Policy* 95: 3–18.

Maren, M. 1997. *The Road To Hell: The Ravaging Effects of Foreign Aid and International Charity.* New York: Free Press.

Mayall, J. ed. 1996. *The New Interventionism: United Nations Experience in Cambodia, Former Yugoslavia, and Somalia.* New York: Cambridge University Press.

Maynes, C. W. 1994. "A Workable Clinton Doctrine." *Foreign Policy* 93: 3–20.

Maynes, C. W., and R. S. Williamson, eds. 1996. *U.S. Foreign Policy and the United Nations System.* New York: Norton.

Mearsheimer, J. J. 1995. "The False Promise of International Institutions." *International Security* 19, 3: 5–49.

Menkhaus, K. 1996. "International Peacebuilding and the Dynamics of Local and National Reconciliation in Somalia." *International Peacekeeping* 3, 1: 42–67.

Mezzalama, F., and S. Schumm. 1993. *Working with NGOs: Operational Activities for Development of the United Nations System with Non-Governmental Organizations and Governments at the Grassroots and National Levels.* Geneva: UN Joint Inspection Unit, document JIU/REP/93/1.

Migdal, J. 1988. *Strong States and Weak Societies: State-Society Relations and State Capabilities in the Third World.* Princeton: Princeton University Press.

Minear, L., et al. 1991. *Humanitarianism Under Siege: A Critical Review of Operation Lifeline Sudan.* Trenton: Red Sea Press.

Minear, L., and T. G. Weiss. 1992–93. "Groping and Coping in the Gulf Crisis: Discerning the Shape of a New Humanitarian Order." *World Policy Journal* 9, 4 (Fall/Winter): 755–88.

———. 1993. "Evolving Humanitarian Standards: Toward a Code of Conduct for Armed Conflicts." In *Humanitarian Action in Times of War: A Handbook for Practitioners.* Boulder, Colo.: Lynne Rienner Publishers.Minear, L., U. B. P. Chelliah, J. Crisp, J. MacKinlay, and T. G. Weiss. 1993. *United Nations Coordination of the International Humanitarian Response to the Gulf Crisis 1990–1992,* Occasional Paper #13. Providence: Watson Institute.

Minear, L., J. Clark, R. Cohen, D. Gallagher, I. Guest, and T. G. Weiss. 1994. *Humanitarian Action in the Former Yugoslavia: The UN's Role 1991–1993*, Occasional Paper #18. Providence: Watson Institute.

Minear, L., and T. G. Weiss. 1995a. *Humanitarian Politics*. New York: Foreign Policy Association.

———. 1995b. *Mercy Under Fire: War and the Global Humanitarian Community*. Boulder, Colo.: Westview Press.

Minear, L., and P. Guillot. 1996. *Soldiers to the Rescue: Humanitarian Lessons from Rwanda*. Paris: Organisation for Economic Co-operation and Development.

Minear, L., C. Scott, and T. G. Weiss. 1996. *The News Media, Civil War, and Humanitarian Action*. Boulder, Colo.: Lynne Rienner Publishers.

Moore, J. 1996. *The UN and Complex Emergencies*. Geneva: UN Research Institute for Social Development.

Natsios, A. 1995. "NGOs and the UN in Complex Emergencies: Conflict or Cooperation." *Third World Quarterly* 16, 3 (September): 418.

———. 1996. Humanitarian Relief Interventions in Somalia: The Economics of Chaos. *International Peacekeeping* 3, 1: 88.

Neuman, J. 1996 *Lights, Camera, War*. Crosslines Special Report 1, New York: St. Martin's.

Ogata, S. 1996. "Opening Address." In *Healing the Wounds: Refugees, Reconstruction and Reconciliation*. New York: International Peace Academy.

Omaar, R., and A. de Waal. 1994. *Rwanda: Death, Despair and Destruction*. London: African Rights.

Palwankar, U., ed. 1994. *Symposium on Humanitarian Action and Peace-Keeping Operations*. Geneva: International Committee of the Red Cross.

Paris, R. 1997. "Blue Helmet Blues: The End of the UN as a Security Organization?" *Washington Quarterly* 20, 1: 191–206.

Pasic, A., and T. G. Weiss. 1997. "The Politics of Rescue: Yugoslavia's Wars and the Humanitarian Impulse 1991–1995." *Ethics and International Affairs* 11: 105–31.

Picco, G. 1994. "The UN and the Use of Force." *Foreign Affairs* 73, 5: 15.

Pieterse, J. N., ed. 1998. *World Orders in the Making: The Case of Humanitarian Intervention*. London: Macmillan.

Pronk, J. 1996. "Keynote Address: Development in Conflict." In *Healing the Wounds: Refugees, Reconstruction and Reconciliation*. New York: International Peace Academy.

Prunier, G. 1995. *The Rwanda Crisis: History of a Genocide*. New York: Columbia University Press.

Randel, J., and T. German, eds. 1997. *The Reality of Aid 1997–1998*. London: Earthscan.

Ratner, S. R. 1995. *The New UN Peacekeeping*. New York: St. Martin's Press.

Reed, L. W., and C. Kaysen, eds. 1993. *Emerging Norms of Justified Intervention*. Cambridge: American Academy of Arts and Sciences.

Rice, E. E. 1988. *Wars of the Third Kind: Conflict in Underdeveloped Countries*. Berkeley: University of California Press.

Rieff, D. 1994–95. "The Humanitarian Trap." *World Policy Journal* 12, 4: 1–11.

Roberts, A. 1993. "Humanitarian War: Military Intervention and Human Rights." *International Affairs* 69: 429–49.

———. 1996. *Humanitarian Action in War: Aid, Protection and Impartiality in a Policy Vacuum*. Adelphi Paper 305. Oxford: Oxford University Press.

Rosenblatt, L. A., and L. Thompson. 1995. "Humanitarian Emergencies: Ten Steps to Save Lives and Resources." *SAIS Review* 15, 2: 91–109.

Rotberg, R. I., and T. G. Weiss, eds. 1996. *From Massacres to Genocide: The Media, Public Policy, and Humanitarian Crises*. Washington, D.C.: Brookings Institution.

Ruggie, J. G. 1996. *Winning the Peace: America and World Order in the New Era*. New York: Columbia University Press.

Salamon, L. M., and H. K. Anheier. 1994. *The Emerging Sector: An Overview*. Baltimore: The Johns Hopkins University Institute for Policy Studies.

Schneider, B. 1988. *The Barefoot Revolution: A Report to the Club of Rome*. London: IT Publications.

Slim, H. 1996. "The Stretcher and the Drum: Civil-Military Relations in Peace Support Operations." Paper presented in Pretoria, South Africa.

Smillie, I. 1995. *The Alms Bazaar: Altruism under Fire—Non-profit Organizations and International Development*. Hartford, Conn.: Kumarian Press.

Smock, D. R. 1996 *Humanitarian Assistance and Conflict in Africa*. Washington, D.C.: U.S. Institute of Peace, Peaceworks No. 6.

Sommer, J. 1994. *Hope Restored? Humanitarian Aid in Somalia 1990–1994*. Washington, D.C.: Refugee Policy Group.

Spiro, P. 1995. "New Global Communities: Nongovernmental Organizations in International Decision-Making Institutions." *Washington Quarterly* 18, 1: 45–56.

Stedman, S. J. 1995. "Alchemy for a New World Order: Overselling Preventive Diplomacy." *Foreign Affairs* 74, 3: 14–20.

Strobel, W. 1997. *Late-Breaking Foreign Policy: The News Media's Influence on Peace Operations*. Washington, D.C.: U.S. Institute of Peace Press.

UN Department of Public Information. 1993. *Mozambique: Out of the Ruins of War*. Africa Recovery Briefing Paper # 8.

———. 1995. Press release SG/SM/5804, 1 November 1995: 2.

UNDP. 1994. *Human Development Report 1994*. New York: Oxford University Press.

UNHCR. 1994, 1995, 1996. *Populations of Concern to UNHCR: A Statistical Overview 1993* and the same publication for 1994 and 1995. Geneva: UNHCR.

———. 1997. *The State of the World's Refugees 1997–98: A Humanitarian Agenda* New York: Oxford University Press

U.S. Committee for Refugees. 1997. *1997 World Refugee Report*. Washington, D.C.: U.S. Committee for Refugees.

U.S. Mission to the United Nations. 1995. *Global Humanitarian Emergencies*. New York.

Uvin, P. 1995. "Scaling Up the Grassroots and Scaling Down the Summit: The Relations Between Third World NGOs and the United Nations." *Third World Quarterly* 16, 3: 496–512.

———. 1996. *Development, Aid and Conflict: Reflections from the Case of Rwanda*. Research for Action 24, Helsinki: World Institute for Development Economics Research.

Väyrynen, R. 1995. *Enforcement and Humanitarian Intervention: Two Faces of Collective Action by the United Nations,* Occasional Paper #8:OP:2. Notre Dame: Kroc Institute.

Walzer, M. 1995–95. "The Politics of Rescue." *Social Research* 62, 1: 53–66.

Wapner, P. 1995. "Politics beyond the State: Environmental Activism and World Civil Politics." *World Politics* 47, 3: 311–39.

Weber, G. 1996. "Introduction: Meeting Standards for Survival." *World Disasters Report 1996:* 6–7.

Weiss, T. G. 1995a. "Military-Civilian Humanitarianism: The 'Age of Innocence' is Over." *International Peacekeeping* 2, 2: 157–74.

———. 1995b. "Overcoming the Somalia Syndrome: Operation Rekindle Hope?" *Global Governance* 1, 2: 171–87.

———. 1995c. "The United Nations at Fifty: Recent Lessons." *Current History* 94, 592: 218–22.

———. 1996a. "Collective Spinelessness: UN Actions in the Former Yugoslavia." In *The World and Yugoslavia's Wars,* edited by R. H. Ullman. New York: Council on Foreign Relations.

———. 1996b. "Humanitarian Action by Nongovernmental Organizations." In *International Dimensions of Internal Conflicts,* edited by M. E. Brown. Cambridge: MIT Press.

———. 1996c. "The UN's Prevention Pipe-Dream." *Berkeley Journal of International Law* 14, 2: 423–37.

———. 1997. "A Research Note about Military-Civilian Humanitarians: More Questions than Answers." *Disasters: The Journal of Disaster Study, Management and Policy* 21, 2: 95–117.

———. 1998a. "Humanitarian Shell Games: Whither UN Reform?" *Security Dialogue* 29, 1 (March): 9–23.

———. 1999. *Military-Civilian Interactions: Intervening in Humanitarian Crises.* Lanham, Md.: Rowman & Littlefield.

———, ed. 1995d. *The United Nations and Civil Wars.* Boulder, Colo.: Lynne Rienner Publishers.

———. 1998b. *Beyond UN Subcontracting: Task-Sharing with Regional Security Arrangements and Service-Providing NGOs.* London: Macmillan.

Weiss, T. G, and K. M. Campbell. 1991. "Military Humanitarianism." *Survival* 33, 5: 451–65.

Weiss, T. G, and C. Collins. 1996. *Humanitarian Challenges and Intervention: World Politics and the Dilemmas of Help.* Boulder, Colo.: Westview Press.

Weiss, T. G, and A. Pasic. 1997. "Reinventing UNHCR: Enterprising Humanitarians in the Former Yugoslavia, 1991–1995." *Global Governance* 3, 1 (January–April): 54–82.

———. 1999. "Dealing with Displacement and Suffering from Yugoslavia's Wars." In *Masses in Flight,* edited by F. Deng and R. Cohen. Washington, D.C.: Brookings Institution.

Weiss, T. G, and L. Gordenker, eds. 1996. *NGOs, the UN, and Global Governance.* Boulder, Colo.: Lynne Rienner Publishers.

Willett, S. 1995. "Ostriches, Wise Old Elephants and Economic Reconstruction in Mozambique." *International Peacekeeping* 2, 1: 34–55.

Wilson, J. Q. 1989. *Bureaucracy: What Government Agencies Do and Why They Do It*. New York: Basic Books.

Wilson, K. B. 1992. *A State of the Art Review of Research on Internally Displaced, Refugees and Returnees from and in Mozambique*. Oxford: Refugee Studies Programme.

Winters, P. A., ed. 1995. *Interventionism: Current Controversies*. San Diego: Greenhaven Press.

World Bank. 1997. *A Framework for World Bank Involvement in Post-Conflict Reconstruction*. Washington, D.C.: World Bank.

Zartman, W. I., ed. 1995. *Collapsed States: The Disintegration and Restoration of Legitimate Authority*. Boulder, Colo.: Lynne Rienner Publishers.

– Chapter 8 –

U.S. FOREIGN POLICY, DEMOCRACY, AND MIGRATION

*David P. Forsythe, with Gary Baker
and Michele Leonard*

All governments of the United States since 1945 have rhetorically associated themselves with the promotion of democracy abroad (Kissinger 1994). The trend has been pronounced since the Carter administration, culminating with Clinton's rhetoric in behalf of a general commitment to democracy in world affairs as a pillar of U.S. foreign policy (Carothers 1997). The U.S. would try to associate itself with global democratic trends whether or not they had any effect on migration. U.S. beliefs and self-image, whether accurate or not, now demand at least the rhetoric of democracy and human rights in foreign policy. But democracy in its several forms, as well as authoritarianism, can have discernible links to migration. Hence U.S. foreign policy on democracy (and other human rights) is an important subject in understanding contemporary patterns of migration.

Concisely put, liberal democracies—those that combine the right of political participation with the protection of other human rights, especially rights of minorities—and that are affluent, do not generate massive flows of emigrants. Liberal democracies, or those aspiring to that status, which are not affluent may have a different effect on emigration. Mexico is a good case for discussion (see Kritz 1995). Illiberal democracies—those that combine the right of political participation with the absence of many civil and minority rights, may indeed generate sizeable emigration, especially if they also lack affluence. Such illiberal democracies as contemporary Iran and Sri Lanka demonstrate some of the patterns. Poor authoritarian countries with weak border controls, like Haiti, are clearly associated with massive emigration (Schmeidl 1995). Other authoritarian countries may not generate large numbers of migrants and refugees, either because of effective border controls (e.g., the former Soviet Union) or because of "soft repression" combined with affluence (e.g., Singapore). Some governments, including a few elected ones, violate civil and minority rights to such an extent that they cause forced migrations (Loescher in this volume; Teitelbaum and Weiner 1995; Zolberg, Suhrke, and Aguayo 1989).

It is evident from the above that the central issue chosen for discussion in this essay is not U.S. foreign policy and democracy per se, but liberal democracy. Democracy, meaning majority (or plurality) rule through free and fair elections for most of the potential electorate, is in fact incompatible with a number of internationally recognized human rights designed to protect individuals or minority groups from the excesses of majority rule (Donnelly 2000). It is a primary role of the judiciary in most liberal democracies to protect individuals and especially members of minority groups from some aspects of majority rule. It was evident from U.S. experience with El Salvador in the 1980s that elections alone, without serious attention to such civil rights as freedom from summary execution, forced disappearance, torture, and free access to an independent judiciary, did nothing to stem the flight of those who feared persecution by, or poverty under, those associated with the elected government. A liberal democracy circumscribes majority rule with a series of rights-protective policies.

After the Cold War, the U.S. has taken a number of widely varying "political" decisions with regard to liberal democracy and related human rights in such places as Bosnia (support for a liberal democratic constitution), Algeria (support for the cancellation of national elections to forestall electoral victory by a fundamentalist Islamic party), and Rwanda (failure to intervene to stop genocide orchestrated under an elected government). In addition to these ad hoc, disparate decisions, the U.S. has launched a systematic program of official Democracy Assistance that combines in varying degrees attention to elections, certain civil rights, and privatization of markets—the latter entailing the workings of the right to private property. This Democracy Assistance is difficult enough to analyze in any one country such as Romania (Carothers 1996b), but it is especially difficult to track when spread over multiple countries in amounts of money that even Washington has trouble accounting for. U.S. policy on these issues is now part of a wider network of support for internationally recognized civil and political rights by most of the industrialized democracies and the intergovernmental and nongovernmental organizations they greatly influence (Karl and Schmitter 1994), which further complicates understanding of the precise U.S. impact (Diamond 1995).

Therefore our thesis in this essay cannot be precise. As the U.S. General Accounting Office noted (1994): "there is no central U.S. government wide democracy program, no overall statement of U.S. policy regarding

U.S. objectives and strategy for democratic development, no specific and common definition of what constitutes a democratic program, and no specificity re the roles of the foreign affairs and defence agencies in promoting democratic processes." We can, however, clarify concepts and trace what the U.S. has attempted in general. We can also delve into the cases of Haiti and Turkey, which show important things about U.S. foreign policy, democracy, and migration. Finally, we can say something about desirable changes in U.S. foreign policy on democracy and human rights.

Background

Political science presents many theories of democracy. It is fair to say, however, as Samuel Huntington (1991) has concluded after a lifetime of inquiry, that no one theory explains why democracy is created and/or consolidated across a variety of countries. Georg Sorensen (1993) agrees, as do Terry Lynn Karl and Philippe Schmitter (1994). Economics can tell us more about how to achieve economic growth, or why it has not been achieved, than political science can tell us about how to create and consolidate liberal democracy. States that are "donors [of foreign assistance] know much less about how to encourage democracy in the unique circumstances of each country than they know about some aspects of economic policy, for instance, how to contain hyperinflation" (Nelson and Eglinton 1996). One school of thought believes that democracy and democratic development is highly dependent on cultural attitudes, or "social capital" such as achievement orientation or trust: since cultures vary, both within and among states, so does the prospect for, or workings of, democratic state capitalism (e.g., Fukuyama 1995; Owens 1987; Putnam 1993). Carothers (1997), however, believes that while no country can be excluded from a democratic future, the ones most likely to attain it manifest a relatively high per capita income, past experience with pluralistic politics, and association with the Western liberal democracies.

In addition to the lack of a precise road map from the social sciences, U.S. foreign policy on democracy and human rights is bedevilled by well-known characteristics in Washington, including the institutional struggle for control of policy. While associating initiatives in foreign policy with different administrations, one cannot exclude the role of Congress. In certain eras, but perhaps not the current one, it has been Congress that has shown more genuine (as opposed to rhetorical) interest in democracy and human rights abroad, by comparison to an executive branch dominated by security managers in the realist tradition of power politics (Forsythe 1988). There is also the ideological struggle between internationalists and isolationists—the latter having reappeared in various disguises after the Cold War. The old idea is now heard once again that the way to advance democracy abroad is to perfect U.S. democracy at home—thus serving as the "shining city on the hill" (Davis and Lynn-Jones 1987). In this view, even American democratic isolationism amounts to international leadership for democracy by example.

The Clinton administration, in its own erratic way, mostly identified with the traditions of executive supremacy and internationalism. But the administration's lofty rhetoric about democracy abroad was accompanied by congressional insistence on low and declining spending on foreign affairs (Muravchik 1996). There was a disconnect between formidable objectives and the means to achieve them. What is also clear is that U.S. foreign policy, fashioned by both the president and Congress, has adopted a shotgun approach to democracy in foreign policy, with a wide variety of public and quasi-public initiatives. This fact closes the circle: given that no one theory predominates in explaining the presence or absence, the stability or instability, of liberal democracy, a shotgun approach makes sense. On the other hand, U.S. spending on democracy may be so low and so dispersed as to make particularly U.S. bilateral efforts marginal to foreign developments (see further Carothers 1996a, 1997; Pastor 1993; Russett 1993).

The third wave (Huntington 1991) of democratization from the 1970s to the present has resulted in some stagnation and retrenchment, numerous ambiguous situations, and some apparent successes thus far (Carothers 1997). It is hardly conceivable that the U.S. played a large and direct role in all these developments. Even for the fifty or so countries receiving some type of U.S. official democracy assistance, its impact seems fairly marginal most of the time (Carothers 1997). U.S. democracy assistance may exist because such an orientation seems the right thing to do and makes us feel good about ourselves (Carothers 1996b).

Finally, in these background remarks we must pay some further attention to economics. In general, U.S. funding for market restructuring abroad is more generous than for democratic assistance. A cynic might be led to believe that under the umbrella of democratic state capitalism, what is really transpiring is pursuit of profit via capitalism, with quite limited action for liberal democracy as the moral fig leaf. After all, U.S. diplomatic history shows periods of rhetoric for democracy when the real thrust of U.S. policy was to secure accommodation of American strategic and commercial interests (Lowenthal 1991; Smith 1994). With regard to Eastern Europe and the former Soviet republics, U.S. policy has probably emphasized security and economics per se, "while promoting democracy is an ancillary goal" (Carothers 1996a). For fiscal 1996 the State Department wanted $504 million for market reform in the newly independent states of the former Soviet Union, and only $148 million for aid to political parties and nonprofit civic groups (draft PL 102-511). Congressional hearings devoted ostensibly to democracy abroad frequently focused on market restructuring and privatization (Commission on Security and Cooperation in Europe 1995).

It is difficult to determine U.S. motivations and priorities in regard to economics and democracy. First of all, economic growth and prosperity do not, historically, correlate with liberal democracy (e.g., Hewlett 1979; Singer and Wildavsky 1996). Matters may or may not be different in contemporary times (see, for example, Abramson and Inglehart 1995; Burkhart and Lewis-Beck 1994). Whatever the evidence, U.S. policymakers may genuinely believe that economic restructuring in favor of private markets is necessary for liberal democracy. And, even while allowing for exceptions, and the overlap between cultural and economic factors, there does seem to be some positive correlation between capitalism, high per capita income, and liberal democracy at least in the modern era. Singer and Wildavsky (1996) believe that there is a high correlation between a modern, high-tech capitalist economy requiring much individual freedom, and eventual democratic politics. Carothers (1997) believes that where new democracies have run into difficulties, it is *not* because of the rigors of market restructuring toward privatization.

Regardless of theories about economics and the creation of democracy, and regardless of the argument that the U.S. could have done more to create democracy in many places (Carothers 1997), the U.S. had demonstrated real interest in the creation of liberal democracy in many states like El Salvador by the time of the Bush and Clinton administrations. In such places, as well as in some of the newly independent states and Eastern Europe, where free and fair elections have taken place, one of the leading issues is whether democracy can be consolidated in liberal form. Here economics would seem to re-enter the picture in terms of the necessity of economic growth with equitable distribution, combined with land reform and a welfare state (Forsythe 1996). Prosperity, and economic assistance, is indeed an important consideration for consolidation of liberal democracy (Diamond 1992, 1996). Even if cultural and institutional factors are important, economics, too, plays a role in the consolidation of liberal democracy—as the fate of the Weimar Republic indicated. (The Weimar Republic was stable for a few years, and while it always had its extremist opponents, it was especially the economic difficulties after the stock market crash of the late 1920s that led to the domination of fascism.)

Bilateral Policy (with Coordination)

U.S. foreign policy, even when nominally unilateral or bilateral, is frequently and informally coordinated with like-minded states. Thus when in 1996 the U.S. suspended foreign assistance to Niger after a military coup toppled an elected leader, the Clinton team coordinated policy with France. Much U.S. foreign assistance is coordinated with the Development Assistance Committee of the OECD, or more narrowly with the G-7 countries. Of course some foreign policies remain unilateral, and sometimes the U.S. and its allies go their separate ways on matters of democracy and other human rights. Be that as it may, one can distinguish U.S.

foreign policy that may be informally coordinated from that which is formally organized through intergovernmental institutions like the United Nations, World Bank, International Monetary Fund, and the like.

Structural Impact

The U.S. has made a structural contribution to democracy abroad, along with its democratic allies, through its emergence as a great power and in particular its role in the Second World War. Had the Fascists and Axis Powers won that war, human rights norms including participatory rights would not have been written into the constituent documents of the United Nations, Organization of American States, and Council of Europe, nor would democracy at the national level have been the beacon it turned out to be. This structural impact was greatest in the North Atlantic area and in Japan, with a certain intangible and unmeasurable radiating effect. As Tony Smith has noted (1994), despite his general enthusiasm for the U.S. record on democracy abroad, this structural impact does not mean that the U.S. was a force for democracy in places like Iran or Guatemala, inter alia, during the Cold War. Still, the U.S. has made a major if elusive impact on the world just by being a dominant great power, and indeed in some times and places a hegemonic power, without abandoning its democratic credentials at home—however imperfectly configured regarding racial minorities and women who were only belatedly treated as equals in law. With regard to the doubling of the number of various types of democracy toward the end of the Cold War, one cannot say precisely what was the structural impact of the U.S. (and other OECD states) as the wealthy and free victors in the seventy-year contest with authoritarian socialism.

Emergency Diplomacy (Reactive)

The U.S. has reacted to wars, political crises, and other emergency situations in ways that sometimes entailed a commitment to democracy. With only moderate overstatement, an Agency for International Development (AID) official testified to Congress that "Democracy is an integral part of all post-crisis agreements ... " (U.S. House 1995a). The response to the coup in Niger in early 1996 has already been mentioned. Likewise, in Guatemala in 1993, the U.S. made clear that unless an attempted departure from constitutional governance was rolled back, Washington's assistance would not be forthcoming.

One clear contemporary example of strong reactive U.S. foreign policy for democracy and human rights has been its central role in the paper construction of a democratic Bosnian state, enmeshed in a series of international human rights agreements—some of which the U.S. has refused to accept itself. Despite subsequent controversies over U.S. support for the arrest of indicted war criminals and over the nature of elections in 1996, at Dayton in 1995 the U.S. clearly supported not simple peace in the former Yugoslavia but a liberal democratic peace. Not since the Versailles Peace Conference and the construction of the Weimar Republic had the U.S. led such an important diplomatic effort to turn an area historically associated with authoritarianism into a liberal democracy. If successful this effort would certainly reduce migration to Germany and other parts of Western Europe. Much the same analysis applies to U.S. policy in Kosovo from 1999.

The U.S. record on responding to other events is more ambiguous in places like China and Myanmar. In the former, a temporary suspension of normal relations after the Tiananmen massacre of June 1989 gradually gave way to business as usual—a policy driven by economic interests. In the latter, again some temporary pressure on behalf of democracy partially gave way to some accommodation in the interests of getting the military rulers to curtail drug traffic. Significant migration from Myanmar, especially to Thailand, did not cause the U.S., or others, to press hard for democracy. In both Asian situations, the reluctance of Japan, with its relatively large assistance and/or investment program, to come down solidly in support of democracy and/or civil rights was a great barrier to U.S. action. As the U.S. voluntarily reduces its spending for foreign assistance under domestic pressures, it cannot hope to be taken as seriously as Japan in foreign capitals. And as long as Japan's endorsement of democracy and human rights abroad is more rhetorical than real (Yokota and Aoi 2000; Arase 1993), U.S. unilateral initiatives will be hampered.

Clearly U.S. ad hoc diplomacy has compiled a quite mixed record on the question of democracy and human rights. In Kuwait in 1991, the expulsion of Iraqi troops was not followed by a concerted effort to produce democracy—liberal or otherwise. The Al-Sabah family has reimposed its essentially authoritarian and elitist ways, despite some quite marginal accommodation to a renewed but toothless parliament.

Likewise in Algeria, and with perhaps more justification, the U.S. has essentially deferred to France and its support of military government despite the canceling of national elections. Faced with the prospect of an Islamic government that, though elected, would engage in numerous violations of civil and political rights on the Iranian model, the U.S., like France, has supported first military government and then an election boycotted by radical Islamic parties. The prospect of another illiberal and Islamic democracy in Algeria, along with a general rise in the level of violence, had already caused significant migration to France. Presumably the long term French and U.S. strategy in Algeria was to support military government in the short run in order to force a moderation in the policies of the Islamic movements, thus leading to a more moderate and stable situation in the long term—with lower rates of migration.

There have been other complicated trade-offs. The Clinton administration avoided public censure of Russian human rights abuses in Chechnya, in the hope that the elected center represented by Boris Yeltsin and Vladimir Putin would hold against a resurgent extremism from both the left and right that could endanger Russian democracy, such as it was, and associated market reforms, however inconsistently pursued. U.S. foreign policy of a reactive or emergency sort does not lend itself to easy generalization with regard to democracy and human rights (see further Carothers 1997).

Programmatic Diplomacy (Preventative/Anticipatory)

By the mid-1990s the U.S. had, in a somewhat crazy-quilt fashion, put together a broad and complicated foreign program to advance democratic state capitalism. This program anticipated the construction or evolution of liberal democracies, and at the same time tried to be a preventative program opposed to backsliding toward authoritarianism. U.S. funding frequently went to international actors, especially transnational nongovernmental organizations active in civic society, making it impossible to draw a sharp line between bilateral and multilateral action. The line between public and private actor was also somewhat fuzzy.

U.S. programmatic democracy assistance was funded from so many different bits and pieces of legislation, and was affected by so many different decisions within executive agencies, that neither the Clinton administration nor Congress could establish just how much was being spent (U.S. House 1995a). It was difficult enough for one agency like AID to come up with a figure for itself (it estimated $447 million for fiscal 1995), much less for the U.S. government in toto. Official democracy assistance involved so many different departments and agencies that it was not always possible to say who was in charge, who reported to whom, or whether the U.S. ambassador to a recipient country knew what was happening (U.S. House 1995a). The State Department might say that its Bureau on Human Rights, Democracy, and Labor was in charge. But AID spent the most money, and the Justice Department ran some legal programs rather independently. The Defense Department resisted control by State, as usual, in places like Haiti and Bosnia.

Congress funded the National Endowment for Democracy, which then made its own programmatic decisions, usually involving grants to other private actors, which in the late 1980s and early 1990s were not always coordinated with official U.S. government agencies. Some improvement in informal consultation occurred over time. Congress also funded the U.S. Institute for Peace, which made its own decisions about what to study and publish, without coordination with studies commissioned by AID or any other agency.

Over time it became evident that U.S. democracy assistance was directed to three general types of activity: support for civic society and the private groups found therein; support for state institution building, including strong parliaments and independent and fair judiciaries; and electoral assistance to guarantee free and fair elections with party competition. There was no general strategy as to which of these was more important, or came first. AID started out with sixteen categories of action, which were vague and overlapping and which were eventually abandoned (Hirschmann 1995). Some of the AID action constituted new wine in old bottles. It already had a program on Women in Development, which was transformed into a democracy program, which had little effect in either form (U.S. House 1995a). The sum total of the three general areas of activity meant that one could use a checklist or shopping list for possible assistance programming directed to a wide range of targets: political parties, elections, rule of law (courts, police), parliaments, civic society (private and advocacy groups), trade unions, and communications media (adapted from Carothers 1996b).

Given the scattershot nature of this programmatic activity, as well as the varying conditions addressed, generalizations are elusive. We will, however, indicate some general statements that can be refined in the future.

- U.S. democracy assistance has been mostly made up of small grants to discrete projects with short time frames, without much general strategy (Carothers 1996a).
- U.S. assistance has been mostly directed to the former communist states of Europe and to the states of the Western hemisphere.
- Funding levels have been generally small, not only compared to the Marshall Plan of the late 1940s but also compared to what Germany has spent on democratic state capitalism in the area of the former East Germany or German Democratic Republic with its 17 million persons (U.S. House 1992). In the early 1990s the West European states were spending more in former communist areas of Europe than was the United States (Grieve 1992–93). The U.S. ranked toward the bottom of all OECD countries in terms of percentage of its GDP directed toward all forms of Official Development Assistance.
- Because of the importance of the democracy rhetoric, AID created a new Center for Democracy and Governance, and experimented with a variety of approaches including an attempt at quantitative measures of democracy—and quantitative formulas for distribution of assistance with attention to democracy—both abandoned.
- Funding for market restructuring in favor of capitalism was almost always much more substantial than direct funding for democracy and human rights assistance (excluding the cost of military deployments in places like Haiti and Bosnia, etc.); no one tried to calculate the cost of diplomacy for democratic order in places like El Salvador.
- Programs were widely dispersed with very little concentration on anyone's conception of pivotal states like Brazil, Mexico, Nigeria, Algeria, Indonesia, etc.; why the U.S. should have a program for democracy assistance in Albania was not addressed, although some thought it was in places like Albania that U.S. assistance

could make a decisive difference; Russia clearly drew more attention than the other former Soviet republics.

- In obviously pivotal or important states routine programmatic concern for democracy and rights lost out frequently to other concerns such as protecting economic interests (China), or advancing strategic interests (Turkey); the very fact of being a pivotal state seemed to reduce the importance of democracy and human rights in relative terms (Neier 1996).
- All the rhetoric about democracy and rights did not alter certain prevalent features of past U.S. foreign policy, such as Israel and Egypt receiving about 50 percent of total U.S. foreign assistance.
- In places like Mexico, transnational private action in support of domestic groups might be more important than direct public action by the U.S. government (Dresser 1996; Sikkink 1996; on the importance of civic society groups in general, see Johnson 1992).
- U.S. democracy assistance was deeply intrusive in foreign societies, creating as it did a linkage between Washington and private actors including opposition political parties; this was not always viewed benignly by foreign governments (Carothers 1996a).

Multilateral Policy

Democratic Standards: Passive and Active

In its recent foreign policy, the U.S. has clearly endorsed democratic standards in the UN, OAS, OSCE, and other general or "political" IGOs. During parts of the Cold War, and especially during the Kissinger-Nixon era (Lowenthal 1991), matters were not always the same. Now the U.S. does indeed fully identify with the view that democratic governance is the only form of legitimate governance (Frank 1992). In this sense the U.S. government formally endorses the "end of history" thesis (Fukuyama 1992), in that democratic values are accepted as the ultimate standard of right rule. (In the meantime the U.S. has no problem in dealing with dictators like President Assad of Syria, who wields effective power.) Its recent leadership for democratic standards has been pronounced especially in the OAS, notably so in its support for the "Santiago Declaration" in which the presence or absence of democracy in hemispheric states was declared to be an international matter and not one of domestic jurisdiction (Bloomfield 1994).

U.S. support for democratic standards in political IGOs has occasionally been active as well as passive. Here we are addressing the use of diplomacy in an effort to produce or protect democratic governance, against the background of internationally recognized democratic standards. It cannot be said that the UN has a long history of attention to democratic behavior (beyond setting standards) via the diplomacy of the

General Assembly or Human Rights Commission, inter alia (Forsythe 1995). Given the presence of many authoritarian states in the UN system, and given the gross violations of essentially civil rights, to the extent that the UN has tried to supervise state behavior on any one theme, it has focused on liberalization of repression rather than democratization per se. The UN has used words to try to pressure states to stop such violations of personal integrity as summary execution and torture, more than it has focused on democracy. U.S. policy has been part of this understandable development. Less understandably, at times in the past the U.S. has used the UN to shield its authoritarian allies—most notably Argentina under military rule during the Reagan era (Guest 1990), but also El Salvador and Guatemala during the same period. After the Cold War, U.S. policy in the UN, OAS, and OSCE has been very supportive of democratic developments in general, going beyond use of words in active and passive standards to support field operations for democracy inside countries (see below).

The U.S. record on passive and active standards for democracy is not so clear in international financial institutions (IFI). Only in the European Bank for Reconstruction and Development has the U.S., like its European allies, clearly endorsed the "intrusion" of democratic and human rights factors into the lending decisions of that multilateral bank. In the World Bank, there is evident confusion as to the meaning of "good governance" and its linkage to democratic and other human rights issues (Forsythe 1997; Gillies 1993; Nelson and Eglinton 1996). Neither the U.S., nor other member states, nor the Bank staff is clear on whether IFI should take a political science or an accounting approach to good governance. The former implies a broad concern with democracy and human rights as part of sustainable development, as the UN secretary-general articulated in his *Agenda for Development* (1994). The latter approach implies sound management, openness to review by international financial institutions, the rule of law, and perhaps some type of citizen consultation on particular development projects.

A similar confusion characterizes the operations of the UN Development Program. Here, unlike in the World Bank, there is passive or rhetorical commitment to democracy. But in the fieldwork of the UNDP, which is frequently undertaken in tandem with the World Bank, it is very difficult to demonstrate a functioning commitment to liberal democracy in national politics. All sorts of development programs are undertaken in authoritarian states, and local citizens—especially indigenous peoples—frequently have no significant say in development projects. The difference between UNDP and the Bank lies in passive standards: UNDP endorses political democracy whereas the Bank cannot make up its collective mind. (The Bank is far more clear in its change to accepting environment standards as a proper lending concern.) In terms of operating standards, there is little systematic difference between the Bank and UNDP. (The Bank is more likely to suspend activities, though somewhat unpredictably, over democratic and human rights issues than is the UNDP.) Both multilateral organizations now say they favor citizen participation in development projects, which may be considered a type of micro- or grassroots democracy.

The International Monetary Fund has never pretended to take human rights standards seriously, being much more adamant than the Bank that democracy and human rights definitely lie outside its proper domain. Yet the IMF, too, suspended drawing rights to China after Tiananmen Square. Regional development banks are similar to the World Bank in their inconsistent and confusing attention to democracy and human rights.

As the U.S. is a major player in these financial multilateral organizations, it bears considerable responsibility for the mixed record on democratic development. The U.S. and Germany led the World Bank into pressuring states like Kenya and Malawi concerning human rights and democratic issues (Nelson and Eglinton 1996). But the U.S. also led the World Bank into continuing loans to the Palestinian authority, despite its evident shortcomings regarding democracy and civil rights. The Bank always rationalizes its decisions in economic terms, but sometimes civil and political rights affect Bank decisions.

IGO Field Operations

The U.S. has been very supportive of IGOs undertaking programs within countries to establish and consolidate liberal democracy. One of the striking developments, especially in the UN and OAS, but also in the OSCE, is the expansion of multilateral electoral assistance. The U.S. government, in addition to it bilateral efforts (and support of NGO action as well), has encouraged the UN and the OAS in particular to supervise elections. In places like El Salvador, Haiti, and Nicaragua these IGOs, with close U.S. support, played important roles in the conduct of free and fair elections (Farer 1996). In Cambodia, the UN not only supervised elections but organized them—including being responsible for the registration of the electorate for the first national election in the country's history (Marks). In 1996 the U.S. threatened to reduce its foreign assistance to Cambodia if the government continued to back away from democratic standards the UN had helped establish, but the decline in those standards continued (Carothers 1997).

In general the U.S. has been supportive of second-generation or complex peacekeeping by the UN, in which the deployment of noncombat military force, with the consent of the parties, along with civilian personnel, is designed not only to secure narrow military objectives but also political ones such as democratic and rights-protective governance (Weiss, Forsythe, and Coate 2000). This can overlap with electoral assistance. In El Salvador, Namibia, Cambodia, Mozambique, and elsewhere, UN complex peacekeeping is directed to construction of democratic order and a liberal democratic state. One of the clear success stories, in relative terms, has been El Salvador and reflects—inter alia—a blending of U.S. bilateral and multilateral policies (Forsythe 1996). Despite congressional hesitancy, U.S. foreign policy continues to pay for about one-third of the costs of this complex peacekeeping, in addition to unilaterally covering the costs of U.S. military deployment in Haiti, and covering the costs of U.S. military deployment in the former Yugoslavia via NATO. So U.S. support for complex peacekeeping as directed toward democratic governance is clear (although resting on shaky domestic foundations). The pattern holds for Kosovo and East Timor at the turn of the century.

The U.S. did not lead on the issue of multilateral involvement in Rwanda during the genocide of 1994 or on Burundi during 1996. Democracy was important in these cases, but the most pressing issue was to stop genocide. Clearly in Rwanda, however, genocide and brutal civil war led to massive migration, and the U.S., smarting from its troubles in Somalia, was slow to react via the UN. It is also fair to say that U.S. commitment to, or leadership for, IGO field operations directed at democratic order may be weak, even when present. Eighteen American military deaths on one day in Somalia, and about forty overall (as many deaths as the Pakistani blue helmets lost in one day) was sufficient to cause the U.S. to start making arrangements for a withdrawal of its forces from that failed state. The U.S. stomach for costly democratic state and nation-building is not strong (Luttwak 1994), even in a multilateral and thus cost-sharing framework.

Finally, the U.S. has supported UN, OAS, and OSCE programs of technical assistance for such things as reform of the judiciary, reconstruction of police forces, protection of minority rights, and civilian superiority over the military. This technical assistance can be authorized through discrete projects or as part of complex peacekeeping. These and similar IGO programs contribute to the construction and consolidation of liberal democracy. U.S. pressure to reduce IGO budgets, however, hurts the ability of the organizations to respond to growing requests for democratic assistance. The UN Human Rights Center still receives only about $18m for its entire global program, or about 1 percent of the UN regular budget. By comparison, the U.S. Justice Department alone was spending some $70 million on rule of law programs abroad in any one year in the mid-1990s. The U.S., perhaps because of congressional pressures, has not been a leader in pushing for the expansion of UN or other IGO human rights funding for liberal democracy. (The U.S. has been the primary supporter, within limits, of the UN Criminal Tribunal for former Yugoslavia, which had been costing some $25 million annually, and which is rose to some $45 million multiple trials get under way.)

Enforcing Democracy

The complicated issue of Kosovo aside, the only place the U.S. has really enforced democracy, as compared to working for its construction or protection through less decisive means, is in Haiti (Maingot 1996). The U.S.

has used IGOs to promote, advance, nurture, and backstop democracy; only in Haiti has it demanded democratic government "now." There, the UN Security Council, having already authorized a mandatory program of economic sanctions, authorized states to use "all necessary means," after which the U.S. and its surrogates such as the Carter Center negotiated an end to authoritarian rule against the background of threat of force. The U.S. then deployed force to secure, at least in the short term, the democratic order that the negotiations had produced. At best this was quasi-enforcement of democracy, since technically the old authoritarian order agreed to step aside. The clear result of these events was a marked decline in migration from Haiti to the U.S. (see below for more details).

There have been other IGO enforcement actions, notably to liberate Kuwait, to guarantee secure humanitarian assistance in Somalia, and to apply the Dayton and Paris peace agreements in former Yugoslavia. The U.S. was centrally involved in all. Kuwait and Somalia were not, strictly speaking, about democracy, although they could have been and should have been. IFOR in the former Yugoslavia, as already noted, is not just about enforcing order, but at least in Bosnia about liberal democratic order—on paper, anyway. At the time of writing IFOR had engaged in essentially peacekeeping action. But it has the legal authority and military muscle to enforce agreements if it had to. That enforcement potential has been more evident on security arrangements than on democracy and human rights. IFOR had mostly resisted demands that it enforce the arrest of those internationally indicted for certain violations of human rights. This was primarily because of U.S. policy.

The U.S. intends to expand NATO membership to include certain democracies in Eastern Europe, at some unspecified time in the future, and in a way—so far unspecified—that does not trigger the paranoia of a Russia that has historically feared Western encirclement. This expanded NATO membership might also be considered a way to enforce, or at least forcefully defend, democracy.

The Case of Haiti

Kosovo aside once again, Haiti provides the best case of U.S. policy to enforce democracy, with policy greatly driven by the pressures of migration (U.S. House 1996a). In fact, the real thorn in the U.S. side was not authoritarianism in Haiti, but unwanted asylum seekers in the U.S. Thus three U.S. administrations had engaged first in a controversial program of interdiction at sea in an effort to keep Haitians beyond U.S. territorial jurisdiction (Loescher and also Ferris in this volume; Teitelbaum and Weiner 1995).

Unlike the situation in Algeria in which authoritarian government was associated with reduced migration (Pierre), Haiti's government during 1991–94 caused tens of thousands of refugees to flee to U.S. shores.

While Florida was already home to approximately 250,000 Haitians, in July 1994 an additional 16 to 21 thousand refugees were interdicted in the course of one month alone (Clary 1995; Hirsch 1995; Willon 1996). This influx of refugees was estimated to cost U.S. taxpayers $1 million per day (U.S. House 1996a), with increasing demands placed on various social services. To mitigate this perceived threat to American society, Operation Uphold Democracy was launched in September of 1994. Since America's democratic values are concurrent with its economic and security interests in Haiti, the U.S. is active in employing both emergency and programmatic diplomacy to pursue its democratic objectives.

During the 1980s, in the context of increasing U.S. attention to the Caribbean and Central America, including the emergence of democracy assistance, the U.S. froze economic aid to Haiti worth $70 million following the violence that accompanied Haiti's first free elections in thirty years (Balutansky 1988). The U.S. made clear that "significant measures" toward democracy needed to be taken if aid was to be resumed. This penalty was not a mere inconvenience since the U.S. had been by far the largest donor in the country. Sanctions did not prevent the September 1991 military takeover, however, nor did subsequent UN and OAS sanctions remedy it. The AID did undertake some democratic initiatives during the three years of the military regime such as legal assistance, civic education, human rights monitoring, and support for four "democratic labor unions" in Haiti (USAID 1995). But it was only after the September 1994 peaceful deployment of the U.S.-led multinational force (MNF) and the negotiated end of authoritarian rule that democracy-building in Haiti received considerable emphasis. From that time Haiti became "the largest recipient of U.S. aid in the Western Hemisphere" (Farah 1994).

U.S. policy since 1994 has clearly been aimed at promoting democratic state capitalism in Haiti. As in other places, funds for market restructuring dominate lesser funds for official development assistance via AID ($57,410,000 vs. $19,260,000 for FY96). American policymakers unquestioningly assume that economic growth and privatization sustain democracy. This belief permeates Congressional statements, AID funding priorities, progress indicators, and even the rhetoric of the Haitian President himself when he referred to democracy as "an economic question" (Preval 1996). According to an AID official, "no matter how successful the Haitian people are at establishing a secure environment or building democratic and legal institutions, stability will elude them without strong, steady, broad-based economic growth" (USAID 1995; see also U.S. State Department 1995a).

Nevertheless, sociopolitical policies aimed at directly engendering democracy in Haiti are receiving substantial support despite their lower spending priority. AID, borrowing language from UN debates and documents, regarded the merger of economic growth and democracy as part of sustainable development. According to one official, "Democratization is an essential part of sustainable development because it facilitates the protection of human rights, informed participation, and public sector accountability" (USAID 1994).

Coordinated Approach

U.S. democracy assistance in Haiti occurs in a multilateral context. Not only have American initiatives received the official sanction of UN Security Council resolutions, but "Donor coordination in Haiti represents an important example of international burden-sharing" (U.S. House 1996a). While in FY94 the U.S. was responsible for nearly 70 percent of international aid flows to Haiti, AID estimates that by the end of FY96 the American contribution to the post-crisis situation will be less than 20 percent—although the U.S. remains the largest single donor (USAID 1995; U.S. House 1996a). Following the 31 March 1995 withdrawal of the MNF, costs for the United States have fallen dramatically as other donors such as the European Union (EU), UN agencies, Germany, Canada, France, and Japan have assumed a larger proportion of the outlays. In addition to the formal organization of assistance to Haiti that is occurring through the UN, EU, IMF, Inter-American Development Bank (IDB), and World Bank, the various bilateral and multilateral economic aid policies were informally coordinated at a consultative group meeting held on 31 January 1995 (Coughlin 1996; U.S. Department of State 1995a). Focal points for democracy-related aid to Haiti have primarily been electoral assistance and strengthening the rule of law (police and judiciary), although support for civil society, parliament, and public sector efficiency also figures into the aid equation.

Electoral Assistance

The U.S. saw the UN as the primary actor for electoral assistance in the 1995 Haitian election. The Center for Electoral Promotion and Assistance (CAPEL), an advisory body formed under the Inter-American Human Rights Institute, also played an important role in the process through its voter education program in Haiti. While these multilateral policies constituted the majority of electoral assistance, the United States also provided bilateral support through AID and the National Endowment for Democracy (NED). AID "controls virtually all of Washington's aid program in Haiti" (U.S. House 1995) and contracts with various NGOs to undertake field operations in the country. During the 1995 elections, AID funded the International Foundation for Electoral Systems (IFES) to train election workers and procure ballots. While the UN Development Program (UNDP) was responsible for the grassroots training effort, IFES was provided with a grant of $231,926 to instruct fifteen core trainers and facilitate the UN's activities. An additional $2,006,268 was spent to procure official ballots by the time of the elections (U.S. Senate 1995).

The National Endowment for Democracy, operating through the International Republican Institute (IRI) and National Democratic Institute (NDI), also played an important role in the Haitian elections. The IRI supplied opposition parties with pre-election tracking reports, sent an observer delegation to the elections, and submitted recommendations on how Haiti's electoral process could be improved (Kirschten 1995). The NDI's approach was nonpartisan and holistic, focusing upon improving the party structure overall through organizing debates and dialogues between parties and candidates (including a party leaders summit), instructing party pollwatchers and an Electoral Monitoring Unit, conducting a civic education program to encourage issue-based campaigns, founding an Electoral Information Center, assisting voter education, and holding seminars for the Haitian media on election reporting (U.S. House 1995a). The Carter Center also sent observers to the elections and submitted reports and recommendations on how Haiti's electoral process could be improved. The short term success of the various multilateral and bilateral efforts was confirmed on 17 December 1995 when Rene Preval replaced Father Aristide and became the first democratically elected president to succeed another democratically elected president in the history of Haiti.

The Rule of Law

U.S. bilateral and multilateral aid designed to foster the rule of law in Haiti is primarily focused upon the creation and strengthening of a civilian police force and the reform of a dysfunctional judicial system. AID is also an important source of funding for these operations, although the U.S. Department of Justice provides funding and actually coordinates the programs through two components of its Criminal Division: the International Criminal Investigative Training Program (ICITAP) and the Office of Professional Development and Training (OPDAT). ICITAP instructs local police forces and was responsible for founding the Haitian National Police Academy in accordance with the UN mandate following the demise of authoritarian rule (U.S. House 1996a). Establishing a professional, apolitical police force is considered an integral part of democracy-building in Haiti since it will be up to the Haitian National Police to enforce the law in a fair and equal manner and secure the confidence of the Haitian people (U.S. House 1996a, 1996b). The U.S., Canada, France, and Norway have all sent experienced instructors to the Academy, and the UN mission's civilian police provide on-the-job training and monitor these new Haitian police officers upon their deployment (O'Neill n.d.; United Nations 1996). As of March 1996 the academy had trained and deployed 5,000 civilian police (at a cost to the U.S. of approximately $35 million—Defense 1996) when the program was "effectively closed down for a month due to the conditions that the administration and Congress established concerning the presence of suspected killers in the security forces" (U.S. House 1996a).

In conjunction with the National Center for State Courts, OPDAT began training Haitian prosecutors and judges in January 1995 and collaborated with the Haitian Ministry of Justice to inaugurate a judicial training academy (L'Ecole de la Magistrature) the following July with Haitian, U.S., French, and Canadian instructors (U.S. House 1996a; O'Neill n.d.). At a cost of $18 million for the four-year project, AID contracted the private firm Checchi and Company to operate the School for Magistrates and tackle judicial reform overall—training judges and coordinating judicial aid (Alphonse 1996; O'Neill n.d.). With U.S. funds, a national prison rehabilitation program was also instituted to provide relief to victims of human rights abuses and their families (U.S. House 1996a).

Perhaps the most dramatic U.S. effort to uphold the rule of law in Haiti was the 29 March 1995 dispatch of an FBI team—under 28 U.S.C. 533(3)—to investigate the murder of a political adversary of President Aristide (U.S. House 1996a). In a country with a long history of political violence it was suspected that such an event could threaten the stability of Haitian democracy if an assiduous investigation was not immediately undertaken (U.S. House 1996a). Congress also responded to these events by passing the Dole Amendment (Section 583 of Public Law 104-107) in January 1996 which conditioned most further U.S. foreign assistance on a serious investigation of "political and extrajudicial killings" (U.S. House 1996a).

Civil Society

Vocational training and job placement programs for thousands of demobilized soldiers are being funded by AID in order to reintegrate them into civil society. A Human Rights Fund was also established to monitor human rights abuses, redress grievances, and promote citizen oversight of the police (U.S. House 1996a). The U.S. hopes that Haitians can overcome the psychological consequences of authoritarian rule and produce an atmosphere conducive to democratic development (U.S. House 1996a). To this end the U.S. supports various programs designed to protect political opposition and community development under the rule of law.

Parliament

AID has been providing technical assistance to the Haitian parliament through such activities as the establishment of a legislative database, renovation of the archives room, provision of office supplies, and the training of administrative staff (U.S. House 1996a). However, it has also provided a grant to the Center for Democracy which has been working closely with the Haitian Parliament and municipal officials. The Center has developed a long-run Legislative-strengthening Project for the Haitian Parliament, while a protocol was signed between Port-au-Prince and New Orleans initiating municipal exchange of mayors and private sector leaders between the two cities (U.S. House 1995a).

Public Sector Efficiency

AID's Policy and Administrative Reform Project was designed to foster efficiency in Haiti's public sector (USAID 1995). This includes support for the Haitian government's Structural Adjustment Program (SAP) that Aristide agreed to as a condition of donor aid. Although the plan primarily focuses on economic reform, with privatization of parastatal companies drawing the most international attention, also on the agenda is civil service reform with reductions targeted at up to 50 percent (U.S. State Department 1995a). The objective is to decentralize the Haitian system and increase the accountability of government officials.

Conclusions on Haiti

Congressional critics of the administration's policy toward Haiti argue that too much assistance has been granted to this emerging democracy at the relative deprivation of other Latin American and Caribbean states (U.S. House 1996a). Clinton's deployment of force and subsequent efforts to democratize Haiti were never very popular beyond southern Florida and with the congressional Black Caucus. Building liberal democratic government takes time and money and incurs risks, especially in countries with little history of democratic rule such as Haiti. In the short term, the U.S. post-invasion record at democracy-building in Haiti was reasonably strong. The military deployment was followed by a serious attempt to produce a sustainable, liberal democracy in Haiti that would protect the civil and political rights of the Haitian people and thus reduce incentives to migrate. Although the relative emphasis in funding was upon economic reform, this emanated more from Washington's belief in a symbiotic relationship between capitalism and democracy than it did from any predatory designs on Haiti's small economic potential. By the turn of the century, however, a number of destablilizing problems had arisen, and Haiti remained far from being a consolidated liberal democracy.

The Case of Turkey

Unlike Haiti, Turkey has been a democratic state off and on for decades, albeit a democracy manifesting serious violations of internationally recognized human rights. Like Haiti, Turkey has been involved in quite serious migration issues, affecting mostly Germany and other European states. There are two general reasons for Turkish migration: slow and inequitable economic growth, and repression—the latter having to do mostly with the Kurdish question.

While many of the Turkish Kurds are assimilated into Turkish mainstream society, there was an active and violent Kurdish separatist party that wished the southeastern part of Turkey to become part of an independent

Kurdistan. Various Turkish governments have reacted to this situation in a very heavy-handed way, using an "anti-terrorism act" to stifle even scholarly discussion of "the Kurdish question."

The U.S. has no programmatic democracy assistance to Turkey, since Turkey holds relatively free and fair elections with party competition (although various manifestations of a Kurdish political party have been periodically repressed). General political freedom, however short lived, was shown by the fact that for a time the senior party in the governing coalition was an Islamic Party, despite misgivings in both Turkish and Western circles about its campaign statements and subsequent governmental policies on a variety of issues. The military eventually forced this party from power. Given the weakness of the U.S. response to this curtailment of democratic opinion, it was clear that strategic concerns are primary in U.S. foreign policy toward Turkey, with democracy and civil rights as distinctly secondary or tertiary issues. Official rationalizations aside, the U.S. tolerates considerable violation of civil rights, and some political rights, in Turkey because of Turkey's historic role as a pro-U.S. member of NATO in an important and unstable part of the world.

According to the UN High Commissioner for Refugees (1994), the number of Turkish asylum seekers abroad reached a peak of 684,000 in 1992. This number constituted the second highest in Europe, behind asylum seekers from the former Yugoslavia, during 1991–94 (Weiner 1995). This flight stemmed mostly from governmental attempts to deal harshly with the Kurdish question. According to the U.S. Department of State in its annual human rights report (1996; see also Commission on Security and Cooperation in Europe 1995; Human Rights Watch 1996), Turkish policy in connection to this Kurdish movement resulted in military attacks on civilian targets, disappeared persons, abuse of detained persons, restrictions on civil and political rights, and other violations of human rights. As long as Turkish citizens did not participate in, support, or write about the Turkish Kurdish movement, Turkish democracy functioned in a basically liberal way. Though there were persistent problems with prison conditions in general, but assimilated Kurdish Turks had few problems. Turkish asylum seekers went mainly to Germany, where there were many Turkish nationals from earlier periods of legal migration in connection to a guest worker program (Weiner 1995).

The U.S. and its European allies periodically addressed these questions of human rights violations by an imperfect democratic partner. Between 1985 and 1995, the U.S. provided some $5 billion to Turkey in military assistance (Morrison 1995). At times the U.S. withheld some small part of military assistance, but perhaps as much because of Turkish actions in Cyprus, which Turkey had invaded in 1974, as because of repression and atrocities in Turkey itself (U.S. State Department 1995c). By 1996 the U.S. was providing $100 million in unrestricted Economic Support Funds to Turkey, plus $5,400,000 via AID to stabilize its population. Military and economic assistance of all types made Turkey the third largest recipient of U.S. foreign assistance. Certain congressional elements wanted to cut some foreign assistance funds on human rights grounds, but the State Department was opposed (New York Times, 28 June 1996: 2). Turkey, having long recognized Israel, had drawn closer to that special state after the Cold War; had served as a logistical base for both the Persian Gulf War and for U.S. intervention into northern Iraq after that war to protect Iraqi Kurds; was temporary home to over 10,000 U.S. military personnel; and was contesting Iranian influence in central Asia. Turkey buys some $1.8 billion in weapons from the U.S. (Human Rights Watch 1996). It was clear from State Department statements (State Department Briefing 1996; Turkish-U.S. Relations Hearings 1995; U.S. State Department 1995b) that the Executive preferred a strategy of constructive engagement, in which the U.S. discussed human rights issues with Turkish officials but did not apply serious sanctions. Withholding 10 percent of military assistance for later release did not appear to be a serious sanction and did not appear to have much impact on most human rights violations—or on patterns of migration. Such withholding did symbolize U.S. concern with improving Turkish democracy—as well as perhaps preempting critics that wanted to do more. John Shattuck, Clinton's first top human rights official in the State Department, also made a blatant appeal for business as usual with Turkey, in the name of American trade and investment (State Department Briefing 1996).

European states, after similar debate, also mostly followed a strategy of constructive engagement. Turkey was allowed to join the European Customs Union in late 1995, despite continuing repression relating to the Kurdish question. This move presumably bound Turkey more firmly in a network emphasizing democratic state capitalism, and encouraged better economic growth. In response to U.S. and European concern, and before the vote on the ECU, the Ciller government, which preceded the Islamic-dominated coalition government, had liberalized the anti-terrorist law and had made other liberal gestures such as becoming a party to various international instruments on human rights (Rouleau 1996). Turkey had finally joined the Council of Europe, become a party to the European Convention on Human Rights, and accepted the supranational authority of the European Court on Human Rights. In 1996 this Court found the Turkish government in violation of regional human rights standards with regard to the destruction of villages in the southeastern region, with the government ordered to make reparations. European states still withheld their ultimate gesture to Turkey: membership in the European Union. This was in part because of the continuing human rights violations (New York Times, 25 September 1996: A4). Thus while the U.S. controlled military assistance to Turkey, the Europeans controlled the most important economic leverage—EU membership. But both needed Turkey as much as Turkey needed them.

Turkey was assuredly not Haiti, and indeed the two countries were not usually compared. In both, however, the U.S. in the 1990s faced questions about democracy and human rights. These questions impacted migration. The major difference between the two, from Washington's point of view, was that in Haiti U.S. strategic, economic, and social concerns all argued for a strong commitment to improved democratic state capitalism. But in Turkey, it was more difficult to press the government about improved democracy through better human rights protection, because of the need to maintain Turkey as a strategic ally and useful military base. Moreover, the rise of the Turkish Islamic Welfare Party, the most popular party from 1995, and its successor party, complicated matters enormously. Thus in Haiti the Clinton administration, despite lack of active and widespread domestic support, took decisive action—though through an indecisive process—in support of liberal democracy, action which also greatly reduced unwanted migration. In Turkey the problem of serious repression, and significant departure from the norms of liberal democracy, went mostly unaddressed by Washington. And significant migration to Germany continued.

Conclusions

The United States does not advocate democracy abroad simply to impact migration, but the size and nature of the liberal democratic community is a structural factor greatly affecting forced and other migrations. Haiti is a perfect example of how authoritarian repression and open borders can create a salient migration problem for neighboring countries, and how a U.S. effort to create liberal democratic state capitalism, combined with tougher border controls, can reduce unwanted migration to a trickle. Turkey also shows that repression of a minority, even in a partial democracy, is correlated with significant migration (although economics also plays a role), and that as long as repression continues so will the flight of asylum seekers.

The U.S., like other important actors in world affairs, now manifests a democracy assistance program of serious pretensions. It exits because of many reasons, although it is funded at miserly levels. In general its effects thus far seem elusive and mostly marginal, although there may be some psychological or moral importance that is difficult to specify. Beyond official democracy assistance, U.S. emergency or reactive diplomacy has been quite important for liberal democracy, in multilateral context, in places El Salvador as well as Haiti—both for the country itself and for migration issues. Other actors of various types are always involved in these situations, but the U.S. has played important roles. The U.S. is also important for the follow-on question of consolidation of liberal democracy.

One cannot arrive at a precise evaluation of U.S. support for democracy abroad (compare Smith 1994). First, the U.S. program or orientation is not a clear and concentrated policy but rather the sum total of various and mostly uncoordinated initiatives. Some initiatives seem to produce greater desired results than others. Some disappointing results are perhaps understandable, maybe even justified. Second, liberal democracy is the likely result of socioeconomic, institutional, and personal factors in a mix that varies with time and place. There is no clear view, in academe or government, about what exactly should be pursued, or when, or where. Thus there is no clear standard against which one can measure U.S. performance. The U.S. has sometimes supported free and fair elections, the development of institutions necessary for liberal democracy such as strong parliaments and independent courts, and agencies making up the civic sector. Results, as expected, have been mixed. Third, U.S. efforts to advance the notion of democratic state capitalism are almost always merged with other state, IGO, and NGO efforts. It is difficult to separate U.S. influences from that of other actors, whether public or private. Fourth, the U.S. record varies from place to place. Haiti is not Turkey.

Questions of peace and war aside (see Russett 1993), it clearly is better to have an enlarged democratic community than not, as long as we mean liberal democracies and not the type of elected governments in Iran and Sri Lanka that have engaged in discrimination of minorities. Illiberal democracies, along with certain authoritarian regimes, and even quasi-liberal democracies like Turkey with pockets of major repression, increase migration problems. So it is well that once again, after the Cold War, the U.S. and others are trying to foster liberal democratic states. Increased funding and a more concentrated focus would seem to be in order, as well as scaled down rhetoric, although none seem to be on the immediate horizon.

References

Abramson, Paul R., and Ronald Inglehart. 1995. *Value Change in Global Perspective*. Ann Arbor: University of Michigan Press.

Alphonse, Henri. 1996. "Haiti-Human Rights: U.S. Role Said to Create Judicial "Anomaly." Inter Press Service (21 March). Available in LEXIS, News Library, Allnws File.

Arase, David. 1993. "Japanese Policy toward Democracy and Human Rights in Asia." *Asian Survey* 33, 20 (October): 935–53.

Balutansky, Edwige. 1988. "Cutoff of U.S. Aid to Haiti Exacts Heavy Toll." *The Reuter Business Report* (June). Available in LEXIS, News Library, Allnws File.

Bloomfield, Richard J. 1994. "Making the Western Hemisphere Safe for Democracy? The OAS Defense-of-Democracy Regime." *The Washington Quarterly* 17, 2 (Spring): 157–69.

Burkhart, Ross E., and Michael S. Lewis-Beck. 1994. "Comparative Democracy: The Economic Development Thesis." *American Political Science Review* 88, 4 (December): 903–10.

Carothers, Thomas. 1994. "The Democracy Nostrum." *World Policy Journal* 11, 3 (Fall): 47–54.

————. 1996a. "Aiding—and Defining—Democracy." *World Policy Journal* 13, 1 (Spring): 97–109.

————. 1996b. *Assessing Democracy Assistance: The Case of Romania.* Washington D.C.: The Carnegie Endowment.

————. 1997. "Democracy Without Illusions." *Foreign Affairs* 76, 1 (January/February): 85–99.

Clary, Mike. 1995. "U.S. Interdictions Rise as Exodus from Haiti Grows." *Los Angeles Times,* 28 November 1995: A1. Available in LEXIS, News Library, Allnws File.

Commission on Security and Cooperation in Europe. 1995. *Briefing on U.S. Assistance to Central and Eastern Europe and the NIS: An Assessment.* 17 February. Washington D.C.: GPO.

Coughlin, Dan. 1996. "Haiti: Haitian Aid Flow Slow in Reaching the Ground." *Inter Press Service* 3 January 1996. Available in LEXIS, News Library, Allnws File.

Davis, T., and S. Lynn-Jones. 1987. "City upon a Hill." *Foreign Policy* 66: 20–38.

Diamond, Larry. 1992. "Promoting Democracy." *Foreign Policy* 87 (Summer): 25–46.

————. 1995. *Promoting Democracy in the 1990s.* New York: Carnegie Corporation of New York.

————. 1996. "Democracy in Latin America: Degrees, Illusions, and Directions for Consolidation." In *Beyond Sovereignty: Collectively Defending Democracy in the Americas,* edited by Tom Farer. Baltimore: Johns Hopkins University Press.

Donnelly, Jack. 2000. "U.S. Foreign Policy and Democracy: Concepts and Complexities." In *The U.S. and Human Rights,* edited by David P. Forsythe. Lincoln: University of Nebraska Press.

Dresser, Denise. 1996. "Treading Lightly and Without a Stick: International Actors and the Promotion of Democracy in Mexico." In *Beyond Sovereignty: Collectively Defending Democracy in the Americas,* edited by Tom Farer. Baltimore: Johns Hopkins University Press.

Farah, Douglas. 1994. "Haitians Await Better Times Aid." *The Washington Post,* 21 October 1994: 3, located on the Internet.

Farer, Tom, ed. 1996. *Beyond Sovereignty: Collectively Defending Democracy in the Americas.* Baltimore: Johns Hopkins University Press.

Forsythe, David P. 1988. *Human Rights and U.S. Foreign Policy: Congress Reconsidered.* Gainesville: University Presses of Florida.

————. 1995. "The UN and Human Rights at Fifty: An Incremental but Incomplete Revolution." *Global Governance* 1, 3 (August): 297–318.

————. 1996. "The United Nations, Democracy, and the Americas." In *Beyond Sovereignty: Collectively Defending Democracy in the Americas,* edited by Tom Farer. Baltimore: Johns Hopkins University Press.

————. 1997. "The United Nations, Human Rights, and Development." *Human Rights Quarterly* 19, 2 (May): 334–49.

————, ed. 2000. *The U.S. and Human Rights.*Lincoln: University of Nebraska Press.

Franck, Thomas M. 1992. "The Emerging Right to Democratic Governance." *American Journal of International Law* 86, 1 (January): 46–91.

Fukuyama, Francis. 1992. *The End of History and the Last Man.* New York: The Free Press.

————. 1995. "Social Capital and the Global Economy." *Foreign Affairs* 74, 5 (September/October): 89–104.

Gillies, David. 1993. "Human Rights, Governance, and Democracy: The World Bank's Problem Frontiers." *Netherlands Quarterly of Human Rights* 1: 3–24.

Grieve, Malcolm J. 1992–93. "International Assistance and Democracy: Assessing Efforts to Assist Post-Communist Development." *Studies in Comparative International Development*, 27, 4 (Winter): 80–101.

Guest, Ian. 1990. *Behind the Disappearances: Argentina's Dirty War Against Human Rights and the United Nations.* Philadelphia: University of Pennsylvania Press.

Hewlett, Sylvia Ann. 1979. "Human Rights and Economic Realities: Tradeoffs in Historical Perspective." *Political Science Quarterly* 94, 3 (Fall): 453–73.

Hirsch, Edward. 1995. "No Homeward Rush by Florida's Haitian Refugees." *Deutsche Presse-Agentur*, 14 April 1995, International News. Available in LEXIS, News Library, Allnws File.

Hirschmann, D. 1995. "Democracy, Gender and U.S. Foreign Assistance: Guidelines and Lessons." *World Development* 23, 8: 1291–1301.

Human Rights Watch. 1995. *Human Rights Watch World Report 1995.* New York: Human Rights Watch.

Huntington, Samuel. 1991. *The Third Wave: Democratization in the Late Twentieth Century.* Norman: Oklahoma University Press.

Johnson, James Turner. 1992. "Does Democracy Travel? Some Thoughts on Democracy and Its Cultural Context." *Ethics and International Affairs* 6: 41–56.

Karl, Terry Lynn, and Philippe C. Schmitter. 1994. "Democratization around the Globe: Opportunities and Risks." In *World Security: Challenges for a New Century*, edited by Michael T. Klare and Daniel C. Thomas. New York: St. Martin's Press.

Kirschten, Dick. 1995. "Haitian Roulette." *The National Journal* 9 (November): Foreign Policy: 3034. Available in LEXIS, News Library, Allnws File.

Kissinger, Henry. 1994. *Diplomacy,* New York: Norton.

Kritz, Mary M. 1995. "Population Growth and International Migration: Is There a Link?" International Center for Migration, Ethnicity and Citizenship, New School for Social Research, New York City.

Lowenthal, Abraham F. 1991. *Exporting Democracy: The United States and Latin America.* Baltimore: Johns Hopkins University Press.

Luttwak, Edward. 1994. "Where Are the Great Powers?" *Foreign Affairs* 73, 4 (July/August): 23–29.

Maingot, Anthony P. 1996. "Haiti: Sovereign Consent versus State-Centric Sovereignty." In *Beyond Sovereignty: Collectively Defending Democracy in the Americas*, edited by Tom Farer. Baltimore: Johns Hopkins University Press.

Marks, Stephen P. 1994. "The New Cambodian Constitution: From Civil War to a Fragile Democracy." *Columbia Human Rights Law Review* 45, 1 (Fall).

Morrison, David C. 1995. "Turkish War a Concern for America." *National Journal* 27, 15 (April): 928–30.

Muravchik, Joshua. 1996. "Affording Foreign Policy." *Foreign Affairs* 75, 2 (March/April): 8–13.

Neier, Arey. 1996. "The New Double Standard." *Foreign Policy* 105 (Winter): 91–102.

Nelson, Joan, and Stephanie J. Eglinton. 1996. "The International Donor Community: Conditioned Aid and the Promotion and Defense of Democracy." In *Beyond Sovereignty: Collectively Defending Democracy in the Americas*, edited by Tom Farer. Baltimore: Johns Hopkins University Press.

O'Neill, William G. N.d. "Building a New Police Force and Justice System." *Crime and Justice International Online* <http://www.acsp.uic.edu/OICJ/pubs/cja/090313.htm.>.

Organization for Economic Co-operation and Development. 1992. *Development and Democracy: Aid Policies in Latin America.*" Paris: OECD Publications Service.

Owens, Edgar. 1987. *The Future of Freedom in the Developing World: Economic Development as Political Reform.* New York: Pergamon Press.

Pastor, Robert A. 1993. "A Discordant Consensus on Democracy." *Diplomatic History* 17, 1 (Winter): 117–27.

Pierre, Andrew J., and William B. Quandt. 1995. "Algeria's War on Itself." *Foreign Policy* 99: 131–48.

Preval, Rene. 1996. *The Newshour with Jim Lehrer.* Transcript. 21 March 1996. Available in Lexis, News Library, Allnws File.

Public Law 102-511 draft. 1995. Freedom Support Act. Available on the Internet.

Putnam, Robert. 1993. *Making Democracy Work: Civic Traditions in Modern Italy.* Princeton: Princeton University Press.

Roberts, Brad, ed. 1990. *The New Democracies: Global Change and U.S. Policy.* Cambridge: MIT Press.

Rouleau, Eric. 1996. "Turkey: Beyond Ataturk." *Foreign Policy* 103 (Summer): 70–91.

Russett, Bruce. 1993. *Grasping the Democratic Peace: Principles for a Post–Cold War World.* Princeton: Princeton University Press.

Schmeidl, Susanne. 1995. "Political Turmoil and Forced Migration." *Working Paper Series.* New York: The International Center for Migration, New School.

Sikkink, Kathryn A. 1996. "Nongovernmental Organizations, Democracy, and Human Rights in Latin America." In *Beyond Sovereignty: Collectively Defending Democracy in the Americas,* edited by Tom Farer. Baltimore: Johns Hopkins University Press.

Singer, Max, and Aaron Wildavsky. 1996. *The Real World Order: Zones of Peace, Zones of Turmoil.* London: Chatham House. Rev. ed.

Smith, Tony. 1994. *America's Mission: The United States and the Worldwide Struggle for Democracy in the Twentieth Century.* Princeton: Princeton University Press.

Sorensen, Georg. 1993. *Democracy and Democratization.* Boulder, Colo.: Westview Press.

State Department Briefing. 1996. Nicholas Burns, 16 January. Available in Lexis, Executive Library, Allnws File.

Teitelbaum, Michael, and Myron Weiner, eds. 1995. *Threatened Peoples, Threatened Borders: World Migration and U.S. Policy.* New York: W. W. Norton, for the American Assembly.

United Nations. 1996. "The United Nations Mission in Haiti UNMIH." 1 July, located on the Internet.

United Nations High Commissioner for Refugees. 1994. *Background Paper on Turkish Asylum Seekers.* Geneva: Centre for Documentation on Refugees, September 1994, on the Internet at http://www.unicc.org/unhcr/country/cdr/cdturk.htm.

UN Secretary-General. 1994. *Agenda for Development.* UN General Assembly Document A/48/935.

USAID (U.S. Agency for International Development). 1994. "Building Democracy: USAID's Strategy." Located on the Internet via USAID (advandem).
———. 1995. "Congressional Presentation FY 96." Located on the Internet via USAID regional information.
U.S. Congress. 1995. *Turkey-U.S. Relations.* Commission on Security and Cooperation in Europe, 104th Cong., 1st sess. 26 September. Washington, D.C.: GPO.
U.S. Department of State. 1993. *Dispatch* 4/39 (27 September). Referring to a speech by National Security Advisor Anthony Lake summarizing a classified document.
———. 1995a. *Dispatch* 6/24 (12 June).
———. 1995b. *Dispatch* 6/17 (24 April).
———. 1995c. *Dispatch* 6/11 (13 March).
———. 1996. *Country Reports on Human Rights Practices for 1995.* Report Submitted to the Congress, Washington, D.C.: GPO.
U.S. General Accounting Office. 1994. *Promoting Democracy: Foreign Affairs and Defense Agencies Funds and Activities—1991 to 1993.* Washington, D.C.: GPO (GAO/NSIAD-94-83, 4 January).
U.S. House. 1992. *United States Assistance to Central and Eastern Europe.* Subcommittee on Europe and the Middle East, House Committee on Foreign Affairs, 102nd Cong., 2nd sess., 7 April 1991. Washington, D.C.: GPO.
———. 1995a. *Assessment of the Current Situation in Haiti.* Hearing, Subcommittee on the Western Hemisphere, House International Relations Committee, 104th Cong., 1st sess., 12 October. Washington, D.C.: GPO.
———. 1995b. *Democracy, Rule of Law and Police Training Assistance.* Hearing, House Committee on International Relations, 104th Cong., 1st sess., 7 December. Washington D.C.: GPO.
———. 1995c. *United States Policy and Activities in Haiti.* Hearing, House International Relations Committee, 104th Cong., 1st sess. 24 February. Washington, D.C.: GPO.
———. 1996a. Domestic Federal Law Enforcement Hearing, Subcommittee on the Departments of Commerce, Justice and State, the Judiciary and Related Agencies, House Appropriations Committee, 104th Cong., 2nd sess. 1 May. Washington, D.C.: GPO.
———. 1996b. *Foreign Operations, Export Financing, and Related Programs Appropriations for 1997.* Part 1, 3: Administrator—U.S. Agency for International Development. Subcommittee on Foreign Operations, Export Financing and Related Programs, House Appropriations Committee, 104th Cong., 2nd sess., 24 April. Washington, D.C.: GPO.
———. 1996c. *Haiti: Where Has All the Money Gone?* Hearing, Subcommittee on the Western Hemisphere, House International Relations Committee, 104th Cong., 2nd sess., 20 June. Washington, D.C.: GPO.
———. 1996d. *Oversight Hearing on FBI Murder Investigation in Haiti.* Subcommittee on Crime, House Judiciary Committee, 104th Cong., 2nd sess., 31 January. Washington, D.C.: GPO.
U.S. Senate. 1995. *Legislative and Municipal Elections in Haiti.* Hearing, Subcommittee on Western Hemisphere and Peace Corps Affairs, Senate Foreign Relations Committee, 104th Cong., 1st sess., 12 July. Washington, D.C.: GPO.
Weiner, Myron. 1995. *The Global Migration Crisis: Challenge to States and to Human Rights.* New York: Harper Collins.

Weiss, Thomas G., David P. Forsythe, and Roger A. Coate. 2000. *The United Nations and Changing World Politics*. 3rd ed. Boulder, Colo.: Westview Press.

Willon, Phil. 1996. "Haiti: A Political Quagmire." *The Tampa Tribune*, 24 May. Nation/world: 6. Available in LEXIS, News Library, Allnws File.

Yokota, Yozo, and Chiyuki Aoi. 2000. "Japan's Foreign Policy toward Human Rights." In *Human Rights and Comparative Foreign Policy*, edited by David P. Forsythe. Tokyo: United Nations University Press.

Zolberg, Aristide, Astri Suhrke, and Sergio Aguayo. 1989. *Escape from Violence: Conflict and the Refugee Crisis in the Developing World*. New York: Oxford University Press.

– Chapter 9 –

MIGRATION AND INTERNATIONAL ECONOMIC INSTITUTIONS

Leah Haus

Introduction

There has been a general trend toward liberalization of the global political economy in the postwar era. Governments have deregulated capital markets. Foreign exchange trading is estimated to be over one trillion dollars daily (Sassen 1996: 40). Trade in services has grown dramatically. Trade in goods is relatively open in comparison with the interwar years, although certain sectors such as textiles are subject to restrictions. This trend toward openness has been reinforced in the last decade with the shift toward liberal-oriented economic policies in some developing countries, particularly in Latin America, and in the former communist countries.

International labor migration constitutes an anomaly for this general trend toward openness (Bhagwati 1984; Zolberg 1991). There has been some transnationalization of the labor market, with or without the consent of governments. However, it lags behind liberalization in other issues. As noted by Jagdish Bhagwati, "immigration restrictions are virtually everywhere, making immigration the most compelling exception to liberalism in the operation of the world economy"(Bhagwati 1984: 680). Bhagwati argued that:

> There is virtually no international Code of Conduct in regard to the question of how immigration restrictions ought to be operated. These restrictions are entirely a matter of national sovereignty, with practically no international constraints systematically sought to be imposed on national action by countries of immigration other than their own conscience, by and large. (Bhagwati 1984: 697)

This chapter focuses on this specific aspect of the anomaly—the question of institutionalization of norms and rules to manage migration at the international, or regional level. It provides a historical review of the extent, or limits, to which governments have delegated authority or undertaken commitments to international and regional institutions on the issue of migration.

Three key institutions were established after World War II to manage the conduct of international economic relations: the International Monetary Fund (IMF), the World Bank, and the General Agreement on Tariffs and Trade (GATT, which has recently been renamed the World Trade Organization). These institutions included neoliberal norms, rules, and procedures and were designed to prevent a return to the discriminatory practices of the interwar years, and to promote an open international economy where economic relations are guided by the market mechanism, with provisions for government intervention to safeguard domestic stability (Ruggie 1983).

The forging of an open economy at that time, which was particularly advocated by the U.S. government, was not extended to migration. No international institution pertaining to migration was established. The subject of migration did reach the agenda of international discussions at that time, and later, although comparatively little in the way of substantive outcome was attained. With regard to regional institutions, the members of the European Union have delegated some authority on migration, although these commitments lag behind the commitments that they have undertaken on other political and economic issues; and the members of NAFTA have for the most part continued to adopt unilateral approaches toward migration.

In short, migration constitutes an anomaly for the overall pattern in the postwar international political economy. Migration is less institutionalized (and less liberalized) than other economic issues. How do we explain the pattern of institutionalization, or lack thereof, on migration issues, and what lessons can be learnt for proposing realistic policy prescriptions for the future?

At a general level this anomaly can in part be explained by the differences between migration and other economic issues. Migrants are sociopolitical actors as well as economic actors, and a person is not a commodity (Piore 1979; Zolberg 1983). A country's right to determine who enters its borders, and on what conditions, has been regarded as the essence of state sovereignty. The right to exclude is often described "as being a natural attribute of national 'sovereignty' … [There is a] notion that the central values and ethos that characterize one's society could be diluted by the entry of individuals and groups who do not share them" (Bhagwati 1984: 681). Thus one may expect governments to be more cautious about committing themselves to international institutional obligations and rules in this issue area than in other economic issue areas that do not so directly impinge on what is considered to be the essence of state sovereignty. Migrant-receiving countries would likely be particularly cautious—more so than governments of migrant-sending countries, as the latter would not face the entry of individuals and groups.

But it is not clear that the close link and central relationship between migration and state sovereignty is a fully sufficient explanation for the degree of institutionalization, or lack thereof, in the issue of international migration. There has been some modest variation in the policies of governments, including those of migrant-receiving countries, which have generally been those countries that had the power to determine the outcomes of discussions over whether to develop and institutionalize international norms and rules pertaining to migration. Thus one needs also to consider the different approaches of governments and the ways in which they have defined their interests.

Governments of some migrant-receiving countries have at times shown some support for granting institutions a modest role on migration issues, as shown in the historical record elaborated in this chapter. In the immediate postwar years the U.S. was not opposed to international cooperation on migration issues in the context of the International Labor Organization, albeit in a limited manner. The U.S. policy then changed to firm opposition as the issue became wrapped up in Cold War politics. Although the commitments were limited, liberal norms on migration were institutionalized in the context of the Organization of European Economic Cooperation (OEEC) in the earlier postwar years. West European approaches at that time separated migrants in their role as economic actors and migrants in their role as sociopolitical actors. They focused on labor procurement policies and overlooked or ignored the question of incorporating immigrants into society and the polity, thereby mitigating the usual concerns over the entry of individuals into the country. Finally, seeking to reap the benefits of a single market, members of the European Union have undertaken some real and substantive institutional commitments on migration issues in recent years, although even here the commitments lag behind those undertaken on other issues.

Solely focusing on the particularly close link and central relationship between migration and state sovereignty in comparison with other economic issues would lead us to expect the historical record to reveal a constant pattern of across-the-board absence of institutionalization in various international and regional forums. This study shows that, generally, this has been the pattern, and that governments have fundamentally resisted committing themselves to institutional obligations on international migration. However, the historical record also reveals some minor variation in government preferences and in outcomes, which suggests that changing circumstances and economic internationalization may lead governments to redefine their preferences toward granting international and regional institutions some role, albeit minor, on migration issues, so as to enhance policy effectiveness.

Causes of Migration

Before exploring how governments have broached the subject of migration in international institutions, it is appropriate to first consider the causes of migration and the role of unilateral government policies, subjects which are considered more extensively in the contribution to this volume by Martin and Taylor.

International migration is small in comparison with other cross-border flows such as capital, and migration remains an anomaly for the trend toward liberalization in the global economy. Although there has been some transnationalization of the labor market, and labor migration is substantial in some areas of the world such as the Middle East, for the most part migration remains small relative to the size of overall populations. The quantity of permanent immigration to the U.S. today is similar to that in the early twentieth century (see Table 9.1). The quantity of travel resulting from promotion of the tourist industry in a world of declining transportation costs is significant. Over 22 million people entered the U.S. as nonimmigrants in 1995, over 17 million of whom were visitors for pleasure. But for the most part this does not involve labor migration (see Table 9.2).

Unilateral government policies have much impact on migration flows. While many of the reasons for migration are rooted in the economy, they are set in motion by government policies through the liberalization of rules of entrance, providing a permissive environment for economic forces to play out. Under such conditions, people sometimes move in response to employer recruitment, in search of work, and in hopes of earning higher wages.

Governments not only play a key role in initiating migration flows when they choose to liberalize rules of entrance, but also retain an important role in suppressing migration flows through unilateral measures when they choose to enact restrictionist rules of entrance. As argued by Zolberg, to explain the anomaly of relatively limited migration flows in an otherwise fairly open international economy and to address the question of why migration flows are not greater than they are, one needs to go beyond overly economistic analyses and to consider politics and the role of the state (Zolberg 1981, 1983, 1991). Moreover, restrictionist rules of entrance not only suppress some potential migration flows, but also contribute to the vulnerable status of those who cross-borders without the consent of governments. In short, unilateral government actions in the field of migration are far from being inconsequential.

However, attempts to regulate migration through unilateral measures under conditions of high cross-border socioeconomic interdependence at times have deleterious consequences for a variety of reasons. As control systems, they lead to evasion and other, unintended consequences (Bhagwati 1984: 683). For example, once the migration process has been set in motion (often by government action through the liberalization of rules of entrance), it sometimes becomes self-sustaining as

Table 9.1: Immigration to the United States for Selected Years, 1900–1995

Year	# Immigrants	Year	#Immigrants
1900	448,572	1960	265,398
1901	487,918	1961	271,344
1902	648,743	1962	283,763
1903	857,046	1963	306,260
1904	812,870	1964	292,248
1905	1,026,499	1965	296,697
1906	1,100,735	1966	323,040
1907	1,285,349	1967	361,972
1908	782,870	1968	454,448
1909	751,786	1969	358,579
1910	1,041,570	1970	373,326
1911	878,587	1971	370,478
1912	838,172	1972	384,685
1913	1,197,892	1973	400,063
1914	1,218,480	1974	394,861
1915	326,700	1975	386,194
1916	298,826	1976	502,289
1917	295,403	1977	462,315
1918	110,618	1978	601,442
1919	141,132	1979	460,348
1920	430,001	1980	530,639
1921	805,228	1981	596,600
1922	309,556	1982	594,131
1923	522,919	1983	559,763
1924	706,896	1984	543,903
1925	294,314	1985	570,009
1926	304,448	1986	601,708
1927	335,175	1987	601,516
1928	307,255	1988	643,025
1929	279,678	1989	1,090,924
1930	241,700	1990	1,536,483
1931	97,139	1991	1,827,167
1932	35,576	1992	973,977
1933	23,068	1993	904,300
		1994	804,400
		1995	720,500

Note: Data for 1989–95 include people who obtained permanent resident status through the legalization program of the 1986 Immigration Reform and Control Act: approximately 478,814 in 1989; 880,372 in 1990; 1,123,162 in 1991; 163,342 in 1992; 24,278 in 1993, 6,022 in 1994; 4,267 in 1995.

Sources: *Statistical Yearbook of the Immigration and Naturalization Service, 1992* (Washington, D.C.: U.S. Government Printing Office, 1993); and *SOPEMI Trends in International Migration: Annual Report 1996* (Paris: OECD, 1997).

Table 9.2. Nonimmigrants Admitted to the U.S. for Selected Fiscal Years,
1985–1995

Year	All Categories	Visitors for Pleasure
1985	9,540,000	6,609,000
1990	17,574,000	13,418,000
1993	21,566,404	16,900,459
1994	22,118,706	17,154,834
1995	22,640,539	17,611,533

Sources: *Statistical Yearbook of the Immigration and Naturalization Service, 1993* (Washington, D.C.: U.S. Government Printing Office, 1994); and *SOPEMI Trends in International Migration: Annual Report 1996* (Paris: OECD, 1997).

cross-border social networks are forged between villages and towns of emigration and regions of immigration, for example between Santo Domingo and Washington Heights, New York City (Georges 1990; Grasmuck and Pessar 1991). These cross-border networks generate chain migration as people move to reunite with family and friends who contribute to transportation expenses and supply information about, and help with finding a place to live and work. These cross-border networks, which have been intensified in the modern era through improved communication technology and declining transportation costs, complicate the task of effectively managing migration flows. For example, an attempt to halt movement by reducing quotas for legal immigration may likely result in an increase in undocumented or illegal immigration and people living and working without social rights and protection.

Likewise, due to cross-issue linkages, government policies in other issue areas, such as capital mobility and trade, may at times have unintended consequences for labor mobility, further complicating the task of unilaterally managing migration. The linkages between capital mobility, trade, and migration are complex and may play out in different ways and have differing impacts in the short run and the long run. With regard to trade, foreign import competition may reduce local employment opportunities in certain sectors in the short run, and thus increase emigration (Martin and Taylor 1996). Government policies to liberalize trade in services promote labor migration due to the inherent cross-issue linkage between the movement of people across borders and the cross-border provision of services. In reverse, greater opportunities for developing countries to export goods may increase employment opportunities and thus reduce emigration. With regard to capital mobility, the industrial jobs relocated to developing countries with foreign direct investment may generate local employment opportunities and thus reduce emigration. But, in reverse, increased capital mobility to the south may downgrade the conditions and opportunities for employment in a developing country, pushing people to emigrate. As argued by Sassen, capital mobility and the associated restructuring of the global economy reinforces labor migration. The relocation of manufacturing jobs to developing countries through foreign direct investment may promote emigration by breaking down traditional work structures and raising expectations. Simultaneously, the growth of the service sector in developed countries increases the demand for immigrant workers by generating a supply of low-wage jobs such as private household cleaners (Sassen 1988).

In summary, although governments have much influence over migration flows, the management of migration through unilateral measures has become complicated in an era of increasing liberalization in other, related economic issues. The intensity of cross-border networks and cross-issue linkages varies in different regions of the world. Among countries that share substantial cross-border networks (such as the members of NAFTA, or the members of the European Union) the effectiveness of policymaking may be enhanced by supplementing unilateral measures with policy cooperation in the context of regional or international institutions.

Labor Migration and International Institutions

The following review considers to what extent governments have historically been willing to delegate authority and undertake commitments on migration in international and regional forums such as the International Labor Organization, the Organization for Economic Cooperation and Development, the European Union, and NAFTA. The review shows that governments have traditionally resisted granting international institutions a substantive role on migration issues. However, it simultaneously shows that there have been some minor variations and that at times even governments of migrant-receiving countries have considered it to be in their interests to give institutions a role—albeit a minor role in comparison with other economic issues. This suggests that as circumstances change with deepening international economic integration, although governments may resist delegating substantial authority to international institutions, they might nonetheless consider it in their interests to supplement unilateral measures by making somewhat more use of international or regional institutions.

International Labor Organization

INTRODUCTION No institution was created after World War II to set out norms and rules to guide international labor migration, and it is thus sometimes erroneously thought that migration was absent from discussions at that time. Migration was discussed in the context of various international forums. In particular, fairly ambitious plans were briefly considered for the International Labor Organization (ILO), but were then abandoned and there was little result in the way of substantive outcome.

How do we explain the lack of substantive results emerging from these discussions in the ILO in the immediate postwar period, at a time when institutions were being forged to guide other aspects of international economic relations? This outcome may in part be attributable to the particularly close connection and central relationship between migration and state sovereignty in comparison with other economic issues.

Moreover, as argued by Zolberg, the U.S., the most powerful country in the immediate postwar period, had little interest in institutionalizing norms and rules on migration in comparison with other economic issues. The U.S. considered it to be in its interest to forge liberal international institutions for other aspects of economic relations. An open international economy would ensure the U.S. with markets for its goods. The reverse situation applied to the issue of migration as the U.S. was a migrant-receiving country (Zolberg 1991: 309). As argued by Zolberg:

> No international regime arose in this sphere because the states which partici-
> pated in the formation of the postwar capitalist political economy shared a
> common outlook with respect to the procurement of foreign labour and were
> in a position to achieve their objectives by acting individually rather than
> having to co-operate with one another.... The more developed countries of
> the capitalist world shared a major objective: to procure a limited supply of
> cheap and disposable foreign labour.... Co-operation was unnecessary be-
> cause, individually and collectively, those states had in effect an unlimited
> supply of such labour at their disposal. In short, they faced a buyers' market
> for what they sought. It is the suppliers who faced an agonizing prisoner's
> dilemma. (Zolberg 1992: 317–18)

To provide a complete explanation, however, one needs to go further. The lack of need for cooperation among the more developed countries fails to explain a switch in U.S. policy. The U.S. position played a crucial role in determining the outcome. But in the earlier stages of the negotiations the U.S. was supportive of granting the ILO some role, albeit limited, on migration issues. The U.S. then changed its policy as the subject became enmeshed in Cold War politics, as explained below (Haas 1964: 172–73). It is thus possible that had Cold War politics not intervened, some institutionalization of international norms and rules on migration might have occurred under the auspices of the ILO at that time of international institution building shortly after World War II.

BACKGROUND The International Labor Organization (ILO) was established in 1919, in the context of the post–World War I settlement. At the conclusion of the war, the Allied governments sought to avoid the outbreak of social conflict in Western Europe and to prevent a spread of the revolutionary movements in Russia. Thus they conceded to trade union proposals for the creation of an international institution designed to draw up international labor conventions, and for labor representation on the organization (Cox 1974: 102; Ghebali 1989: 6–7; Haas 1964: 140–41).

The ILO aims to promote social justice by focusing on such issues as freedom of association, collective bargaining rights, working conditions and welfare programs. The institution, unlike other international economic organizations, has a tripartite structure, with participation by representatives of government, labor and business. The subject of migration has always been on the ILO's agenda, and one of the institution's constitutional goals is to protect "the interests of workers when employed in countries other than their own" (ILO 1995).

GOVERNMENT PREFERENCES During the course of World War II, the postwar planners in the U.S. and the U.K. focused their attention on plans for creating institutions to guide trade and monetary issues. They gave little attention migration issues—a subject of less importance to them. Postwar plans for migration were only briefly considered by governments in the context of an ILO meeting held in Philadelphia in May 1944. At this meeting an agenda was drawn up for the ILO's Permanent Migration Committee, which was to consist of representatives of governments interested in the issue, and was to convene after the war. It was agreed that the Permanent Migration Committee would provide a forum for the exchange of views on postwar migration prospects and on the forms of international cooperation that could facilitate an organized resumption of migration after the war.[1]

The United States was one of the 25 countries represented at the Permanent Migration Committee's first meeting after the end of the war, in 1946. The U.S. representative had been instructed to support the continuation of the Committee's work in the field of economic migration, including studies and recommendations on such issues as labor recruitment, resettlement, and treatment of employed foreign workers.[2]

The need for international cooperation on migration was stressed by many government representatives at this meeting in 1946. The Committee unanimously approved a resolution pointing to the desirability of coordinated international responsibility for migration problems. Issues that were to be coordinated included the collection of information on migration, the sending of study missions at the request of the governments concerned, and the giving of advice to emigration and immigration countries.[3]

A consensus on the appropriateness of the ILO as an institution to oversee the international coordination of migration issues developed over the next year. The ILO's Permanent Migration Committee was opposed to creating a new institution to coordinate migration issues, and considered that the ILO's role should be increased to include more practical action, such as the creation of an international employment information service. The Committee's spokesperson argued that the problems of migration, in conjunction with manpower problems, constituted "the most important matter confronting the International Labor Organization at present. It was therefore felt that priority should be given to migration problems in regard to any possible extension of staff and of the facilities needed to secure results."[4] The importance of the role of the ILO in dealing with migration issues also began to be shared by other international institutions.

This consensus on the need to increase the ILO's role in migration was noted in a statement by the British representative in 1948:

> The debate had shown that the Governing Body as a whole shared the [ILO] Director General's view as to the importance of the matter and as to the rightness of the principle which underlay his proposals, namely, that the time had come for the Organization to embark on operational activity and no longer to confine itself, as in the past, to research work and semi-legislative action.... The extension of this principle which was now proposed had been welcomed by the whole Governing Body and certainly by the Government of the United Kingdom.[5]

Although Britain was a potential country of immigration (and emigration) and thus one may expect it to be concerned to avoid international commitments on the particularly sensitive subject of migration, the British representative nonetheless pointed to the limits of national action:

> The problem was not a new one, but it was particularly acute at the present time. It could not be solved merely by national measures, and some kind of international action was required. It was significant that within recent months other international organizations had gradually become convinced that the International Labour Organization had primary responsibility in this field.[6]

The justification given for this position reflected what was to soon become the dominant approach among West European governments—a tendency to view migrants solely in their role as economic actors, or manpower, and to overlook or ignore the prospective incorporation of foreigners into the society and polity. Reflecting this tendency, the British representative noted that "[t]he essential problem which the proposals were designed to solve was that of securing the best use of manpower with a view to increasing the happiness and prosperity of all people everywhere."[7]

During the course of the next year the ILO's activities in the field of migration included studies, exchanges of information, training schemes, collection and exchanges of information on labor shortages and surpluses, and technical assistance to governments on training facilities and employment services.

The suitability of the ILO as an institution for dealing with migration issues was reiterated at an international conference, known as the Preliminary Conference on Migration, held in Geneva in April 1950. The general resolution that emerged from the conference was that the ILO should intensify its activities on migration and draw up, after consultations with governments, proposals for cooperation at the international level to deal with migration.[8]

The U.S. delegation was at that stage in general agreement with the conference recommendations and regarded the conference as a success.[9] The U.S. delegation had been instructed to seek an extension of ILO field-work in Europe and overseas to facilitate migration in accordance with the approach that the U.S. had taken at ILO meetings in the previous two or three years. The U.S. favored supporting European governments, which were concerned with the need for migration and which were seeking to overcome what the U.S. considered to be "one of the most dangerous obstacles to economic recovery and social progress."[10]

The ILO, under the leadership of Director-General David Morse, accordingly developed an ambitious proposal to create a Migration Administration within the ILO. The proposal envisioned that the Migration Administration would be designed to facilitate orderly migration, and would oversee and fund such activities as developing immigration plans, recruitment, vocational training, loans for transportation of migrants, placement facilities, and loans to assist migrant settlement.[11]

The general consensus on the need to grant the ILO a role, albeit a comparatively modest role, then fairly suddenly collapsed. The ILO's proposal to create a Migration Administration, when it was discussed at the Naples Conference in October 1951, was promptly axed due to a switch in the U.S. position. To understand why the original postwar plans of the late 1940s failed to materialize, one needs to turn to the subject of Cold War politics. The U.S. delegation had been instructed to take a very guarded position at the Naples Conference in October 1951. They "were to oppose any scheme involving the instrumentality of the ILO."[12] The U.S. administration had its hands tied by Congress, where there was clear opposition to any ILO responsibility on migration issues, and where the ILO's proposal was regarded as "unsellable" by Congressman Walter, Chair of the Subcommittee on Immigration.[13]

In a meeting held in September 1951, a few weeks before the Naples Conference, between the chief of staff of the immigration subcommittee of the House and officials from the Departments of State and Labor, it was made clear that Congress would oppose the ILO's proposal. At the meeting, executive branch officials urged support for some kind of a migration administration within the ILO, albeit different from the specifics of the ILO's proposal. They also noted that no communist governments had been invited to the forthcoming Naples Conference. However, the immigration subcommittee's chief of staff pointed to very major obstacles and emphasized that to his knowledge many interested members of Congress would oppose any plan for organizing migration under the auspices of the ILO, which was an institution whose membership included communist countries.[14]

The issue was further complicated by the fact that at that same time Congress was concluding consideration of Congressman Walter's "uphill fight" to gain authorization in the Mutual Security Act for funds for interim arrangements to facilitate migration by taking over the shipping facilities of the International Refugee Organization—an institution which was being terminated. The chief of staff considered that this other effort to obtain funds for interim arrangements to facilitate migration would be seriously prejudiced if a proposal regarding the ILO was introduced. Shortly before the Naples Conference, Congress's Conference Committee on the Mutual Security Act did allocate funds for the alternative interim arrangements to facilitate migration, and made clear its intent that none of the funds should be allocated to any international organization which had in its membership any communist governments.[15]

In short, as noted by Ernst Haas: "The enthusiasm of Australia, Britain, and the United States for a true international program remained intact from the earlier period; but they were unwilling to have it delegated to an organization in which the enemy might participate" (Haas 1964: 173).

The switch in the U.S. position, when Cold War politics took over, is not particularly surprising from the point of view of U.S. interests on the specific issue of migration. The U.S. was a country with comparatively little interest in institutionalizing an international program to facilitate migration, and thus the U.S. had relatively little to lose by abandoning its previous support for delegating some limited role to the ILO.

The U.S. position was not shared by all governments. In particular Italy, as a potential migrant-sending country and with substantial interests in liberalizing migration at the international level, continued to favor granting some role to the ILO on migration issues at the Naples Conference in 1951. Thus Italy, with some other countries, supported a compromise proposal. But, in the words of the Chairman of the U.S. delegation, the "moderate compromise proposal, which provides a means for broader international collaboration, [was] rendered sterile by reservations on the part of the U.S., [which] represented a distinct failure on our part to recognize important political realities."[16]

ILO ACTIVITIES Despite being denied a substantive role, the ILO has since undertaken various activities pertaining to migration, including drawing up conventions, data collection and dissemination, the convening of meetings, and technical assistance, for example, for the formation of policies and institutional structure of what became the Federal Migration Service of Russia.

Several conventions that seek to protect migrant workers have been adopted by the ILO, such as the Migration for Employment Convention, the Equality of Treatment Convention, and the Maintenance of Social Security Rights Convention. The first multilateral attempt to tackle the issue of illegal migration was undertaken under the auspices of the ILO, resulting in the Migrant Workers' Convention of 1975. The Convention specifies measures that are to be taken to provide basic protection to irregular migrant workers, measures to detect and halt illegal migration and employment, and measures to halt the organizers of illegal migration. The measures include the exchange of information between countries, consultation of employers' and workers' organizations for information, and the definition and application of sanctions with regard to illegal employment of migrant workers and the organization of such migrations (ILO 1980, 1996b).

However, ratification of ILO conventions on migration by the member states has been slow and particularly limited among migrant-receiving countries, pointing to a general reluctance of governments to undertake commitments on the issue of migration. Some migrant-receiving countries, such as France, Germany, Norway and Sweden have ratified some of these conventions, but the United States has not ratified any of them.[17]

Data collection and dissemination has in recent years been an important focus of the ILO. To increase the provision of information, the institution has gathered and disseminated data on migration flows, cross-issue linkages between flows of goods, services, capital, and labor, and national legislation and practices. Recent ILO studies include a comparative analysis of the means to combat labor market discrimination against immigrants and ethnic minorities in 11 industrialized countries, such as Germany and the U.S.; and a study of regulations, or lack thereof, for social security protection of migrant workers in 22 countries (ILO 1996a, n.d.).

The ILO disseminates the results of its studies through seminars, working reports, information bulletins, and newsletters, with the aim of increasing awareness and providing a means for policy learning by giving officials in different countries an opportunity to learn about the experiences of other countries (ILO 1996a).

United Nations

The ILO has traditionally been regarded as the international institution with the competence to draw up standards and conventions pertaining to migration. However this role was taken up by the UN General Assembly in the late 1970s as a result of initiatives from developing countries who considered that their interests would be better served in this forum than in the ILO. This shift to the UN as a forum for institutionalizing standards on migration occurred contrary to the preferences of the advanced industrialized developed countries, who favored retaining the ILO as the appropriate forum for this purpose (Bohning 1991: 700; Lonnroth 1991: 726).

Lengthy negotiations (which were marked by clear conflicts between sending and receiving countries) under the auspices of the UN culminated in the International Convention on the Protection of the Rights of All Migrant Workers and Members of Their Families, which was adopted by the UN General Assembly in December 1990.

The final results of these negotiations in the UN forum, however, point to the need to base policy prescriptions on a realistic recognition that countries are unwilling to undertake international commitments on migration issues, particularly in the context of universal institutions such as the UN. During the course of the negotiations, provisions that reflected the original intent to protect the rights of individuals evolved into provisions that upheld the interests of states (Lonnroth 1991: 722). Despite this evolution, no advanced industrialized receiving countries have ratified the Convention. Only thirteen countries had ratified the Convention by December 1997, and it has thus not come into force.[18]

Organization for Economic Cooperation and Development

Although no international institution was set up after World War II to liberalize migration along the lines of the institutions established to cover trade and monetary issues, the gap was less noticeable in the European context. European governments favored liberalizing migration. Institutionalization of norms pertaining to migration, and other economic issues, emerged under the auspices of the Organization for European Economic Cooperation (OEEC). Migration did not stand out as such an extreme anomaly in comparison with other economic issues in the context of this institution. European governments were willing to institutionalize liberal norms in this instance to open the labor market at the regional level. This outcome may be attributable to their tendency at that time to equate migrants with manpower. They assumed migrants would follow the market and exit when no longer needed. They overlooked or ignored the question of incorporating immigrants into the society and polity. Moreover, the degree of commitments taken on were minor, and the liberal norms that were agreed to proved flexible to adaptation when the governments changed their national policies toward restrictionism with the onset of the recession in the 1970s.

The Organization for European Economic Cooperation (OEEC) was an institution that was created in 1948 to administer Marshall Plan Aid and to guide postwar reconstruction in Europe. It was replaced by the Organization for Economic Cooperation and Development (OECD) in 1961. The OECD's goal is to promote economic growth and employment through the efficient allocation of resources. The institution, which has a limited membership of twenty-nine (primarily developed) countries, conducts studies on a range of economic issues and serves as a forum for economic policy coordination in an interdependent economic world, where the outcomes of one government's economic policies depend not only on its actions but also on the reactions of other governments (Cooper 1968).

In the years shortly after World War II, the OEEC gave significant attention to the subject of migration. At that time its goal was to find ways to make effective use of available personpower through cooperation in the reduction of obstacles to the free movement of labor, and it set up a Manpower Committee to deal with this question in July 1948. Over the course of the next few months the Committee concluded that the OEEC alone could not effectively deal with the problem of surplus labor in such countries as Italy, and displaced persons, because of difficulties in absorbing them into OEEC member states, and that "unless some further outlet is found these persons will have to be maintained in idleness, and will constitute a drag on the economy of Europe and a threat to social stability, while, on the other hand, they could contribute elsewhere to raising the economic levels of other countries."[19] Thus the OEEC expanded its horizons on the migration front in the late 1940s to countries in Latin America, working in conjunction with the more universal institution of the ILO. The OEEC supported giving the ILO a greater role in migration issues, granting it some funds for this purpose until, as noted above, the ILO's potential became a victim of Cold War politics in late 1951.[20]

During the 1950s and 1960s, the OEEC and its successor, the OECD, continued to view migrants as factors of production and to view cross-border population flows as a means to enhance an efficient allocation of resources, economic growth, and full employment. As noted in a later review by the OECD, since the OEEC was "elaborating 'codes' of liberalization of trade and payments, it was natural to try and do the same for manpower movements" (OECD 1975: 8). A report that was approved at the ministerial level at an OEEC Council meeting in 1952 devoted considerable attention to "manpower" issues under the general subject of "available resources." The report argued that labor immobility was the basic obstacle to offsetting shortages and surpluses in different regions and sectors, and recommended "that the international objective for the five-year period should be to establish among Member countries that all that is possible should be achieved toward the elimination of restrictive rules, formalities and other obstacles to the free movement of workers across national boundaries, even though it is clearly impracticable to dispense with these entirely during the period" (OEEC 1952: 11–12).

The OEEC subsequently adopted more specific recommendations to facilitate implementation of its model, and engaged in various activities such as drawing up an international classification of occupations to assist matching cross-border labor demand and supply, and the adoption of detailed standards of employment service organization (*International Labor Review* 1959). "Labor deficit" West European governments played an active role in the liberalization of migration flows, as countries such as Germany, France, and Switzerland instituted "guest-worker" programs permitting large scale migration (anticipated as temporary) from "labor surplus" countries such as Italy, Portugal, and Turkey.

The OECD's liberal norms in the sphere of labor migration, however, only continued as long as this fit with the national approaches of its members. When recession set in during the early 1970s, West European governments changed their national policy preferences toward restrictionism, and the OECD's focus accordingly shifted. The OECD began to focus on what it termed the "migratory chain"—emigration, residence abroad, and return. Concerned with questions of return and re-integration of migrants in their "home" country of origin, the OECD drew up a program of activities to facilitate return, such as providing information on employment possibilities in countries of origin, and it initiated a series of studies on experiences of return migration from, for example, Germany to Turkey and France to Algeria (OECD 1975: 29, 1978).

In recent years the OECD has been active in the field of migration through the provision of information and the convening of occasional conferences, facilitating policy learning. In particular, the OECD has for several decades coordinated an annual report on trends in migration and migration policy (known as the SOPEMI report), which is an influential publication among policy analysts, generating some transgovernmental convergence in policy knowledge. The reports include detailed statistical data on trends in migration flows, and summaries of changes in national migration policies during the previous year. The reports focus on particular issues to facilitate policy learning. For example, the 1989 report included a comparative analysis of the experiences of the regularization (amnesty) programs in France, the U.S., Italy, and Spain, providing policymakers and analysts with an opportunity to learn from the experiences of other countries.

The International Organization for Migration

The International Organization for Migration (IOM) is an institution that emerged in 1989 from what was originally known as the Intergovernmental Committee for European Migration (ICEM), which was created in December 1951, with support and funds from the U.S. among others, shortly after the ILO's plans to develop a Migration Administration became a victim of Cold War politics. The ICEM, which excluded communist countries, was originally only intended to be a provisional or interim arrangement designed to facilitate movement of refugees and what were referred to as "surplus populations" from Europe (e.g., Italy and Greece) to such countries as Brazil, Chile, Venezuela, and Australia.[21] Since that time the institution has expanded its regional coverage and now addresses all regions of the world.

Much of the IOM's activities has traditionally focused on refugee issues. But it has also addressed labor migration, often working in cooperation with other international institutions. For example, it has provided language courses for migrant workers, it has collected and disseminated information, and has convened various conferences. It has also provided technical aid to governments, such as technical assistance given to the Soviet Union's successor states in the formulation of immigration legislation.

The World Trade Organization

Cross-issue linkages between migration and other economic activities that have been increasingly liberalized have led to some increase in the inclusion of migration onto the agenda of international institutions in recent years. This is particularly evident in the European Union, but there are also some signs of a similar process at work, albeit in an extremely limited manner, in the context of the World Trade Organization (WTO), which is the successor institution to the GATT.

With the expansion of the service sector in advanced industrialized countries in recent decades, these countries, particularly the United States, have sought to liberalize trade in this sector. The issue was a major component of the multilateral trade negotiations, known as the Uruguay Round, which were concluded in 1993, and resulted in the broadening of the institution's norms and rules to cover new issues, such as trade in services. This brought aspects of labor migration onto the agenda of the WTO for the first time due to the inherent cross-issue linkage between the movement of people across borders and the cross-border provision of services. One of the four "modes of supply" of services covered by the final agreement is the provision of services requiring the temporary movement of people—service suppliers or persons employed by a service supplier who is a national of a country that is a party to the agreement (Hoekman 1994: 87).

The European Union

The European Union (EU) is the one institution where governments have been willing to pool sovereignty and undertake substantive commitments on migration issues, specifically with regard to citizens of the EU member states. However, even within the EU, member governments have consistently resisted allowing migration policy toward non-EU countries to reach the agenda.

The subject of migration within the European Union has been on the agenda since its founding in 1957. In this earlier period, discussion was limited to the subject of migration for workers of the member states. Migration policy toward people from non-EU countries was not discussed at that time, but was instead considered as an issue falling within the jurisdiction of national competence and outside the competence of the EEC (Callovi 1992: 355).

The Treaty of Rome, which established the European Economic Community in 1957, specified in Article 48 that there was to be free movement of workers among the member states of the European Economic Community. Subsequent regulations gave more detailed guidelines for implementation of Article 48, clarifying, for example, how the term "worker" was to be defined.[22]

Discussions on migration have reemerged since the rejuvenation of the Community in the mid-1980s. The cover of passports was changed to state both "European Community" and the name of the member state. Other policy developments have proceeded along different routes, generating a complex situation that reflects a firm will of the member states to not abandon traditional notions of the function of state sovereignty and to not pool sovereignty or cede much authority to the Community on immigration policy, while simultaneously acknowledging the need to address the countervailing forces arising from the cross-issue linkages involved in implementing a single European market.

The different pieces of what has been labeled as the "jig-saw puzzle" of EU migration policy are not all yet in place, and what will emerge in the future remains unclear (Callovi 1992; Convey and Kupiszewski 1995). The more advanced route centers on the Schengen Agreement, which was signed in 1985 and came into force in 1995. It includes many, but not all members of the EU. The Agreement involved the abolition of all border checks and controls between its members, which necessitated coordinating and harmonizing policies on linked issues such as police cooperation, drugs, controls and checks at territorial borders with nonmembers, and visa and immigration policies toward nonmembers.[23]

The second route began with the Single European Act, which was signed in 1987 and aimed to create an internal market by December 1992. Freedom of mobility, which had previously been limited to workers, was now extended to persons. Article 8a stated that "The internal market shall comprise an area without frontiers in which the free movement of goods, persons, services and capital is ensured." Implementation of measures to ensure the free movement of people has been slow, with the exception of issues pertaining to those working in professional occupations, such as engineers and accountants.[24]

The Maastricht Treaty, signed in 1992, constitutes the third avenue through which migration policy is emerging in the EU. The Treaty moves beyond freedom of mobility for persons and addresses the subject of citizenship. The Treaty states that every person holding the citizenship of a member state shall be a citizen of the Union (the question of who was a citizen of a member state was left to the member state to decide). The Maastricht Treaty envisioned that EU citizenship includes rights such as the right to move and reside within the Union, and the right to vote and stand for election in local and European Parliamentary elections in the citizen's place of residence. However, it did not broach the subject of the right to vote in national elections in the citizen's place of residence, leaving EU citizens who work or reside in a member state other than their country of origin disenfranchised. Thus, while the Community has extended social rights to EU nationals who migrate to, and reside in a member state other than their country of origin, the issue of political rights remains as yet unresolved (Koslowski 1994).

These developments in EU rules on migration and citizenship for people who are nationals of the member states are substantive and real, and represent the main exception to the general pattern of government resistance to undertaking meaningful commitments in international institutions on the issue of migration. This general pattern of resistance to ceding authority on migration issues has however also displayed itself in the EU. EU member governments have resisted pooling sovereignty or transferring authority to the EU on migration policy toward people who are not nationals of EU member states. The Maastricht Treaty only included very small changes that would bring immigration policy to non-EU countries under the competence of Community law. The legal competence to determine those non-EU countries whose nationals would require visas to enter the EU was transferred from the member governments to the Community, opening the path to the establishment of a common visa policy. However, on other issues power was left with national governments. The Treaty did include provisions on other issues (for example, conditions of entrance, and measures pertaining to undocumented immigration). But these issues were to be dealt with through the process of intergovernmental cooperation and outside the framework of Community institutions.[26]

NAFTA

The North American Free Trade Agreement (NAFTA), which came into effect in January 1994, is geared toward liberalization of capital mobility and trade. Policy cooperation on migration issues under the auspices of NAFTA lags very far behind that in the European Union. Almost no regulations pertaining to migration were incorporated into the agreement. Provisions on migration were limited to those that permit the temporary entrance of business people, intracompany transferees, and some categories of professionals (i.e., highly skilled workers).

Due to potential cross-issue linkages between migration and other economic activities that were liberalized by NAFTA, the subject of migration did figure prominently in the debates over NAFTA before it was finalized. Arguments were presented on both sides. Some argued that NAFTA would generate migration, particularly in the short-medium term, due to provisions to ease the mobility of capital south, which, through cross-issue linkages, might intensify the mobility of labor north; and due to provisions that would open the Mexican market to import competition from U.S. producers, which might reduce opportunities for employment in certain sectors of the Mexican economy, such as corn and wheat. Others argued that NAFTA would reduce Mexican emigration by generating employment opportunities in Mexico as a result of the increased opportunities for Mexican exports of goods and agricultural produce, and particularly in the longer term, by promoting conditions conducive to overall development of the Mexican economy (Smith 1997).

While regulations to manage migration were largely excluded from the agreement, NAFTA has provided a forum for facilitating communications between U.S. and Mexican officials and for fostering regular and frank discussions on migration, among other issues (Weintraub 1997).

Conclusion and Policy Implications

Migration presents an anomaly for the trend toward liberalization of international economic relations in the postwar era. No international institution exists that includes meaningful norms and rules pertaining to migration, and it is thus sometimes erroneously thought that no international discussions were held on the subject. Labor migration has not been absent from discussions in the context of international and regional institutions in the postwar period. However, for all the discussions, for the most part little in the way of substantive outcome has emerged.

This relative absence of institutionalization reflects a strong unwillingness by governments to delegate authority and undertake international commitments on an issue that is often considered to be the essence of state sovereignty. This has been particularly evident with regard to migrant-receiving countries, which would face the entrance of individuals and groups. And it is these countries that have also been the more advanced industrialized countries with the capabilities to determine the outcomes of international discussions.

But a complete account of the degree of institutionalization, or lack thereof, also requires addressing those limited instances where the migrant-receiving advanced industrialized countries have shown a preference to grant international institutions some role on the issue of migration. The U.S. was willing to grant the ILO a limited role in the late 1940s until the issue became wrapped up in Cold War politics. The U.S. position in the late 1940s came in the context of a period of international institution building, and in a period when it was considered that migration in Europe would facilitate postwar reconstruction. Liberal norms were subsequently institutionalized at the European level in the context of the OEEC. These norms fit with national preferences and approaches, which tended to equate migrants with manpower and to overlook or ignore migrants in their role as sociopolitical actors and the question of integrating migrants into society and the polity. This limited institutionalization of liberal norms did not involve any transfer of authority, and the norms became irrelevant when they no longer fitted with the national preferences of the member governments in the 1970s. The European Union is a major exception to the general pattern, and here governments have been willing to share authority on questions pertaining to migration for nationals of the member states in their desires to reap the economic benefits of an integrated single market. But even here the member governments have resisted transferring competence to the Community on migration policy toward non-EU countries.

In summary, on the whole governments have clearly resisted undertaking substantive commitments on migration at the level of international institutions, pointing to limitations that need to be considered when developing realistic policy prescriptions. But there are minor exceptions to this rule, which show that governments at times perceive it to be in their interests to make some use of international institutions on the issue of migration.

Is there a scenario under which the U.S. might be disposed to make greater use of international and regional institutions to manage migration in the future? In what ways could the U.S. make greater use of such institutions in the future?

Cross-issue linkages between migration and other economic issues that have been increasingly liberalized may lead the U.S. to consider migration issues in international economic institutions in the future. This happened recently in a limited way when the U.S. sought to broaden the coverage of the WTO's neoliberal norms and rules to include trade in services. The inherent cross-issue linkage between the movement of people across borders and the cross-border provision of services pushed the subject of the temporary movement of people onto the WTO's agenda.

Another avenue through which the U.S. could make greater use of international institutions would be through the adoption and implementation of a social clause at the international level, for example under the auspices of the WTO. Although the subject of a social clause laying out provisions on working conditions is usually discussed in the context of other economic issues such as trade, it is simultaneously relevant to migration issues. Norms and regulations that improve work conditions in developing countries, by reducing emigration pressures (supply), would supplement and complement alternative proposals to reduce immigration pressures (demand) through greater enforcement of labor legislation in developed countries. Recent proposals to incorporate a social clause into the WTO, drawing on key ILO conventions, have received support from the U.S. government and organized labor in the United States. A social clause has also received support from other developed countries, including France.[26] The subject has generated some discussion, but has not to date advanced far onto the agenda due to opposition from some developed countries and due to opposition from developing countries—countries that may consider that a social clause would provide a means of trade protectionism for advanced industrialized countries. However, a social clause is unlikely to be adopted in the near future and, if it is, the possibilities for implementation remain thin. NAFTA's side agreement on labor lacks substance.

A related route may be for the U.S. to grant the ILO more of a role on migration issues in the post–Cold War world. The U.S. favored granting the ILO a modest role in the late 1940s, until the issue became wrapped up in Cold War politics. When developing countries sought to transfer the task of setting standards on migration from the ILO to the UN General Assembly in the late 1970s, developed countries were opposed and considered that this task should remain with the ILO. In the context of trade and the WTO, the U.S. has shown some support for a social clause, apparently with the goal of protecting human rights and improving work conditions. U.S. ratification of ILO conventions on migration would advance this goal. Some other advanced industrialized migrant-receiving countries, such as Germany, France, Sweden and Norway, have ratified some of these conventions, presenting a puzzle as to why the U.S. has not done so.

An alternative way in which international institutions could be used more extensively to enhance policy effectiveness would be to make more use of these institutions as forums to provide information, to facilitate policy learning by providing officials with an opportunity to learn about the experiences of other countries, and to provide meeting places for discussions on a frequent and routine basis.[27] Some such activities are already underway in institutions such as the ILO and the OECD.

With regard to the United States, it shares strong cross-border socioeconomic linkages with Mexico and Canada. However, in contrast with the EU, the development of institutions has lagged behind the deepening socioeconomic integration between the NAFTA countries. Despite increasing cross-border socioeconomic linkages, the U.S. has generally adopted a unilateral approach to migration issues. Policy effectiveness may be enhanced by further developing institutional mechanisms that, for example, increase the provision of information by formalizing the cross-border collection and dissemination of data on issues pertaining to migration, such as in-depth studies that explore to what extent and in what ways cross-issue linkages and cross-border networks impact on migration. There has been some minor change in this direction in recent years. Since the mid-1990s there has been more dialogue between U.S. and Mexican officials on the subject of migration in the context of the Working Group on Migration and Consular Affairs of the Mexico-U.S. Binational Commission. In addition to increasing dialogue, the Commission has begun to address the need for cross-border collaborative studies, as shown by the decision to undertake the Mexico-U.S. Binational Study on Migration, a study that was conducted between 1995 and 1997. More regular, cooperative transborder studies would provide a more reliable database for policy formation; and more regular dialogue might generate more prudent policies. Even in light of the unwillingness of governments to delegate authority and undertake substantive commitments on migration in the context of international or regional institutions, this is a realistic scenario for making more use of such institutions in the near future.

Notes

1. ILO, *Minutes of the 92nd Session of the Governing Body*, April–May 1944: 27.
2. Instructions to the U.S. Government Representative to the First Session of the Permanent Migration Committee of the ILO. In National Archives, Decimal File 1945–49, 500.C115, Box 1967.
3. ILO, *Minutes of the 99th Session of the Governing Body*, September 1946: 80, 83–84.
4. Ibid., *Minutes of the 104th Session of the Governing Body*, March 1948: 61.
5. Ibid., *Minutes of the 107th Session of the Governing Body*, December 1948: 30.

6. Ibid., p. 31.
7. Ibid.
8. Telegram to Secretary of State, 24 May 1950; and enclosures to Assistant Secretary of State, 9 May 1950. In National Archives Decimal File 1950-54, 398.06ILO, Box 1500.
9. Telegram to Secretary of State, 9 May 1950. In National Archives, Decimal File 1950-54, 398.06ILO, Box 1500. Report of the U.S. Delegate to the ILO Preliminary Conference on Migration. In National Archives, Decimal File 1950-54, 398.06, Box 1501.
10. Instructions to the U.S. Delegate to the Preliminary Conference on Migration of the ILO, Geneva, April 1950. In National Archives Decimal File 1950-54, 398.06ILO, Box 1500.
11. *International Labor Review* (1952): 173–75.
12. Report to the Secretary of State on the Second Conference on Migration called by the ILO, Naples, Italy, 29 November 1951. In National Archives, Decimal File 1950-54, 398.06ILO, Box 1504.
13. Memorandum of Conversation, 19 September 1951. In National Archives, Decimal File 1950-54, 398.06ILO, Box 1504.
14. Ibid.
15. Memorandum of Conversation, 19 September 1951. Note from U.S. Department of State to American consul in Naples, 3 October 1951. In National Archives, Decimal File 1950-54, 398.06ILO, Box 1504.
16. Report to the Secretary of State on the Second Conference on Migration called by the ILO, Naples, Italy, 29 November 1951. In National Archives, Decimal File 1950-54, 398.06ILO, Box 1504.
17. ILO, "Social Security for Migrant Workers," n.d.; and ILO *Migration*, November 1992.
18. United Nations (1998), "International Instruments: Chart of Ratifications as at 31 December 1997."
19. "The Activities of the OEEC since its inception in regard to the surplus manpower problem." Paper submitted 6 June 1951 to Committee of Experts on the Question of Refugees and Over-Population, of the Council of Europe. In National Archives Decimal file 1950-54, 740.00, Box 3391.
20. Ibid.
21. Memorandum, 14 November 1951. Instructions for U.S. Delegate to Conference to Facilitate Movement of European Migrants, 21 November 1951; and Note, 13 January 1953. In National Archives Decimal File 1950-54, 398.18ICEM, Box 1538.
22. A ruling by the European Court of Justice characterized a worker as someone with a relationship of employment or offer of employment, and specified that the employment was to be real and effective. The question of the right to migrate in search of work was left more ambiguous. It was clarified that the right to migrate extended to the worker's spouse and children under the age of twenty-one (Davidson 1989: 120–21).
23. The Schengen Accords are not part of EU law. The Accords state that Schengen provisions apply only insofar as they are compatible with Community legislation (Schutte 1991).
24. The General Systems Directive, enacted in 1988, aimed to eliminate barriers to cross-border movement in professional occupations. The Directive "stipulates that all higher education diplomas of three or more years' duration

leading to a professional qualification are recognized as valid for practice of that activity in other Member States" (Orzack 1991: 137).

25. The Commission was given some limited powers of initiative on some of these issues, but no power to oversee implementation, nor to formulate recommendations (Niessen 1992).

26. *Financial Times*, 22 and 24 July 1996.

27. For a theoretical account of why institutions may facilitate cooperation through the provision of information under those conditions where common interests between countries exist, see Keohane 1984.

References

Bhagwati, J. 1984. "Incentives and Disincentives: International Migration." *Weltwirtschaffliches Archiv* 120, 4.

Bohning, R. 1991. "The ILO and the New UN Convention On Migrant Workers." *International Migration Review* (Winter).

Callovi, G. 1992. "Regulation of Immigration in 1993: Pieces of the European Community Jig-Saw Puzzle." *International Migration Review* 26 (Summer).

Convey, A., and M. Kupiszewski. 1995. "Keeping Up with Schengen: Migration and Policy in the European Union." *International Migration Review* 29 (Winter).

Cooper, R. 1968. *The Economics of Interdependence*. New York: McGraw-Hill.

Cox, R. 1974. "ILO: Limited Monarchy." In *The Anatomy of Influence: Decision Making in International Organizations*, edited by R. W. Cox and H. K. Jacobson. New Haven: Yale University Press.

Davidson, S. 1989. "Free Movement of Goods, Workers, Services and Capital." In *The European Community and the Challenge of the Future*, edited by J. Lodge. New York: St. Martins Press.

Georges, E. 1990. *The Making of a Transnational Community: Migration, Development, and Cultural Change in the Dominican Republic*. New York: Columbia University Press.

Ghebali, V. 1989. *The International Labor Organization*. Boston: Martinus Nijhoff Publishers.

Grasmuck, S., and P. R. Pessar. 1991. *Between Two Islands: Dominican International Migration*. Berkeley: University of California Press.

Haas, E. B. 1964. *Beyond the Nation-State: Functionalism and International Organization*. Stanford: Stanford University Press.

Hoekman, B. 1994. "Services and Intellectual Property Rights." In *The New GATT: Implications for the United States*, edited by S. M. Collins and B. P. Bosworth. Washington D.C.: Brookings Occasional Papers.

ILO (International Labor Organization). 1980. "Migrant Workers: General Survey by the Committee of Experts on the Application of Conventions and Recommendations." Geneva: ILO.

———. 1995. "ILO Activities Concerned with International Labor Migration and Migrant Workers." Geneva: ILO (April).

———. 1996a. "Combatting Discrimination Against (Im)Migrant Workers and Ethnic Minorities in the World of Work." Information Bulletin No. 3 (January). Geneva: ILO.

———. 1996b. "International Migration and Migrant Workers" (March). Geneva: ILO.

———. n.d. "Social Security for Migrant Workers." Geneva: ILO.

International Labor Review. 1952. "The I.L.O. and Migration Problems" (February).

———. 1959. "Recent Developments in the Clearance of Manpower Between Western European Countries" (February).

Keohane, R. O. 1984. *After Hegemony: Cooperation and Discord in the World Political Economy.* Princeton: Princeton University Press.

Koslowski, R. 1994. "Intra-EU Migration, Citizenship and Political Union." *Journal of Common Market Studies* 32 (September).

Lonnroth, J. 1991. "The International Convention on the Rights of All Migrant Workers and Members of Their Families in the Context of International Migration Policies: An Analysis of Ten Years of Negotiation." *International Migration Review* (Winter).

Martin, P., and J. E. Taylor. 1996. "Managing Migration: The Role of Economic Policy." Occasional Paper #2, Migration Policy in Global Perspective Series, International Center for Migration, Ethnicity and Citizenship, New School for Social Research.

Niessen, J. 1992. "European Community Legislation and Intergovernmental Cooperation in Migration." *International Migration Review* 26 (Summer).

OECD. 1975. *The OECD and International Migration.* Paris: OECD.

———. 1978. *The Migratory Chain.* Paris: OECD.

OEEC. 1952. *European Economic Cooperation.* Paris: OEEC.

Orzack, L. 1991. "The General Systems Directive and the Liberal Professions." In *The State of the European Community*, edited by L. Hurwitz and C. Lequesne. Lynne Rienner Publishers.

Piore, M. 1979. *Birds of Passage: Migrant Labor and Industrial Societies.* New York: Cambridge University Press.

Ruggie, J. G. 1983. "International Regimes, Transactions and Change: Embedded Liberalism in the Postwar Economic Order." In *International Regimes*, edited by S. Krasner. Ithaca, N.Y.: Cornell University Press.

Sassen, S. 1988. *The Mobility of Labor and Capital: A Study in International Investment and Labor Flow.* New York: Cambridge University Press.

———. 1996. *Losing Control? Sovereignty in an Age of Globalization.* New York: Columbia University Press.

Schutte, J. 1991. "Schengen: Its Meaning for the Free Movement of Persons in Europe." *Common Market Law Review* 28.

Smith, P. H. 1997. "NAFTA and Mexican Migration." In *At the Crossroads: Mexico and U.S. Immigration Policy*, edited by F. D. Bean, R. O. De La Garza, B. R. Roberts, and S. Weintraub. New York: Rowman and Littlefield Publishers.

Weintraub, S. 1997. "U.S. Foreign Policy and Mexican Immigration." In *At the Crossroads: Mexico and U.S. Immigration Policy*, edited by F. D. Bean, R. O. De La Garza, B. R. Roberts, and S. Weintraub. New York: Rowman and Littlefield Publishers.

Zolberg, A. R. 1981. "International Migrations in Political Perspective." In *Global Trends in Migration*, edited by M. M. Kritz, C. B. Keely, and S .M. Tomasi. New York: Center for Migration Studies.

———. 1983. "Contemporary Transnational Migrations in Historical Perspective." In *U.S. Immigration and Refugee Policy*, edited by M. M. Kritz. Lexington: D.C. Heath and Co.

———. 1991. "Bounded States in a Global Market: The Uses of International Labor Migrations." In *Social Theory for a Changing Society*, edited by P. Bourdieu and J. S. Coleman. Boulder, Colo.: Westview Press.

———. 1992. "Labour Migration and International Economic Regimes: Bretton Woods and After." In *International Migration Systems: A Global Approach*, edited by M. M. Kritz, L. L. Lim, and H. Zlotnik. Oxford: Clarendon Press.

– Chapter 10 –

DEVELOPMENT ASSISTANCE AND INTERNATIONAL MIGRATION

Richard E. Bissell and Andrew S. Natsios

Introduction

As concern over immigration rises in the U.S., policymakers have begun to look to conditions in the source countries of those migrants. Some observers hope that the improvement of economic conditions abroad will result in fewer immigrants into the U.S., that incentives to stay home will take the place of economic opportunities in the U.S. The presence of many program funding agencies in the U.S. encourages policymakers to think about proactive support of job creation abroad. Outside the U.S. in recent years, dramatic movements of people between developing countries, from Africa to Europe, and from Latin America to the U.S., have caused additional speculation about possible remedies. Development assistance is one of those remedies, and the question to be addressed here is its exact role.

Economists and development specialists have been less than forthcoming about the true potential for using development assistance to meet the refugee challenge. The long-term nature of most economic development investments has made for a difficult match with the short-term attention drawn to refugee movements and large-scale migration. The payoff from traditional development programs is never measured in months, rarely in a few years, and commonly by decades. The investments that show the highest payoff in the long term—human resources—are also the slowest to have an impact on the decisions of people considering emigration. The stimulation of economic growth in developing countries with sufficient impact throughout societies to change migration patterns takes many years. In the meantime, forces of changes (including development assistance) may be the source of internal migration that spills over into migration abroad, especially when complemented by "pull" forces such as the U.S. has exerted on Latin America (Zolberg and Smith 1996: 18–19).

Two changes of the last decade have brought development practitioners closer to the concerns of migration policymakers. On the issues of migration and refugees, there has been substantial recharacterization of the issues. For bilateral development assistance agencies, the enhancement of disaster relief functions has given them more effective tools that have standing in their own right as well as in relation to long-term development efforts.

The post–Cold War world has changed the focus of the spotlight in international disorder. Where much had been attributed to the U.S.-Soviet conflict in proxy states throughout the developing world, and both countries clearly played a role in catalyzing refugee flows over forty years, it is now evident that involuntary migration is not simply a function of superpower policies. Southeastern Europe, Central Africa, Southeast Asia, and East Africa, for example, show few signs of controlling human flows on their own, and observers wonder about the adequacy of short-term relief alone. There are thus efforts to develop longer-term solutions, whether economic, political, military, or social. In that context, the quest for economic reconstruction is much more than a matter of dollars spent on housing and roads; it also seeks to include a structure of incentives that will encourage adversaries to begin to work together in a functional manner. Just as some of the early proponents of post–World War II integration in Europe argued for "functionalism" as the guiding principle of enlightened cooperation among former enemies, so those who wish to heal some of the perennial sources of refugees among developing countries argue for hope in simple transactions. Trade, multiethnic workplaces, and integrated economies on a regional or national scale are seen by some as development tools to heal noneconomic problems.

On the side of development agencies, the cost of pure relief operations in the 1980s began to cause a reconsideration of how best to invest in troubled regions. The recurrence of such emergencies—in the 1980s, generally resulting from wide-scale famines on top of the usual man-made disasters—not only destroyed much development investment of prior decades through emigration of skilled manpower and destruction of infrastructure, but it also demonstrated that aid alone could not prevent the kind of destructive events that recurred. As the U.S. share of meeting the needs of displaced people in Africa and Asia, in particular, climbed into hundreds of millions of dollars annually, in addition to the cost of destroyed development investments, aid policymakers began to see the coherence of their international resources in tatters, driven more by emergencies than long-term strategies. In the U.S. government, the U.S. Agency for International Development questioned the existing structures, asking how one might begin to better align those short and long-term aid resources to be mutually supportive, rather than competing with one another for scarce budget dollars.

In addition, USAID officials pressed for answers about their comparative advantage: in the arena of global burden-sharing for these cauldrons of refugees, what support could the U.S. most advantageously provide? One characteristic that set the U.S. apart from other development assistance donors was the plethora of nongovernment organizations (NGOs) with U.S. roots, dedicated to the relief of poverty and disastrous conditions in developing countries. Many of these NGOs, still relying overwhelmingly on private donations, developed closer ties to the U.S. government in order to ensure their funding. Indeed, so many developed large international programs that it was argued that the multitude of NGOs that emerged to combat emergency situations were better managed by an outside agent such as USAID than by the local government. Such a role for USAID, with its capacity for private sector cooperation unique among donor nations, was possible primarily where the local government has completely collapsed and is thus incapable of exercising sovereign rights over foreign organizations.

The U.S. saw a comparative advantage in being able to bring greater coherence to many of the institutional actors, such as NGOs, and to provide resources in the form of food and money. Development assistance is, above all, hard currency, and while traditionally deployed in the context of long-term development investments with a need for imports, those specializing in refugees began to understand better how such hard currency assistance could, in fact, be the best tool for intervention in improving people's lives. The famines and civil wars in Ethiopia and Somalia in the 1980s and 1990s were testing grounds for new, indirect approaches to famine alleviation that showed promising results in follow-on evaluations.

The encounter of humanitarian and development assistance programs in the U.S. government has been salutary for all involved. The impulse to charity on the part of Americans, documented annually in the public and elite surveys conducted by the Chicago Council on Foreign Relations, has needed to come to terms with creating economic incentives that better people's lives. The American predilection to treat the displaced as refugees, and to find permanent new homes for refugees outside their country of origin was sustainable when the numbers were small, and when most refugees made the move on their own as individuals and families rather than as ethnic groups or communities. Today, civil wars have resulted in the shift of so many people into neighboring countries, sometimes as intact communities, that the need for investments to enable them to repatriate to their homes is manifest. That requires more than the traditional tools of U.S. refugee and relief policy; it requires the social and economic tools of nation-building (as it used to be called) to enable communities to reintegrate into a national fabric.

The challenge for the U.S. today is thus twofold: to deal with a world of migration and refugees that has changed substantially from earlier decades, and to deal with movements of people between third countries as well as from those countries to the U.S. While more distant from direct U.S. interests, the scale of movement is much larger abroad, and therefore a major concern to the U.S. The U.S. must also deal with an abundance of development assistance-like instruments, both within the government and outside, that threaten to be random events on a suffering landscape of people instead of heading in the same direction. Such diverse application of resources can be much more than wasteful; it is easily contradictory, each negating the value of other resources. This is particularly the case where long-term remedies are at stake. The U.S. government (USG) can apply its limited resources as it will, can only partially influence the direction of NGO resources (so long as the USG does not directly challenge the values or ideology of a given NGO), and has very little influence over actions of other governments; as a policy question, then, how can the range of development assistance resources be well spent?

* * * *

IN THIS CHAPTER, we shall examine three policy areas. The first is how people move in response to short-term disasters, whether natural or manmade. The U.S. can make investments either before or after the onset of such disasters that have long-term consequences. The second is that of complex emergencies, those sustained conflicts and disasters in developing countries that create terrible dilemmas for donor countries: how long and where to deploy resources in support of refugees outside their countries. The last area is that of how people respond to long-term economic prospects as potential migrants. The U.S. has long wrestled with this issue in Latin America, and through its experience there, may be able to share lessons with other countries.

Phase One: The Effect of Humanitarian Assistance on Population Migration during Natural and Manmade Disasters

Population movements during and immediately following natural disasters tend to be short term; indeed, studies indicate that people will return to the site of their homes and remain there, trying to construct temporary shelter, even if their homes have been destroyed and the area of their old neighborhood is highly disaster prone. The two variables which affect this calculus are social class and climate. The lower the economic class the greater the proclivity toward an immediate return to their home sites. Families that do not return to their homes owing to weather conditions or the absence of essential services or commodities such as water or food will frequently stay with family or close friends, the most common coping

mechanism of disaster victims. Natural disasters do not generally produce much in the way of refugee populations unless the natural disaster
occurs simultaneously with a complex humanitarian emergency.

The degree of internal population displacement resulting from a natural disaster will inevitably rise over the next several decades in lower
income countries as this displacement is directly related to high rates of
population growth and the increasing use of marginal land by the poor
for housing. These growth rates are highest among lower income populations and lowest among upper income populations. The poor do not
have the assets to purchase good land for housing and thus tend to take
marginal land, which is highly prone to natural disasters: land around
active volcanoes, low lying land along storm and flood-prone coastal and
riverbank areas, and earthquake fault lines. Intense population pressure
in Bangladesh has pushed an estimated two million poor people onto the
flood plain and unstable islands of the Brahmaputra and Ganges river
systems which is highly prone to periodic flooding and onto coastal
islands only a few feet above sea level. Those islands have been completely inundated from tropical storms twice in the last twenty years,
killing hundreds of thousands. In both cases, the squatter settlements on
those marginal areas have almost immediately been reestablished by
those who have survived the disasters in spite of the clear and continuing danger—because they have no other option.

Most long-term population displacement, internal or refugee, results
not from natural disasters, but from complex humanitarian emergencies
which commonly share five characteristics: (1) internal ethnic or religious
conflict accompanied by widespread human rights abuses; (2) food insecurity and epidemics of communicable diseases resulting in very high
morbidity and mortality rates; (3) macroeconomic collapse with hyperinflation, depression-level unemployment and net declines in the GNP;
(4) deterioration or disappearance of public sector services and political
authority; and (5) large-scale population movements affecting between
25 and 75 percent of the people. In the case of Liberia, after six years of
particularly destructive civil war, only 10 to 20 percent of the population
still lives in their original homes. In most cases, humanitarian organizations have provided relief for displaced and refugee populations forced
from their homes in these massive emergencies.

Structure as Program

Practitioners and scholars alike have known for some years that the provision of humanitarian relief during natural and manmade disasters can
strongly attract populations under stress away from their homes and villages to refugee and displaced persons camps where food and physical
safety are thought to be. What has not been much studied is how the
choice of provider of humanitarian assistance and the structure of donor
aid agencies indirectly influence population movements during times of

crisis. The United Nations High Commissioner of Refugees (UNHCR) has had since its inception in 1951, a clear mandate for assisting refugees, defined as at-risk persons crossing a national boundary, while no such mandate presently exists for internally displaced persons (IDPs) who have left their homes but not their country. This UN refugee mandate has meant there has been an institutional focal point for raising and spending money and running field operations, which does not exist for IDPs. In fact the mandate for IDPs has vaguely rested with the United Nations Development Program (UNDP) under precedents and decisions by the secretary general. UNDP has been uninterested, unprepared, and by temperament ill-disposed to carry out the mandate: its work is longer term development not humanitarian relief to IDPs, a perspective which has sharply skewed its focus away from relief operations of any kind.

UNHCR has stepped into this void left by UNDP's disinterest, diverting a modest proportion of its budget for internally displaced persons. (Much of this increase, however, is attributable to disputes over how to categorize as IDPs or refugees those people who have been displaced in Bosnia and to a lesser degree other conflicts where the nation state, and therefore national boundaries, no longer exist as an identifiable entity.) In recent years, Sadako Ogata, the UN High Commissioner for Refugees, tried to expand the inherent institutional mandate of UNHCR to assist only refugees, with innovative efforts at providing support for IDPs before they leave the country and become refugees. UNHCR in Bosnia, Afghanistan, Cambodia, and Tajikistan has made modest efforts to initiate developmental relief programs among IDPs so they might remain in their own countries during their national crisis. While this trend in UNHCR is encouraging, it has met with only limited success; it is far from standard operating procedure both because of donor government resistance to diverting funds for refugees to developmental relief interventions for IDPs and because of resistance within UNHCR which since its founding assiduously avoided expanding its mandate to IDPs. U.S. policymakers should make it national policy to redress the resource allocation disparity between IDPs and refugees in the international system, thus focusing more resources inside the country in crisis. In addition, UNHCR should be pressed to accelerate these reforms, making them standard operating procedure, and should be given the financial resources to carry them out. The design and implementation of these developmental relief interventions among IDPs require donor oversight and evaluation, as the UN's record at reform and innovation is not a happy one. Should UNHCR in a particular crisis revert to its traditional interpretation of its mandate which would preclude assistance to IDPs, donor governments should consider diverting funding to those humanitarian agencies that will provide this assistance: ICRC, IOM (International Organization for Migration), and NGOs.

Maintaining refugee camps and carrying out the protection function for refugees remains the central work of UNHCR. It is noteworthy how many refugee camps remain operational over a decade or more (e.g., Afghans in Pakistan, Cambodians in Thailand, Eritreans in Ethiopia, and Palestinians in Gaza), while it would be difficult to recall many examples of IDP camps anywhere in operation for more than five years. This disparity is only partially a function of the greater security afforded by the camps outside rather than inside the country in crisis, which certainly has some effect on their longevity. Without UNHCR, these camps would never have survived for so long; in some cases, camps which have outlived their usefulness, or which have become embarrassments because they have been turned into military bases by armed elements, continued because of UNHCR subsidies. The very organizational existence of a UN agency to protect refugees has focused considerable assistance outside rather than in the countries in conflict and crisis. Perhaps the most recent example of this is the Great Lakes region of Africa, one of the most violent and conflict-prone regions of the world, where nearly a million Rwandan Hutu refugees—many of whom participated in the genocide against the Rwandan Tutsis (and some moderate Hutus) in the spring and summer of 1994—remain in Tanzanian and Zairean camps. At a time of major development assistance reductions by donor governments with no corresponding cuts in refugee and disaster relief funding, little money has been provided by Western countries to help rebuild Rwanda, investments which might well have improved life enough to attract home some of the refugees in the camps, if personal security issues for returnees could also have been addressed. Structure then profoundly influences program and policy.

Not only do UN mandates and organizational structures affect assistance to refugees and IDPs, so too do the ways in which donor governments structure their foreign assistance programs. In the case of the United States, unlike most other Western democracies, the refugee and IDP functions are organizationally separated—refugees are the responsibility of the State Department and IDPs the USAID—with separate budget line items that are not transferable and separate staffs that communicate only irregularly.

The State Department refugee office, formally known as the Office of Population, Refugees, and Migration (PRM) has three characteristics: it is not operational in the field; as a rule, it funnels most of its budget to UNHCR with a small portion to NGOs; and it sees the focus of its advocacy efforts, almost exclusively, as influencing UNHCR's operations and decision making. In FY01, the Office of Migration and Refugee Assistance requested $658 million, up from a $622 million budget in FY00. Of that amount, $457 million was designated for overseas assistance, primarily to UNHCR. Assistance to IDPs is provided by informal agreement through the Office of Foreign Disaster Assistance (OFDA) in USAID. OFDA is operational in the field, works through the NGOs, UN agencies and the International Committee of the Red Cross (ICRC) with a budget request in FY01 of $165 million, as opposed to a budget of $152 million in FY00.

This organizational bifurcation has several consequences which directly affect population movements: (1) it makes the design of comprehensive strategies for emergencies where there are IDPs and refugees quite difficult; (2) it prevents the transfer of funding between offices in a particular year when more funding is needed for one or the other population; and (3) it biases refugee assistance toward relief and camp maintenance and away from developmental relief and rehabilitation. The direct operational presence of the U.S. governmental humanitarian relief offices on the ground can force a higher level of accountability, coordination, and collaboration among the operational actors, and can design strategies to deal with the crisis by the application of U.S. government funding toward specific strategic objectives.

The choice of UNHCR by PRM to provide services to refugees instead of the ICRC, or other UN agencies, such as UNICEF and NGOs, affects ground operations in several ways. UNHCR historically had provided services to refugees in camps through the government ministries of the country in which the refugee camp was located or through local NGOs, and sometimes international NGOs. The rise of complex emergencies since the end of the Cold War has placed new demands on UN agencies, including UNHCR, which have responded by developing internal operational capacity. While USAID does employ some developmental NGOs to provide humanitarian assistance—in FY93, 300 NGOs received grants of $300 million to provide these services—the relationship is contractual and subordinate. NGOs which do both longer term development and relief work tend to handle the transition from refugee relief assistance to rehabilitation, reconstruction, and development more easily.

Most of the major PVO players in emergencies provide what is known as developmental relief interventions, that is, relief interventions with a heavy developmental component such as agricultural recovery, food-for-work projects which build infrastructure, or job creation through mass employment programs. One report on the Somalia relief operation indicated that over 50 percent of the relief grants made by OFDA to NGOs went for developmental relief programs. The developmental relief approach is something which UNHCR, indeed UN agencies generally, have yet to be comfortable with nor have they developed any internal expertise in how it is best done. Thus the U.S. governmental structure is inherently biased toward UNHCR and therefore toward a custodial rather than an innovative approach to assistance to refugees: camp maintenance over resettlement in the country of origin, refugees over IDPs, and relief over developmental relief and rehabilitation.

The Movement of Elites in Crisis

One unintended but salutary consequence of major relief operations in times of crisis is the hiring of local employed professional people by humanitarian agencies. Those relief providers which do heavy local hiring within a country in conflict—and most NGOs, the ICRC, and the UN agencies (other than UNHCR) do this when they are operational—create a magnet which keeps the educated elite within their own country. During Somalia's famine of 1992, an ICRC accountant who kept their financial records devoted his entire salary to feeding over 100 members of his extended family. In developing countries a breadwinner is obligated by custom and family pressure to provide for a much larger universe of people than the nuclear family in the Western tradition. So, the magnetic effect of these jobs is much broader than simply the employees of the NGOs, but reaches out to their extended families as well. Without this employment, these elites will more likely leave the country for refugee camps or venture to other countries, even if they do not seek refugee status. During emergencies, these humanitarian relief agencies become the major employers in the country, particularly given the collapse of the local economy, a general characteristic of complex emergencies. The magnetic effect of this employment by NGOs is obviously only operative when their work is in the country in crisis among the IDP population or the populations which have not left their homes in the first place. If the same indigenous staff were hired to work in refugee camps, its effect would be pernicious. Employing local elites to manage camps would draw them out of their own country.

The educated elites in most societies are the most mobile members of society by virtue of their wealth, employability, and the contacts they have across national borders, including relatives who have emigrated to other countries. They have more options than the working class, rural farmers, or the poor. In a country suffering through a complex humanitarian emergency, the educated elites are usually the first to leave, not only because of this mobility but also because of the risks they face: those who are educated are often targeted by rival factions wishing to deprive their adversaries of skilled leaders and administrators; their wealth and possessions are coveted by the contestants; and they are generally more visible. And yet, the elites are the most critical element for rehabilitation and reconstruction to a country after a conflict; they can bring stability to a traumatized society needed to make a peace agreement work or negotiate it in the first instance.

Phase Two: Spontaneous Repatriation of Refugees and Resettlement of IDPs

Just as the choice of institutions by donor government aid agencies to assist refugee and IDPs during crises profoundly influences population movements, so too do the substantive strategies chosen, if any, to address the refugee crisis by these same donor agencies. Traditionally three strategies have been employed by donor governments and UNHCR as more durable solutions to refugee crises: (1) local resettlement in the country to which the refugee has fled; (2) resettlement in a third country (such as the United States during the Cambodian, Laotian, and Vietnamese refugee population resettlements in the 1970s and early 1980s); and (3) repatriation of refugees back to their homes. It is instructive to note that this third alternative—clearly the most desirable from any number of perspectives—is the least researched and studied. Seminal research from two extensive studies conducted by Fred Cuny and his associates on voluntary repatriation of refugees produced some well documented, but unconventional, conclusions about international assistance as it influences repatriation efforts. The conclusions are worth quoting at length:

> Today, most voluntary repatriations occur during conflict, without a decisive political event such as national independence, without any change in the regime or the conditions that originally caused flight.... The fact that large number of refugees choose to return without the "protection" of the UN tells us something about efficacy of the protection process and the fact that many are willing to forgo assistance indicates how aid is regarded during this point in a refugee's exile.... This new perspective calls for assistance agencies to work with and react to the refugee's decisions rather than attempting to design and direct returns before seeking refugee participation. (Stein, Cuny, and Reed 1992:15)

The natural bias in the international humanitarian response system against extensive studies of or reporting on spontaneous (unorganized) repatriation of refugees has skewed data collection on repatriation toward that which is undertaken formally and away from its spontaneous manifestation. In fact, the same study concludes that *the number of refugees who repatriate voluntarily may be ten times greater than those who are assisted by humanitarian organizations.* Traditional repatriation assistance seen from this perspective may be peripheral to the general movement of refugee populations. This suggests that aid resources might be more effectively used if directed toward alternative strategies rather than in the manner currently employed by the international response system. These alternative strategies might include directing funding to support refugee-initiated repatriation efforts which are ongoing rather than UN-initiated efforts.

Why do people leave their homes and communities? When and under what circumstances do they decide to return? Refugee and displaced populations too often are treated analytically as one group of people leaving a particular country, with the focus on "why they leave," rather than "who they are." Refugee populations must be disaggregated in order to analyze more precisely their decision making processes. Not surprisingly, the wealthy and educated more often leave in the early stages of an emergency and avoid registering as refugees and entering refugee camps: this pattern has been documented for the population movements in the Sri Lankan and Cambodian civil wars. For people accustomed to a higher standard of living, camp life is particularly depressing and becomes intolerable for extended periods of time. Educated elites confined to camps, particularly older men, experience disproportionately high rates of suicide. Those populations that do not register with the international system and avoid camps, typically return to their countries and homes spontaneously, assiduously avoiding organized repatriation efforts. Those people who avoid the official system, regardless of social class, have good reasons for doing so: they do not wish political factions back home to associate them with one side or the other, a fear which is well-founded as camps are frequently controlled by one faction or another, used as a base of military operations, a source of new recruits for the militias, and a source of food and supplies. This was the case with Cambodian camps in Thailand, the Hutu camps in Zaire, and the Sudanese camps in Ethiopia. The camps are seldom politically neutral, and a refugee's registration with them can be dangerous.

In the case of the Cambodian camps in Thailand many people would leave the camps, return to their homes and then go back to the camps in a seasonal movement to plant their crops or check on their farms and property. Surveys showed the bulk of the people in these camps were small farmers. This same pattern of seasonal visits to homes and farms repeated itself in the Liberian camps in neighboring countries during the five-year civil war. Frequently when an organized repatriation takes place under duress, people who still feel insecure once resettled in their home communities, will return to the border areas near the camps with which they had been associated: this took place in the Cambodian refugee crisis.

This is all to say that refugees and IDPs will return to their homes when they are ready to: they make their decisions based on a complex set of conflicting calculations. These include:

- concern about security along the route they will travel between the camp and their homes,
- security in their home village or neighborhood,
- comparative living conditions in the camps versus their home villages (in some cases the camps provide better housing, medical care, cleaner water, and food than they would have if they return home),
- the militias which informally control their camps may have threatened them if they return without permission or don't return when they are told to,
- they have no assurance of being able to support themselves economically if they return home,
- the rest of their village, extended family, clan or tribal elders decide to return to their homes (the security offered by other kinsmen and family does act as a powerful incentive to draw people back to their homes).

Repatriation assistance efforts should be programmatically organized around this complex matrix of incentives and disincentives or it will ultimately fail or have limited effects. Refugees and IDPs find ways of returning home unassisted, and resisting organized repatriation and resettlement efforts if they are not comfortable with these conditions. Their resistance is quite effective over the longer term since the international community cannot monitor the repatriation process permanently.

These findings suggest several approaches to policymakers who must deal with the problem of population movements, particularly in conflict situations. The people who are being repatriated or resettled need to be consulted on an ongoing basis during the process to ensure their continuing support; this requires the collection of hard data from survey instruments designed to monitor refugee views on repatriation, since their opinions will evolve over time. The refugee populations should be disaggregated and discrete groups should be treated separately, not in terms of financial or logistical support, which should remain constant among all returning populations, but in terms of other incentives to return such as security. Services in refugee and IDP camps should be carefully designed so they are not significantly more comfortable than their home villages: they should be Spartan but adequate to sustain life at no more than a subsistence level. This more Spartan approach was taken in the construction of the Kurdish holding areas in northern Iraq in 1991, which precluded those areas from working at cross purposes with the U.S. government strategy to encourage the Kurds to leave the mountains and move back into their homes.

Generally, repatriation and resettlement efforts are officially initiated just after a political settlement has been approved by the warring parties. Evidence from case studies challenges the wisdom of this traditional prescription. People will frequently repatriate during a conflict if the area into which they are returning is secure and prosperous even if the end of hostilities is not in sight. Rehabilitation and reconstruction work likewise can be initiated during a conflict in areas that are more remote from the hostilities, work which itself can act as a magnet for drawing people to their homes (Cuny and Tanner 1995: 12–20). Effort to stimulate local markets, through the monetization of food aid and other critical items, can have the effect of creating economic activity, jobs which will keep people in their villages and increase family assets and thereby improve food security. This can prevent population movements caused by food insecurity during a famine, whether during peaceful times or during conflict.

Security during Repatriation Efforts

In virtually all complex humanitarian emergencies, threats to personal and ethnic group security, along with food insecurity, act as the driving motivation for population movements. These security issues have become the central challenge of the international humanitarian response system in several ways: (1) while the very presence of humanitarian agencies in insecure areas does sometime restrain some of the violence against at-risk populations, they cannot stop it; (2) UNHCR (or any other agency) has no protection mandate for IDPs as it does for refugees; and (3) the UN agency with this newly created mandate—UNHCR—has not yet demonstrated the operational competence, or strategic vision, or resources to provide this protection. Additionally, the UNHCR requires the consent of the national government to work, consent which is likely to be denied since it may be this consenting government that is committing or abetting the atrocities in the first instance. More funding, more experience, and more staff, trained in developmental relief interventions might render UNHCR a useful tool to policymakers wishing to improve security in some crisis where the international community has some leverage over the national government and can thus guarantee access.

Clearly the security issue can sometimes only be properly addressed by military force. Given the levels of unrestrained violence, ethnic cleansing, and genocide directed against at risk ethnic groups in most complex emergencies, the security issue has become even more important. Solve this problem and population movements—refugee or IDP—would dramatically subside. Military intervention has now become an acceptable alternative under some circumstances, other options having been found inadequate. A thorough analysis of the doctrine of military intervention in complex humanitarian emergencies is beyond the scope of this essay, however, some reflection on the direct effect of the presence of peacekeeping or peace enforcement soldiers on population movements is appropriate. How the intervening military forces are perceived by the local population generally has had profound effects on population movements. In the few weeks following the U.S.-led international intervention in Somalia in December 1992, the ICRC reported a 25 percent increase in the population they were serving in their chain of soup kitchens in and around Mogadishu. The U.S. military decision to phase the entrance of U.S. troops into the country by first securing Mogadishu caused this large increase in the population being served by the ICRC. Thus a decision taken for sound logistical reasons—the port and largest airfield were in Mogadishu—had a pernicious effect in almost every other regard. Somalis within traveling distance of Mogadishu understandably saw the U.S. troops as a source of security and food—neither of which they had enough—and so they quickly moved to get more of what they required.

This population movement has another decidedly undesirable consequence: it became a very effective recruitment tool for the militia led by General Aideed, the most powerful and disruptive warlord in the country. Refugee and IDP camps frequently serve as rebel supply bases, rest and medical care areas for the wounded, and fertile rebel and militia recruitment grounds as young men in the camps became demoralized, disoriented, and bored with camp life, and the influence of traditional authority figures who might act as a restraint on their passions diminishes under the stress of the crisis. The larger the size of the militias, which are chronically undisciplined and poorly provisioned, the more havoc they caused in the countryside, further increasing population displacement. Had the military intervention in Somalia taken place simultaneously in all of the nine cities it eventually secured, instead of in phases, this pernicious effect would have been avoided.

Military intervention carefully conceived and executed can have a salutary effect on the course of a conflict. The allied intervention in northern Iraq during the emergency in 1991 provides another useful case study in how altering the security equation in a deliberate way can affect population movements, in this case for the better. USAID and allied military efforts to construct temporary holding centers, with rudimentary accommodations, to care for the nearly one million Kurdish IDPs and refugees along the border with Turkey, combined with a security plan to protect the Kurds, led to the successful resettlement of this population over a three month period back to their home cities and villages. The U.S. government created a security perimeter enforced by the U.S. Air Force in Turkey and northern Iraq, across which Baghdad's military forces were prohibited from traveling, which remained in effect for five years. After the perimeter was created in 1991, groups of Kurdish elders were taken by USAID and the U.S. military back to their home villages to convince them that the route home was safe and that their homes were not destroyed and that there were no Iraqi military forces in the area. Once these elders returned to the camps they convinced their people that it was safe to return. The speed of the response was a critical factor in avoiding the creation of permanent camps. The military instrument in refugee and IDP emergencies will continue to be an option for policymakers. It should, however, be employed with some care and humility, when other options have failed; its very power can have salutary consequences or quite harmful, though unintended, ones as well.

Organized repatriation efforts by the international system and the package of resettlement assistance that accompany these efforts—through UNHCR, national governments, and NGOs—can affect the incentive mix, but alone may not be sufficient to alter the decision of a refugee or IDP to move to their homes. Military and political interventions may also be needed. Policymakers should see resettlement assistance in this larger context: influential, but not decisive, an option for some, but peripheral or irrelevant to the decisions of many more.

Phase Three: Development Assistance in Repatriation/ Resettlement Assistance and Migration Prevention

Some Americans have been particularly concerned in recent decades with the question of assisting potential migrants in their country of origin. The putative intent of such assistance is clear: to encourage independent decisions by potential emigrants not to leave their country, but rather to see the possibilities for satisfactory political, social, and economic conditions.

This concern on the part of Americans has been encouraged by the apparent increase in immigration from Latin America, both the large-scale Cuban migration in the post-1960 period as well as from Mexico and other areas of Latin America. The assumption behind such assistance is that people would prefer to stay in their ancestral homes, and that they emigrate only due to intolerable conditions of one kind or another.

It is clear from decades of scholarship that the picture is more complicated. While individual scholars may emphasize one aspect over another, it takes a combination of economic, social, and political factors in both the source and the target country for people to move (see Alba 1978; Diaz-Briquets and Weintraub 1991; Portes and Bach 1985). The accumulation of studies shows a range of "pull" and "push" factors at work. Nevertheless, in this chapter we are primarily interested in the cases where emigration was a function of internal developments in the source country. As noted by many observers, urbanization has played a crucial catalytic role, as a symptom of the destruction of a stable, integrated social and economic system. The introduction of new technologies (particularly labor-saving devices in the traditional economy) and an uneven distribution of growth served to stimulate emigration. In that sense, the infusion of development assistance could be seen as encouraging or discouraging emigration, depending upon how it was spent.

Certain factors often proposed as stimulative of immigration appear to have little historical evidence. The rate of population growth in the source country has only an indirect effect. Absolute income differentials between source and target country do not have much effect, unless related to overall growth opportunities for one economy. Building rural infrastructure in the source country is sometimes proposed as a means of improving the standard of living; its impact is more probably to ease the emigrant's exit. Expansion of education in rural areas may also have the perverse effect of increasing emigration—first internally and then abroad, since most jobs for educated people are in the cities or abroad.

Finally, past studies show that long-term emigration patterns rely less and less upon internal conditions in the source country as migration habits build. For neighboring countries with significant differentials in income, social and economic patterns of moving across borders for income will develop. Networks of related people in several countries will evolve over time to allow either short-term or permanent movement to achieve an adequate income level. This pattern is particularly clear between the U.S. and its southern neighbors, where it is abetted by U.S. laws allowing for family reunification. This allows for an enhanced comfort level for immigrants in the U.S., for ready income redistribution through repatriation of earnings, and the improvement of rural life in the source country fed by foreign earnings. While this pattern was initially limited primarily to Puerto Rico and Mexico with the U.S., there are now numerous Latin American countries with similar circular relationships with American society. Indeed, in some countries USAID support inadvertently encouraged the creation of such emigration support mechanisms: first, by paying for the education of thousands at U.S. universities annually; second, by supporting joint projects involving U.S. and foreign nationals with ongoing cooperation; and third, by encouraging more open economic policies that tend to engender greater international movement. Studies show that the mere reduction in the real cost of transportation and communication in recent decades encourages migration.

The case of Mexico is particularly dramatic. The sustained circular flow of people and over $2 billion annually in repatriated earnings has been noted by many. Few, however, realize that those earnings constitute nearly 10 percent of Mexico's total exports to the U.S., and thus serve as a major source of economic growth in Mexico. There is no conceivable way that the U.S. could provide similar development assistance to substitute for those flows. The money reaches Mexican people at the grass roots, and supports consumption and investment of extensive families able to thereby remain in their traditional social setting (Durand, Parrado, and Massey 1996). The American public is largely unaware of such long-term effects, focusing instead on their anxieties associated with the short-term presence of such Mexican workers in the U.S.

American concern about the emergence of these patterns has led to a variety of laws and programs initiatives in recent decades. The Kissinger Commission on Central American Assistance recommended a drastic increase in resources to enhance job creation in those countries in the mid-1980s. Similarly, the creation of the Caribbean Basin Initiative, and the related Section 936 program for Puerto Rico were intended to accelerate export growth and job creation for the unemployed in those countries. While there was a variety of reasons for launching such initiatives, they drew upon concern about immigration levels to some degree in obtaining passage in Congress and obtaining continuing funding.

In areas outside Latin America, there has been greater reluctance to link development assistance to such long-term issues. If anything, the flow of refugees and large-scale emigration have been reasons to terminate development assistance, as symptoms of instability in societies where economic investments would not make sense. If a country qualified for disaster or refugee relief, by this logic, it became disqualified for development assistance. While those funds generally came from the same budgetary account of the U.S. government, there has historically been little coordination. Even the provision of food assistance was channeled through different pieces of authorizing legislation: Title II of Public Law 480 for relief, and Title I of the same act for development. Thus, when Africa was hit by recurrent droughts and famines in the 1980s in various countries and subregions, the onset of famine relief to the refugees appeared at the same time as development assistance was drastically scaled back in those countries. Authority for the country program moved from one section of the USAID bureaucracy to another. Given the high threshold for qualifying for development assistance, such countries had difficulty resuming a "development relationship" with the U.S. The "unsettled" condition of the population made it impossible for development programs to continue, even when the migrants themselves were doing a remarkable job of taking care of themselves, through circular emigration and self-repatriation (as in Mali, see Findley 1994).

Development assistance took on a new mandate in the last decade with the emergence of new, more ambitious ideas to "prevent emigration." The realization that emigration could be spurred by political and social conditions in addition to economic issues led USAID to expand its program offerings. The introduction of a small grants program in human rights was an attempt to improve conditions of civil rights, first in Latin America, and then expanded to include Africa and Asia. The creation of an "administration of justice" program in the early 1980s was an indication of the importance of the rule of law. The support for elections and other democratic processes initiated in the late 1980s were important for creating an assurance for orderly transitions of power in societies unaccustomed to democracy. Aid was used in many countries, through small grant programs, to support the emergence of nongovernmental organizations, all part of the civil society infrastructure underpinning greater public participation in decision making.

Likewise on the social side, development assistance was designed in many countries to focus on structural poverty left untouched by the national government. In order to avoid the severe disparities that are known to cause migration, USAID supported extensive projects outside the cities, and indeed, in many countries USAID chose to avoid work in the cities unless absolutely urgent for fear of creating an environment more attractive to rural-urban emigration. Social coherence, experts recognized, was threatened by the economic forces unleashed through development assistance programs, but with modification and targeting, experts also thought that the benefits could reach all segments of society. In that way, social cohesion could be proactively sustained even in the face of rapid economic change. As it happened, there were probably as many cases where such targeting was unsuccessful as where it was successful, but to our knowledge, USAID never commissioned a retrospective, comparative study of the effectiveness of such efforts that was able to distinguish clearly the effect of development assistance from other factors.

USAID and other development assistance donors have been generally ineffective when attempting to intervene in emerging group conflicts. The flowering of ethnic civil wars in the post–Cold War era has created a challenge for which the international system is ill suited, and it is evident in the behavior of aid agencies. Emerging ethnic conflicts occur in a context of sovereignty (Moynihan 1994). While the United States and the post–World War II global structure have done much to protect individual rights, this has emerged at the price of de-emphasizing the group rights that were prominent in the interwar period. The resurgence of problems of "group rights" in the last decade has posed a challenge where development agencies are not prepared with norms to apply. The international community is effectively hamstrung, and the price has been paid in the tragic situations in Rwanda, Burundi, Lebanon, Liberia, Yugoslavia, and elsewhere.

The second area where development assistance played an expanded role was in following up the refugee experience. USAID's experience in this regard has been limited but a source of extensive learning. The repatriation of Mozambique's refugee population was a rapid process, even if largely informal, but the demands of those returnees for economic support was great. USAID launched a major program to reintegrate the population, even carrying out conversion of soldiers to become productive civilian members of the population (Colletta, Kostner, and Wiederhofer 1996). Likewise in Central America, USAID supported a number of programs for returnees, attempting to find ways of bringing government and rebels together in an acceptable political and social compact. In the former Yugoslavia, the U.S. has attempted to create multiethnic enterprises and economic zones, in the belief that repatriated refugees could find a "comfort zone" that crosses the ethnic boundaries clearly drawn by the warring parties. Interestingly, the situation in Ethiopia has taken several different turns. In Eritrea, émigrés self-repatriated to their native country, and then very selectively accepted international assistance in the belief that they needed to control the direction of their country. In the remainder of Ethiopia, by contrast, a great deal of social tension and personal pain has been associated with repatriation, frequently from other parts of the country, and foreign assistance has been unevenly applied to mitigate those difficulties.

What development assistance cannot directly resolve is the insecurity of the repatriated persons—physical protection must come from other sources, as illustrated in highly unusual situations such as the Kurdish enclave in northern Iraq where cooperation with the U.S. military could create a no-fly zone. Cooperation with the U.S. military has not always been so smooth; note the USAID experience in Panama following Noriega's overthrow. In some postconflict situations, some degree of security has been assured through international involvement in political reconciliation—supervision or monitoring of the holding of elections being the most common. UN or regional peacekeeping forces are also in high demand. In such instances, returnees can at least be assured of some international attention to violations of commitments to peace. Legal recourse, however, in the current international system is rare. Assistance can do more to alleviate food insecurity, if the original source of migration was famine. Assistance agencies have learned better what combination of seed, tools, and food are most useful for returnees, although experience in some situations would indicate that cash grants may be most useful. For support of repatriated persons in the country, development assistance is a relatively slow-response mechanism. Some international agencies such as

UNHCR have spoken of "Quick-Impact Projects," rapidly designed and administered in a manner to benefit all people in an area, not just the returnees (Ogata 1992). The track record of UNHCR with this program initiative is laid out above.

As U.S. activities have expanded in pre and postmigration situations, problems have arisen in the way in which such activities are administered by the U.S. government. We have already referred to some of the complications engendered by the presence and importance of U.S.-based nongovernmental organizations. Equally important is the plethora of U.S. official agencies with a role in the policy nexus of migration, refugees, and development assistance. The roles of the Department of State, USAID, and the Department of Defense have already been discussed. As the U.S. government attempts to become more instrumental in its foreign economic policies, however, Commerce, USTR, and Treasury also become relevant. In the 1980s, for instance, when USAID was attempting to use foreign assistance and the CBI to encourage economic growth in the Caribbean countries, other parts of the executive branch went along with a reduction in the sugar quota that cost those same countries $600 million annually and countless jobs. Coordination thus becomes an issue, and within most recent administrations, little attention has been given to these issues. The composite of development policies, humanitarian policies, and security policies has no single focal point outside crisis mode in the executive branch, nor in the oversight mechanisms of Congress. Too often, contradictory policies emerge. It is little wonder that coordination is difficult in and among international institutions, if the national members cannot get their internal agencies well focused. Far too often the international arena becomes another place for national agencies to play out their rivalries and disagreements over policy and resources rather than a place to overcome such difficulties.

Equally important to the issue is the fact that immigration is generally managed as a "domestic issue," not a foreign policy issue. Interest in the U.S. over immigration stems from two sources: the economic anxiety that Ross Perot characterized in the 1992 presidential election as the "giant sucking sound" of jobs being taken south of the border, but, which can be equally applied to low-wage immigrants coming to the U.S.; and the ethnic identification of many U.S. voters that leads them to favor or oppose potential immigration from various parts of the world. These are not new issues, for just as Irish immigrants were blamed in the mid-nineteenth century for wage stagnation, so Mexican labor is blamed today. The unanswered question at this historical juncture is whether the American electorate will resort to the old reaction—closing the border to new immigrants—or whether they can see the ameliorative effect of supporting development in the countries from which immigrants arrive. Even within the executive branch, these domestic politics of immigration rarely intersect with the international programs that might help to solve these problems.

A final structural problem that makes addressing the long-term migration issues with development assistance more difficult is the shift of resources from bilateral agencies to international financial institutions and the private sector. Twenty years ago it could be argued that USAID was the premier development agency. Today the locus of policy leadership and the vast bulk of development resources are elsewhere. The shrinkage of USAID since 1989 has been dramatic and pervasive, both in terms of skilled, long-term officers as well as program resources. The resulting reduction of options for U.S. leadership in the field of development should not have been a surprise. In its place, the presence of the World Bank and related regional development banks dominate policy consultations on development issues, to the point that when it came time for reconstruction and repatriation in Bosnia in 1996, the international community turned overwhelmingly to the World Bank for leadership in such a situation for the first time. Relief activities, however are generally excluded from Bank support; instead, it provides Emergency Recovery Loans and encourages a policy dialogue with the government to prevent future crises. Until recently, the Bank has been reluctant to step into a coordination role in the recovery from disasters and civil wars, but with growing disenchantment over the capabilities of UN agencies to provide such coordination, the Bank is becoming much more visible. In Bosnia, the Bank had prepared $940 million in reconstruction projects by August 1996, including $235 million in Bank funds. These projects included $67 million for landmine clearance as well as $50 million for emergency housing repair. For the Bank to view landmine clearance as the first step in reconstruction is undoubtedly helpful for accelerating donor activity in this area, and a significant move toward the relief end of the "relief-development spectrum." The policy leadership of the Bank has thus grown with Bosnia, along with development of a general framework for involvement in situations of conflict. This framework is meant to apply to countries without effectively functioning governments and lacking access to normal Bank lending—thus a program exceptional to most Bank norms. Being outside the usual Bank lending boundaries, the framework allows for Bank involvement in conflict prevention in at-risk countries, a watching brief in conflict countries, assessment and planning as soon as resolution is in sight, early reconstruction activities, and emergency operations. The challenge for the Bank, as it is drawn into these activities, will be to keep its sights on the long-term development horizon.

With regard to financial resources, however, the leadership has shifted to the private sector. Private flows of development capital now so outweigh official development assistance, that any plan for application of international resources to the immigration question would have to include consideration of incentives for private sector flows. This, of course, highlights a contradiction—private capital has little history of choosing to invest in insecure environments. Thus, more and more attention in bilateral agencies as well as the World Bank is given to the creation and availability of guarantees in order to encourage, at relatively low cost, the flow of private funds to insecure countries. In the medium-term time frame, there is no donor substitute for the private sector. If a country cannot create policies and a regulatory framework friendly to private sources of capital and trade, there will be an economic collapse when the short-term donor-funded reconstruction assistance fades out.

Ultimately, the utility of development assistance to deal with unwanted migration flows, whether preemptively or after the fact, will depend upon better warning systems, a greater legitimacy for intervention in the affairs of collapsing states, and improved cooperation among governments, international financial institutions, and private sector institutions. Given the diversity of value systems in the world today, it is unlikely that the international community will reach agreement on those issues globally, but rather regionally. The pace of change in an increasingly open international economic and social system can only have the effect of encouraging more migration; what is unclear is whether a uniform response can be developed by the international community. One element of that response could be the use of development assistance, based on experiences to date. But such official assistance is unlikely to play a dominant role in the face of current trends.

Development assistance to refugees, whether short-term humanitarian assistance or longer-term aid to the economy, has too often been a substitute for a concerted strategy instead of being an integrated piece of a broader national effort by the U.S. The reasons for this situation have been touched upon already, but are magnified when one considers the most desirable option of repatriation for refugees. It has historically been much easier to advocate resettlement in a third country or integration into a local host country, than to undertake the complicated, long-term commitment of achieving voluntary repatriation of migrants to their home country.

To some extent we have explained the historical and cultural reasons for this emphasis in U.S. policy. The understanding and advocacy of repatriation flies in the face of a carefully constructed, although very fragile and largely unenforceable, system of protecting the legal rights of individual refugees. For American policymakers, this is reinforced by a national tradition of individualism and absence of communal rights. Even where the U.S. recognizes the threat to specific communities abroad, it is administered in a way that obliges the refugee to prove that he or she is an oppressed member of that community. It would thus be a major leap for the U.S. to shift its emphasis away from a set of policies that has led to millions resettling in the U.S. in the last decade.

Nevertheless, we live in a world with many new institutions and assumptions arising from events of the last decade, and there is no reason to assume that our management of refugees would not take on a similarly new cast. Changes, however, would have to occur in USG agencies, in the mechanisms for coordinating U.S. policy, in international organizations, and among the many private sector agencies involved in refugee affairs. Such an agenda does not augur well for a rapid change in policies.

The first area of policy change is the point of engagement with displaced people. After much experience, we know that international refugees do not generally spring forth from a static situation. Prior internal displacement, whether from accelerated rural-urban migration or from internal conflicts, creates the instability that enhances the likelihood of refugee creation. For the U.S. to wait until refugees cross the international border is to lose a major opportunity to prevent further flows. Development programs and projects have rarely taken such internal dynamics into account. The breakdown of internal social structures, from the family to the ethnic community, has rarely been considered a calculable element in development assistance, but it needs to be included. Opportunities exist in current programs to pay more attention to this internal mobility, especially in the orientation of urban development programs, and to help people maintain their roots in their own cultures.

Policy must also be better informed about the nature of the migration flow being addressed. There is no "cookie-cutter approach" to assistance. Indeed, the U.S. has had enough direct experience in the last decade to support much better analysis of the appropriate measures. The fact that refugees suffer from insecurity in attempting to repatriate does not mean that they all need the U.S. Army to escort them to their home country. On the other hand, when refugees face the likelihood of air bombing, as the Kurds did in confronting the Iraqi Air Force, it is likely that anything short of the U.S. Air Force will be inadequate to meet the threat. In order to understand the changing nature of a particular refugee issue, government needs to understand that much of the most accurate information lies in the NGO sector, not the government, and yet will often be presented with a bias quite self-serving for the institutional purposes of the source. This kind of information is invaluable both in understanding the source of migration as well as the eventual construction of incentives for repatriation. The need for careful liaison among people who have information pertinent to policy makes this task hazardous at best; distrust between government agencies and NGOs has a long historical basis, and is unlikely to be dissolved as a general proposition. Only in specific instances, where shared interests outweigh visceral distrust can better information be shared.

Similar hazards await those who call for greater integration and coordination among government agencies in meeting refugee challenges. While textbooks always call for such measures, the reality is that coordination slows and dilutes the responsiveness of policy. Each institutional player wants to have his interests represented in the outcome. As a result, it make sense where speed and a targeted policy is required that the U.S. spend less energy coordinating, and do more to reduce the number of agencies involved. Recent years have witnessed a proliferation of nontraditional players in refugee matters; in some cases, there have been justifiable additions. At some point, however there has to be a shakeout, to reduce the number of players at the policy table. For long-term development efforts, it makes sense to add departments and agencies that can bring useful resources and energy to the effort after a consensus-building process. For short-term implementation of measures to meet a crisis or to repatriate refugees out of a complex humanitarian emergency, fewer agencies may be the better course, with an administrative structure that allows for rapid, clear impacts.

The U.S. needs to apply this organizational principle to refugee flows abroad, and even more to the issue of illegal migration into the U.S. While the responsiveness of short-term measures can be improved, the U.S. is particularly deficient in addressing the long-term solutions that should be considered. American understanding of the economic and social dynamics of circular immigration into the U.S. is sorely lacking, and without a stronger basis, policy solutions will not be generated. Amidst all those solutions, development assistance could be desirable in applying lessons learned from other countries, but seriously inadequate as a financial mechanism to address the magnitude of the problem. Assistance thus needs to be considered in its broadest sense, in order to include all financial and economic mechanisms that could make a difference.

The transition from short-term to long-term assistance deserves much greater attention. The traditional posture of aid agencies has been to wait until the social and political situation is so "stabilized" inside the target country that traditional development programs and projects can be sustained. We now know that such a time is too late to capture the many opportunities that come earlier. The balance of aid—between refugee camps on the outside and reconstruction projects on the inside— must be addressed much earlier, in order to ensure adequate incentives for refugees to return home to a viable society. The administration of aid programs internally must be structured in a way to ensure employment of the talented and educated classes in the process of reconstruction. Too much reliance on external technical assistance means that elites have fewer reasons to return home, and without their leadership it is hard for damaged societies to heal. Development assistance needs to step into the process of repatriation early, to ensure that aid is given to entire communities, not just to returnees; it is community development that is required, with medium- to long-term commitment from donors, rather than just short-term enrichment of refugees. Nevertheless, it is also important to ensure that repatriated farm families do have access to essential supplies to get through the first growing season (seeds, tools, food, and fuel); such may require coordination among donors and agencies to ensure such an integrated response. In other words, the humanitarian agencies cannot simply hand off their responsibility abruptly, and move on. The overlap with development agencies is counterintuitively desirable, though indeed necessary to provide refugees with the confidence to return home.

The U.S. faces a new century with a growing understanding of the refugee problem, a set of weakened institutions to address it, and an uncertain political mandate from the public to deal with it preemptively. Some policymakers recognize that the place to deal with refugees is before they attain that status. To initiate actions after people arrive in camps from foreign countries should be the last resort, not the first choice. The U.S. has the ability and the resources (if coordinated with NGOs and other official donors) to engage displaced people before they cross borders. To intervene earlier requires the application of development assistance in more flexible formats, both short term and long term. The U.S. needs better information about situations within countries, now less feasible with the reduction of official presence in much of the developing world. Yet the agency that would deliver it for the U.S. is a shadow of its former self. The U.S. has a choice to make, and can readily re-create that capacity to avoid the disorder and refugee crises predicted by many. Indeed, that capacity could be improved significantly to meet future challenges. It can do so by reducing the number of bureaucratic players, and thus spending less time on coordination. Managing the continuum from short-term to long-term assistance would then be much more feasible. Whether the U.S. will do so depends upon the emergence of a new consensus within the government and American society that such investments are worth making.

References

Alba, Francisco. 1978. "Mexico's International Migration as a Manifestation of its Development Pattern." *International Migration Review* 12.

Colletta, Nat J., Markus Kostner, and Ingo Wiederhofer. 1996. *Case Studies in War-to-Peace Transition: The Demobilization and Reintegration of Ex-Combatants in Ethiopia, Namibia, and Uganda.* Washington: The World Bank.

Cuny, Frederick C., and Victor Tanner. 1995. "Working with Communities to Reduce Levels of Conflict: Spot Reconstruction." *Disaster Prevention and Management* 4: 12–20.

Diaz-Briquets, Sergio, and Sidney Weintraub, eds. 1991. *Determinants of Emigration from Mexico, Central America, and the Caribbean.* Boulder, Colo.: Westview Press.

Durand, Jorge, Emilio A. Parrado, and Douglas S. Massey. 1996. "Migradollars and Development: A Reconsideration of the Mexican Case." *International Migration Review* 30, 2: 423–44.

Findley, Sally E. 1994. "Does Drought Increase Migration? A Study of Migration from Rural Mali during the 1983–1985 Drought." *International Migration Review* 28, 3: 539–53.

Moynihan, Daniel Patrick. 1994. *Pandaemonium.* New York: Oxford University Press.

Ogata, Sadako. 1992. "Refugees: A Multilateral Response to Humanitarian Crises." 1992 Sanford S. Elberg Lecture in International Studies. Berkeley: Institute for International Studies.

Portes, Alejandro, and Robert Bach. 1985. *Latin Journey: Cuban and Mexican Immigrants in the United States.* Berkeley: University of California Press.

Stein, Barry N., Frederick C. Cuny, and Pat Reed, eds. 1992. *Refugee Repatriation during Conflict: A New Conventional Wisdom.* Papers from a Conference in Addis Ababa, Ethiopia. Dallas: The Center for the Study of Societies in Crisis.

Zolberg, Aristide R., and Robert C. Smith. 1996. "Migration Systems in Comparative Perspective: An Analysis of the Inter-American Migration System with Comparative Reference to the Mediterranean-European System." Report Submitted to the U.S. Department of State. Mimeo: 18–19.

– Chapter 11 –

AFTER THE WARS ARE OVER: U.S. POLICY IN RECONSTRUCTION

Elizabeth G. Ferris

Although peace agreements represent important turning points in the transition from war to peace, conflict-ravaged countries face multiple and simultaneous challenges of reconstruction, rehabilitation, and reconciliation. This process is a fragile one; efforts in Liberia, Angola, and Afghanistan to produce a durable framework for peace are evidence that negotiated agreements do not automatically mean an end to bloodshed. In some cases, agreements collapse in a renewed round of generalized warfare. In other cases, renewed fighting in some parts of the country occurs simultaneously with a return to normal life in other parts of the country. Even in cases, such as Cambodia, where the transition to democratic government has been largely accomplished, the threat of renewed fighting is a constant shadow.

This study focuses on the rebuilding process after peace agreements have been signed, with a particular focus on the way in which refugees are repatriated and incorporated into the peace process. Reconstruction is the term generally used to refer to the process of rebuilding social, political, and economic institutions after the conflicts have ended. In practice, this is somewhat of a misnomer as it implies that functional institutions existed prior to the conflict. The aim of reconstruction policy is usually more ambitious: to create institutions that will prevent subsequent outbreaks of violence. Thus, in Haiti, an essential component of reconstruction policy was the creation of a civilian and politically neutral police force, which was a new development in Haiti.

In all reconstruction processes, the complex mix of tasks to be accomplished in order to translate an agreement into reality is daunting: soldiers have to be disarmed, elections held, infrastructure repaired, the economy rebuilt, law and order established, human rights monitored, confidence restored, jobs found for demobilized soldiers, claims for justice satisfied, and immediate assistance needs met. These tasks must all be done at the same time and typically are begun in a climate of suspicion and doubt. The return of refugees—which was often a driving force in international pressure for a peace agreement—is an added pressure on all the other tasks the peacekeeping troops and the newly constituted government are attempting to carry out. How can refugees be returned to an area infested with landmines? How can they be returned if they are still afraid? Why should they receive preferential treatment over nationals who have endured the years of war? How can they be returned in a way that does not overwhelm local absorptive capacity?

Governments of countries of exile are typically anxious for the refugees to be returned quickly. Zaire and Germany, for example, are currently pressing for the speedy return of their respective Rwandan and Bosnian refugee populations while most international observers fear that a rapid return of these refugees would not only destabilize fragile political and economic conditions, but could trigger the collapse of the fragile peace agreements. The office of the United Nations High Commissioner for Refugees (UNHCR) is often caught in the middle in these debates. Eager on the one hand for refugees to be returned quickly, UNHCR has learned that refugee repatriation is inherently tied to larger-scale peace processes. UNHCR reports, for example, that in both Angola and Afghanistan

> foreign troops have withdrawn, the external support provided to the combatants has been scaled down, and formal peace agreements have been signed. But in both cases the fighting and suffering has continued, generating new population displacements and limiting the number of refugees who are prepared to repatriate. Thus 2.7 million Afghans and 175,000 Angolans continue to live in exile, while in both countries much larger numbers of internally displaced people wait for the day when they can go back to their own town or village. (UNHCR 1996a: 22)

Even when peace agreements hold, refugee repatriation is far more than a logistical exercise of moving people home. As Sadako Ogata, UN High Commissioner for Refugees, explained with respect to Bosnia:

> During these past four years, as my office struggled against all odds to deliver humanitarian aid in the midst of conflict, what motivated us was the thought that, one day, we would be able to provide durable solutions to these innocent victims of war. That day has finally come. Ironical as it may seem, our work in this time of peace will, in many ways, be more complex than it was in war. The obstacles ahead are enormous. (UNHCR 1996b)

This study begins with the premise that an effective response by the international community—and by the U.S. government in particular—to support reconstruction begins long before a peace agreement is achieved. Rather than seeing postconflict assistance as a response to a new situation, the study argues that there is a continuum of assistance from relief to reconstruction. Provision of humanitarian relief in conflict situations and political efforts to reach a peace agreement are major determining factors in reconstruction. The way in which refugees are returned—the planning, the pace, the logistics, the coordination, the hand-off of responsibilities to other actors—is a major component of reconstruction policy.

Following a description of some of the effects of long-term conflict situations which affect subsequent reconstruction and refugee repatriation, the cases of Mozambique and Haiti are examined in more detail. These two cases are very different in terms of the type of conflict, the involvement of major powers, the peace processes, and the particular difficulties of returning refugees (or in case of Haiti, asylum-seekers). But, in both cases, the return of refugees was a driving force in reaching a settlement and UN intervention in both cases set the stage for reconstruction and for return. The two cases also point out the limits of international assistance for postconflict societies. The article concludes with an assessment of policy implications for the international community and for the governments of countries facing the challenges of reconstruction after the wars are over.

Conflicts Today

Almost all of the world's ongoing armed conflicts are internal wars. The outbreak of violence in places such as Tajikistan, Georgia, Rwanda, and Burundi, coupled with the seeming intractable conflicts in places such as Liberia, Sri Lanka, and Angola suggest that internal conflicts will continue to characterize warfare in the coming years. Deepening ethnic and religious tensions in countries such as the Democratic Republic of the Congo, Nigeria, and India are clear warning signs that new outbreaks of civil violence may occur at any time. In fact, some have argued that war as an institution for resolving interstate conflicts is becoming obsolete (Mueller 1990).

Prolonged civil conflict and the absence of a central government able to assert control, create a generalized climate of violence. In Angola and Sierra Leone, Sri Lanka and southern Sudan, armed groups ravage the country and fight rival armed groups, creating a climate of terror and fear which has led to the displacement of millions of people. In these countries, civil strife has resulted in a breakdown of societal norms and violence has acquired a seemingly random nature. Power has passed into the hands of local warlords. In these situations it is obviously more difficult to negotiate cease-fires and peace agreements as the actors change and leaders of armed factions may not, in fact, be able to control their soldiers.

In these types of conflicts, mass population displacement has become an explicit objective of warring parties. The three million people uprooted in the former Yugoslavia are not unintended consequences of war. Rather, the point of the conflict was to force people to leave. In Rwanda, Burundi, Armenia, Azerbaijan, and Georgia, the forced displacement of the population was a central objective of the warring factions. In these types of conflicts, the numbers displaced are extraordinary. Over 50 percent—and perhaps as high as 80 percent—of Liberia's population has been displaced by the war. Somalia produced 500,000 refugees and many more internally displaced in a relatively short period of time. In Rwanda half a million people were massacred in the first half of 1994, followed by an exodus of around 2 million refugees to Tanzania and Zaire, most of whom fled from their homeland within a single week. These sudden, mass influxes produce enormous strain on the international humanitarian system. As UNHCR notes, "while the number of refugee-producing conflicts has not increased significantly in recent years, the number of people displaced in each conflict has become much larger" (UNHCR 1996a: 23).

But the nature of armed conflicts today also has major implications for the peace process and for eventual reconstruction of countries devastated by long-term war. Three characteristics of today's conflicts have specific implications for reconstruction policy: landmines; high civilian casualties; and widespread economic damage. These three characteristics are all interrelated and all affect both the course of refugee repatriation and the outcome of reconstruction efforts.

Landmines

One of the most striking characteristics of modern warfare is the extensive use of landmines. Estimates are that there are 100 million landmines in 64 countries and 250,000 landmine-disabled people in the world with 26,000 new victims each year. The direct medical and rehabilitation costs for the world's landmine victims is estimated at $750 million and it will take decades and a minimum cost of $33 billion to clear the world's landmines, this based on the somewhat dubious assumption that no new landmines will be laid (Roberts and Williams 1995: 3). However, the costs of landmines are far greater than even these figures indicate. For example, many kinds of landmines are designed deliberately to maim, rather than kill, their victims. This places a tremendous drain on medical resources and on family members who must care for the victims of the mines, often for extended periods. As Roberts and Williams report in their comprehensive study of the effects of landmines in seven severely mined countries:

> The impact of the mine explosion extends far beyond the individual casualty. From the moment of an incident, others are involved in evacuation and emergency care, in transport to the hospital, in surgery and postoperative treatment, and in rehabilitation services and vocational training. In most instances

a family member must not only accompany the victim to the hospital, but also stay there to ensure that food and other basic needs are met. In countries investigated for this report, families reported having to spend an amount equivalent of up to two-and-one-half times their annual income on immediate costs related to mine injuries. (1995: 9)

Although most mine victims are adult males, the impact of mines on families and children are substantial, as are the economic costs when dams, electrical installations, and transportation infrastructure are rendered unusable. "Market systems have been seriously disrupted or abandoned because farmers and herders have been unable to move over mined roads and footpaths to bring their produce to market. Such disruption has a direct impact on employment, and rising prices for goods and services (made scarce by such restricted movement) contributes to inflation" (Roberts and Williams 1995: 6).

Mine clearance is dangerous, labor-intensive, and very expensive; with the exception of Kuwait, countries that are heavily mined simply do not have the resources to fund mine clearance on anywhere near the scale that is needed. The cost for UN mine clearance programs ranges from $300 to $1,000 per landmine.[1] Moreover, mine clearance is complicated by the lack of maps and by the fact that many different warring factions are usually involved in laying mines.

The presence of landmines obviously affects the displacement of the population. On the one hand, people leave areas that are heavily mined. At the same time, the presence of mines complicates the return of refugees and internally displaced people. Refugees are afraid to go back to heavily mined areas and the added expense of mine awareness and mine clearance programs is an additional cost for repatriation schemes. In comparison with the population that did not leave, returning refugees or internally displaced people are also more unfamiliar with the location of mines. Thus in 1992 when Afghan refugees returned, estimates were that 77 percent of mine victims were returnees (Roberts and Williams 1995: 15). Moreover, "in many instances, displaced persons return home to find that the most productive and mine-free lands have been occupied by families who did not leave during the fighting. Competition for mine-free land can exacerbate other postconflict pressures and threaten peace" (11).

The presence of landmines complicates reconstruction policies on almost every issue, including the return of displaced populations, efforts to reconstruct the economy, confidence in the government's ability to improve the situation, and the psychological climate of a country that is now officially at peace, but where the legacy of the war claims victims for decades.

Civilian Casualties

Wars in the 1990s increasingly target civilians as casualties. This is partly a function of technology; landmines, as we have seen, are a threat to civilian populations and aerial bombardment has extended the potential battle zone to entire national territories. In conflicts within states, battlefields are the villages and suburban streets. "In this case, the enemy camp is all around, and distinctions between combatant and non-combatant melt away in the suspicions and confusions of daily strife" (UNICEF 1996: 14). Women have been particularly vulnerable to violence. In Rwanda rape has been systematically used as a weapon of ethnic cleansing to destroy community ties. In some raids, virtually every adolescent girl who survived an attack by the militia was subsequently raped. Many of those who became pregnant were then ostracized by their families and communities. Some abandoned their babies, others committed suicide (19).

UNICEF has analyzed the impact of today's warfare on children, concluding that families and children are also being targeted as a result of ethnic conflict, as a "perilous logic" clicks in when ethnic loyalties prevail. "The escalation from ethnic superiority to ethnic cleansing to genocide can become an irresistible process. Killing adults is then not enough; future generations of the enemy—their children—must also be eliminated. As one political commentator expressed it in a 1994 radio broadcast before violence erupted in Rwanda, 'to kill the big rats, you have to kill the little rats'" (UNICEF 1996: 19).

This violence has an obvious long-term impact on children—and on the future reconstruction of their countries. A survey by the Christian Children's Fund in Angola in 1995 found "that 66 percent of children had seen people being murdered, 91 percent had seen dead bodies and 67 percent had seen people being tortured, beaten or hurt. In all, more than two thirds of children had lived through events in which they defied death" (UNICEF 1996: 23).

Children are not only innocent victims of violence. They are also increasingly drawn into the wars as soldiers. The proliferation of light weapons, the forced recruitment of ever-younger children, the large number of orphans, and the greater availability of drugs has meant an increase in the number of child soldiers. As conflicts drag on for years, fighting (and looting and raping) becomes their way of life. When a peace agreement is signed, and even after troops are demobilized, the reintegration of child soldiers into the fabric of normal life is a daunting task. As one NGO worker with years of experience in working with child soldiers in Sierra Leone explained, "it's not just a question of putting these kids back with their loving families. Fighting has become their preferred way of life and the rewards of power, money, recognition and belonging which they get from the gangs are hard to replicate in normal life."[2]

Economics

Armed conflicts have serious economic costs. Most immediately, wars kill people and displace them from their homes which, of course, damages the human resource base of a country or a region. Agricultural production typically plummets as people are forced to abandon their farms. The availability of food decreases while prices of local produce increase. People flock to the cities, but urban employment suffers as a consequence of the war. The economic and social infrastructure is often devastated with factories destroyed, transportation and communications networks rendered unusable. Unemployment in Bosnia, for example, is estimated at over 70 percent. The long-term economic effects of closed schools and deteriorating health services are enormous. Government funds are taken away from social spending and economic investment to pay for armies and counterinsurgency campaigns.

When combined with the debt—often used to purchase arms to continue the war—the economic costs of war are mammoth. In El Salvador in the early 1990s, 41 percent of the government's budget went for servicing the foreign debt and an additional 26 percent was spent on the military. So, 67 percent of the government's resources were devoted to debt and war. The Philippine government spent 44 percent on external debt service and 12 percent on the military, for a total cost of 56 percent of the government's budget (George 1992: 163). Those are resources which cannot be used to improve the social and economic well-being of the Salvadoran and Filipino people. The typical pattern is for governments of countries with internal conflict to borrow heavily for military spending. About two-thirds of the countries involved in war in 1991 are considered to be heavy debtors. Of the twenty-seven states involved in war for more than a decade (and for which data on debt were available), three-fourths—have heavy debt burdens (145–46).

Frances Stewart analyzed the economic impact of sixteen conflicts between 1970 and 1990 in which more than half of 1 percent of the population died as a result of war. She found that civilian deaths accounted for two-thirds of the total deaths in 12 of the 16 cases and only in Iraq and Iran were military deaths much higher than civilian (Stewart 1992). All of the countries that were at war in the 1980s (for which data are available), experienced declining per capita income. The worst were Mozambique (-6 percent per year), Liberia (-4.6 percent), Nicaragua (-4.3 percent), Afghanistan (-2.7 percent) and Guatemala (-2.6 percent). These declines were significantly worse than the regional averages and can almost certainly be attributed to the war. Food production per capita fell in most of the countries at war, ranging from a decline of 55 percent in Cambodia in the 1970s to 42 percent in Nicaragua, 30 percent in Sudan and 19 percent in Angola and Mozambique (Stewart 1992: 11–20).

Armed conflicts have a dramatic impact on the health of the population; the effects go far beyond those who are maimed by landmines or killed by bombs. In fact, most of the casualties of war are caused by disease and famine rather than bullets. One 1980 study in a war zone in Uganda attributed only 2 percent of the deaths to violence, while 20 percent were caused by disease and 78 percent by hunger. And when war is combined with drought, the death toll can be enormous. In Somalia during 1992, half or more of all the children under five on 1 January were dead by 31 December—and around 90 percent of these died from the interaction of malnutrition and disease. War interrupts the distribution of food, destroys agricultural land and ruin the infrastructure, including the provision of safe water. In Lebanon in 1990, one study found that "66 percent of urban water sources were contaminated and that one-third of urban communities were using cesspools for sewage disposal. In Mozambique between 1982 and 1986, over 40 percent of health centers were destroyed. In Uganda between 1972 and 1985, half the doctors and 80 percent of the pharmacists abandoned the country in search of better opportunities elsewhere" (UNICEF 1996: 20–23). The economic consequences of war influence every aspect of reconstruction.

Reconstruction Policy

These characteristics of warfare today—ethnic conflict, the widespread use of landmines, generalized violence as a result of the breakdown of social order, the high proportion of civilian casualties (most of which result from hunger and disease), the forced displacement of large sectors of the society, and the serious economic consequences of long-term strife—create certain common imperatives in reconstruction policy. Most immediately, the postconflict government must provide security for its population by disarming and demobilizing the armed forces and by restoring popular confidence in new political institutions. The population—and particularly the armed forces—must become confident that the new political institutions will last and that they will provide a forum for nonviolence conflict resolution.

Although there is typically a lot of talk about reconciliation, there is little consensus about the meaning of the term. For some, reconciliation refers to overcoming the differences which provoked the conflict; for others reconciliation can only occur after justice has been carried out and those who were responsible for the violence have been punished. In other words, while some want to "forgive, forget, and get on with it," others are adamant that there can be no reconciliation without trials (and punishments) for those found to be guilty of crimes committed during the conflict. Fundamental disagreements on how to reconcile warring factions is in itself a very divisive issue and one which influences the process of negotiating the peace agreement. In some agreements, amnesties have been an explicit part of political arrangements to bring an end to the conflict. Obviously, negotiation setting out the terms of the amnesty can be a very contentious process.

The decision in recent years to create internationally sanctioned processes for bringing justice to Rwanda and former Yugoslavia mark a turning point in the international community's involvement in these justice/reconciliation issues. It is still too early to judge the effectiveness of these tribunals in promoting reconciliation, although it is widely recognized in both cases that the judicial processes will be primarily symbolic. In Rwanda, for example, the number of individuals involved in the killing is thought to number in the tens of thousands. Even if judicial structures had the capacity to handle this volume and funds were made available to support the process, it is unlikely that bringing 30,000 to 100,000 people to trial would contribute to political stability in Rwanda. The long delays in actually setting up these judicial processes are also a cause for concern.

While the most immediate pressure on postconflict governments is to provide security for their populations, economic needs are equally urgent. In the short term, this means continuing distribution of food and other relief items to people who are unable to provide for themselves. Paradoxically, meeting survival needs may actually be easier in war-affected societies than in ones that have not experienced large-scale conflict because of the development of institutional capacity. Thus, for example, in the southern African drought of 1991–92, it was easier to provide additional food supplies to Mozambique than to Zimbabwe because capacity had been developed during the long years of war in Mozambique (Green 1994: 44).

Restoration of the economy is a multifaceted endeavor ranging from repairing damaged infrastructure to negotiating foreign debt service payments. As we have seen, the main cause of civilian casualties during war is hunger and disease, and thus priority must be given to restoring agricultural production. Reconstruction must make a priority of reestablishing agricultural life, which is the basis of subsistence for most countries of the South. While mine clearance is usually too expensive to be carried out on a wide scale, programs of landmine awareness and marking landmined areas are essential if people are to return to their land and be able to produce sufficient food for the country. In the short term, international assistance can play a role in providing needed relief but reconstruction policy must place an immediate priority on subsistence agriculture. This is rarely as "glamorous" as restoring power lines or rebuilding bridges, but is probably more important in the long term.

The economic pressures of reconstruction are daunting: meeting the immediate economic needs of the civilian population; mobilizing funds for rebuilding the country's economic, transportation, energy, and communication infrastructures; negotiating reduction in foreign debt payments; rebuilding factories and schools; recreating social service systems; and mobilizing investment. Moreover, while priorities can be set, basically these tasks must all be done simultaneously. The government, which is typically a brand new democracy, has a very short grace period. The success of the government will be judged in large part by how well it is able to manage and carry out the economic aspects of reconstruction. Can people find jobs? Will children be able to go to school? Will electricity be restored? While immediate security needs are the most pressing popular demand, a new government cannot ignore the economic needs of its population—particularly at a time when expectations are likely to be high as a result of a long-awaited peace agreement.

Moreover, reconstruction costs a lot of money; demobilization of soldiers, for example, has substantial economic costs, as does restoration of the judicial system and training teachers. Fortunately, the coming of peace frees up funds for economic and social expenditures. Armies are demobilized, international funds are sometimes made available for reconstruction, and agricultural productivity can increase as fields and markets become safe. There is a peace dividend for countries in which conflict has ended. In Ethiopia, half a million soldiers were demobilized in 1992, the military's share of total government expenditure has fallen from almost 60 percent to just over 30 percent and spending on health and education has risen from 12 percent of the budget in 1989–90 to almost 20 percent in 1992–93 (Grant 1994: 50).

The role of the international community in mobilizing funds for reconstruction is essential. When funds are urgently needed for reconstruction—in Eritrea or Mozambique, El Salvador or Nicaragua, Cambodia or Afghanistan—formerly war-torn countries may find that international attention has passed them by and that humanitarian relief funds are now being channeled to helping the victims of new or ongoing conflicts rather than being used to sustain the peace once it is established. Demobilization of soldiers and the return of refugees are areas where the international community has provided more support.

Reconstruction and Demobilization

Disarmament and demobilization of armed forces has become an essential component reconstruction. Although the details vary from case to case, typically, the armed factions negotiate a timeframe in which armed forces will report to an assembly or cantonment area, turn over their weapons, be registered and then discharged from the army and given some kind of assistance for their reintegration. While this process is going on (and it can take many months), there must be a concurrent "remobilization" of the country's armed and/or police forces in order to provide immediate security to the population and to restore confidence in the government's ability to protect its people.

The timing of demobilization is critical. Until armed forces are disarmed and soldiers demobilized, it is difficult to begin the processes of economic and political reconstruction. However, it is sometimes difficult to drum up the necessary financial support to implement plans—particularly plans calling for substantial monetary assistance to demobilized soldiers. On the one hand, "donors want assurances that their investment will not be lost to continued fighting, and yet demobilization often takes place in a context of fragile peace and instability where no such guarantees can be given" (Refugee Policy Group 1994: 22). Nongovernmental organizations often find it difficult to provide funds to demobilized combatants when there are urgent unmet needs among civilian "victims." While the argument is that in the absence of alternatives, the demobilized troops will return to violence, the evidence is inconclusive on the impact of such assistance programs. As the Refugee Policy Group/UN Department of Humanitarian Affairs conference on this theme pointed out, even countries such as Zimbabwe where demobilized soldiers were given substantial assistance and access to civil service jobs, unemployment rates among demobilized soldiers remain higher than for their civilian counterparts (Refugee Policy Group 1994: 14).

Moreover, as Margaret McKelvey points out:

> Advantaging the former military over other groups only exacerbates cleavages. Finally, I believe that the popular vision of providing vocational education for demobilized soldiers in order to provide alternative lifestyles to those of thieving and abusing civilians is little more than an appealing mirage. We have not figured out how to do it well in our own country which has an incredibly varied and relatively robust economy. How can a devastated economy such as Mozambique's or Somalia's provide jobs for tens of thousands of demobilized soldiers outside of subsistence agriculture and animal husbandry? (1995: 63)

While questions remain about how to assist demobilized soldiers and how to ensure that they do not pose a continuing security threat, the fact remains that reconstruction depends on the disarmament and demobilization of fighting forces. In comparison with other groups with specific needs—widows, orphans, returning refugees and internally displaced people, disabled, elderly, etc.—it is likely that demobilized soldiers will receive a disproportionate share of the limited resources, precisely because of the threat they embody. In some cases, such as Mozambique, UNHCR's program of reintegration assistance targets geographical areas where there are large numbers of returnees, but within those areas, provides assistance to all groups—including demobilized soldiers—with particular needs.

Reconstruction and Repatriation

The return of displaced populations depends on the postconflict government's ability to provide security and subsistence in rural areas. Refugee repatriation is based on the premise that return should be voluntary and that refugees should be able to go back to areas where they will be able to survive.[3] During long-term conflicts, people are displaced from rural to urban areas; their ability to return to their communities depends on their perception that it is safe to do so and that they can begin to farm again. While the postconflict government is typically anxious for the internally displaced to return (in part to relieve the pressure in the cities), there is less interest in refugee repatriation. In fact, it is in the best interests of the postconflict government for the refugees to remain in exile; their return increases the pressure on the postconflict government. Economically, hard-pressed governments will have to assume responsibility for their livelihood—and survival. Politically, the refugees may be a destabilizing force because of their ethnicity, perceived culpability in the violence, or their political demands. Refugees may have become accustomed to a certain level of service provision, which the government back home is unable to match. The demands of returning refugees for land are serious pressures, highlighting the impact of landmines and increasing pressures on fledgling judicial institutions to resolve questions of land tenure and restoration of property. Moreover, in at least some cases, the return of refugees means a decrease in foreign remittances—and foreign exchange —for the country.

But while it is in the interests of governments to delay refugee repatriation until the country is better able to cope with their demands, the pressures from the governments of neighboring countries and from international donors are to return the refugees as quickly as possible. Routine use of the term "voluntary" repatriation, for example, is giving way to a more nuanced awareness of a continuum from facilitating to promoting to encouraging to coercing repatriations. This is coupled with a growing recognition that repatriation can't be delayed until the conflict is completely over or the postconflict government feels ready to absorb the refugees. As a U.S. State Department spokesperson explained, "it will almost always be impossible for recovery from war to totally precede refugee repatriation. It would be manifestly unfair to countries of asylum (and to the donor community) to ask that refugees be kept on until their home countries are fully prepared to reabsorb them easily" (McKelvey 1995: 62).

The host and donor governments together with UNHCR thus try to balance their needs for rapid refugee repatriation with the longer-term needs of the postconflict government. Infusions of cash for reconstruction, particularly with UNHCR's Quick Impact Projects, and agreements to assist both returnees and other affected populations, coupled with the political need for governments to be seen as welcoming their refugees home, usually result in a formal repatriation agreement.

While governments and UNHCR negotiate the details and logistics of such agreements, much repatriation occurs outside of formal channels. As Stein and Cuny state "[c]ountless number of refugees return home in the face of continued risk, frequently without any amnesty, without a repatriation agreement or program, without 'permission' from the authorities in either the country of asylum or country of origin, without international knowledge or assistance, and without an end to the conflict that caused the exodus" (Stein and Cuny 1994: 174).

We turn now to examination of two case studies—Mozambique and Haiti—to explore the interconnections between reconstruction and repatriation.

Mozambique

Almost from the time of its independence in 1975, Mozambique has been at war. In 1977 with Rhodesian support, the Mozambique National Resistance (Renamo or MNR) was formed and began carrying out guerrilla raids against the government. Later with South African support, Renamo intensified its attacks, targeting schools, health centers, and transportation links. The war expanded as the Frelimo (Front for the Liberation of Mozambique) government was unable to counter growing Renamo violence. As Renamo came to control large portions of Mozambican territory, Frelimo forces responded with increasing violence. Lawlessness and banditry, became widespread. The violence took a heavy toll. As many as a million Mozambicans died as a result of the violence or the war-induced famine. By the late 1980s, nearly half of all primary schools and a third of the rural health network had been destroyed or forced to close down. By 1993, some 1.7 million Mozambicans had fled the country as refugees while perhaps four million were displaced within the country.

The economic toll was high. A 1989 study by the UN Economic Commission for Africa estimated Mozambique's total economic losses as a result of the war from 1980 to 1988 at a staggering $15 billion—more than five times the country's actual gross domestic product (Harsch 1990: 13) Between 1980 and 1986 the country's real GDP fell by 21 percent and commodity exports dropped by 72 percent. By 1989 cultivated land areas had fallen to less than half the levels in 1983 and cattle herds had been decimated. By the end of the decade, Mozambique was importing 85 percent of its food requirements. At independence, Mozambique had a GDP per capita of U.S. $117—one of the poorest countries in the world. By 1992, as a result of the war and the drought, the GDP per capita had fallen to $64. Life expectancy was 47.5 years. And as if the war and its economic destruction were not enough, in 1991–92, the drought that hit Southern Africa took a particularly heavy toll in Mozambique (UNHCR 1995: 2).

The Peace Process

In early 1990 Frelimo began a process of political liberalization and in July 1990, Renamo and Frelimo began negotiations. The peace negotiations, largely carried out in Rome under the auspices of the Vatican, reached agreement on a number of substantive issues. When the intensification of the drought in 1992 brought new fears of widespread suffering, the two parties agreed on a series of "guiding principles for humanitarian assistance" in July 1992. These provided security for international relief personnel and operations, and assured access to Mozambicans living throughout the country. The two sides also agreed to ask the United Nations to chair a committee to coordinate and supervise all humanitarian assistance operations in the country. Three months later, the General

Peace Accord with seven separate protocols and many clauses, was signed—offering hope for an end to the sixteen-year-old war.

The peace agreement established a Control and Supervisory Commission to oversee the peace process to be chaired by the UN Secretary General's Special Representative in Mozambique and made up of representatives from the government, Renamo, the Organization of African unity, and five of the nations that signed the peace agreement. In December 1992, the UN Security Council constituted ONUMOZ (UN Operation in Mozambique, acronym for the name in Portuguese), a peacekeeping force which eventually grew to 7,500 soldiers and another 600 military and civilian observers. Like other peacekeeping initiatives it was to be a multidimensional operation, with responsibilities for:

- facilitating and supervising the peace accords;
- monitoring and verifying the cease-fire, the withdrawal of foreign forces, the destruction of armaments, the demobilization of military forces, including the disbanding of private and irregular armed groups and establishing security for vital infrastructure and the country's transport corridors;
- assisting and monitoring the entire electoral process, including technical help, voter registration, a new electoral law, and fielding a large team of international observers for the 1994 elections;
- coordinating and monitoring all humanitarian assistance operations, including resettlement of refugees and displaced persons, food aid, emergency relief (including relief to demobilized forces), and for the rehabilitation process (Harsch 1990: 13).

The timetable for accomplishing these tasks was clearly specified—but ONUMOZ got off to a slow start. The deployment of ONUMOZ troops was delayed as the Security Council dickered over the financing of the operation. The original timetable called for implementation of the General Peace Accord to begin on 15 October 1992 with elections scheduled for a year later. However, delays in implementing the accord—particularly with the deployment of ONUMOZ troops and the demobilization of combatants—led to a decision to postpone elections for an additional year. ONUMOZ representatives arrived in October 1992, but by February 1993, less than 100 were in place. ONUMOZ wasn't adequately staffed until May 1993.

The immediate priority was to disarm and demobilize 110,000 combatants and to reestablish security throughout the country. As has been the case in other peacekeeping operations, the election date became the central organizing imperative. Political reform was to be accomplished by October 1994; most of the refugees were to be returned by then—in order to participate in the elections.

The challenges facing ONUMOZ and the international community in bringing about a durable peace in Mozambique were daunting. The long years of war, with atrocities committed on both sides, had created a climate of fear and suspicion. The pressures of landmines, economic devastation, millions of refugees and internally displaced people, and the presence of tens of thousands of armed combatants meant that reconstruction would be a politically difficult and expensive undertaking. Moreover, the stakes were high for the United Nations. As the peace process took shape in Mozambique, the international community was conscious of the UN's failure just the year before to implement a peace agreement in Angola. The success of the UN, it was recognized at the time, depended on all its component parts. As Kofi Annan, head of the UN's Peacekeeping operations, explained:

> Without sufficient humanitarian aid, and especially food supplies, the security situation in the country may deteriorate and the demobilization process might stall. Without adequate military protection, the humanitarian aid would not reach its destination. Without sufficient progress in the political area, the confidence required for the disarmament and rehabilitation process would not exist. The electoral process, in turn, requires prompt demobilization and formation of the new armed forces, without which the conditions would not exist for successful elections. (Cited by Harsch 1990: 4)

LANDMINES AND ECONOMIC DEVASTATION The U.S. State Department estimates that between 1 and 2 million mines were laid in Mozambique during almost 10 years of war. The mines were laid by both Renamo and government forces—around military bases, economic infrastructure (including electrical lines from the Cahora Bassa Dam and other power plants), railway tracks, airfields, bridges, and roads (U.S. Department of State 1993: 127). The presence of landmines inhibited agricultural production and re-establishment of economic markets, contributing to food shortages, inflation and hunger (Human Rights Watch 1994: 14–15).

Mozambique's massive Cahora Bassa Dam had been a major source of foreign exchange as the government exported electricity to South Africa. The power lines stretch over 980 kilometers supported by pylons—which have been mined. While the generators remained operational throughout the war, the power generated cannot be exported, due to the landmines. Economically, the country's imports of electricity increased from $1 million in 1980 to $10 million in 1988 (Hanlon 1990) while the cost of repairing the power lines is estimated at $125 to $150 million (not including the costs of removing mines from all of the paths which lead to the lines).

As a consequence of the war and its devastating economic impact on the country, Mozambique acquired a massive foreign debt. Military spending, for example, consumed 38 percent of the government's expenditures in the years preceding the peace agreement and much of this was borrowed from international sources. From $2.7 billion in 1985, Mozambique's debt grew to $4.7 billion in 1991 and to $5.4 billion in 1996—more than four times the country's GDP. This is the highest ratio of debt to

GDP in Africa. Scheduled debt servicing obligations in 1992 of over $500 million, if actually paid, would have been equivalent to 133 percent of export earnings.[4]

DEMOBILIZATION While debt servicing provisions were being implemented, the immediate priority of ONUMOZ was demobilization. Although the cease-fire largely held, security problems were constant. Gangs of bandits and irregular troops without means of livelihood attacked food convoys and caused panic among citizens. Delays in negotiations between Renamo and Frelimo over the cantonment areas and the pace of demobilization created problems, including mutinies by soldiers and lower than expected numbers of volunteers for the new Mozambican army. Cantonment did not begin until November 1993, and demobilization did not start until March 1994. But once it began, it happened very quickly. By late August 1994, the combatants had been disarmed and demobilized. In their fascinating study of demobilization, Borges Coelho and Vines concluded that demobilization in Mozambique achieved "an unprecedented level of success in comparison with other UN operations of its kind. It cantoned, disarmed and demobilized practically all the combatants of the contingents from both sides. As a result, far from being just one other stage in the timetable, the conclusion of demobilization had a very positive impact by decreasing tension and reducing the possibility of hidden agendas of military solutions for political problems" (Borges Coelho and Vines 1994: 13). Although somewhat marred by a late start, demobilization of combatants was amazingly successful and provided an impetus for other elements of the reconstruction plan. There were criticisms of course—particularly fears that not all arms were turned in and that reintegration of combatants was insufficient.

On the political front, the government embarked on a series of reforms designed both to open up the political system and to move toward a market economy. Elections were scheduled—and then, as noted above, postponed a year. The elections took place on 27–28 October 1994 and were monitored by international observers. Frelimo won the election and was sworn in as head of state on 9 December 1994, and a new government was formed. When ONUMOZ's mandate expired on 15 November 1994, many of the UN agencies set up to oversee the transition left the country or were reorganized for the postelection period. The last ONUMOZ representatives departed Mozambique in mid-1995.

Although ONUMOZ is generally credited with doing a good job of pulling off fair elections and although the political climate that has emerged has generally been much more successful than originally anticipated, the governmental capacity to lead and carry out the reconstruction plan has been much more limited. The success of reconstruction policy ultimately depends on the capacity of the government to deliver public services. As a result of the protracted conflict and the response of the international humanitarian community, the capacity of the government to meet the needs of its citizens had been weakened. As several observers have noted, during the long years of war and breakdown of social order, Mozambique had become a laboratory for international assistance. According to UNDP, in the 1988–90 period, there were no less than 26 UN agencies, 6 non-UN multilateral agencies, and 44 bilateral donors and official agencies from 35 countries, as well as 143 external NGOs from 23 countries active in Mozambique. These posed obvious problems of coordination, but they also raised questions about the viability of government institutions. For example, nongovernmental organizations operated major programs throughout Mozambique, often bypassing the government and creating parallel power structures. Joseph Hanlon argues that the NGOs, in providing humanitarian relief, severely hampered the ability of the government to function (Hanlon 1991).

At the same time the international community was trying to support the peace process and offer humanitarian assistance to the victims of the war, there were efforts at long-range planning for reconstruction. The 1993–94 UN humanitarian assistance program sought to channel about half the resources raised for long-term reconstruction needs, such as restoration of water services and agricultural production.

Mozambican Refugees and Internally Displaced People

UNHCR estimates that nearly half of Mozambique's 12 million people left their homes at some point during the war in the 1980s. At the time of the peace agreement in October 1992, 1.3 million to 2 million refugees were in five host countries and an additional 4.5 million people were internally displaced. With the signing of the agreement, many refugees started to return to their country unassisted. As the election drew nearer, the pace of repatriation increased. A report from Zimbabwe notes

> as the Mozambican general elections of October 1994 approached, there was increasing concern expressed by refugees in the camps in Zimbabwe about their participation. Some felt very strongly that they must vote; others actually delayed their repatriation until after October so as to avoid the necessity of voting.... [U]nofficially the word was that the camp populations were considered possibly too volatile to expose them to the direct party campaigning which would take place once they were seen to be potential voters. Through the Mozambican news media we also learned that Renamo had demanded the omission of refugees from the voter rolls because of suspected influence by host government and communities hostile to their party. (Christian Care 1995: 1)

So, as the election approached, and as news got out to the refugees that there was a good harvest, that food was available in Mozambique and access roads to the areas of origin had been improved, people started to move. There was also an inherent push factor as the governments of neighboring countries made it clear that refugee camps were being closed and as food distribution was shifted from refugee camps to settlements in Mozambique (UNHCR-Malawi 1994: 2).

Over a two-year period, UNHCR facilitated the return of more than 1.7 million refugees, and provided transportation to 271,000 refugees from six countries (Malawi, Zimbabwe, Zambia, Tanzania, Swaziland, and South Africa) in fact almost 80 percent of the refugees returned on their own. As of early 1995, refugee camps and settlements in nearly all the surrounding countries were being closed and UNHCR was phasing down its operations, although nearly 100,000 Mozambicans remained refugees at the end of 1995 (U.S. Committee for Refugees 1996: 59).

The repatriation to Mozambique was the largest and most logistically complicated repatriation in African history. Not only did UNHCR plan for the repatriation of 1.7 million refugees and actually transport about 270,000 refugees, but the assistance to returnees was substantial. More than 800 Quick Impact Projects (QIPs) were implemented, and food assistance was provided to all UNHCR-assisted returnees for about ten months; at the height of the operation almost one million returnees were receiving food from UNHCR. From the beginning of repatriation planning, it was agreed that rather than singling out returnees for special assistance, UNHCR would focus on priority geographic areas, rather than specific population areas. Thus, UNHCR concentrated its reconstruction assistance efforts on areas where there was (1) a high concentration of returnees, (2) lack of basic infrastructure, (3) a need to improve access, and (4) a lack of significant rehabilitation activities. In practice, this meant that UNHCR assistance was targeted not just to returnees but also to internally displaced populations, demobilized soldiers, and other people affected by the war.

While UNHCR was planning assistance for the return of refugees, the larger numbers of internally displaced people were returning on their own. Roberts and Williams report that by 1995, about 30 percent (1.5 million) of the internally displaced had returned to their home communities, mostly on their own. Another three million, particularly those in the south, had not returned due to the presence of landmines (Roberts and Williams 1995: 246). By the end of 1995, the U.S. Committee for Refugees reported that about 500,000 people were still internally displaced and about 100,000 refugees had not returned—in spite of the formal closure of UNHCR's program of repatriation.

While it is still too early for definitive evaluation of Mozambican reconstruction policy, by most measures, Mozambique has been a splendid success. The fighting has stopped. The soldiers have gone home. Refugees have returned. Monumental problems remain, of course. While the economy is beginning to rebound, increasing by 5.4 percent in 1994 and 5.5 percent in 1995, poverty is still a reality for most Mozambicans. There are not enough schools or clinics to meet the population's needs; it will be years before agricultural production reaches prewar levels. Unemployment rates are high and there is concern about demobilized combatants who have not found jobs. Since ONUMOZ's departure, there has been an escalation of crime, banditry, and lawlessness, but the atrocities that characterized the long war have largely disappeared. The State Department's Report on human rights in Mozambique details a long list of human rights concerns, but they are the sort of problems that most developing countries experience (U.S. Department of State 1996b).

Haiti

Haiti has long been the poorest country in this hemisphere, characterized by extreme concentration of wealth in the hands of a powerful elite and by frequent U.S. intervention in its political and economic life. In 1990, the Haitian people elected a populist Catholic priest, Jean-Bertrand Aristide, as president and hopes were high that democratic rule would bring about needed reforms. But a military coup on 30 September 1991 forced Aristide into exile after only eight months in power. The military regime unleashed a reign of terror with thousands of people murdered and hundreds of thousands forced into hiding within the country. The violence also produced a wave of refugees embarking in small boats for the United States. This refugee influx—and fears of further refugee flows—was a catalyst for U.S. action to restore democratic rule in Haiti.

Over the past decade, thousands of Haitians have sought to escape the poverty and repression in their homeland by setting sail in boats bound for U.S. territory. Unlike its policy toward Cubans seeking the same destination by the same means, the U.S. has followed a policy of preventing Haitians from entering U.S. territory to apply for asylum. A policy of interdiction, worked out through an exchange of letters between the two governments in 1981 provided for the interdiction of ships leaving Haiti, screening of the passengers to see if they had grounds for asylum, and return of the remaining Haitians. From 1981 until the coup in September 1991, 22,716 Haitians were returned to Haiti, while only 28 were allowed to enter the United States to pursue asylum claims (United States Committee for Refugees 1996: 180). Although human rights groups and refugee advocates denounced this policy, it remained the cornerstone of U.S. policy for most of the three years of the military regime.[5]

Immediately after the coup, the number of Haitians fleeing by boat increased dramatically. As violence directed against Aristide supporters escalated, criticism of the U.S. interdiction policy also increased. But it was not until a court ruling in November 1991 that the policy was changed. Instead of screening the Haitians on board the U.S. Coast Guard cutters, the interdicted Haitians were to be taken to Guantánamo Naval Air Station for screening. Those who were found to have a credible basis for refugee status were allowed to come to the United States to pursue asylum claims. Those who were screened out were returned to Haiti. This policy lasted from November 1991 to June 1992.

While Haitians had left Haiti in varying numbers for more than a decade, the outflow resulting from the 1991 coup was alarming to the U.S. government. Credible reports of widespread persecution, couple with the rise of paramilitary groups and the absence of an imminent political solution, increased the pressure for the U.S. to respond to the protection needs of refugees without serving as a magnet for further flows. In February 1992, the U.S. government set up "in-country processing" inside Haiti through which Haitians could apply for refugee status while still in Haiti. But the program was slow getting started (only 54 refugees were approved in fiscal year 1992) and the number of Haitians being screened on Guantánamo continued to increase (Americas Watch 1993).

In response, U.S. policy changed again. On 24 May 1992, President George Bush issued a directive known as the "Kennebunkport order" putting an end to the Guantánamo screening. Henceforth all Haitian boats would be interdicted at sea and Haitians would be returned to Haiti. There would no longer be any screening to determine whether any of the Haitians had grounds for asylum claims. The existence of an in-country processing mechanism was used to justify the return; after all, the argument went, Haitians with credible fears of persecution could come to the United States as refugees without leaving Haiti. After May 1992, in-country processing was the only option for Haitians to get to the United States.

In spite of presidential candidate Bill Clinton's promise to reverse this policy if elected, he continued the policy of forced return and actually increased the number of Coast Guard cutters patrolling the waters off the island to beef up the interdiction efforts. In June 1993, the U.S. Supreme Court ruled that the principle of non-refoulement does not apply to Haitian refugees interdicted on high seas, thus legitimizing the government's interdiction policy. While UNHCR protested the decision (characterizing it as a setback to modern international refugee law), UNHCR was never a major player in policies affecting the Haitian refugees. Decisions about treatment of Haitian asylum-seekers were made by the U.S. government; UNHCR was usually informed of policy changes, but this was not a consultative process.

Immediately after the coup, the United Nations and the Organization of American States condemned the coup and imposed limited trade sanctions on Haiti which were largely ineffective. But as the violence continued—and as the refugees continued to leave Haiti—the U.S. began to push harder for a solution. In July 1993, an agreement was worked out, known as the Governors Island Accord, and signed by Aristide and the military ruler of Haiti, General Raoul Cedras, which provided the general framework for the return of constitutional government. Aristide was to name a prime minister to be confirmed by a reconstituted Parliament. This was to be followed by the lifting of international sanctions, the retirement of army commander Cedras, the creation of an independent police force and, by 30 October 1993, the return of Aristide as president. A month after the agreement was signed, the UN Security Council suspended its sanctions against Haiti.

But the Governors Island Accord was not implemented. Instead the violence and repression inside Haiti escalated.[6] Sanctions were imposed again; again, they had little impact. The pressure of refugee departures continued. While the U.S. government continued to insist that those leaving Haiti by boat were economic migrants, the number of Haitians applying for refugee status through the in-country processing program increased. But the in-country option was characterized by major shortcomings. The program was administered by the State Department, which consistently downplayed the scope of human rights violations. Although approval rates increased from 8 percent to 30 percent over the program's three years, it was widely understood that overall admissions numbers should remain low. Procedurally, the process was flawed as there was no way to protect the anonymity of applicants, raising serious protection issues. Haitians waiting in line to fill out forms or be interviewed did so publicly and were vulnerable to harassment and intimidation. The interviews themselves were carried out in a crowded room. Even Haitians who were approved—and thus found to have a well-founded fear of persecution—would often wait for months while their papers were processed before being moved to the United States. As the likelihood of a peaceful resolution of the conflict decreased, pressure grew on the U.S. government to come up with a better plan.

While refugees continued to apply for refugee status through the in-country program, they also left Haiti in ever greater numbers. The interdiction policy continued with some 2,329 Haitians returned in 1993. While U.S. Embassy staff met the returned Haitians on the docks, the reports of violence directed at forcibly returned Haitians increased. And throughout 1993, the level of civil violence grew and prospects for a solution seemed remote.

In March 1993, the joint UN/OAS Mission deployed human rights observers throughout the country—but their role was limited to observation and monitoring. They were unable to take actions to prevent the abuse from occurring and few of the observers felt that their presence was deterring violence. In at least some cases, the observers reported that paramilitary forces deliberately committed acts of violence within sight of the monitors. This blatant disregard for international opinion and for the United Nations, coupled with escalating violence, created a climate of despair. The high-profile political assassinations of Aristide's justice minister Guy Malary and political supporter Antoine Izmery in September and October 1993 provoked a round of popular protests, followed by increased repression. The human rights observers were evacuated.

Political pressure mounted on the U.S. government to change its interdiction policy. In April 1994, President Aristide notified the U.S. government that he was ending the interdiction agreement because of the lack of progress in returning him to power and the latest upsurge in killings. The same month Randall Robinson, Executive Director of TransAfrica, began a well-publicized hunger strike in Washington, D.C. on behalf of the Haitians.

On 8 May 1994, President Clinton again changed the policy toward the Haitian refugees, to institute shipboard screening of Haitians interdicted at sea. The screening took place aboard a U.S. ship, the *U.S.S. Comfort*, which was stationed in the harbor of Kingston, Jamaica. Those Haitians who were found to be refugees were taken to Guantánamo for processing; Haitians found not to be refugees were returned to Haiti. Immediately the flow of Haitian boats leaving the country increased, overwhelming the capacity of the U.S. government to screen refugees on board ship. After only a month of shipboard processing, Clinton announced a new policy. Interdicted Haitians would be taken to Guantánamo for refugee determination. The flow accelerated.

On 4 July, a total of 3,247 Haitians were intercepted in a single day— more than the entire number of interdictions in all of 1993. On 5 July, Clinton announced that the policy would be changed yet again. Haitians would continue to be intercepted and they would not be forcibly returned to Haiti, but neither would they have a possibility for permanent resettlement in the United States. Rather, interdicted Haitians would be given a choice of voluntary return to Haiti (where they could apply for refugee status through the in-country processing program) or given safe haven in Guantánamo or other locations to be worked out in the Caribbean. They would be allowed to stay in these safe havens until the situation was judged safe for them to return to Haiti. The number of Haitians leaving Haiti declined. By August 1994, there were 14,000 Haitians in Guantánamo.

Meanwhile, the situation inside Haiti was worsening. The UN/OAS observer mission was expelled and the level of violence was tremendous. The U.S. intensified its efforts to find a solution, supporting much more rigorous economic sanctions, including the freezing of assets and denial or abrogation of visas for military and civilian backers of the regime. By May 1994, some 106,000 Haitians had filled out questionnaires for the U.S. resettlement program. But the situation was deteriorating rapidly. On 27 July 1994, the last commercial flight departed Haiti, stranding a thousand Haitian refugees who had been approved for travel to the United States.

Threats of military force were finally implemented. On 19 September, a U.S.-led Multinational Force (MNF) of 20,000 troops entered Haiti and took control of the country. The Multinational Forces entered Haiti with a specific mandate: "to use all necessary means to facilitate the departure from Haiti of the military leadership, consistent with the Governors Island Agreement, the prompt return of the legitimately elected President and the restoration of the legitimate authorities of the Government of Haiti, and to establish and maintain a secure and stable environment that will permit implementation of the Governors Island Agreement" (Celli 1995: 8).

A series of carefully orchestrated measures were implemented in the next month. Parliament resumed deliberations under the protection of the MNF. The Chamber of Deputies then adopted an amnesty act and a week later, on 13 October, General Raoul Cedras left the country. On 15 October, Jean-Bertrand Aristide returned to take his position as president. Two weeks later, the chamber of Deputies adopted the National Police Act, establishing a civilian police force. On 17 December, a presidential decree established the Commission on Justice and Truth. In January 1995, the majority of the Haitian armed forces were dismissed and training began for the civilian police force. By January 1995, the number of troops in the Multinational Force had dropped to 7,500.

During these months, most of the Haitians on Guantánamo chose to return to Haiti. In fact, the U.S. Justice Department recruited 718 refugees on Guantánamo to serve as "public safety trainers," unarmed auxiliaries for Haiti's new interim police force. In late December, the U.S. troops said that the remaining 5,000 Haitians would be returned to Haiti and their forced repatriation was carried out by mid-January 1995. UNHCR refused to participate in screening the Haitians for return, denouncing the procedures as seriously flawed. The primary exception to this return was a group of unaccompanied children, most of whom were sent back to Haiti after the UNHCR had traced their families. By the end of June 1995, all of the children were either back in Haiti or with relatives in the United States.

By early 1995, the Haitian government had also concluded repatriation agreements with nearby countries providing for the return of Haitians from their countries. Thus it was agreed that up to 800 Haitians could be returned every month from the Bahamas and up to 4,000 per month from French Guyana. The Haitian government set up a National Office of Migration to assist returning Haitians. However, the Office was understaffed, underfinanced, and unable to offer much assistance. While UNHCR facilitated the repatriation of a few hundred Haitians from other countries, it was largely marginal to the process—as it had been during the whole saga of the Haitian refugee exodus.

As in Mozambique, the international forces organized elections, with international monitors to assure the legitimacy of the results. The presidential elections were held on 17 December 1995; Rene Preval, the candidate of the Lavalas (Aristide) party defeated thirteen opponents to win the election with 88 percent of the vote. Preval took office on 7 February 1996.

The U.S.-led Multinational Force came to an end in March 1996, with the departure of the last U.S. troops in February. The UN Mission in Haiti (UNMIH) which originally had 6,000 peacekeeping troops and 900 civilian police, was also scheduled to withdraw in February, but an extension was negotiated to enable it to remain until November 1996 at a reduced level of 1,900 soldiers and 300 police monitors. The mandate of UNMIH was "to assist the democratic Government of Haiti in sustaining the secure and stable conditions established during the initial phase and protecting international personnel and key installations; the professionalization of the Haitian Armed Forces and the creation of a separate police force; and to establish an environment conducive to the holding of the legislative, local-authority and presidential elections" (Celli 1995: 9).

Reconstruction Policy

Although the nature of the violence and of UN engagement was very different in Mozambique and Haiti, in both cases the demobilization and disarmament of the armed forces was a central prerequisite for the holding of elections. While the Haitian military was demobilized and a new national police force created, the intervention was not successful in its disarmament efforts. The Multinational Force confiscated only 30,000 weapons, many of which were reportedly heavy artillery not used against the general population, and also arms of questionable utility, that were acquired through a controversial "buy-back" program (Richardson 1996: 11). It is widely believed that the paramilitary forces have hidden large caches of arms throughout the country (Celli 1995: 6–8).

By December 1995, the Haitian National Forces had been reduced from 7,000 to 1,500. President Aristide had wanted to abolish the army (a suggestion that was resisted by the U.S.). Most of the officers corps were dismissed by Aristide after they protested over salaries in late 1994. Many soldiers simply deserted from the military after the Multinational Forces came in, taking their weapons with them. While most of the remaining enlisted personnel received vocational training as part of the demobilization process, they have found it very difficult to find jobs. With unemployment estimated at 50 percent of Haiti's population, the economic pressure for survival is acute.

At the same time the Haitian military was being reduced, a civilian police force was created. This police force presently numbers about 6,000; all of its members have received basic training from the international forces. However, there is a widespread belief that many former military and paramilitary members have been incorporated into the police force. Although the police force has been trained in human rights, there are still problems with inadequate equipment, leadership, and experience (Slavin 1996: 4–5). The lack of judicial reform and adequate prison facilities are serious obstacles to reforming the security scene.

As in Mozambique, the reestablishment of democratic institutions has been accompanied by a resurgence in crime and banditry (U.S. Department of State 1996a). Richardson reports that the number of violent acts in the capital has increased from 75 per day to more than 200 (Richardson 1996: 12). The donor governments' meeting in July 1996 agreed on the need for emergency measures to strengthen the police forces before the withdrawal of UN forces in November.

Economically, the Preval government depends on the international community for assistance, with two-thirds of its budget coming from aid. The conditions required by the donors have been difficult. The donors had already held up $100 million that had been promised in 1996, and when the Haitian government missed the July 1996 deadline set by the International Monetary Fund to enact new laws on privatization, the donors agreed to withhold additional funds. Moreover, the U.S. Congress passed legislation suspending U.S. assistance until investigations have been carried out on several politically motivated murders. While the return to democracy and the repeated promises of help have created high public expectations, the immediate economic pressures are substantial. Unemployment is high, foreign reserves are dropping, many reconstruction projects are on hold and there is fear that the government will soon run out of money to pay its employees (Rohter 1996: A12).

As in Mozambique, the key to long-term reconstruction in Haiti lies in the government's ability to provide security for its population and to restore rural agricultural production. Two-thirds of Haiti's labor force works in subsistence farming which has shrunk by 7 percent since 1990 as a result of the violence and uncertainty. The delays in international assistance, coupled with the lack of effective disarmament and continuing poverty create an uncertain climate for Haiti's political future.

Reconstruction and Repatriation

In both Mozambique and Haiti, the international community played the decisive role in implementing peace agreements. In both cases, it was international troops that carried out the demobilization of the military, supervised elections, and monitored compliance with established timetables. But in the case of Haiti, it was the U.S. government which made the crucial decisions, including the deployment of armed forces in September 1994. The need to prevent further refugee arrivals in Florida was the driving force in U.S. efforts to restore Aristide to power. The treatment and return of Haitian refugees was carried out by the State Department; UNHCR was a minor player in influencing these policies. In Mozambique, UNHCR was clearly the driving force in planning the repatriation of almost 2 million refugees, although as we have seen, the vast majority of the Mozambican refugees returned on their own. The sustained attention that UNHCR gave to assisting reintegration and targeting assistance for up to a year after the refugees returned was a major component in the country's reconstruction policy. In Haiti, UNHCR presence in monitoring the return of Haitians was minimal; its role in providing reintegration assistance was all but nonexistent. In part this difference is due to the fact that the Mozambican refugees were clearly recognized as refugees and thus as falling under UNHCR's mandate. In contrast, the Haitians were generally seen as asylum-seekers (and later as rejected asylum-seekers).

The dominant role exercised by the U.S. government in dealing with the Haitians left little room for UNHCR to operate—as did the fact that the U.S. remains a major donor to UNHCR.

Although repatriation has been completed, the presence of large numbers of both Mozambicans and Haitians in neighboring countries will continue to be a factor in the longer-term reconstruction of both countries. Approximately 100,000 Mozambicans work in South Africa, sending remittances to family members. Although the South African government is coming under pressure to limit or expel foreign workers, such a move would have a disastrous impact on the struggling Mozambican economy. Similarly, the large number of Haitians working in the United States is an important source of foreign exchange for the Haitian economy. Efforts by the government of the Dominican Republic in the past year to crack down on the estimated 500,000 Haitian migrants have caused fears about the destabilizing effects of large-scale returns.

Although the devastation in Mozambique is worse than in Haiti, the immediate political problems facing the postconflict governments are similar: inadequate governmental capacity, corruption, slow judicial reform, increased banditry and criminal violence, dependence on international donors and their conditions, high popular expectations that life will improve, and insufficient resources for meeting those expectations. Although the peace agreements have been signed, armies demobilized, refugees returned, and elections held, reconstruction will take a long, long time.

Notes

1. See, for example, United Nations (1994); see also U.S. Dept. of State (1994).
2. Personal interview with author, Freetown, June 1996.
3. The growing literature on repatriation explores changes in conceptual understanding of repatriation in conflict situations. See for example, Guy Goodwin-Gill (1989); Enoch Opondo (1992); Dennis Gallagher (1994); Fred Cuny and Barry Stein (1989); also see *First International Emergency Settlement Conference: New Approaches to New Realities*, 15–19 April 1996, University of Wisconsin Disaster Management Center, topic 11; as well as the annual publications of UNHCR, *The State of the World's Refugees*.
4. Africa Recovery Briefing, UN Department of Public Information, 16
5. For a description of U.S. policies toward Haitians, see L. Guttentag and L. Daugard (1993); also Bill Frelick (1993).
6. See, for example, Human Rights Watch and National Coalition for Haitian Refugees (1994a, 1994b).

References

Americas Watch, National Coalition for Haitian Refugees and Jesuit Refugee Service/U.S.A. 1993. "No Port in a Storm: The Misguided Use of In-Country Refugee Processing in Haiti." Washington D.C.

Amnesty International. 1994. "The Price of Rejection—Human Rights Consequences for Rejected Haitian Asylum-Seekers." London: Amnesty International.

Borges Coelho, Joao Paulo, and Alex Vines. 1994. "Pilot Study on Demobilization and Reintegration of Ex-Combatants in Mozambique." Oxford: Refugee Studies Program.

Celli, Marco Tulio Bruni. 1995. "Situation of Human Rights in Haiti." Report submitted to the UN Commission on Human Rights, 6 February.

Christian Care (Zimbabwe). 1995. *Mozambican Repatriation Report* (February).

Cuny, Fred, and Barry Stein. 1989. "Prospects for and Promotion of Spontaneous Repatriation." In *Refugees and International Relations*, edited by Gil Loescher and Laila Monahan. New York: Oxford University Press.

Frelick, Bill. 1993. *Haitian Boat Interdiction and Return: First Asylum and First Principles of Refugee Protection*. Washington D.C.: U.S. Committee for Refugees.

Gallagher, Dennis. 1994. "Durable Solutions in a New Political Era." *Journal of International Affairs* 47, 2: 429–50.

George, Susan. 1992. *The Debt Boomerang*. London: Zed Books.

Goodwin-Gill, Guy. 1989. "Voluntary Repatriations: Legal and Policy Issues." In *Refugees and International Relations*, edited by Gil Loescher and Laila Monahan. New York: Oxford University Press.Grant, James. 1994. *The State of the World's Children 1993*. New York: UNICEF.

Green, Reginald H. 1994. "The Course of the Four Horsemen: Costs of War and Its Aftermath in Sub-Saharan Africa." In *War and Hunger: Rethinking International Responses to Complex Emergencies*, edited by Joanna Macrae and Anthony Zwi. London: Zed Books.

Guttentag, L., and L. Daugard. 1993. "United States Treatment of Haitian Refugees: The Domestic Response and International Law." *International Civil Liberties Report* 1, 2 (June).

Hanlon, Joseph. 1990. *Mozambique: The Revolution under Fire*. London: Zed Books.

———. 1991. *Mozambique: Who Calls the Shots?* London: James Currey.

Harsch, Ernest, with Roy Laishley. 1990. "Mozambique: Out of the Ruins of War." *Africa Recovery Briefing Paper* 8, 13.

Human Rights Watch. 1994. *Landmines in Mozambique*. New York: Human Rights Watch.

Human Rights Watch and National Coalition for Haitian Refugees. 1994. *Rape in Haiti: A Weapon of Terror*, 6, 8.

———. 1994. *Terror Prevails in Haiti: Human Rights Violations and Failed Democracy*. New York: Human Rights Watch.

McKelvey, Margaret. 1995. "Refugee Assistance, Repatriation and Integration." In *African Refugees: Human Dimensions of the Continuing Crisis in Africa: Proceedings of the Second National Conference of the Ethiopian Community Development Council*. Washington, D.C.

Mueller, John. 1990. "The Obsolescence of Major War." *Bulletin of Peace Proposals* 21, 3 (September): 31–28.

Opondo, Enoch O. 1992. "Refugee Repatriation during Conflict: Grounds for Scepticism." *Disasters* 16, 4: 359–62.

Refugee Policy Group. 1994. *Challenges of Demobilization and Reintegration: Background Paper and Conference Summary.* Washington: Refugee Policy Group.

Richardson, Laurie. 1996. "Disarmament Derailed." *NACLA Report on the Americas* 29, 6 (May/June).

Roberts, Shawn, and Jody Williams. 1995. *After the Guns Fall Silent: The Enduring Legacy of Landmines.* Washington: Vietnam Veterans of America Foundation.

Rohter, Larry. 1996. "Freeze I U.S. Aid Hampers New Haitian President's Recovery Effort." *The New York Times,* 29 April 1996: A12.

Slavin, J. P. 1996. "The Haitian Police: Struggling with Inexperience and Leadership Woes." *Haiti Insight* (April/May): 4–5.

Stein, Barry N., and Frederick C. Cuny. 1994. "Refugee Repatriation During Conflict: Protection and Post-Return Assistance." *Development in Practice* 4, 3.

Stewart, Frances. 1992. "War and Underdevelopment: Can Economic Analysis Help Reduce the Costs?" Mimeo. Oxford: International Development Center.

UNHCR. 1995. *Repatriation and Reintegration of Mozambican Refugees: 1993 Progress Report and 1994 Activities.* Geneva: UNHCR.

———. 1996a. *State of the World's Refugees: In Search of Solutions.* Geneva: UNHCR.

———. 1996b. "UNHCR Presents Bosnia Repatriation Plan." UNHCR Update, 17 January.

UNHCR-Malawi. 1994. Update, 9 May.

UNHCR-Mozambique. 1994. "Reintegration Strategy." Draft working paper.

UNICEF. 1996. *State of the World's Children.* New York: UNICEF.

United Nations. 1994. *Assistance in Mine Clearance: Report of the Secretary-General.* New York: United Nations.

United States Committee for Refugees. 1996. *World Refugee Survey 1995.* Washington, D.C.: USCR.

U.S. Department of State. 1993. *Hidden Killers: The Global Landmines Crisis.* Washington D.C.: Department of State.

———. 1996a. *Haiti Human Rights Practices 1995.* Washington D.C.: Department of State

———. 1996b. *Mozambique Human Rights Practices 1995.* Washington D.C.: Department of State.

University of Wisconsin Disaster Management Center. 1996. "New Approaches to New Realities." First International Emergency Settlement Conference. Madison.

NOTES ON CONTRIBUTORS

Peter M. Benda is Associate Director, Center on Policy Attitudes, Washington, D.C. He served as Associate Director of the New School University's International Center for Migration, Ethnicity, and Citizenship from September 1994 to January 2001. Previously he served for three years (1991–94) as Program Associate for Public Policy at The Pew Charitable Trusts, and before that as Program Officer at the Eisenhower Exchange Fellowships, Inc. A summa cum laude graduate of Swarthmore College, where he majored in philosophy, he subsequently pursued graduate studies in political science, with a concentration in public law and jurisprudence, at the University of Chicago and Princeton University. His prior professional experience includes three years as a researcher in the Government Division of the Congressional Research Service, U.S. Library of Congress, and faculty appointments at the University of Virginia and Swarthmore College.

Richard E. Bissell is the Executive Director of the Policy Division at the National Academy of Sciences. Prior to this position, he was Chairman of the Inspection Panel at the World Bank. As a specialist in economic and social development, Richard Bissell was a senior manager in the U.S. Agency for International Development (AID) from 1986 to 1993. He was first appointed to the number three position at AID, as Assistant Administrator for Program and Policy Coordination, where he served until 1990, overseeing the budget, policy development, coordination with other aid donors, and evaluation of AID programs. From 1990 to 1993, he headed AID's programs in research and technical support to the field missions, as the Assistant Administrator for Research and Development. In the latter position, he oversaw all technical sectors, from agriculture and the environment, to education, health, population, and women in development. Prior to joining AID, he taught at the University of Pennsylvania, Georgetown University, and the Johns Hopkins School of Advanced International Studies. He previously served as editor of *The Washington Quarterly* and as managing editor of *Orbis*. Dr. Bissell has published a number of books and many articles on international affairs. Among his books are *The Missing Link* (Duke University Press) *Strategic Dimensions of Economic Behavior* (Praeger) and *South Africa and the United States: Erosion* *of an Influence Relationship* (Praeger). Dr. Bissell was educated at Stanford University (B.A.) and then received his M.A. and Ph.D. at the Fletcher School of Law and Diplomacy at Tufts University.

Elizabeth G. Ferris is Executive Secretary for International Relations at the World Council of Churches in Geneva, Switzerland where she is responsible for global analysis and advocacy on refugees, internally displaced and forced migrants. From 1993–98, she served as Director of the Immigration and Refugee Program of Church World Service which is the humanitarian relief and development arm of the National Council of Churches of Christ in the United States. From 1991–93, she served as Research Director for the Life & Peace Institute in Uppsala, Sweden and from 1985–91, as Study and Interpretation Secretary for the Refugee Service of the World Council of Churches. From 1976–85, she was a professor of Political Science at several U.S. universities, including Miami University of Ohio and Lafayette College in Easton, PA. From 1981–82 she was a Fulbright professor at the Universidad Autonoma de Mexico where she taught courses in International Relations and U.S.-Latin American Relations. She earned her bachelor's degree in history from Duke University, her master's degree in Latin American studies and Ph.D. degree in political science from the University of Florida. She has had over thirty articles and monographs and six books published. Her most recent book, *Uprooted: Refugees and Forced Migrants* was published by Friendship Press in 1998.

David P. Forsythe is Professor and Chair of Political Science at the University of Nebraska-Lincoln. He is the author or editor of more than a dozen books and some fifty shorter publications on international law, organization, and human rights. These include the widely used *The United Nations and Changing World Politics* (with Tom Weiss and Roger Coate), second edition 1997. He is editor of *Human Rights and Comparative Foreign Policy*, recently published by the Brookings Institute, and has also recently completed work on *Human Rights and International Relations*, forthcoming from Cambridge University Press.

Leah Haus is a member of the Department of Political Science at Vassar College, where she teaches international political economy and European politics. Her publications include "The East European Countries and Gatt," in *International Organization* (Spring 1991); and "Openings in the Wall: Transnational Migrants, Labor Unions, and U.S. Immigration Policy," in *International Organization* (Spring 1995). Her current research project focuses on labor unions and immigration policy in France and the U.S. in the twentieth century.

Mary M. Kritz, sociologist and demographer, currently holds positions as Senior Research Associate, Department of Rural Sociology and as Associate Director, Population and Development Program, at Cornell University.

From 1974–89, she worked in the Social Sciences and Population Divisions at the Rockefeller Foundation. She has published numerous books and articles on international migration and currently serves on the Editorial Board *of International Migration Review,* and on the Advisory Board of the Center for Migration Studies. From 1986–89, she served as Chairman of the International Union for the Scientific Study of Population's (IUSSP) Committee on International Migration. Other positions include member of the Steering Committee for the PAA's Special Interest Group on International Migration (1986–90); PAA Board member (1989–92); Secretary and Newsletter Editor, for the ASA's Sociology of Population Section (1980–83); and member of the IUSSP's Working Group on the Economics of International Migration (1980–81). Her migration research focuses on two dimensions: comparative patterns of international migration and differentials in settlement and integration processes of immigrant groups in the United States.

Gil Loescher is a professor of international relations at the University of Notre Dame. Recently, he served as a senior advisor to the Office of the United Nations High Commissioner for Refugees (UNHCR) Geneva. He is also member of the External Research Advisory Board for UNCHR's *State of the World's Refugees* and has been its past chair. He had been a Research Associate at the International Institute for Strategic Studies (IISS) in London and a Visiting Fellow at Princeton, Oxford and the London School of Economics, and a Visiting Scholar at the U.S. State Department's Bureau of Humanitarian Affairs. He is the author of the Twentieth Century Fund book *Beyond Charity: International Cooperation and the Global Refugee Problem* (1993) and an IISS Adelphi Paper "Refugee Movements and International Security" (1992). He is also co-author of *Calculated Kindness: Refugees and America's Half-Open Door, 1945 to Present* (1986) and co-editor of *Refugees and International Relations* (1989) among other works. His new book *The UNHCR and World Politics* is forthcoming from Oxford University Press.

Philip L. Martin studied Labor Economics and Agricultural Economics at the University of Wisconsin-Madison, where he earned a Ph.D. in 1975. He is Professor of Agricultural Economics at the University of California-Davis, and Chair of the University of California's sixty member Comparative Immigration and Integration Program. Martin has published extensively on farm labor, labor migration, economic development, and immigration issues. He has testified before Congress and state and local agencies numerous times on these issues, and was the only academic appointed to the Commission on Agricultural Workers to assess the effects of the Immigration Reform and Control Act of 1986 on U.S. farmers and workers. Since 1987, Martin has chaired the WRCC-76, a group of thirty-five researchers from land-grant universities that meets annually to discuss research on the effects of immigration reform on U.S. agriculture.

Martin has been asked to develop practical solutions to complex and controversial migration and labor issues in many countries. Between 1988 and 1990, he assessed competing predictions of how many Turks might emigrate if Turkey were admitted to the European Union. In 1994, he evaluated the effects of immigration on Malaysia's economy and its labor markets. In 1995, he assessed the effects of the peso devaluation on Mexican migration to the United States. Martin was awarded UCD's Distinguished Public Service award in 1994.

Andrew S. Natsios is the Secretary of Administration and Finance for the Commonwealth of Massachusetts. Prior to assuming this position in 1998, he was Vice President of World Vision-U.S. and Executive Director of World Vision Relief and Development. From 1991–93, he was the Assistant Administrator of the Bureau of Food and Humanitarian Assistance at the U.S. Agency for International Development (AID). Natsios also served as the Director of the AID's Office of Foreign Disaster Assistance. He was a Massachusetts State Representative from 1975–87, the Massachusetts Republican Party Chair from 1980–87, and served in the U.S. Army Reserves from 1972–95. Natsios's recent publications include *American Foreign Policy and the Four Horsemen of the Apocalypse* (Praeger), the article "A Commander's Guidance: A Challenge of Complex Humanitarian Emergencies," which appeared in *Parameters* (1996), and contributions to *Learning Somalia: The Lessons of Armed Humanitarian Intervention* (edited by Walter Clarke and Jeffrey Herbst, Westview Publishing) and *From Massacres to Genocide: The Media, Public Policy and Humanitarian Crisis* (edited by Robert Rothberg and Thomas Weiss, Brookings Institution).

Susanne Schmeidl, a native of Germany, received her Diploma in social work from the Evangelische Stiftungsfachhochschule für Sozialpädagogik (Nürnberg, Germany, 1987) and her M.A. and Ph.D. in sociology from the Ohio State University (Columbus, 1989 and 1995). She worked at the Centre for Refugee Studies (York University, Canada) as a postdoctoral researcher (1995–96), coordinator of the Prevention/Early Warning Unit (1996–97), coordinator of the interim secretariat of the Forum on Early Warning and Early Response (1996–97), and as a consultant for the Food and Statistics Unit of the UN High Commissioner for Refugees (Geneva, 1997). In 1998 Dr. Schmeidl joined the Swiss Peace Foundation, Institute for Conflict Resolution as a senior research analyst for FAST (Early Recognition of Tension and Fact Finding) and the lead for South Asia. Her research on early warning of humanitarian disasters and the dynamics of forced migration has resulted in several articles in refereed journals, edited volumes, and an edited book with Howard Adelman, *Early Warning and Early Response* (Columbia International Affairs Online, Columbia University Press, 1998). After serving in several positions for the section on Ethnicity, Nationalism and Migration of the

International Studies Association (ISA), Dr. Schmeidl was recently elected as section chair for 2000–01.

Robert C. Smith is Assistant Professor in the Sociology Department at Barnard College, and directs the Transnational Migration module of the Hewlett Program on Mexico at the Institute of Latin American and Iberian Studies at Columbia University. His dissertation, "Los Ausentes Siempre Presentes: The Imagining, Making and Politics of a Transnational Community Between Ticuani, Puebla, Mexico and New York City" (Columbia, 1995), was nominated for the Bancroft Prize. He is author, most recently, of "Transnational Localities: Technology, Community and the Politics of Membership within the Context of Mexico-U.S. Migration" forthcoming in *the Journal of Comparative Urban and Community Research,* "Transnational Migration, Assimilation and Political Community" in Margaret Crahan and Alberto Vourvoulias-Bush, eds., *The City and the World: New York in the Global Context New York* (Council on Foreign Relations, 1997); and co-author, with Aristide Zolberg, of "Migration Systems in Comparative Perspective: An Analysis of the Inter-American Migration System with Comparative Reference to the Mediterranean-European System," a 1996 report prepared for the U.S. Department of State, Bureau of Population, Refugees and Migration. He has held fellowships from the Social Science Research Council, the National Science Foundation, and other institutions.

J. Edward Taylor is Professor of Agricultural Economics at the University of California-Davis, and an expert on migration and development. His research focuses on determinants of migration, the effects of remittances on local economies, and the effect of immigration on U.S. labor markets. Professor Taylor is author of *Micro Economy-wide Models for Migration and Policy Analysis* (Paris: OECD, 1995), *Development Strategy, Employment and Migration: Insights from Models* (Paris: OECD, 1996), and, with Irma Adelman, *Village Economics: The Design, Estimation and Use of Villagewide Economic Models* (Cambridge University Press, 1996).

Thomas G. Weiss is Presidential Professor at The Graduate Center of The City University of New York, where he is co-director of the United Nations Intellectual History Project and one of the editors of *Global Governance.* From 1990 to 1998 as a Research Professor at Brown University's Watson Institute for International Studies, he also held a number of administrative assignments (Director of the Global Security Program, Associate Dean of the Faculty, Associate Director), served as the Executive Director of the Academic Council on the UN System, and co-directed the Humanitarianism and War Project. He has also served as executive director of the International Peace Academy, a member of the UN secretariat, and a consultant to several public and private agencies. His latest book is *Military-Civilian Interactions: Intervening in Humanitarian Crises* (1999).

William B. Wood is Director of the Office of the Geographer and Global Issues which is part of the Bureau of Intelligence and Research at the U.S. Department of State. He received his undergraduate degree from the University of California at Berkeley and his Ph.D. in Geography from the University of Hawaii. His graduate research focus (sponsored by the Population Institute, East West Center) was on urbanization and regional development, particularly in Southeast Asia. In 1985, he joined the Office of the Geographer as a geographic analyst. Since 1990, he has served as the Geographer for the Department of State and is responsible for research and analysis on a wide range of global issues: boundary and territorial disputes; refugee and migration flows; humanitarian interventions; population trends and policies; ethnic distribution patterns; war crimes and atrocities; transboundary environmental, energy, and resource problems; and United Nations activities. Dr. Wood is co-editor (with George J. Demko) of *Reordering the World: Geopolitical Perspectives on the Twenty-first Century,* second edition (Westview Press, 1999).

Aristide R. Zolberg is University-in-Exile Professor at the Graduate Faculty of the New School University in New York City, and Director of the New School's International Center for Migration, Ethnicity, and Citizenship. He has served twice as Chair of the Department of Political Science and is a member of the Committee on Historical Studies as well as Chair of the New School component of the New York City Consortium on European Studies. He is a member of the Social Science Research Council's Committee on International Migration, of the editorial board of *International Migration Review*; of the advisory boards of *Actes de la Recherche en Sciences Sociales* (Paris), *Politique* (Quebec), and *Journal of Refugee Studies* (Oxford). He is also a member of the Council on Foreign Relations and serves on the Advisory Board of Human Rights Watch/Africa, as well as on the Scientific Advisory Board of the Fondation Médecins sans Frontières (Paris).

Professor Zolberg has written extensively in the fields of comparative politics and historical sociology, on ethnic conflict and immigration and refugee issues, in both English and French. Recent major works include *Working-Class Formation: Nineteenth Century Patterns in Western Europe and the United States* (Princeton, 1986; co-authored and co-edited with Ira Katznelson); *Escape from Violence: Conflict and the Refugee Crisis in the Developing World* (Oxford, 1989; co-authored with Astri Suhrke and Sergio Aguayo; translated into Dutch); and *The Challenge of Diversity: Integration and Pluralism in Societies of Immigration* (co-editor, with Rainer Bauboeck and Agnes Heller; Avebury, 1996). Other recent publications include "Global Movements, Global Walls: Responses to Migration, 1885–25," in Wang Gongwu, ed., *Global History and Migrations* (Boulder: Westview Press, 1997); "Why Islam is Like Spanish" (with Long Litt Woon), *Politics and Society*, 1999; and "Matters of State: Theorizing Immigration Policy," in Charles Hirschman, Philip Kasinitz, and Josh DeWind, eds., *The*

Handbook of International Migration: The American Experience (New York: Russell Sage Foundation, 1999).

Professor Zolberg is currently completing a book on the role of immigration policy in American political development, tentatively titled *Designing Immigration: American Projects and Policies, 1750–2000*. Other pending research and publications concern the democratic management of cultural difference, and the emergence of anti-immigrant parties in Europe (with Martin Schain and Patrick Hossay).

INDEX

Africa. *See also* Rwanda
  controlling human flow, 298
  development assistance, 312–13
  Great Lakes region, 192, 303
  famine relief, 312
  grant programs in human rights, 313
  list of forced migration by country of
      origin, 86
  trends in forced migration, 65, 70, 72
African pastoralists, 53–54
aid. *See* foreign aid
*Alien Nation: Common Sense about America's
  Immigration Disaster* (Brimelow),
  5–6, 7
Amazonian resources, 55–56
American Immigration Control Federation,
  4, 6
Amnesty International, 190
Apodaca on refugees and violence and
  human rights, Terri, 79
armed forces in war zones advantages, 213
arms expenditures, 191
Asia
  comparison to Central America, 146–47
  controlling human flow, 298
  economic growth players in, 107
  geopolitical ties and immigration to
      United States, 37
  grant programs in human rights, 313
  list of forced migration by country of
      origin, 87
  NAFTA's effects on East Asian exports,
      154n. 8
  trends in forced migration, 70–71, 72
assistance and protection
  addressing growing problem of internal
  closing gap between, 193–200
  displacement, 196–97
  empowerment of international human
      rights regime, 194–95
  protection role for human rights NGOs,
      198

refugees, UN peacekeeping, and out-
      side military forces, 199–200
asylum mechanisms in host states, weaken-
      ing of, 178–79
Atwood on money spent for humanitarian
      assistance and peacekeeping
      (1994–1995), Brian, 190
Australia and "white Australia" policy, 3
authoritarian rule and refugees, 14

Berlin Wall coming down and exodus of
      East Germans, 5
Bhagwati on immigration restrictions,
      Jagdish, 271
bilateral policy (with coordination), United
      States, 247–52
  emergency diplomacy (reactive), 248–50
  programmatic diplomacy (preventive/
      anticipatory), 250–52
  structural impact, 248
Bissell, Richard E.
  on development assistance and interna-
      tional migration, 297–321
  on development assistance resources, 15
Bouvier on population pressures in Mex-
      ico, Leon, 123–24
Bracero Program, 99–100, 126–27, 147,
      152n. 2
Brimelow on United States becoming
      "Alien Nation," Peter, 5–6

Camp of the Saints (Raspail), *The*, 3–4, 97
  Hart on, Jeffrey, 4
  National Review on, 4
  re-release of, 4
Canada versus United States in number of
      migrants, 20–21, 38n. 1
Calvillo's 1995 survey of Maquila workers,
      Pinal, 137
Caribbean migration. *See* Central American
      and Caribbean migration; Latin
      America and Caribbean

Carothers, Thomas
  on attaining democracy, 245
  on new democracies and difficulties, 247
Castaneda on "moral hazard" of U.S.
    bailouts in Mexico, Jorge, 140–41
Central America and Caribbean, 130–32,
    143–47. *See also* Latin American and
    Caribbean
  Asian model comparison to, 145–46
  assessing policy alternatives, 145–47
  Caribbean Basin Initiative (CBI), 145,
    312, 315
  development assistance, 312
  migration, 130–32
  NAFTA, 146–47
  peace, political processes, and migra-
    tion, 143–45
  repatriation, 314
  tariffs and sugar producing nations, 145
Childers on unified UN-system emergency
    machinery and volunteer NGOs,
    Erskine, 222
China
  floating population, 54
  foreign investment in, 108, 117nn. 16, 17
  internal migration, 115n. 2
Christoper on consolidation of UN agencies,
    Warren, 218
civil war and failed states victims, 183
climate change influence on population
    movements, 51
Clinton, President Bill
  "assertive multilateralism," 207
  Chechnya and, 249–50
  democracy abroad, 246
  Emergency Financing Mechanism pro-
    posal, 141
  on foreign policy commitment to
    democracy, 243
  Haiti policies, 134, 152n. 4, 261
  on loan guarantees to Mexico, 109
  population-limiting programs in devel-
    oping world, 2
Cold War
  Central America policies during, 131
  forced migrations and, 62
  foreign intervention in intrastate con-
    flicts, 77
  ideological alignments versus ethnic
    affiliation, 76
  ILO during, 13
  immigration numbers during and after,
    12–13
  intrastate conflicts, 77, 78
  trends in forced migration and, 64–65

Colombia lobbying United States, 134–35
communications revolution, 102
Conflict and forced migration (1964–1995),
    62–94
  Africa, 65, 70
  approach to quantitative review of,
    62–64
  Asia, 70–71
  Cold War and after trends, 64–65
  conclusions, 83–85
  economic factors and population pres-
    sures role, 82–83
  findings from empirical analysis, 73–83
  internal displacement by region, 67, 69
  interstate wars, 73–75
  intrastate conflicts, 75–78
  introduction, 62
  Latin American and Caribbean, 71–72
  list of forced migrations by country of
    origin, 86–89
  Middle East, North Africa, and South-
    west Asia, 72
  refugee stock changes analysis, 89
  repressive states, 78–82
  Soviet bloc and its aftermath, 72–73
  trends, 64–73
Connelly, Matthew
  on *Camp of the Saints*, 4, 5
  on poor countries' growth, 8
  on population pressure, 45
  on rapid population growth in develop-
    ing countries and global migra-
    tion trends, 19
control efforts on migration, 20
Cornelius, Wayne
  on hope factor that inhibits migration,
    138
  on potential migrants from various
    areas of Mexico, 137
Correlates of War (Singer), 76, 77, 90n. 9
country characteristics and U.S. immigra-
    tion, 31
Crenshaw on population density measur-
    ing social complexity, Edward, 83
criminal tribunals, international, 181–82
Cuba, 133
Cuny on international assistance and repa-
    triation efforts, Fred, 306
current dilemmas and future prospects of
    inter-American migration system,
    121–67
  actual or potential challenges for U.S.
    policy, 135–47
  conclusion, 147–52
  emergence of, 126

introduction, 121–22
migration between United States and
    Mexico, Central America, and
    Caribbean, 126–35
population growth, state capacity, and
    unauthorized immigration,
    123–126

delivery system for wars, humanitarian.
    See reforming international humani-
    tarian delivery system for wars
demand-pull factors, 97, 98, 99–100
DeMars on humanitarian organizations
    manage and report information on
    human rights abuses, Bill, 198
democracy definition, 244
democratization to reduce forced move-
    ments, 14
demographic and economic inequalities
    contribution to international migra-
    tion, 21
developed countries (DC) migration
    to other DCs, 38
    to LDCs, 38
developing nations rapid population
    growth fueling migration, 20
development assistance and international
    migration, 297–321
    financial resources, 316–17
    introduction, 297–300
    movement of elites in crisis, 304–5
    natural and manmade disasters, 300–5
    repatriation/resettlement assistance
        and migration prevention, 310–20
    security during repatriation efforts,
        308–10
    spontaneous repatriation of refugees
        and resettlement of IDPs, 305–10
    structure as program, 301–4
displacement problem, 179
distance between sending country and
    United States, 29, 31, 32, 33, 38
Dominican Republic, 133
Dresser on rise in political violence in Mex-
    ico, Luis Hernandez, 141

East bloc list of forced migrations by coun-
    try of origin, former, 88
ecomigration, 10, 42–61
    analysis dearth, 44–45
    categories of, 50–51
    conclusions about, 58–59
    eco definition, 46–47
    environment influenced mobility, 44–45
    environmental refugees versus, 46–47

frayed umbrella, 47–49
government reactions, 55–56
green walls, 56–57
introduction, 42–44
men effected by, 48
natural disasters, 50, 51
obstacles, 52
patterns and predictability, 50–53
questions for, 43
relationship between environmental
    causes and societal effects, 42
resourced-based, 50, 53–55
umbrella economics, 49–50
urban industrial disasters, 50–51
urbanization/international trade revo-
    lution, 49
women and children affected by, 48
economic and demographic inequalities
    contribution to international migra-
    tion, 21
economic factors and population pressures,
    82–83
economic growth and social welfare in
    sending countries to United States,
    29, 30, 33, 38
economic institutions and migration. *See*
    international economic institutions
    and migration
economic migrants definition, 126
economic migrations, 14, 98–103
economic policies role, 95–120. *See also*
    managing migration
Edmonston on economic hardship and
    refugee migration, Barry, 85
El Salvador
    conflicting aid to, 231
    elections not enough in, 244
    migration, 130–32
    new police force, 144–45
    paying for services in United States to
        help asylum applicants, 135
    peace process in, 143
    peacekeeping efforts in, 254, 255
    remittances, 135
    United Nations and, 144
    United States interest in democracy
        in, 247
emigration pressures, reducing, 96, 103–14
    definition, 116–17n. 11
    foreign aid, 110–12
    foreign investment, 96, 107–10
    intervention, 112–14
    migration hump, 96, 105–7
    trade, 96, 104–7
employer sanctions, 128, 147, 149

employers recruiting foreign labor, 11
employment, international migration for, 98
environmental change and migration linkages, 42–61. *See also* Ecomigration
environmental pressures, 50
environmental refugees. *See* Ecomigration
Environmentally Induced Population Displacements and Environmental
Impacts Resulting from Mass Migrations symposium, 44
Ethiopia and repatriation, 314
ethnic community size in United States and
effect on immigration volume, 21
ethnic ghettoes, 56–57
ethnic lobbying, 133–34, 149
Europe on family reunion and asylum, 12
European Union (EU)
as model for United States, Mexico, and
Central and South America,
151–52
asylum procedures, 178
cross-border networks, 277
labor migration and, 287–89, 290
migration policies, 272, 273

family considerations and migration decisions, 103–4
family reunions, 11, 149, 311
cross-borders networks, 276
Europe on, 12
Mexico and sponsoring relatives in
United States, 128
United States laws, 311
farms, disappearance of, 101
Fein, Helen
on genocide as cause of refugee
migration, 81
on genocide definition, 80–81
on human rights violations, 80
Ferris, Elizabeth
on repatriation and reconstruction, 15
on U.S. policy in reconstruction, 322–49
fertility rates and U.S. immigration. *See*
total fertility rates (TFR) as related
to U.S. immigration
financial resources for development assistance, 316–17
Fitzpatrick on distance between sending
countries and United States, Gary, 29
forced migration. *See* conflict and forced
migration (1964–1995)
foreign aid, 96, 110–12
foreign-born stock and immigration to
United States, 31, 32, 33

foreign direct investment (FDI), 107–8, 109,
118n. 21, 118n. 22
foreign investment, 96, 107–10
Forsythe, David
on liberal democracy, 14
on spread of democratization and liberalization, 206
on United States foreign policy, democracy, and migration, 243–70
France
Algeria and, 249
encouraging immigration from fertile
neighboring counties, 9–10
Niger and, 247
zero population growth, 7
free trade, 13
Freedom House index of civil liberties, 80
Freeman on employer sanctions in United
States, Gary, 125

Gelb on "wars of national debilitation,"
Leslie, 207
genocide definition, 80, 81
Geographical Information System (GIS), 29
geopolitical ties and Asians immigrating to
United States, 37–38
Germany and fear of "yellow peril," 7
Gibney on refugees and violence and
human rights violations, Mark, 79
global warming, 51
government reactions, 55–56
government repression definition, 79
Grahl-Madsen on asylum in foreign country, Atle, 201
Green Revolution, 52
green walls, 56–57
Gregory on rate of Mexico's per capita
income to reach half of United
State's, Peter, 138
gross domestic product (GDP) growth and
immigration to United States, 31,
32, 33
Gurr, Ted Robert
on genocide and forced migration, 81
on measure of ethnic rebellion, 76

Haas on international migration program
problem, Ernst, 282
Haiti, 256–61
aid withheld, 257
attributes of civil war in, 233n. 1
border controls and massive emigration, 243–44
coordinated approach for aid to, 258
decline of, 55

electoral assistance, 258–59
forced migration, 71
human rights abuse, 185
military humanitarianism, 213
parliament in, 260
police and judiciary system, 259–60
policy changes and intervention by
    United States to avoid stem of
    refugees from, 134
public sector efficiency, 261
Turkey and United States policy versus,
    263–64
United Nations failure in, 206
United States changing policies about
    immigration, 112–13
United States demand for democratic
    government in, 256
United States military invasion, 208
United States policy driven by
    unwanted asylum seekers, 256
United States policy in, 256–61
voter education programs in, 258
Harff on genocide and forced migration,
    Barbara, 81, 84
Harkovirta on government repression and
    refugee exodus, Harto, 79
Hart on *Camp of the Saints,* Jeffrey, 4
Hartung on arms trade, William, 78
Haus on international economic institu-
    tions, Leah, 13, 271–96
Hmong refugees from Southeast Asia, 5
Hughes on export agriculture workers in
    northern Mexico, Allie, 138
human development index (HDI), 30, 31,
    32, 33, 40n. 8
human rights
    and refugee regime, 184–88, 194–95
    tied to foreign aid and access to United
        States markets, 151
    tied to peacekeeping efforts, 194
    violations versus severe threats to life,
        78–82
humanitarian action. *See* protection and
    humanitarian action in post–Cold
    War era
humanitarian assistance on population
    migration during natural and man-
    made disasters, 300–5
humanitarian delivery system for wars,
    reforming international, 206–42
Huntington on democracy, Samuel, 245

Immigration and Naturalization Service
    (INS), 22, 23, 39n. 5
    budget increase for, 148

entrant-tracking technology at border, 125
on undocumented immigrants, 148
warrant need and entering farm fields,
    128
Immigration Reform and Control Act
    (IRCA), 23, 39n. 4, 128, 149
immigration to United States
    1910–1995, 275
    1989–1993, 23
Indochinese, 70–71
industrial disasters, 50, 51
Ingram on linking of humanitarian efforts,
    James, 225
institutional human rights violations ver-
    sus severe threats to life, 78–82
inter-American migration system. *See* cur-
    rent dilemmas and future prospects
    of inter-American migration system
intergovernmental organization (IGO)
    enforcement actions of, 256
    field operations, 254–55
    United States support for democratic
        standards in, 252
internally displaced people (IDPs)
    addressing growing problems of, 196–97
    Guiding Principles adapted by United
        Nations, 197
    NGOs and, 209
    reasons for returning home, 307
    record numbers of, 206, 207
    Refugee Watch organizations, 198
    by region, 67, 69
    resettlement of, 305–10
    solutions to problem of, 200
    United Nations and, 196–97, 218, 302–3
    United States handling of, 303, 304
International Association of Peacekeeping
    Training Centres, 233n. 3
international capitalism, 9
International Committee of the Red Cross
    (ICRC), 187, 189, 190, 225, 226, 303,
    305, 309
international criminal tribunals, 181–82, 195
international economic institutions and
    migration, 271–96
    causes of migration, 274–77
    conclusion and policy implications,
        289–92
    introduction, 271–73
    labor migration and, 277–89
international environment changes for
    humanitarian action, 172–75
international financial institutions (IFI) and
    governance approach, 253, 254

international human rights regime, empowerment of, 194–95
international humanitarian law and mandates, inadequacy of existing, 193
international humanitarian system weakness, 196
International Labor Organization (ILO), 13, 277–83, 291–92
  activities, 282–83
  background, 278–79
  government preferences, 279–82
  IDA and, 110–11
  introduction, 277–78
  structures of, 279
international migration and development assistance. *See* development assistance and international migration
international migration for employment, 98
International Organization for Migration (IOM), 286
international protection system gaps, 184–93
international refugee law, 185–86
International Union for the Scientific Study of Population, 8
interregional linkages, 53
interstate wars, 73–75
intervention as means to contain refugee movements, 175–78
intrastate conflicts, 75–78, 207
  aid instead of solutions, 177–78
  as civil wars, 207
  definition, 75
  displaced and trapped people within own country, 196
  ethnic and nonethnic internal wars, 76
  foreign intervention, 77
  internally displaced people (IDPs), 196
  post–Cold War, 171
introduction, 1–41

Jonassohn on genocide as cause of refugee migration, Kurt, 81

Kennar on prosperity sucking in poverty from adjacent regions, George, 20
Kennedy, Paul, 4
  on *Camp of the Saints*, 4, 5
  on fertility and immigration, 123
  on global population explosion for twenty-first century, 2–3
  on poor countries' growth, 8
  on population and refugee migration, 13
  on population pressure, 45

on rapid population growth in developing countries and global migration trends, 19
on strategic overstretch, 208
Kritz on population growth and international migration, Mary, 10, 19–41

labor migration, international, 271, 274, 276, 277
  European Union (EU), 287–89
  institutions and, international, 277–89
  international labor organization, 277–83
  International Organization for Migration (IOM), 286
  managing, 97–103
  NAFTA, 289
  Organization for Economic Cooperation and Development, 284–86
  United Nations, 283–84
  World Trade Organization, 286–87
Latin America and Caribbean. *See also* Central America and Caribbean
  development assistance, 312
  grant programs in human rights, 313
  list of forced migrations by country of origin, 87
  trends in forced migration, 71–72
less developed countries (LDCs) migration
  to developed countries (DCs), 21, 36
  to other LDCs, 38
liberalization of exit, 11
lobbying, 133–34, 135, 149
Loescher, Gil
  on humanitarian assistance, 14–15
  on protection and humanitarian action in post–Cold War era, 171–205
  on refugee problem and repressive societies, 79

managing migration, 95–120
  conclusion, 114–15
  demand-pull, 97, 98, 99–100
  instruments to reduce unwanted migration, 96, 103–14
  networks, 97, 98, 102–3
  reducing emigration pressures, 96, 103–14
  supply-push, 96, 97, 98, 100–2
  toward international cooperation?, 114
Mandelbaum on UN conducting military operations, Michael, 215
manmade disasters, 300–5
Martin, Philip
  on free trade, 13

on hope factor that inhibits migration, 138

on managing migration, 95–120

mass migration, 19, 97

Massey on skepticism of effectiveness of U.S. regulations for immigration, Douglas, 8

material resources and demographic growth, 19

May, Cordelia Scaife, 4

Maynard on NGOs role in conflict resolution, mediation, and reconciliation, Kimberly, 198

Maynes on "benign realpolitik," Bill, 215

McCann on refugees and violence and human rights, Jay, 79

McCarran-Walter Act (1952), Texas Proviso, 128

McCoy on effects of tariffs and Caribbean sugar producing nations, Terry, 145

Mercosur, 147

Mexican trends in population growth and U.S. immigration, 34–37

Mexico, 127–29, 135–43
  Bracero Program, 99–100, 126–27, 147, 152n. 2
  challenge facing United States regarding migrants from, 140–42
  civil conflict, 142–43
  corn subsidies elimination, 137–38
  debt servicing, 129
  documented versus undocumented immigration to United States, 124
  drug traffickers, 141–42, 152–53n. 5, 153n. 6
  ecomigration and, 58
  economic development and migration, 136–38
  economic policies leading to migration, 129
  farmers, 104
  foreign investment reliance example in, 109–10
  human rights, 143
  immigration to United States and government of, 85
  Import Substituting Industrialization (ISI), 129
  INDENT system, 148, 149, 150
  maquiladoras (border assembly plants), 136–38
  military and antidrug campaigns, 141–42, 152–53n. 5
  money sent by immigrants in United States, 104, 127, 312

NAFTA, 109, 110, 129, 135, 136–38, 140, 145

nortenizacion, 127

Operation Hold the Line, 149, 150

poli-narcos, 142

political or economic instability, 139–43

political parties and elections in, 139–40, 141

political violence rise, 141

population growth in, 123–24, 125, 129

population pressures in, 123

potential migrant or refugee creating developments, 139–43

poverty level in, 139

PRI, 139–40, 141, 142

relatives sponsoring relatives cycle, 128

remittance economies in, 104, 127, 134

trade expansion with United States, 107

trade liberalization and increase in migration, 136

trends in population growth and U.S. immigration, 34–37

Mexico-U.S. migration, 126–129

Middle East, North Africa, and Southwest Asia
  list of force migrations by country of origin, 88
  trends in forced migration, 73

migration and international economic institutions. *See* International economic institutions and migration

migration, causes of, 274–77

migration hump, 13, 14, 96, 105–7

migration, prevention of involuntary, 211–12

migration versus population growth percentages, 12

military humanitarians, 212–17
  accountability, 216
  evaluating downside, 213–14
  functions of, 212–13
  guaranteeing access, 214
  monitoring of behavior, 216
  in natural disasters, 213

Modlin on distance between sending countries and United States, Marilyn, 29

money sent back to Mexico/Central America by immigrants in United States, 127, 147

Moore on UN's fragmented and feudal nature, U.S. Ambassador Jonathan, 217

movement of elites in crisis, 304–5

moving world, 96–97

multilateral foreign policy, United States, 252–56

multilateral foreign policy *(cont.)*
    democratic standards, 252–54
    enforcing democracy, 255–56
    IGO field operations, 254–55

national immigration policy goals and
    actual results gaps, 8–9
Natsios, Andrew
    on development assistance and interna-
        tional migration, 297–321
    on development assistance resources, 15
    on linking UN and NGOs, 224
    on public funding of NGOs, 227
natural disasters, 50, 51, 300–5
networks for immigration, 10, 97, 98, 99,
    102–3
new economics of labor migration (NELM),
    103–4
nongovernmental organizations (NGOs)
    defining when to intervene, 207, 220
    distribution figures, 209–10
    during war, 218, 219
    employing local elites, 305
    and human rights protection of
        refugees, 189–90, 198
    humanitarians, 223–29
    number of, 225
    post-World War II, 213
    professional standards, 226, 227, 228
    regulation of, 228
    reliance on, 209
    subcontracting for humanitarian deliv-
        ery services, 208, 209
    United Nations versus, 209, 223–24
    UNHCR and, 304
    United States distrust of, 318
    United States funding to, 303, 304
    United States influence on direction of, 300
    United States roots of, 299
nonimmigrants admitted to United States
    (1985–1995), 276
North American Free Trade Agreement
    (NAFTA), 13, 103, 109, 110, 129, 135,
    136–38, 140, 145, 146, 151, 273, 277,
    289, 291

Official Development Assistance (ODA),
    110, 112, 113, 114
Operation Hold the Line, 149–50, 154n. 9
Operation Turquoise, 180
Operation Wetback, 148
Organization for Economic Cooperation
    and Development (OECD), 110, 112,
    114, 284–86, 292

Organization for European Economic
    Cooperation (OEEC), 284–85, 290

policy and theory implications, 147–52
political objectives with idealism, coinci-
    dence of, 200–1
poor countries' population growth and
    U.S. immigration trends, 20
population density as related to U.S.
    migration, 25, 28–29, 31
population growth and international
    migration link, 10, 19–41, 301
    empirical link between U.S. immigra-
        tion and population pressure,
        22–25
    introduction to, 19–22
    Mexican trends in population growth
        and U.S. immigration, 34–37
    population and other mediating factors
        in U.S. immigration, 29–33
    rapid population growth in developing
        nations fueling migration, 20, 30
    statistics, 19, 24, 39n. 6
    trends and future patterns, 34, 36,
        37–38
    U.S. immigration and other population
        dimensions link, 25–29
population growth, state capacity, and
    unauthorized immigration, 123–126
population-limiting programs in develop-
    ing world, 2
population migration during natural and
    manmade disasters, humanitarian
    assistance effect on, 300–5
population pressure
    in El Salvador, 130
    index, 21
    in Mexico, 123
    and U.S. immigration empirical link,
        22–24
population size as related to U.S. immigra-
    tion, 25, 27, 30, 31, 32, 33, 36–37
population trends and future migration
    patterns, 34–38, 301
population versus migration percentages,
    12, 13
post-Cold War
    Central America, 144
    conflicts and "refugee hump," 14
    forced migrations, 62
    humanitarian crises characteristics, 207–9
    humanitarianism efforts, 190
    protection and humanitarian action in
        era of, 171–205

refugee crises affecting security of sending and receiving states, 172
trends in forced migration, 64–65, 83–84
prevention approach for protection of refugees pitfalls, 174
prevention of involuntary migration, 211–12
Program for Mexican Communities Abroad, 135
prosperity sucking in poverty from adjacent regions, 20
protection and humanitarian action in post–Cold War era, 171–205
assistance and protection gap closing, 193–200
changing international environment for humanitarian action, 172–75
coincidence of political objectives with idealism, 200–1
empowerment of international human rights regime, 194–95
existing mandates and international humanitarian law inadequacy, 193
existing resource base inadequacy, 190–93
failure of policies and tactics, 179–84
gaps in international protection system, 184–93
human rights and refugee regime, 184–88
internal displacement, addressing growing problem of, 196–97
international criminal tribunals, 181–82
intervention as means to contain refugee movements, 175–78
need for more systematic temporary protection, 183–84
NGOs and human rights protection of refugees, 189–90
protection role for human rights NGOs, 198
refugees and human rights regime, 188–89
refugees, United Nations peacekeeping, and outside military forces, 199–200
safe havens, 181
safe zones, 179–81
weakening of traditional protection and asylum mechanisms in host states, 178–79
protection system gaps, international, 184–93
human rights and refugee regime, 184–88
inadequacy of existing mandates and international humanitarian law, 193

inadequacy of existing resource base, 190–93
NGOs and human rights protection of refugees, 189–90
refugees and human rights regime, 188–89
quotas and undocumented and illegal immigration, 276

rapid population growth in fueling international migration, 20, 37–38
Raspail, Jean, 13
Camp of the Saints, The, 3–4, 97
on Indians from Calcutta setting out for French Riviera, 97
on Third World paupers immigrating to Europe, 3
rate of natural increase (RNI), 23, 31
Reagan, President Ronald
asylum and refugee status granting, 133
El Salvador and administration of, 130–31
population-limiting programs in developing world, 2
Red Cross. *See* International Committee for the Red Cross
reducing emigration pressures, 103–14
reforming international humanitarian delivery system for wars, 206–42
after wars, 229–32
before wars, 211–12
characteristics of humanitarian crisis, 207–10
during wars, 212–29
military humanitarians, 212–17
nongovernmental organizations (NGOs) humanitarians, 223–29
prevention of involuntary migration, 211–12
United Nations humanitarians, 217–23
what can be done, 210–32
refugee
definition, 46, 126
definition in international law, 82
refugee camps and nonneutrality of them, 307, 309
"refugee hump," 14
refugee law, international, 185–86
refugee migration by region, 66
refugee movements containment by intervention, 175–78
refugee-sending countries by region, numbers for, 68
Refugee Watch organizations, 198
refugees and human rights regime, 188–89

refugees remaining in region of origin, 9, 14
refugees, United Nations peacekeeping, and outside military forces, 199–200
Reimers on migration chain for relatives sponsoring relatives, David, 128
remittances as source of foreign exchange, 104, 114, 132, 134, 135, 150–51
repatriation
    development assistance and migration prevention, 310–20
    efforts, security during, 308–10
    of refugees and resettlement of IDPs, spontaneous, 305–10
Replacement Agricultural Workers (RAW), 128
repressive states, 78–82
resettlement
    development assistance and migration prevention, 310–20
    of IDPs and repatriation of refugees, spontaneous, 305–10
resource-based ecomigrations: regional perspectives, 53–55
resource-based exploitation and degradation, 50–51
rights revolution, 103, 116n. 10
Russell on LDC to DC migrations, Sharon, 21
Rwanda, 177
    conflicting objectives in, 201
    emergency aid to, 212
    French intervention, 208, 215
    human rights abuse, 185
    international tribunals to prosecute war criminals, 179, 181, 182
    invasion by Tutsi refugees, 5
    lack of protection or peace efforts by international community, 192
    lack of United States intervention, 244
    military humanitarianism, 213
    NGOs and, 228–29
    refugee camps, 177, 303
    Rwandan Patriotic Front, 211
    safe zones, 180
    UN failure in, 206, 218
    UNAMIR, 177
    UNHCR and, 174, 177, 179, 192, 199, 221–22
    United States slowness to react to genocide in, 255

safe havens, 181, 183, 201, 208, 215
safe zones, 179–81, 183, 199
Sassen on labor migrants, S., 276–77
Saudia Arabia, 2

Schengen Agreement, 178
Schmeidl, Susanne
    on Cold War and refugees, 12–13
    on democratization, 14
    on refugees remaining in region of origin, 9
secessionist claims, 76, 90n. 6
security during patriation efforts, 308–10
Sen, Amartya, 9
    on "population bomb," 1
    questioning third link in chain, 8
    on racial balance, 6–7
    on south to north movements, 9
Shawcross on war tribunals, Lord Hartley, 182
Sierra Club and anti-immigration, 5
Simcox on population pressures in Mexico, David, 123–24
Singer on correlation between capitalist economy and democratic politics, Max, 247
Singer on interstate versus intrastate conflicts, J. David, 76, 90n. 7
Smillie on greatest problems facing NGOs, Ian, 226
Smith on development of inter-American migration system, Robert, 9, 121–67
Smith on United States record on democracy abroad, Terry, 248
social and economic welfare in sending countries to United States, 29, 30, 33, 37–38
societal and environmental pressures, 47–49
Sollenberg on interstate wars, M., 75
Somalia
    famine alleviation programs, 299
    IGOs enforcement actions in, 256
    international humanitarian relief operations, 175–76
    military intervention in, 213
    NGOs failure in, 218
    Red Cross operation in, 305
    relief operation in, 304
    regional versus more global powers to handle problems in, 215
    United Nations shortcomings and failures in, 206, 207, 208, 218
    United States aid to, 118n. 28, 309
south generating masses to migrate, 11
Soviet bloc and aftermath trends in forced migration, 72–73
specialized labor, 9
Stanley on violence level in El Salvador and refugee flight, William D., 79
state repression definition, 79

Stedman on prevention as alchemy, Stephen, 212
subcontracting for military services and humanitarian delivery services, 209–9
supply-push factors, 96, 97, 98, 99, 100–2
Taylor, Edward
    on free trade, 13
    on managing migration, 95–120
Teitelbaum, Michael, 2
    on LDC to DC migration, 21
temporary immigrants adjusting to permanent immigration states, 22, 39n. 3
Temporary Protect States (TPS), 95, 132
temporary protection, need for more systematic, 183–84
Third World
    conflicts between migrants and natives, 57
    ecomigration in, 52
    population mobility, 44
    Raspail on, Jean, 3–4
    voluntary migration from, 2
Torres-Rivas, Edelberto
    on economic migrants definition, 126
    on refugee definition, 126
total fertility rates (TFR)
    to U.S. migration, 25, 26, 30, 31, 32, 33
    lack of variation over time, 40n. 7
    Mexico, 34–37
    sending migrants and, 36
tourist numbers, 96, 115n. 1
trade, 96, 104–7, 117n. 12
transnationalization and interactive relationship of domestic and foreign politics, 132–35
transportation revolution, 102–3
trends in forced migration, 64–73
    Africa, 65, 70
    Asia, 70–71
    Cold War and after, 64–65
    Latin America and Caribbean, 71–72
    Middle East, North Africa, and Southwest Asia, 72
    Soviet bloc and aftermath, 72–73
Turkey
    asylum seekers numbers, 262
    European Union (EU) and, 263
    Haiti and United States policy versus, 263–64
    Kurdish movement, 262
    migration, 261
    United States foreign policy, 261–64
    United States tolerance of civil and political rights abuses in, 262

Tutsi refugees invasion of Rwanda, 5

undocumented immigration, 148, 149, 150
UNICEF, 190, 221, 223
United Nations
    Central America and, 144
    consolidation of organizations of, 217–23
    democracy commitment, 253–54
    and failed or collapsed states administration, 230, 231
    focus, 252–53
    growth in demand for soldiers from, 207, 208
    human rights machinery of, 188, 189, 191, 195
    humanitarian interventions by, 175
    humanitarians, 217–23
    for institutionalizing standards on migration, 283–84
    former Yugoslavia and, 176, 180–81, 184
    internally displaced people (IDPs) and, 196
    involvement in elections, 254
    Iraq and, 175
    Macedonia and troops from, 211
    mandates, 303
    military inadequacies of, 214–15
    nongovernmental organizations (NGOs) versus, 209, 223–24
    peacekeeping, refugees, and outside military forces, 199–200
    Rwanda and, 180, 182
    shortcomings and failures, 206–7
    Somalia and, 175–76
United Nations High Commissioner for Human Rights (UNHCHR), 15, 195
    budget, 195
    field presence, 195
    focus of, 195
    internally displaced people (IDPs) and, 197
    office of (OHCHR), creation of, 194
United Nations High Commissioner for Refugees (UNHCR), 63, 174–75, 183, 186–87, 315
    assistance for conflict in former Yugoslavia, 172
    asylum issues, 186
    budget, 190, 191, 192
    decision-making abilities hampered, 174, 184
    emphasis on assisting refugee camps and negotiating for support, 172
    former Yugoslavia and, 174, 192, 196, 199, 200

United Nations High Commissioner for
 Refugees (UNHCR) *(cont.)*
 human rights conditions, 185, 187
 humanitarian action when outside military forces involved, 221
 inability to resolve refugee problems
  alone, 194
 internally displaced people (IDPs) and,
  302–3
 international refugee law, 185
 mandates of, 202n. 7, 302–309
 on number of refugees and internally
  displaced people, 171
 Official Development Assistance (ODA)
  and, 110–11
 Rwanda and, 174, 177, 179, 192, 199,
  206, 221–22
 on "soft intervention," 186
 strategies for refugee crises, 305–6
 working both sides of borders where
  there is conflict, 172–73, 202n. 5
United Nations Human Rights Center,
 188, 189
United States
 back door policy and Mexicans, 127–28
 borders laxity, 12
 Bracero Program, 99–100, 126–27, 147,
  152n. 2
 Canada in number of migrants versus,
  20–21
 challenge for handling Mexican
  migrants, 140–42
 challenge for today, 300
 country characteristics and immigration
  to, 31
 distance between sending country and, 29
 documented versus undocumented
  Mexican immigrants, 124
 economic growth and social welfare in
  sending countries, 29
 employer sanctions in, 125
 foreign aid money spent versus GNP, 191
 foreign-born proportion in, 12
 foreign policy and immigration, 132–35,
  152n. 3
 foreign policy democracy and migration,
  243–70
 immigration numbers (1900–1995), 275
 as largest receiver of migrants, 21
 Mexico as largest sender of migrants to,
  34, 40n. 9
 migration from Mexico, Central America, and Caribbean, 126–35
 nonimmigrants admitted (1985–1995),
  276

 permanent residency visa, qualifying
  for, 37
 policy challenges, 135–47
 policy changes needed, 318–20
 population and other mediating factors
  in immigration, 29–33
 remittances as source of foreign
  exchange, 132
 safe havens at Guantánamo Bay naval
  base, 181
 Saudia Arabia versus on immigration, 2
 unauthorized immigration deterrent, 126
urban industrial disasters, 50, 51
urbanization, rapid, 51–52
urbanization/international trade revolution, 49
U.S. Commission on Immigration, 2
U.S. Committee for Refugees (USCR), 63
U.S. foreign policy, democracy, and migration, 243–70
 background, 245–47
 bilateral policy (with coordination), 247–52
 case of Haiti, 256–61
 case of Turkey, 261–64
 conclusions, 264–65
 emergency diplomacy, 248–50
 enforcing democracy, 255–56
 funding for democracy assistance, 250
 general statements, 251–52
 Japan and, 249
 multilateral policy, 253–56
 reactive foreign policy, 248–50
U.S. immigration and population pressure
 empirical link, 22–25
 statistics, 24, 39n. 6

Väyrynen on need for new multifaceted
 international mechanism for humanitarian intervention, 218

Wallensteen on interstate wars, P., 75
Walker on duration of average humanitarian relief operation, Peter, 172
war and international humanitarian delivery system, 206–42
 after war, 229–32
 before war, 211–12
 during war, 212–29
war durations, 171–72
Weiner, Myron, 5
 on international economy approach, 5
 on intrastate conflicts, 75
 on oppressive authoritarian and revolutionary regimes and refugee
  migration, 79, 82

on refugee populations size and population growth, 83
Weintraub on effect of growth rate and increased income in Mexico, Sidney, 138
Weiss, Thomas
  on assistance delivery difficulties, 15
  on reforming international humanitarian delivery system for wars, 207–42
  responses to humanitarian disasters, 194
  on World Food Program and UNICEF, 190
Western Europe
  developed regions as source of migrants, 36
  developing regions as source of migrants to, 20
  foreign-born proportion, 12
white race decline anxiety, 6, 7, 8
Wildavsky on correlation between capitalist economy and democratic politics, Aaron, 247
Wood on ecomigration, William, 10, 42–61
worker as defined by European Court of Justice, 287, 293n. 22
World Bank
  on classification of countries, 98, 115–16n. 3, 116n. 4
  on countries that attracted foreign direct investment (FDI), 108
  on Dominican Republic, 113
  as leader on development issues, 316
  on number of people living and working outside their country of citizenship, 96

World Food Program (WFP), 190
world on the move, 96–97
World Tourism Organization on number of tourists, 115n. 1
World Trade Organization (WTO), 114, 286–87, 291

Yang, Philip
  on population pressure index, 21
  on role of mediating forces in shaping U.S. immigration, 21, 38–39n. 2
  on size of immigrants' ethnic community in United States and effect on immigration volume, 21
Yates on NAFTA effect on Caribbean, Alexander, 146
"Yellow peril," 7

Zabin on export agriculture workers in northern Mexico, Carol, 139
Zlotnik, Hania, 10
  on developing regions and migration, 20
  on population and migration growth percentages, 12
Zolberg, A.R.
  on labor migration, 278
  on limited migration flows, 274